McGraw-Hill Ed

SAT* SUBJECT TEST

LITERATURE

McGraw-Hill Education

SAT* SUBJECT TEST

LITERATURE

Fourth Edition

STEPHANIE MUNTONE

New York   Chicago   San Francisco   Athens   London   Madrid
Mexico City   Milan   New Delhi   Singapore   Sydney   Toronto

1 2 3 4 5 6 7 8 9   LHS   23 22 21 20 19 18

ISBN   978-1-260-14275-4
MHID   1-260-14275-2

e-ISBN   978-1-260-14276-1
e-MHID   1-260-14276-0

Special Contributor: Wendy Hanks

SAT is a registered trademark of the College Board, which was not involved in the production of, and does not endorse, this product.

McGraw-Hill Education products are available at special quantity discounts to use as premiums and sales promotions or for use in corporate training programs. To contact a representative, please visit the Contact Us pages at www.mhprofessional.com.

Contents

McGraw-Hill Education

SAT* SUBJECT TEST

LITERATURE

PART I

Introduction

All About the SAT Literature Test

The SAT Literature Test is one of the Subject Tests offered by the College Board. The test is a one-hour exam consisting of approximately 60 multiple-choice questions. It is designed to measure how well you have learned to read and interpret literature.

The SAT Subject Tests (formerly known as the SAT II Tests or Achievement Tests) are the lesser-known counterpart to the SAT, offered by the same organization—the College Board. While the SAT covers general verbal, writing, and mathematical reasoning skills, the SAT Subject Tests cover specific knowledge in a variety of subjects, including English, mathematics, history, science, and foreign languages. SAT Subject Tests are only one hour long and thus are significantly shorter than the SAT. Furthermore, you can choose which SAT Subject Tests to take and how many (up to three) to take on one test day, but you cannot register for both the SAT and the SAT Subject Tests on the same test day.

The SAT Literature Test usually includes six to eight literary texts. Each text is followed by a set of questions based on that text. The test covers the topics shown in the table:

GENRE	PERCENTAGE
Prose passages (primarily excerpts from fiction and essays)	40–50%
Poetry (primarily entire poems, though some selections are excerpts from larger works)	40–50%
Drama and other (included in Prose passages) (many tests, but not all, contain one dramatic selection)	0–10%
Period	
Before 1700	30%
Between 1701 and 1900	30%
After 1900	40%
National Tradition	
Authors from the United States	40–50%
Authors from Great Britain	40–50%
Authors from other English-speaking traditions (India, Ireland, Canada, and the Caribbean)	0–10%

The SAT Literature Test measures not only how well you understand the subject matter of each text, but also how well you understand specific literary concepts, such as theme, genre, tone, and characterization. You may be asked about the structure and organization of a text, or you may be asked about the author's use of narrative voice. You may also be asked about syntax, diction, vocabulary, and the author's use of figurative language, including imagery. You should be familiar with these concepts from your English and language arts classes.

When determining which SAT Subject Tests to take and when to take them, consult your high school guidance counselor and pick up a copy of the "Taking the SAT Subject Tests" bulletin published by the College Board. Research the admissions policies of colleges to which you are considering applying to determine their SAT Subject Test requirements and the average scores students receive. Also, visit the College Board's web site to learn more about which tests are offered (www.collegeboard.org).

Use this book to become familiar with the content, organization, and level of difficulty of the SAT Literature Test. Knowing what to expect on the day of the test will allow you to do your best.

When to Take the Test

For the SAT Literature Test, the College Board simply recommends that you have as much experience as possible in reading and carefully analyzing a variety of American and British literary works from different historical periods and in different genres. The more texts you have read and closely studied, the better prepared you will be. Note, however, that there is no specific reading list for the test, so you cannot know beforehand which literary works you will encounter on the exam you take.

Many students take the SAT Literature Test at the end of their junior year or at the beginning of their senior year. If you are unsure when you should take this exam, consult your teacher or school counselor.

Colleges look at SAT Subject Test scores to see a student's academic achievement, because the test results are less subjective than are other parts of a college application, such as grade point average, teacher recommendations, student background information, and the interview. Many colleges require at least one SAT Subject Test score for admission, but even schools that do not require SAT Subject Tests may review your scores to get an overall picture of your qualifications. Colleges may also use SAT Subject Test scores to enroll students in appropriate courses. If English is your strongest subject, then a high SAT Literature score, combined with good grades on your transcript, can convey that strength to a college or university.

To register for SAT Subject Tests, pick up a copy of the *Student Registration Guide for the SAT and SAT Subject Tests* from your guidance counselor. You can also register at www.collegeboard.org or contact the College Board directly at:

(866) 756-7346

General inquiries can be directed via e-mail through the College Board's website e-mail inquiry form or by telephone at the number listed above.

The SAT Literature Test is administered six Saturdays (or Sunday if you qualify because of religious beliefs) a year in October, November, December, January, May, and June. Students may take up to three SAT Subject Tests per test day.

Scoring

The scoring of the Literature test is based on a 200–800-point scale, similar to that of the math and verbal sections of the SAT. You receive one point for each correct answer and lose one quarter of a point for each incorrect answer. You do not lose any points for omitting a question. In addition to your scaled score, your score report shows a percentile ranking indicating the percentage of students scoring below your score.

Score reports are mailed, at no charge, approximately 5 weeks after the test day. Score reports are available approximately 3 weeks after the test day at www.collegeboard.org. Just as with the SAT, you can choose up to four college/scholarship program codes to which to send your scores, and the College Board will send a cumulative report of all of your SAT and SAT Subject Test scores to these programs. Additional score reports can be requested, for a fee, online or by telephone.

Test-Taking Strategies for the Literature Test

Test-Taking Strategies for the Literature Test

The SAT Literature Test will present you with several poems and prose passages, all originally written in the English language. In many cases, the poems and passages will be excerpted from longer works; in some cases, they will be complete. Each passage will have the date of its original publication at the end. (Knowing when the passage or poem was written will often help you as you approach the questions.) You will not be expected to identify the authors or to have read these works before.

This section contains a number of strategies that you can use to help yourself earn a high score on the SAT Literature Test. The first strategy will help you prepare for the test before you take it. The other strategies address the types of questions on the test and describe some methods that will help prevent you from making careless or unnecessary errors in choosing your answer. Each strategy is accompanied by a sample question. Try using the strategy to answer the question, and then go over the answer explanation provided.

On the actual SAT Literature Test—as well as on the practice tests in Part III of this book—each poem or passage will be followed by a set of approximately four to ten questions. Read the passage or poem, then answer the questions. Try these strategies on the practice tests to help prepare yourself for the actual test day.

STRATEGY: Read fiction, nonfiction, poetry, and drama actively and often.

The best way to get a high score on the SAT Literature Test is to be an avid and active reader. You won't be required to have read any specific literary works or to memorize authors' names or lists of the books and poems they wrote. Prior familiarity with the passages that appear on the test probably won't affect your score. However, it will help to be generally familiar with literature of different periods, because writing styles and vocabulary changed a great deal between the Renaissance and modern times.

It is also best to get into the habit of thinking about what you read, because that is what the test will ask you to do. You will have to analyze passages, to identify specific details, and to draw conclusions. You can practice this skill the same way as any other. Every time you read a book or a story, ask yourself questions about it as you go. Use homework assignments from English class to help yourself prepare for the test. The more accustomed you are to thinking about what you read, and to picking up clues and implications in a text, the stronger position you will be in to do well on the Literature Test.

STRATEGY: Skip difficult poems or passages and return to them later.

The literary works and excerpts that appear on the SAT Literature Test were chosen with college-bound high school students in mind. In other words, these works should be appropriate to your current reading level. However, everyone brings different knowledge and experience to literature, and everyone has different areas of difficulty.

The best way to earn a high score on the test is to choose as many correct answers as possible and as few wrong answers. Therefore, it is a smart strategy to read through, or at least glance at, all the passages before you look at any of the questions. Begin with the easiest selection, then go back and work on the more challenging ones. Because you are free to answer the questions in any order you choose, it's best to concentrate on the easy poems and passages first. This will give you confidence and help you accumulate a stock of correct answers to build on.

With some questions, you may be able to eliminate two or even three wrong answer choices. If you can narrow your choices down to two or three from the original five, it's probably a good idea to answer these questions. However, you should only go back to them after you have answered all the questions of which you are sure of the answers.

STRATEGY: Weigh three given options to decide if one, two, or all three are correct.

The SAT Literature Test uses a question format you may not have encountered before. Some of the questions will ask you which of three options is correct. It then will give you five lettered choices that show different combinations of those three options. Any one, any two, or all three of the options may be correct.

First, read the three options and eliminate any that do not answer the question correctly. Cross out the Roman numerals of those options in your test booklet. Any remaining options should constitute the correct answer. Look among the five answer choices to see if there is one that agrees with your answer. If there isn't, go back and check the numbered options against the original passage.

Read the following passage, then try the sample question that follows.

The grill-room clock struck eleven with the respectful unobtrusiveness of one whose mission in life is to be ignored. When the flight of time should really have rendered abstinence and migration imperative the lighting apparatus would signal the fact in the usual way.

5 Clovis approached the supper-table, in the blessed expectancy of one who has dined sketchily and long ago.

"I'm starving," he announced, making an effort to sit down gracefully and read the menu at the same time.

"So I gathered," said his host, "from the fact that you were nearly punctual. I ought to
10 have told you that I'm a Food Reformer. I've ordered two bowls of bread-and-milk and some health biscuits. I hope you don't mind."

Clovis pretended afterwards that he didn't go white above the collar-line for the fraction of a second.

"All the same," he said, "you ought not to joke about such things. There really are such
15 people. I've known people who've met them. To think of all the adorable things there are to eat in the world and then to go through life munching sawdust and being proud of it."

"They're like the Flagellants of the Middle Ages, who went about mortifying themselves."

"They had some excuse," said Clovis. "They did it to save their immortal souls, didn't they? You needn't tell me that a man who doesn't love oysters and asparagus and good
20 wines has got a soul, or a stomach either. He's simply got the instinct for being unhappy highly developed."

(1911)

Example

1. The author most likely wrote this work from which this passage is taken in order to

      I. persuade readers not to eat health food
      II. entertain readers with an amusing story
      III. inform readers what it is like to be a Food Reformer

(A) I only
(B) I and II only
(C) II only
(D) II and III only
(E) III only

Read the question, then read options I–III. Cross out any options that do not answer the question correctly. Then look at the lettered choices to see if your answer is among them. That will be the correct answer.

Remember that any one, any two, or all three of the numbered options may be correct. Do not hesitate to choose any of the lettered answers simply because they contain one, two, or all of the three options.

The writer does not mention any benefits that would accrue to the reader from eating health food, so you can cross out option I. The story is entertaining and amusing, so option II is correct. The writer does not dwell on what it's like to be a Food Reformer. He mentions the idea of health food simply in order to create an amusing moment between the host and Clovis. Therefore, you can cross out option III.

Only option II is left, which means only choice C can be the correct answer.

STRATEGY: Learn how to answer questions about vocabulary.

The SAT Literature Test will ask you to choose the correct definition of a word from a passage or poem. The best way to answer such a question is to go back to the passage to find the word, then mentally replace it with each of the five answer choices. The correct answer will be the one that best fits the sense of the sentence in the original.

The question may ask about a word you have never seen before. Don't panic. Often, the context in which a word is used will make the meaning clear, or at least will enable you to eliminate two or three obviously wrong answers. You will then have good odds of guessing the correct answer.

Use your knowledge of prefixes, suffixes, and roots when asked about unfamiliar vocabulary words. For example, you know that the prefix *uni-* means "one." This would help you define the word *unicycle* if you had never seen it before.

Never answer a vocabulary question without looking back at the word in the original passage. Many English words have more than one meaning. *Cleave,* for instance, can mean "to cling together" or "to split apart." If you don't look back at the passage, you won't know which definition of a multiple-meaning word is correct.

The sample question refers to the passage above.

Example

2. The word "unobtrusiveness" in the first sentence (line 1) means

(A) anger
(B) inconspicuousness
(C) heartiness
(D) sullenness
(E) invisibility

If you know the meaning of *unobtrusiveness,* good; you can answer the question without taking any further time. If not, go back to the passage and circle the word. Try each of the five answer choices in its place. Which one makes the most sense?

The context clues are "respectful" and "mission in life is to be ignored." Therefore you are looking for a word that conveys a meaning of quietness, modesty, and keeping a low profile. *Anger* and *heartiness* clearly do not fit with the notion of being ignored. *Invisibility* is too extreme and does not fit the idea of a clock striking, which is a sound rather than a sight. *Sullenness* goes with the idea of being ignored, but not with being respectful. Choice B, *inconspicuousness,* is a perfect synonym for *unobtrusiveness. Inconspicuous* means "not obvious, apparent, or noticeable." It makes perfect sense in the context and is the correct answer.

STRATEGY: If you don't know the answer, make an educated guess.

Most questions on the SAT Literature Test will refer you back to the passage, asking you to draw a conclusion or correctly identify a detail. However, some questions will ask about literary terms. If you don't know the definitions of those terms, you may have trouble with the question. It is a good idea to study the meaning of literary terms such as *allusion, sonnet,* and *metaphor* before you take the test. See Chapter 1 of this book for a glossary of common literary terms.

If you come across unfamiliar literary terms on the test, you should still be able to make an educated guess. You will probably recognize one or two of the terms in the answer choices. You may be able to figure out the meaning of others just by looking at them. For instance, the word *simile* looks enough like the word *similar* that you might be able to approximate its meaning for the purposes of answering a multiple-choice question.

Read the poem, then try the sample question that follows.

The Man He Killed

"Had he and I but met
By some old ancient inn,
We should have sat us down to wet
Right many a nipperkin!

5 "But ranged as infantry,
And staring face to face,
I shot at him as he at me,
And killed him in his place.

"I shot him dead because—
10 Because he was my foe,
Just so: my foe of course he was;
That's clear enough; although

"He thought he'd 'list, perhaps,
Off-hand like—just as I—
15 Was out of work—had sold his traps—
No other reason why.

"Yes; quaint and curious war is!
You shoot a fellow down
You'd treat, if met where any bar is,
20 Or help to half-a-crown."

(1917)

Example

3. This poem represents or includes all of the following EXCEPT

  (A) enjambment
  (B) dialect
  (C) dramatic monologue
  (D) exact rhyme
  (E) ballad

If you know the meaning of the five literary terms in the answer choices, then you can answer this question right away without wasting any time. If you only know one or two of them, you are in a good position to make an educated guess.

Go through the terms one by one. You may not recognize *enjambment*; if not, move on to the next choice. You probably will remember that *dialect* refers to colloquial or regional speech, which you can see in the poem in such expressions as "wet / Right many a nipperkin." You can use your knowledge of word parts to break down the word *monologue* and define it as "a speech made by one character." This poem, which is spoken aloud by one person, fits that meaning. You should conclude that the term *exact rhyme* is self-explanatory; it refers to words that rhyme exactly. Such pairs as *perhaps/traps* and *down/crown* show that this poem includes exact rhymes. You may or may not know exactly what kind of poem a *ballad* is.

You have eliminated three of the five choices. Now you have a 50% chance of guessing the correct answer, and you probably should take a chance on it. It is probably best to go through the rest of the questions first, answering all the ones you are quite sure of, then return and answer questions like this one, which you have a good chance of answering correctly.

(In fact, *enjambment* refers to lines of poetry that do not end in punctuation marks, but instead continue a sentence or complete thought to the next line or lines without pause. A *ballad* is a narrative poem that features four-line stanzas with alternate lengths of six and eight syllables. This poem does feature enjambment; several of the lines carry a thought on to the next one without a pause. It is clearly influenced by the ballad form, but does not quite fit the definition, as each stanza has a different pattern of syllables. Therefore, *ballad* is the one term that is not included or represented in the poem, and E is the correct answer.)

STRATEGY: Learn how to answer quotation questions.

The SAT Literature Test will feature a number of questions that quote a specific sentence, line, or phrase in the passage or poem. The best strategy in this case is to read the question, go back to the passage, read the phrase or line in its context, and then look at the answer choices to see which one is best.

Read the poem, then try the sample question that follows.

That time of year thou may'st in me behold
When yellow leaves, or none, or few, do hang
Upon those boughs which shake against the cold,
Bare ruined choirs, where late the sweet birds sang.

> 5 In me thou see'st the twilight of such day
>   As after sunset fadeth in the west;
>   Which by and by black night doth take away,
>   Death's second self, that seals up all in rest.
>   In me thou see'st the glowing of such fire,
> 10 That on the ashes of his youth doth lie,
>   As the deathbed whereon it must expire,
>   Consumed with that which it was nourished by.
>   This thou perceiv'st, which makes thy love more strong.
>   To love that well which thou must leave ere long.

(1609)

Example

4. "Death's second self" (line 8) refers to

    (A) sleep
    (B) twilight
    (C) night
    (D) old age
    (E) sunset

You notice that the question tells you the line number where you can find this phrase in the original poem. The SAT Literature Test will always provide you with the line number of a quotation so you won't have to reread the entire passage to find it.

Look back at line 8 of the poem to find the reference to "Death's second self." Read back a few lines to find the beginning of the sentence. Remember that in poems, lines are not the same thing as sentences. In this case, the sentence begins at line 5, "In me thou see'st." In line 7 you find the phrase "black night," which is what the speaker describes as "Death's second self." The correct answer is choice C.

STRATEGY: Understand archaic word order and usage.

The SAT Literature Test will feature selections from the premodern era. For example, the sonnet you read for question 4 comes from the English Renaissance of the late sixteenth and early seventeenth centuries. At that time, English usage differed from the modern usage to which you are accustomed. For example, this poem uses a verb tense that we no longer use: the familiar second-person pronoun *thou* and the verbs that go with it, ending in *–st*. When questions ask you about the meanings of words and phrases, you need to consider carefully how those words and phrases are being used in a selection that dates back to a time before 1800. This is especially true of poetry.

The sample question refers to the sonnet above.

Example

5. Which of the following best paraphrases the final two lines of the sonnet (lines 13–14)?

(A) Your love for me is stronger than my love for you.
(B) Since you can see how old I am, there is no sense in you loving me so much.
(C) Your love is strong because I am too old for you.
(D) You are brave to love me when you know that you are bound to lose me to death before long.
(E) I love you, so I regret that I will die long before you will.

This question asks you to rephrase two lines of a poem in modern language. The best way to do that is to go over those two lines to be sure you understand exactly what they say. You may want to rewrite the lines yourself, then see which answer comes closest to your version. Remember that a paraphrase must include all the same ideas as the original.

"This thou perceiv'st, which makes thy love more strong.

To love that well which thou must leave ere long."

You need to know that *ere* means *before* and that *thou perceiv'st* means *you perceive*. You also need to know that *thy* is the possessive form of *thou*.

Your version might say:

"Your ability to see my old age makes your love more admirable.

It takes great strength to love someone who will soon leave you because he will soon die of old age."

This paraphrase includes all the ideas expressed in the original. Note that you have to read back a little further than line 13 to figure out exactly what the speaker means.

You can see right away that the speaker does not refer at all to his own feelings toward the person he is addressing; therefore you can eliminate choices A and E. You can eliminate choice B because the speaker says nothing about the love being unwise. Choice D encompasses the important ideas expressed in the two lines and is the correct answer.

STRATEGY: Pay attention to capitalized words in the questions, such as NOT and EXCEPT.

Make sure you do not carelessly misread a question. Some questions on the SAT Literature Test contain the capitalized word NOT or EXCEPT. If you miss this word, you will misinterpret the question and choose the wrong answer. The best strategy is to circle this word when you see it in a question. That will help you concentrate on what the question is really asking you to find.

Read the passage and then try the sample question that follows.

When Jane and Elizabeth were alone, the former, who had been cautious in her praise of Mr. Bingley before, expressed to her sister how very much she admired him.

"He is just what a young man ought to be," said she, "sensible, good-humored, lively; and I never saw such happy manners!—so much ease, with such perfect good-breeding!"

5   "He is also handsome," replied Elizabeth; "which a young man ought likewise to be, if he possibly can. His character is thereby complete."

"I was very much flattered by his asking me to dance a second time. I did not expect such a compliment."

"Did not you? *I* did for you. But that is one great difference between us. Compliments
10   always take *you* by surprise, and *me* never. What could be more natural than his asking you again? He could not help seeing that you were about five times as pretty as every other woman in the room. No thanks to his gallantry for that. Well, he certainly is very agreeable, and I give you leave to like him. You have liked many a stupider person."

"Dear Lizzy!"

15   "Oh! you are a great deal too apt, you know, to like people in general. You never see a fault in anybody. All the world are good and agreeable in your eyes. I never heard you speak ill of a human being in my life."

"I would not wish to be hasty in censuring anyone; but I always speak what I think."

"I know you do; and it is *that* which makes the wonder. With *your* good sense, to be so
20   honestly blind to the follies and nonsense of others! Affectation of candour is common enough—one meets it everywhere. But to be candid without ostentation or design—to take the good of everybody's character and make it still better, and say nothing of the bad—belongs to you alone."

(1813)

Example

6. Which of the following does NOT characterize Jane?

   (A) friendliness
   (B) perceptiveness
   (C) pleasantness
   (D) popularity
   (E) modesty

Circle the word NOT in the question. This word tells you that four of the choices should describe Jane accurately, while the other one does not. The one that does not describe her accurately is the correct answer.

Look over the four choices. Anyone who sees the good in others and never comments on the bad is bound to be friendly, popular, and pleasant. In addition, because *friendly* and *pleasant* mean more or less the same thing, they must both be either wrong or right. Because there is only one right answer to every test question, both must be wrong. Therefore you can eliminate choices A, C, and D. Elizabeth's statements "Compliments always take you by surprise" and "you were about five times as pretty as any other woman in the room" make it clear that Jane is modest; a pretty woman should not be surprised at a compliment, unless she is unusually modest about her own good looks. This leaves choice B, *perceptiveness*. You know from Elizabeth's comment "so honestly blind to the follies and nonsense of others" that Jane sees the good but not the bad in people. This makes her kind, but not truly perceptive. Choice B is the correct answer.

Diagnostic Test

The following diagnostic test is designed to be just like the real SAT Subject Test in Literature. It matches the actual test in content coverage and degree of difficulty.

Once you finish the diagnostic test, determine your score. Carefully read the answer explanations of the questions you answered incorrectly. Identify any weaknesses in your literary skills by determining the areas in which you made the most errors. Review those sections of this book first. Then, as time permits, go back and review your strengths.

Allow one hour to take the test. Time yourself and work uninterrupted. If you run out of time, take note of where you stopped when time ran out. Remember that you lose a quarter point for each incorrect answer, but you do not lose points for questions you leave blank. Therefore, unless you can eliminate one or more of the five choices, it is best to leave a question unanswered.

Use the following formula to calculate your score:

(number of correct answers) − ¼ (number of incorrect answers)

If you treat this diagnostic test just like the actual exam, it will accurately reflect how you are likely to perform on test day. Here are some hints on how to create test-taking conditions similar to those of the actual exam:

- Complete the test in one sitting. On test day, you will not be allowed to take a break.
- Tear out the answer sheet and fill in the ovals just as you will on the actual test day.
- Have a good eraser and more than one sharp pencil handy. On test day, you will not be able to go get a new pencil if yours breaks.
- Do not allow yourself any extra time; put down your pencil after exactly one hour, no matter how many questions are left to answer.
- Become familiar with the directions on the test. If you go in knowing what the directions say, you will not have to waste time reading and thinking about them on the actual test day.

Answer Sheet

Tear out this answer sheet and use it to mark your answers.

1. Ⓐ Ⓑ Ⓒ Ⓓ Ⓔ	16. Ⓐ Ⓑ Ⓒ Ⓓ Ⓔ	31. Ⓐ Ⓑ Ⓒ Ⓓ Ⓔ	46. Ⓐ Ⓑ Ⓒ Ⓓ Ⓔ
2. Ⓐ Ⓑ Ⓒ Ⓓ Ⓔ	17. Ⓐ Ⓑ Ⓒ Ⓓ Ⓔ	32. Ⓐ Ⓑ Ⓒ Ⓓ Ⓔ	47. Ⓐ Ⓑ Ⓒ Ⓓ Ⓔ
3. Ⓐ Ⓑ Ⓒ Ⓓ Ⓔ	18. Ⓐ Ⓑ Ⓒ Ⓓ Ⓔ	33. Ⓐ Ⓑ Ⓒ Ⓓ Ⓔ	48. Ⓐ Ⓑ Ⓒ Ⓓ Ⓔ
4. Ⓐ Ⓑ Ⓒ Ⓓ Ⓔ	19. Ⓐ Ⓑ Ⓒ Ⓓ Ⓔ	34. Ⓐ Ⓑ Ⓒ Ⓓ Ⓔ	49. Ⓐ Ⓑ Ⓒ Ⓓ Ⓔ
5. Ⓐ Ⓑ Ⓒ Ⓓ Ⓔ	20. Ⓐ Ⓑ Ⓒ Ⓓ Ⓔ	35. Ⓐ Ⓑ Ⓒ Ⓓ Ⓔ	50. Ⓐ Ⓑ Ⓒ Ⓓ Ⓔ
6. Ⓐ Ⓑ Ⓒ Ⓓ Ⓔ	21. Ⓐ Ⓑ Ⓒ Ⓓ Ⓔ	36. Ⓐ Ⓑ Ⓒ Ⓓ Ⓔ	51. Ⓐ Ⓑ Ⓒ Ⓓ Ⓔ
7. Ⓐ Ⓑ Ⓒ Ⓓ Ⓔ	22. Ⓐ Ⓑ Ⓒ Ⓓ Ⓔ	37. Ⓐ Ⓑ Ⓒ Ⓓ Ⓔ	52. Ⓐ Ⓑ Ⓒ Ⓓ Ⓔ
8. Ⓐ Ⓑ Ⓒ Ⓓ Ⓔ	23. Ⓐ Ⓑ Ⓒ Ⓓ Ⓔ	38. Ⓐ Ⓑ Ⓒ Ⓓ Ⓔ	53. Ⓐ Ⓑ Ⓒ Ⓓ Ⓔ
9. Ⓐ Ⓑ Ⓒ Ⓓ Ⓔ	24. Ⓐ Ⓑ Ⓒ Ⓓ Ⓔ	39. Ⓐ Ⓑ Ⓒ Ⓓ Ⓔ	54. Ⓐ Ⓑ Ⓒ Ⓓ Ⓔ
10. Ⓐ Ⓑ Ⓒ Ⓓ Ⓔ	25. Ⓐ Ⓑ Ⓒ Ⓓ Ⓔ	40. Ⓐ Ⓑ Ⓒ Ⓓ Ⓔ	55. Ⓐ Ⓑ Ⓒ Ⓓ Ⓔ
11. Ⓐ Ⓑ Ⓒ Ⓓ Ⓔ	26. Ⓐ Ⓑ Ⓒ Ⓓ Ⓔ	41. Ⓐ Ⓑ Ⓒ Ⓓ Ⓔ	56. Ⓐ Ⓑ Ⓒ Ⓓ Ⓔ
12. Ⓐ Ⓑ Ⓒ Ⓓ Ⓔ	27. Ⓐ Ⓑ Ⓒ Ⓓ Ⓔ	42. Ⓐ Ⓑ Ⓒ Ⓓ Ⓔ	57. Ⓐ Ⓑ Ⓒ Ⓓ Ⓔ
13. Ⓐ Ⓑ Ⓒ Ⓓ Ⓔ	28. Ⓐ Ⓑ Ⓒ Ⓓ Ⓔ	43. Ⓐ Ⓑ Ⓒ Ⓓ Ⓔ	58. Ⓐ Ⓑ Ⓒ Ⓓ Ⓔ
14. Ⓐ Ⓑ Ⓒ Ⓓ Ⓔ	29. Ⓐ Ⓑ Ⓒ Ⓓ Ⓔ	44. Ⓐ Ⓑ Ⓒ Ⓓ Ⓔ	59. Ⓐ Ⓑ Ⓒ Ⓓ Ⓔ
15. Ⓐ Ⓑ Ⓒ Ⓓ Ⓔ	30. Ⓐ Ⓑ Ⓒ Ⓓ Ⓔ	45. Ⓐ Ⓑ Ⓒ Ⓓ Ⓔ	60. Ⓐ Ⓑ Ⓒ Ⓓ Ⓔ

DIAGNOSTIC TEST

Time: 60 Questions/60 Minutes

Directions: This test consists of selections from literary works and questions on their content, form, and style. After reading each passage or poem, choose the best answer to each question, and then fill in the corresponding oval on the answer sheet.

Note: Pay particular attention to the requirements of questions that contain the words NOT or EXCEPT.

Questions 1–10. Read the following excerpt carefully before you choose your answers.

I don't know why I should write this. I don't want to. I don't feel able. And I know John would think it absurd. But I *must* say what I feel and think in some way—it is such a relief!

5 But the effort is getting to be greater than the relief. Half the time now I am awfully lazy, and lie down ever so much.

John says I musn't lose my strength, and has me take cod-liver oil and lots of tonics and things, to say nothing of ale 10 and wine and rare meat.

Dear John! He loves me very dearly, and hates to have me sick. I tried to have a real earnest reasonable talk with him the other day, and tell him how I wish he would let me go and make a visit to Cousin Henry and Julia.

15 But he said I wasn't able to go, nor able to stand it after I got there; and I did not make out a very good case for myself, for I was crying before I had finished.

It is getting to be a great effort for me to think straight. Just this nervous weakness, I suppose.

20 And dear John gathered me up in his arms, and just carried me upstairs and laid me on the bed, and sat by me and read to me till it tired my head.

He said I was his darling and his comfort and all he had, and that I must take care of myself for his sake, and 25 keep well.

He says no one but myself can help me out of it, that I must use my will and self-control and not let any silly fancies run away with me.

There's one comfort, the baby is well and happy, and 30 does not have to occupy this nursery with the horrid wallpaper.

If we had not used it that blessed child would have! What a fortunate escape! Why, I wouldn't have a child of mine, an impressionable little thing, live in such a room for 35 worlds.

I never thought of it before, but it is lucky that John kept me here after all. I can stand it so much easier than a baby, you see.

Of course I never mention it to them any more—I am too 40 wise—but I keep watch of it all the same.

There are things in that paper that nobody knows but me, or ever will.

Behind that outside pattern the dim shapes get clearer every day. It is always the same shape, only very 45 numerous.

And it is like a woman stooping down and creeping about behind that pattern. I don't like it a bit. I wonder—I begin to think—I wish John would take me away from here!

(1892)

1. Which of the following does the first paragraph establish?

   (A) the speaker's mental discomfiture
   (B) the speaker's relationship with John
   (C) the cause of the speaker's inner conflict
   (D) the absurdity of the speaker's introspection
   (E) the speaker's consummate ability as a writer

2. The phrase "to say nothing of" conveys that

   (A) the speaker is at a loss for words
   (B) John has prescribed that the speaker abstain from ale, wine, and rare meat
   (C) the speaker's diet currently consists of all the items mentioned in lines 9–10
   (D) John refuses to discuss the speaker's preference for food and beverages
   (E) the speaker is unwillingly silent on the matter of sustenance

3. Which of the following lines contains the LEAST convincing evidence of the narrator's malady?

   (A) "I don't know why I should write . . . feel able."
   (B) "He says no one but myself . . . run away with me."
   (C) "It is getting . . . nervous weakness, I suppose."
   (D) "There are things . . . clearer every day."
   (E) "I wish John would take me away from here!"

4. What can be inferred about life during the nineteenth century by the speaker's phrase "but I did not make out a very good case for myself"?

   (A) the predominant patriarchal ideology of the time
   (B) the extralegal ramifications for women pleading mental insanity
   (C) the hopeless position of young mothers with physician husbands
   (D) the loss of individual rights in cases of female hysteria
   (E) the widespread practice of quarantine for the mentally disturbed

5. It can be inferred that the discernible tension between the speaker and her husband, John, is attributable to which of the following?

   I. The speaker is skeptical of her husband's prescribed methods for her recovery.
   II. Their marriage is molded by misogynistic social mores.
   III. The husband is unconvinced of the seriousness of her illness.

   (A) I only
   (B) III only
   (C) I and II only
   (D) I and III only
   (E) I, II, and III

6. The phrase "What a fortunate escape!" is ironic for all of the following reasons EXCEPT

(A) a nursery is meant to be occupied by a baby

(B) the narrator is placed under house arrest by her physician husband

(C) the narrator is genuinely thankful that her child is spared the experience and confines of the nursery

(D) the narrator feels helpless and incapable of escaping her mental, emotional, and physical state

(E) the narrator's illness has taken such a toll on her family that they share in her misfortune during this retreat to this country

7. "This nursery with the horrid wallpaper" has primarily affected the speaker by

(A) allowing her the freedom for self-examination

(B) bringing her closer to terms with her mental illness

(C) eliciting further feelings of paranoia

(D) inspiring her to practice her passion for writing

(E) unnerving her beyond the bounds of sanity

8. In context, "Of course . . . will" (lines 39–42) can best be described as

(A) an insinuation of the speaker's elevated IQ

(B) evidence of the wallpaper's mirage-like quality

(C) autobiographical testimony of the feminine plight during the nineteenth century

(D) an example of the woman's increasingly bold delusions

(E) a stream of consciousness style of inner monologue

9. All of the following literary devices appear in the excerpt EXCEPT

(A) personification

(B) hyperbole

(C) indirect dialogue

(D) allusion

(E) double entendre

10. The narrator's tone suggests that her emotions, beliefs, and actions are guided by

(A) socially conscious dysphoria

(B) whimsical illusion

(C) psychological degradation

(D) hysterical insinuation

(E) wry self-deprecation

GO ON TO THE NEXT PAGE ⟹

Questions 11–19. Read the following poem carefully before you choose your answers.

One Art

The art of losing isn't hard to master;
so many things seem filled with the intent
to be lost that their loss is no disaster.

Lose something every day. Accept the fluster
5 of lost door keys, the hour badly spent.
The art of losing isn't hard to master.

Then practice losing farther, losing faster:
places, and names, and where it was you meant
to travel. None of these will bring disaster.

10 I lost my mother's watch. And look! my last, or
next-to-last, of three beloved houses went.
The art of losing isn't hard to master.

I lost two cities, lovely ones. And, vaster,
some realms I owned, two rivers, a continent.
15 I miss them, but it wasn't a disaster.

—Even losing you (the joking voice, a gesture
I love) I shan't have lied. It's evident
the art of losing's not too hard to master
though it may look like (*Write* it!) like disaster.

11. The structural form of the poem is that of

(A) a villanelle
(B) a paean
(C) an Italian sonnet
(D) a ballad
(E) an elegy

12. The repetition of "The art of losing isn't hard to master" (line 1) throughout the poem mainly serves to

(A) emphasize a concept the speaker wants to memorize by heart
(B) compress an esoteric concept into a singsong verse
(C) undermine the seriousness of the poet's intent
(D) extemporize within variations-on-a-theme poetic form
(E) unify both the form and the content of the poem

13. In listing the items the speaker has lost, she

(A) denies her absentmindedness
(B) builds a catalog of increasingly dear personal effects and memories
(C) underscores her overly possessive tendencies
(D) forces herself to reexamine her priorities
(E) criticizes the "art of losing" as impervious to mastery

14. Which of the following devices is used more fully as the poem goes on?

(A) enjambment
(B) end rhyme
(C) interruptive punctuation
(D) irregular cadence
(E) subtle irony

15. Which of the following best characterizes how the poem progresses in the first three stanzas?

    (A) The speaker proposes a novel idea, elaborates on its efficacy through specific illustrations, and then legitimizes her point by introducing its counterpoint.

    (B) The speaker declares a belief, defends her view with universal occurrences, and then justifies her confidence in the infallibility of her belief.

    (C) The speaker shares a personal mantra, includes a brief log of daily life experiments, and then extrapolates the natural conclusion from these results.

    (D) The speaker states a thesis, provides supporting evidence, and then offers further examples that bolster her argument.

    (E) The speaker makes an assumption, posits a rationale underlying the assumption, and then gives reasons as to why the rationale is foolproof.

16. The caesura that begins the final stanza illustrates all of the following EXCEPT

    (A) the speaker's momentary lapse of memory

    (B) the dwindling firmness of the speaker's intent

    (C) the speaker's sudden loss of self-assurance

    (D) a break in the poem's adherence to form

    (E) evidence of the speaker's art in belying her guilt

17. Which of the following interpretations best illustrates the poet's attitude by the end of the poem?

    (A) Life is busy, possessions come and go, and our minds are often occupied by the past when we should be focused on the present in order to distract ourselves.

    (B) The goal of mastering the art of losing is full of folly and self-delusion since we will never get over the loss itself.

    (C) It is human to miss what we once had in our possession but have suffered the loss of, be they concrete or abstract things; this universal experience, however, is no disaster.

    (D) There is always the possibility of disaster when we lose something, but life inculcates the idea that we can write off the loss with cool detachment.

    (E) It is too easy to lose things, therefore one must learn by practicing the art of losing objects, people, places, and concepts daily, so that endurance leads to mastery.

18. The overall tone of the poem is

    (A) dramatically ironic
    (B) endearingly self-aware
    (C) stoically disaffected
    (D) pedantically moralistic
    (E) gently sardonic

19. The momentum that drives "One Art" is a mounting conflict between

    (A) self-possession and pathologies surrounding "love"

    (B) living in the present and outliving the haunting past

    (C) human faculty and that which exceeds our reason

    (D) mastery of self and the necessity for companionship

    (E) artistic efforts and the constraints of reception

Questions 20–26. Read the following passage carefully before you choose your answers.

What opium is instilled into all disaster! It shows formidable as we approach it, but there is at last no rough rasping friction, but the most slippery sliding surfaces. We fall soft on a thought . . . People grieve and bemoan
5 themselves, but it is not half so bad with them as they say. There are moods in which we court suffering, in the hope that here, at least, we shall find reality, sharp peaks and edges of truth. But it turns out to be scene-painting and counterfeit. The only thing grief has taught me, is to
10 know how shallow it is. That, like all the rest, plays about the surface, and never introduces me into the reality, for contact with which, we would even pay the costly price of sons and lovers. Was it Boscovich[1] who found out that bodies never come in contact? Well, souls never
15 touch their objects. An innavigable sea washes with silent waves between us and the things we aim at and converse with. Grief too will make us idealists. In the death of my son, now more than two years ago, I seem to have lost a beautiful estate,—no more. I cannot get it nearer to me.
20 If tomorrow I should be informed of the bankruptcy of my principal debtors, the loss of my property would be a great inconvenience to me, perhaps, for many years; but it would leave me as it found me,—neither better nor worse. So is it with this calamity: it does not touch
25 me: something which I fancied was a part of me, which could not be torn away without tearing me, nor enlarged without enriching me, falls off from me, and leaves no scar . . . I grieve that grief can teach me nothing, nor carry me one step into real nature.

(1844)

[1] Roger Joseph Boscovich, SJ (1711–1787) was a Croatian Jesuit mathematician, physicist, and scholar who conceived the first coherent description of atomic theory in his work *Theoria Philosophiae Naturalis*. In it, he states that bodies are not composed of continuous matter but of countless "point-like structures" or "atoms."

20. In line 1, opium is used figuratively for its capacity to

(A) dull the senses
(B) corrupt the soul
(C) weaken the will
(D) produce euphoria
(E) intensify fantasies

21. According to the speaker, "we court suffering" (line 6) at times because we believe that

(A) pain is easier to relish than pleasure or truth
(B) pain carries us closer to contact with reality
(C) pain makes us more steadfast and augments our integrity
(D) pain earns us the compassion and absolution of others
(E) to bring an end to pain is to usher in pleasure

22. The clause "the things we aim at and converse with" (lines 16–17) signifies about the same thing as the phrase

(A) "slippery sliding surfaces" (line 3)
(B) "innavigable sea" (line 15)
(C) "beautiful estate" (line 19)
(D) "principal debtors" (line 21)
(E) "real nature" (line 29)

23. The phrase "no more" (line 19) most nearly means

(A) no longer in existence
(B) nothing deeper
(C) I can endure no more pain from my grief
(D) I cannot remember my grief
(E) I am bankrupt and abandoned by my grief

24. The speaker's experience with grief has left him

      I. bereft of any heirs
     II. mortally wounded beneath the surface
   III. woebegone and acquiescent

(A) I only
(B) I and II
(C) II only
(D) II and III
(E) III only

25. Most of the passage's imagery and figurative expressions are achieved through the poet's use of diction, which is generally

(A) oriented around scenic and landscape painting
(B) histrionic and out of fashion
(C) unpretentious and monochromatic
(D) self-consciously stripped of all sentimentality
(E) humdrum and unsophisticated

26. The speaker suggests all of the following aspects of grief EXCEPT its

(A) paralyzing effect on the grief-stricken
(B) intimidating approach but impassive appearance
(C) eventual disintegration
(D) permanent mark on those who suffer
(E) infantilization of the dead

Questions 27–30. Read the following passage carefully before you choose your answers.

We deplore the outrages which accompany revolutions. But the more violent the outrages, the more assured we feel that a revolution was necessary. The violence of those outrages will always be proportioned to the ferocity and
5 ignorance of the people: and the ferocity and ignorance of the people will be proportioned to the oppression and degradation under which they have been accustomed to live. Thus it was in our civil war. . . . There is only one cure for the evils which newly acquired freedom
10 produces—and that cure is freedom. When a prisoner leaves his cell, he cannot bear the light of day;—he is unable to discriminate colors, or recognize faces. But the remedy is not to remand him into his dungeon, but to accustom him to the rays of the sun. The blaze of truth
15 and liberty may at first dazzle and bewilder nations which have become half blind in the house of bondage. But let them gaze on, and they will soon be able to bear it. In a few years men learn to reason . . . Many politicians of our time are in the habit of laying it down as a self-evident
20 proposition that no people ought to be free till they are fit

to use their freedom. The maxim is worthy of the fool in the old story who resolved not to go into the water till he had learnt to swim! If men are to wait for liberty till they become wise and good in slavery, they may indeed wait
25 forever.

(1895)

27. The passage contains an example of

(A) epic simile
(B) mythological allusion
(C) anaphora
(D) argument by analogy
(E) dramatic verse

28. What primary effect does the inclusion of "Thus it was in our civil war" (line 8) have?

(A) It provides contextual clues that ground the speaker's lofty rhetoric in lived experience and humble optimism.

(B) It underscores the linearity of the rise and fall of empires.

(C) It lends credibility to the authority of the speaker.

(D) It draws parallels across historical eras and civilizations.

(E) It reinforces the speaker's urging for a second civil war.

29. The speaker's use of repetition, bracketed syntax, and juxtaposition has the effect of

(A) the absolute height of emphasis

(B) indisputable reverence for certain words and the values they embody

(C) deferential reserve for words that will signify the same thing to his audience as they do for him

(D) flippant disregard for posturing simply to gain a king's regard

(E) all of the above

30. In the maxim referred to in lines 21–23, "water" is symbolic of

(A) liberty

(B) reason

(C) violence

(D) tyranny

(E) revolution

Questions 31–40. Read the following passage carefully before you choose your answers.

I have one word to say upon the subject of profound writers, who are grown very numerous of late; and I know very well, the judicious world is resolved to list me in that number. I conceive therefore, as to the business of being
5 profound, that it is with writers as with wells—a person with good eyes may see to the bottom of the deepest, provided any water be there; and that often, when there is nothing in the world at the bottom, besides dryness and dirt, though it be but a yard and half under ground, it
10 shall pass, however, for wondrous deep, upon no wiser a reason than because it is wondrous dark.

I am now trying an experiment very frequent among modern authors; which is to write upon *Nothing*; when the subject is utterly exhausted, to let the pen still move
15 on; by some called the ghost of wit, delighting to walk after the death of its body. And to say the truth, there seems to be no part of knowledge in fewer hands, than that of discerning when to have done. By the time that an author has writ out a book, he and his readers are become
20 old acquaintances, and grow very loth to part; so that I have sometimes known it to be in writing, as in visiting, where the ceremony of taking leave has employed more time than the whole conversation before. The conclusion of a treatise resembles the conclusion of human life,
25 which has sometimes been compared to the end of a feast; where few are satisfied to depart, *ut plenus vitae conviva*. For me will sit down after the fullest meal, though it be only to doze, or to sleep out the rest of the day. But, in this latter, I differ extremely from other writers, and shall
30 be too proud, if, by all my labours, I can have anyways contributed to the repose of mankind, in times so turbulent and unquiet as these.

(1704)

31. In terms of the comparison of writers to wells, "water" (line 7) is best understood as

(A) content

(B) mere appearance

(C) imagination

(D) style

(E) practical value

GO ON TO THE NEXT PAGE ⟹

32. Given the terms of comparison in lines 5–11, "dryness and dirt" (lines 8–9) is best interpreted as

    (A) barren thoughts
    (B) inflexible beliefs
    (C) pornographic fancies
    (D) down-to-earth realities
    (E) conventional attitudes

33. Which of the following is the most appropriate interpretation of the figurative language in lines 5–7 ("it is . . . be there")?

    (A) If writing is to be truly profound, the ideas must be conveyed in a complicated style.
    (B) If the writing has any substance, it can be understood by an intelligent reader.
    (C) A complicated style of writing is often a disguise for a shallow intelligence.
    (D) If the writing is truly profound, it is beyond ordinary human understanding.
    (E) The true meaning of a work is whatever an intelligent reader wants it to be.

34. The speaker uses "wondrous" (lines 10–11) to convey

    (A) a perverse delight in light and shallow literature
    (B) critical approval of literary and philosophical profundity
    (C) the response the speaker wants others to have toward the speaker's own works
    (D) the naive enthusiasm of uncritical readers
    (E) an awed response to genuine literary achievements

35. In its metaphorical context, "body" (line 16) refers to

    (A) an author
    (B) the substance of the work
    (C) a completed text
    (D) an edited and published work
    (E) the author's talent

36. Which of the following best paraphrases the sentence "And to say the truth . . . to have done" (lines 16–18)?

    (A) Authors seldom get their works into the proper hands.
    (B) Few authors know when to stop writing.
    (C) Authors seldom know anything about what other authors have done.
    (D) Few authors really know how to express themselves clearly.
    (E) Authors seldom know where to obtain the knowledge they require.

37. Which of the following best defines "his readers" in line 19?

    (A) friends the author has made through his writings
    (B) loyal friends on whom the author can depend to read his books
    (C) the readers who have purchased the author's work
    (D) acquaintances the author has sent his manuscript to
    (E) the readers the author imagines he is addressing as he writes

38. Given the speaker's attitude toward modern authors, the word "profound" (line 1) is best understood to mean

    (A) morbidly pessimistic
    (B) engagingly witty
    (C) intellectually pretentious
    (D) psychologically deep
    (E) authentically philosophical

GO ON TO THE NEXT PAGE ⟼

39. Given the speaker's attitude toward modern authors and their readers, "judicious" (line 3) is best interpreted as

(A) unnecessarily precise
(B) critically inept
(C) acutely discriminating
(D) intellectually challenging
(E) unpleasantly hypercritical

40. The second paragraph wittily illustrates

(A) the notion that most writers are truly profound
(B) a philosophical argument on the nature of existence
(C) the very technique the author is criticizing
(D) the nature of the relationship between writers and readers
(E) the importance of leave-taking ceremonies as social convention

Questions 41–50. Read the following poem carefully before you choose your answers.

Sympathy

I know what the caged bird feels, alas!
When the sun is bright on the upland slopes;
When the wind stirs soft through the springing grass,
And the river flows like a stream of glass;
5   When the first bird sings and the first bud opes,
And the faint perfume from its chalice steals—
I know what the caged bird feels!

I know why the caged bird beats his wing
Till its blood is red on the cruel bars;
10 For he must fly back to his perch and cling
When he fain would be on the bough a-swing;
And a pain still throbs in the old, old scars
And they pulse again with a keener sting—
I know why he beats his wing!

15 I know why the caged bird sings, ah me,
When his wing is bruised and his bosom sore,—
When he beats his bars and he would be free;
It is not a carol of joy or glee,
But a prayer that he sends from his heart's deep core,
20 But a plea, that upward to Heaven he flings—
I know why the caged bird sings!

(1899)

41. The style of the poem is that of

(A) a villanelle
(B) an English ode
(C) a paean
(D) a ballad
(E) a limerick

42. In line 1, the speaker's expressive sigh "alas!" conveys a sense of the speaker's

(A) dismay and ability to identify with the caged bird
(B) world-weariness and self-loathing to the point of despair
(C) exasperation with maintaining caretaking duties for the bird
(D) frustration with the speaker's lack of freedom in the social sphere
(E) distress and compulsion for intrusive commentary about social constructs

43. In line 11, the phrase "When he fain would be" can be understood to mean

(A) "When he would be faint"
(B) "While he would wish instead to be"
(C) "Were he elsewhere, he would be"
(D) "When he would feign be"
(E) "Whenever he would be, in vain"

44. Which of the following BEST paraphrases lines 10–11?

    (A) The bird must return to the perch even though he would rather be on a swing.
    (B) The bird stays in his cage because his injuries might cause him to faint.
    (C) The bird has to stay in the cage when he would rather be perched on a swinging tree branch.
    (D) The bird stays on his perch because he is afraid of the wind.
    (E) The bird reciprocates the cruelty of the bars of his cage by violently flapping his wings and maiming himself.

45. In line 13, the speaker's use of "keener" to describe the sting felt by the bird can be interpreted as all of the following EXCEPT

    (A) more painfully
    (B) more intensely
    (C) more acutely
    (D) more intelligently
    (E) more stridently

46. The poet compares the caged bird's song to a

    (A) lullaby
    (B) symphony
    (C) prayer
    (D) carol of joy
    (E) pulse

47. Lines 12–14 suggest that

    (A) the bird is so crippled he will never be able to enjoy freedom
    (B) as the bird gains years of experience, his desire for freedom intensifies
    (C) the bird could enjoy his captivity if only he would stop fighting
    (D) the bird has not given up hope despite a lifetime of captivity
    (E) the bird perpetuates his chronic pain by endeavoring to escape his futility

48. According to the speaker, how does the caged bird feel?

    (A) bright, springy, perfumed
    (B) constrained, oppressed, imprisoned
    (C) faint, clingy, ill
    (D) alarmed, persecuted, fearful
    (E) restless, bitter, bruised

49. Which of the following BEST explains the poem's title, "Sympathy"?

    (A) The speaker pities the caged bird because of his injuries.
    (B) The speaker admires the caged bird's courage.
    (C) The speaker is critical of the caged bird's reasons for singing.
    (D) The speaker shares the caged bird's desire for freedom.
    (E) The speaker yearns for compassion and connection to the natural world.

50. Which of the following would the author of the poem MOST LIKELY agree with?

    (A) Birds are the highest symbol of purity to which man can compare himself.
    (B) It is essential to express one's aspirations, even when circumstances make them unattainable.
    (C) Animals in captivity share an ancestry with humans who have experienced enslavement.
    (D) For introspection, social engagement, and civic responsibilities, the caged bird is not the likeliest of models to study.
    (E) If civilized men only treated each other with the same respect they devote to their domesticated animals, human cruelty would cease to exist.

Questions 51–60. Read the following poem carefully before you choose your answers.

Leda and the Swan

A sudden blow: the great wings beating still
Above the staggering girl, her thighs caressed
By the dark webs, her nape caught in his bill,
  He holds her helpless breast upon his breast.

5 How can those terrified vague fingers push
The feathered glory from her loosening thighs?
  And how can body, laid in that white rush,
But feel the strange heart beating where it lies?

A shudder in the loins engenders there
10 The broken wall, the burning roof and tower
And Agamemnon dead.

                    Being so caught up
So mastered by the brute blood of the air,
Did she put on his knowledge with his power
15 Before the indifferent beak could let her drop?

                                        (1923)

51. The most dominant sound of the first stanza is
established through

(A) repetition
(B) sibilance
(C) alliteration
(D) consonance
(E) assonance

52. Which of the following best describes the nature
of the poem?

(A) a subtle polemic against the ravages of
patriarchal ideology
(B) a disguised narrative of civilization's
progress and disintegration
(C) a sober meditation on the extant
consequences of violence from antiquity
(D) a moving panegyric on feminine resilience
in the face of trauma
(E) a nuanced allegory on sexual and cultural
appropriation

53. The poet makes use of all of the following
literary devices EXCEPT

(A) slant rhyme
(B) apostrophe
(C) caesura
(D) allusion
(E) synecdoche

54. The violence conveyed in the poem is primarily
achieved through which of the following means?

(A) hyperbolic language and mythical imagery
(B) rich imagery and blank verse with slight
interruptions
(C) dramatic diction and poetic asides
(D) ambiguous adjectives and misplaced
modifiers
(E) understatement and rhetorical questions

55. Compared to the first stanza, the second stanza
contains

(A) an elevated urgency to convey Leda's doubts
(B) a heightened atmosphere with more
graphic detail
(C) an investigative tone and suggestive line of
conjecture
(D) impossible foreknowledge of internal
conflict
(E) an intrusion by the author, underscoring the
swan's sudden assault

56. Which of the following pairs in opposition is
NOT a source of the poem's central conflict?

(A) predator versus prey
(B) human versus nature
(C) human versus divine
(D) myth versus history
(E) outer versus inner

GO ON TO THE NEXT PAGE ⟹

57. Based on the questions posed in lines 5–6 ("How can . . . thighs?") and lines 7–8 ("And how . . . it lies?"), what can be inferred about Leda's reaction to the swan?

    I. Leda regards the swan with aversion but perceives an inner strength by which to endure the violation.
    II. Leda is ambivalent toward the swan but mindlessly acquiesces to his physical might.
    III. Leda's bodily attempts to escape the swan belie the curiosity, allure, and empowerment she feels in the moment.

    (A) I only
    (B) I and II
    (C) I and III
    (D) II only
    (E) I, II, and III

58. Which of the following is NOT a possible substitute for the phrase "put on" (line 14)?

    (A) affect
    (B) present
    (C) register
    (D) equate
    (E) gain

59. Which of the following is NOT a consequence ascribed to the interaction portrayed in the poem?

    (A) the death of Agamemnon
    (B) the departure of the swan
    (C) the birth of offspring fathered by the swan
    (D) the Trojan War
    (E) the suffering of Leda

60. As a whole, the poem emphasizes which of the following?

    (A) the cathartic pathos of human frailty
    (B) the barbaric exploitation of mortals by deities
    (C) the mutability of myth and folklore
    (D) the ambiguity of traumatic memory
    (E) the cause-and-effect nature of human history

STOP

If you finish before time is called, you may check your work on this test only.

Do not turn to any other test in this book.

Answer Key

1. A	16. E	31. A	46. C
2. C	17. D	32. A	47. B
3. E	18. A	33. B	48. B
4. A	19. C	34. D	49. D
5. E	20. A	35. B	50. B
6. C	21. B	36. B	51. B
7. C	22. A	37. E	52. C
8. D	23. D	38. C	53. B
9. D	24. E	39. B	54. B
10. A	25. A	40. C	55. B
11. A	26. D	41. D	56. D
12. E	27. D	42. A	57. C
13. B	28. A	43. B	58. B
14. C	29. E	44. C	59. C
15. B	30. A	45. D	60. E

Answers and Explanations

1. **(A)** is correct because the speaker clearly states that she doesn't want to and doesn't feel capable of writing how she feels; if she did, it would make her feel better. This shows some kind of internal conflict and discomfort.

2. **(C)** is the correct answer because "to say nothing of" is another form of introducing an additional point.

3. **(E)** is correct because the speaker is just suggesting that her husband take her away; she does not explain from where or why. Choices A, B, C, and D all give convincing evidence that our narrator is unstable—for example, she is not able to write how she feels and is the only one who knows and sees things in the wallpaper.

4. **(A)** is correct because the speaker's husband is the one who decides everything for her. Our speaker lives in a patriarchal society—she tries to tell her husband why it's a good idea that she visit her cousin, but he decides against it. Even through the rest of the passage, we see how the speaker's husband controls everything she does.

5. **(E)** is correct because we can see from the speaker's dialogue that, first, her husband doesn't allow her to go outside or visit her family. Second, John takes care of her more as though he's treating a patient/child than his wife. The speaker makes a point of this when she mentions the things he says she should and shouldn't do. Third, the husband doesn't really know what is going on with his wife. From what the speaker tells us, we know he thinks she has an ailment but not to what extent.

6. **(C)** is correct because the narrator states that she would rather be the one in the room with the wallpaper because she is capable of tolerating it better than her child; her child won't suffer the same fate as she does. It is ironic because the wallpaper adds to her mental instability.

7. **(C)** is correct because toward the end of the text the speaker tells us she knows of things the paper is hiding, and she sees a shadow resembling a woman in the wallpaper itself. These are evident signs of paranoia and delusions.

8. **(D)** is the correct answer because in these lines the speaker tells us she knows of things in the wallpaper of which no one else is aware. These delusions draw her further into the wallpaper, which she starts to look at as a sense of self.

9. **(D)** is the correct answer because the passage contains no reference of any historical, literary, cultural, or political significance.

10. **(A)** is correct because the speaker shows us her unease throughout the passage. She is socially conscious in the way that she isn't allowed to do anything other than what her husband tells her because of her illness. Choice B is not correct because she is not being playful or amusing in any way. Choice C is wrong because she is not shaming herself over her psychological state of mind. Choice D is not correct because she's not implying that anything is funny, and choice E is also wrong because she's not being humorous or criticizing herself.

11. **(A)** is the correct answer because the poem is composed of 19 lines with five tercets and one quarain. Choice B is wrong because the poem is clearly not joyful or praising anything. Choice C is incorrect because the poem isn't composed of octaves or sestets. And choice E is wrong because an elegy mourns the loss of a loved one; its voice is one of sadness and loss. Although the author talks about the art of losing and mentions losing a loved one, it is not focused solely on death but mostly on losing material things.

12. **(E)** is correct because the repetition of this line builds up the structural form of the villanelle and connects the content with the art of losing something. Choice A is incorrect because we clearly see the poet isn't trying to memorize anything; rather, things are meant to be/should be lost. Choice B is incorrect because everyone understands what it means to lose things; this is not limited to certain individuals. Choices C and D are wrong because the repetition only helps explain the poet's intentions.

13. **(B)** is the correct answer because as the poem progresses the author keeps building up things she has lost that have greater value—door keys, places, names, a watch, her home, and finally a loved one.

14. **(C)** is correct because the poem's stanzas are mostly enjambments—they don't really have any pauses before they end, especially in stanza 5. Interruptive punctuation (commas, periods) is used here to make the reader pause while reading, which draws the reader in to what has been lost.

15. **(B)** is correct because in the first stanza the speaker introduces us to her belief that things are meant to be lost, and it's really not a big deal (line 3). In the second stanza she says people lose something every day, hence, the universal part; you have to accept things will be lost, like keys or time (line 5). In the third stanza the speaker declares that the art of losing things should be practiced, justifying her belief about lost things even further.

16. **(E)** is correct because the speaker doesn't feel any guilt in what she is portraying to her readers. A caesura represents an interruption or a dramatic pause that results in a strong impact on its readers.

17. **(D)** is the correct answer because throughout the poem the speaker mentions all the possibilities for disaster, including objects and people lost, but in the end it is all about being able to detach oneself from all the loss.

18. **(A)** is correct because we see the speaker dramatize the phrase "The art of losing isn't hard to master," as the poem progresses. It's ironic because she's making it seem as though that should be a goal or an achievement. Another reason it is dramatically ironic is because she's attempting to mask the seriousness of the loss of someone she loved, and that is very hard to master.

19. **(C)** is correct because we are conscious and constantly thinking about things, specifically things lost in this poem. The act of losing something or someone exceeds our reason to understand why we lose these things and why we keep thinking about them.

20. **(A)** is the correct answer because opium is a drug that suppresses pain and literally dulls the senses. The speaker says that opium makes you unaware of disaster.

21. **(B)** is correct because the speaker states that we welcome suffering "in the hope that . . . we find reality, sharp peaks and edges of truth."

22. **(A)** is the correct answer because the things we aim at are slippery, elusive, and lie on the surface. It is not choices C, D, or E because those are specific things or bodies that do not elude our grasp and we are not fetching. It is not choice B, because we cannot hope to steer ourselves along an "innavigable sea."

23. **(D)** is correct because, according to the speaker, grief contains no depth; it doesn't go deeper than the surface. The speaker is telling us he does not remember the grief he felt for his lost son because he never experienced it; it never touched him.

24. **(E)** is the only correct answer because the speaker clearly states that grief has done nothing for him. He isn't mortally wounded beneath the surface because grief doesn't "touch" him—it's something he hasn't felt/doesn't feel; it leaves him with "no scar." Even though he lost his son (an heir), it's as if he never knew he had one.

25. **(A)** is correct because the speaker mentions sharp surfaces, the sea with its silent waves, and beautiful estates—he uses nature as his focal expressive point.

26. **(D)** is correct because the speaker states that grief is not something that goes deeper than the surface. He even says it "can teach him nothing, nor carry [him] one step into real nature"; it doesn't leave a mark on anyone.

27. **(D)** is correct because the speaker is arguing that violence and war come from the anger of the people, who are led on by the oppression of how they are used to living. He also argues that when you let a man out of his cell, he must become accustomed to the light—to his freedom. A is incorrect because although he makes comparisons to get his point across, he isn't comparing one specific thing, but several. Choice B is wrong because there is no mention of mythology. Choice C is wrong because no specific or certain word is repeated to emphasize anything. Choice E is wrong because this is not a dramatic work.

28. **(A)** is correct because by including the Civil War, the speaker shows why acts of violence come about.

29. **(E)** is correct because the speaker uses all of these literary devices to draw readers in and help them to clearly understand what he is trying to portray.

30. **(A)** is correct because the speaker is implying that if you do not do something to liberate yourself when you can, you will never possess freedom.

31. **(A)** is correct because the water would be the subject matter of the well. The water is the content, it represents materials—written works of art. A person who keeps searching in the well will eventually find the water if there is any water there. Just like a writer will eventually find content—inspiration for writing—if there is anything to be written.

32. **(A)** is correct because essentially, dryness and dirt do not produce anything, which is a comparison to having nonexistent thoughts.

33. **(B)** is correct because when a well has water, it has substance in it, meaning it can be seen and understood.

34. **(D)** is correct because the speaker is saying that even those who cannot see the content of what they are reading pretend to be excited and knowledgeable about it; they are not analyzing it to understand it.

35. **(B)** is correct because the "death of its body" refers to the author's substance in his or her work.

36. **(B)** is correct because the speaker is saying that a writer keeps writing just to write instead of knowing when to stop. Modern authors keep writing even when there is nothing left to say on the subject.

37. **(E)** is correct because when an author writes a book, he writes to people he can connect with and address. Every author has a reader in mind while writing, but these types of authors know their reader well because they write endlessly with no substance.

38. **(C)** is correct because the speaker thinks these authors believe they are intellectually superior because they write endlessly but with no substance.

39. **(B)** is correct because throughout the passage the speaker states that modern writers do not have any substance to their writing, and they keep writing mindlessly even when their subject is already done. According to the speaker, modern authors have no critical writing skills.

40. **(C)** is correct because although the speaker tells us that modern writers do not know when to stop writing, he continues writing about the exact thing he is saying modern authors do. He is contradicting himself by doing so.

41. **(D)** is the correct answer because the speaker is telling us a story about the caged bird. A is incorrect because a typical villanelle poem has 19 lines with a fixed form. Choices B and C are wrong because the speaker is not enthusiastically or triumphantly praising the caged bird. Choice E is incorrect because the poem is in no way humorous.

42. **(A)** is correct because the speaker is acknowledging that she understands how the caged bird feels.

43. **(B)** is correct because the poet is expressing to us how the bird is locked in a cage and wishes he were elsewhere, on a tree branch instead of trapped.

44. **(C)** is correct because the bird has nowhere else to go. The speaker explains that the caged bird beats his wings until they are bruised to express his longing for freedom.

45. **(D)** is correct because the bird is showing persistent efforts to get out of the cage by keenly flapping its wings against the cage bars. "Keen" means to show enthusiasm or be determined to do something. Choices A, B, C, and E all represent the bird's efforts.

46. **(C)** is correct because the poet's expression of the bird is that he is crying out for help, which is essentially what you do when you pray. The poet also states that the bird is actually sending out a prayer from his heart every time he beats his wings.

47. **(B)** is correct because line 12 says the bird's old scars throb in his attempts to free himself from the cage. They sting more because he does not give up even after years of being captive.

48. **(B)** is correct because the bird is being held captive; he is imprisoned in a cage.

49. **(D)** is correct. We can see how the speaker shares the caged bird's desire for freedom with the repeating lines of, "I know what the caged bird feels." She also says she knows why he sings (line 8) and why he beats his wings (line 15).

50. **(B)** is correct because the speaker shows us how the bird tries to be free even though he knows he won't be. The poet also tells us that the bird has been captive for years because old scars begin to surface. The fact that the bird is oppressed does not stop him.

51. **(B)** is correct because while we read the stanza, we hear the repeated *s* or hissing sound, which is a sibilance.

52. **(C)** is correct because the poem talks about the rape of a young woman, something that still happens today.

53. **(B)** is correct because the speaker never introduces another audience in the poem.

54. **(B)** is correct because while reading the poem we can actually envision what is going on. We can see the "great wings beating still above the . . . girl," and how the entire poem comes together. We can also see this through the poet's use of blank verse; the lack of rhyming makes it sound like a story is being told.

55. **(B)** is correct because the speaker uses more adjectives to heighten the atmosphere and describe Leda's weakness and helplessness—"terrified," "vague," "loosening." He also uses words indicating powerful action being taken, like "beating." We can imagine how this is happening and see how the swan takes possession of her.

56. **(D)** is correct because although the speaker is telling us the poem derives from mythology, no historical facts are introduced into the poem. Choice A is incorrect because the swan is the predator while Leda is his prey. Choice B is incorrect because we see a human being tormented by an animal, the swan (nature). Choice C is incorrect because the speaker does show us the interaction of human versus divine, the divine being a god coming down to earth. Choice E is incorrect because we see Leda's inner struggle with herself at what is happening, she is helpless (line 4) and terrified (line 5). The outer or external force Leda is dealing with is the swan.

57. **(C)** is correct because we see Leda is terrified and tries to push the swan away, but we can also see, in lines 7–8, how even though she is entangled with the swan and feels the violation, she feels his heart beating against hers. This contradicts her actions to push him away; she feels curious and empowered at that moment.

58. **(B)** is correct because Leda did not introduce any knowledge; it was introduced to her.

59. **(C)** is correct because we do not see any children being born or introduced to the poem after the swan's violation of Leda. Choice A is incorrect because the downfall of Agamemnon is mentioned. Choice B is incorrect because after the swan drops her, he leaves. Choice D is incorrect because the mention of the death of Agamemnon (choice A) was during the Trojan War. Choice E is incorrect because we see how Leda suffers both internally and externally throughout the poem.

60. **(E)** is correct because Leda's violation (cause) led to the downfall of civilization (effect). It shows the violence of human history.

How To Calculate Your Score

Count the number of correct answers and enter the total below.

Count the number of wrong answers. Do NOT include any questions you did not answer.

Multiply the number of wrong answers by 0.25 and enter the total below.

Do the subtraction. The answer is your raw score. Use the scoring scale to find your scaled score.

$$\overline{\text{(number of correct answers)}} - \overline{\text{(number of wrong answers} \times 0.25)} = \overline{\text{(raw score)}}$$

RAW SCORE	SCALED SCORE	RAW SCORE	SCALED SCORE	RAW SCORE	SCALED SCORE	RAW SCORE	SCALED SCORE	RAW SCORE	SCALED SCORE
60	800	44	710	28	560	12	420	−4	260
59	800	43	700	27	550	11	410	−5	250
58	800	42	690	26	540	10	400	−6	240
57	800	41	690	25	530	9	390	−7	230
56	800	40	680	24	520	8	380	−8	220
55	800	39	670	23	510	7	370	−9	210
54	790	38	660	22	500	6	360	−10	200
53	790	37	650	21	500	5	350	−11	200
52	780	36	640	20	490	4	340	−12	200
51	770	35	630	19	490	3	330	−13	200
50	760	34	620	18	480	2	320	−14	200
49	750	33	610	17	470	1	310	−15	200
48	740	32	600	16	460	0	300		
47	740	31	590	15	450	−1	290		
46	730	30	580	14	440	−2	280		
45	720	29	570	13	430	−3	270		

Note: This is only a sample scoring scale. Scoring scales differ from exam to exam.

PART II

Literature Topic Review

Literary Terms

Literary Terms

Literary terms are the words and phrases students and scholars use to discuss and interpret works of literature. This chapter contains an alphabetical glossary of literary terms likely to appear in questions and answer choices on the SAT Literature Test. You can use this chapter to review the meaning of these literary terms. The examples are all taken from literary works like those you will find on the SAT Literature Test.

Chapter 1 concludes with a sample passage, a sample poem, and questions, which you can use to test your knowledge of the literary terms.

Alliteration

Alliteration occurs when two or more words in a line of verse or a sentence of prose begin with the same sound. There are two types of alliteration: when the repeated sound is a vowel, it is sometimes called *assonance*. When the repeated sound is a consonant, it is sometimes called *consonance*.

> **EXAMPLE:** To sit in solemn silence in a dull dark dock,
> In a pestilential prison with a lifelong lock,
> Awaiting the sensation of a short sharp shock
> From a cheap and chippy chopper on a big black block!

Allusion

An **allusion** is a reference to a person, place, thing, or event in history, literature, or the arts. Authors do not explain allusions because they expect their readers to recognize these references automatically.

EXAMPLE: In geometry Anne met her Waterloo.

"It's perfectly awful stuff, Marilla," she groaned. "I'm sure I'll never be able to make head or tail of it."

(The author expected her readers to get the allusion to Waterloo—the battle in which Napoleon met his final defeat. If you don't recognize it, you can use context clues to figure out that geometry lessons are defeating Anne.)

Argument

An **argument** can also be called a thesis. It is a strong statement of opinion that an author sets out to prove. The term *argument* is usually used in discussion of nonfiction; it can also be applied to certain kinds of poetry.

EXAMPLE: The history of the present king of Great Britain is a history of repeated injuries and usurpations, all having in direct object the establishment of an absolute tyranny over these states. To prove this, let facts be submitted to a candid world.

Audience

The term **audience** refers to the intended readers of a particular literary work. The author chooses the tone, diction, and content of the writing based on what he or she knows about the audience.

Blank Verse

Blank verse refers to unrhymed lines of **iambic pentameter** (see below). Elizabethan plays were largely written in blank verse. Authority figures, royalty, and members of the nobility usually speak in blank verse, while clowns, servants, and commoners usually speak in prose. Elizabethan playwrights used blank verse because the regular rhythm made the dialogue easier for actors to memorize and the rhythm of iambic pentameter closely approximates the natural rhythm of English speech. In addition, blank verse has a certain stately and majestic quality appropriate to the royal, heroic, and/or noble characters who speak it.

EXAMPLE:

GLOUCESTER.   Now tell me, brother Clarence, what think you
                Of this new marriage with the Lady Grey?
                Hath not our brother made a worthy choice?

CLARENCE.   Alas, you know, 'tis far from hence to France;
                How could he stay till Warwick make return?

SOMERSET.   My lords, forbear this talk. Here comes the King.

Character

The term **character** has two meanings:

1. a person or animal who plays a role in a literary work

2. the personality traits and type of the person or animal

The process of creating and describing a literary character is called **characterization.** In **direct characterization,** an author tells the reader what a character is like. In **indirect characterization,** the author leaves the reader to infer this from the character's words and actions.

EXAMPLE OF DIRECT CHARACTERIZATION:

> Oh! but he was a tight-fisted hand at the grindstone, Scrooge! a squeezing, wrenching, grasping, scraping, clutching, covetous old sinner! Hard and sharp as flint, from which no steel had ever struck out generous fire; secret, and self-contained, and solitary as an oyster.

Connotation

The **connotation** of a word is its implied meaning rather than its literal meaning (**denotation**). Often, the author uses a specific word to evoke emotional or cultural associations.

EXAMPLE: The words *slim* and *skinny* have the same basic meaning, but *skinny* has a negative connotation and *slim* has a positive one.

Denotation

The **denotation** of a word is its literal meaning, the dictionary definition.

EXAMPLES: Here are the literal meanings of the words *skinny* and *slim*:

> *Skinny*: very lean or thin

> *Slim*: thin; slenderly built

Dialect

Dialect is colloquial, idiomatic speech used in everyday conversation among uneducated characters. Dialect also refers to speech patterns used in a specific geographic region. The grammatical and spelling patterns of dialects differ from those of Standard English.

EXAMPLES:

BRITISH DIALECT (LONDON, EAST END)	AMERICAN DIALECT (MISSOURI REGIONAL)
"Let me lay here quiet, and not be chivied no more," falters Jo, "and be so kind any person as is a-passin' nigh where I used fur to sweep, as jist to say to Mr. Sangsby that Jo, wot he known once, is a-moving on right forards with his duty, and I'll be wery thankful."	Pap was standing over me looking sour—and sick too. He says: "What you doin' with this gun?" I judged he didn't know nothing about what he had been doing, so I says: "Somebody tried to get in, so I was laying for him." "Why didn't you roust me out?" "Well, I tried to, but I couldn't; I couldn't budge you." "Well, all right. Don't stand there palavering all day …"

Dialogue

Dialogue refers to the words spoken by characters in fiction, poetry, or drama and by the real people who are quoted in works of nonfiction. In a play, the character's name appears at the start of each speech he or she makes. In prose and narrative poetry, dialogue is enclosed in quotation marks.

EXAMPLES:

DIALOGUE IN DRAMA	DIALOGUE IN PROSE
PHYLLIS. There's really nothing to choose between you. If one of you would forgo his title, and distribute his estates among his Irish tenantry, why, I should then see a reason for accepting the other. LORD M. Tolloller, are you prepared to make this sacrifice? LORD T. No! LORD M. Not even to oblige a lady? LORD T. No! not even to oblige a lady.	"What did you say his name was?" he asked. "Scratchy Wilson," they answered in chorus. "And will he kill anybody? What are you going to do? Does this happen often? … Can he break in that door?" "No, he can't break down that door," replied the barkeeper. "He's tried it three times. But when he comes, you better lay down on the floor, stranger."

Diction

Diction is the author's choice and use of words and phrases in a piece of writing. Together with tone, the diction creates the style of the writing. Diction is determined by the author's purpose and audience and is used to create a certain effect. Types of diction include **formal, informal, colloquial,** and **slang.**

> **EXAMPLE:** Ah, happy, happy boughs! that cannot shed
> Your leaves, nor ever bid the spring adieu.

(Keats chooses the phrase "bid the spring adieu" instead of "say good-bye to spring" to create a formal, respectful diction.)

End Stopping/Enjambment

An **end-stopped** line of verse ends in a punctuation mark that indicates a pause or a full stop. **Enjambment** occurs when lines do not end in punctuation marks, but rather express thoughts or ideas that continue without pause to the following line(s).

> **EXAMPLE:** That's my last Duchess painted on the wall,
> Looking as if she were alive. I call
> That piece a wonder, now; Fra Pandolf's hands
> Worked busily a day; and there she stands.

(Lines 1 and 4 are **end-stopped***; lines 2–4 are an example of* **enjambment***, because the complete thought begun on line 2 continues to the end of line 4.)*

Figurative Language

Any figure of speech that has a meaning beyond the literal definition of the words is called **figurative language.** Types of figurative language include **hyperbole, metaphor, simile,** and **personification** (see definitions and examples below).

Free Verse

Free verse is "free" because it does not employ a regular rhythm, meter, or rhyme scheme. However, not all unrhymed poems are free-verse poems. A poem with rhythm and meter is not a free-verse poem, even if it is unrhymed.

EXAMPLES:

FREE VERSE	UNRHYMED POETRY; NOT FREE VERSE
I sang to you and the moon But only the moon remembers. I sang O reckless free-hearted free-throated rhythms, Even the moon remembers them And is kind to me.	Gipsy queen of the night, wraith of the fire-lit dark, Glittering eyes of ice, sharp as glacier green, Lisping falling kisses, syllabled flakes of snow, Down on the stubbled fields, over my eyes and hair; If on my mouth one falls, it is tasteless and light and cold.

(The regular rhythm and meter of the excerpt on the right prevent it from being free verse.)

Genre

The **genre** of a piece of writing is its type or category, which is characterized by a certain content, form, and style. Literature has five primary genres: **fiction, non-fiction, poetry, prose,** and **drama.** Each genre has certain features that separate it from the others, and each serves a different function.

Hyperbole

Hyperbole refers to gross exaggeration that no one could mistake for a literal statement of fact. It is usually used for humorous effect.

> **EXAMPLE:** "How long can you hold him?" asks Bill.
> "I'm not as strong as I used to be … but I think I can promise you ten minutes."
> "Enough," says Bill. "In ten minutes I shall cross the Central, Southern, and Middle Western States, and be legging it trippingly for the Canadian border."

Iambic Pentameter

This term denotes a specific **rhythm** and **meter** (see below) used in verse and verse drama. **Pentameter** refers to a line of verse that has five metric feet (*penta-* is Latin for "five"). **Iambic** means that each metric foot has a weak syllable followed by a strong one. Elizabethan playwrights wrote in iambic pentameter (see **blank verse,** above). **Sonnets** (see below) are also written in iambic pentameter, which is generally a very popular meter for English poetry. Couplets with a meter of iambic pentameter are called **heroic couplets**.

> **EXAMPLE:** KING   The mercy that was quick in us of late
> By your own counsel is suppress'd and kill'd.
> You must not dare, for shame, to talk of mercy,
> For your own reasons turn into your bosoms,
> As dogs upon their masters, worrying you.
> See you, my princes and my noble peers,
> These English monsters!

Imagery

Imagery is any descriptive language that appeals to one or more of the five senses. It occurs in all types of writing.

> **EXAMPLE:** Ah, what can ever be more stately and admirable to me than mast-hemm'd Manhattan?
> Rivers and sunset and scallop-edg'd waves of floodtide?
> The sea-gulls oscillating their bodies, the hay-boat in the twilight, and the belated lighter?
> What gods can exceed these that clasp me by the hand, and with voices I love call me promptly and loudly by my nighest name as I approach?

(Details in this excerpt appeal to the senses of sight, touch, and hearing.)

Inference

To make an **inference,** a reader must study the details of a literary text and decide what they mean. Authors do not tell readers everything directly; they often leave readers to figure out meaning for themselves. The reader must **infer** from what the author **implies.**

> **EXAMPLE:** True! nervous, very, very dreadfully nervous I have been and am; but *why* will you say that I am mad? … Hearken! and observe how healthily, how calmly, I can tell you the whole story.
>
> It is impossible to say how first the idea entered my brain … I loved the old man. He had never wronged me. He had never given me insult. For his gold I had no desire. I think it was his eye! Yes, it was this! One of his eyes resembled that of a vulture—a pale blue eye with a film over it. Whenever it fell upon me my blood ran cold, and so by degrees, very gradually, I made up my mind to take the life of the old man, and thus rid myself of the eye for ever.

(The reader might reasonably infer that the narrator is in custody for the old man's murder and that he is insane, because his motive for murder is irrational.)

Irony

Irony is the use of words or a situation with an intended meaning that is different from the actual meaning. There are two main types of irony. **Verbal irony** is the use of words that mean the opposite of what the speaker actually means. Sarcasm is a type of verbal irony. **Situational irony** is when a situation ends up being quite different from what is generally anticipated. Another type of irony, related to situational irony, is **dramatic irony**. In situational irony, both the characters and the audience are aware of the irony. In dramatic irony, only the audience is aware of the irony; the characters are clueless.

> **EXAMPLE:** Water, water, everywhere,
> Nor any drop to drink.

Main Idea

The **main idea** of a literary work is the most important concept the author is writing about—the one he or she most wants the reader to think about. The main idea of a nonfiction work is similar to the **theme** (see below) of a work of fiction, poetry, or drama.

> **EXAMPLE, WITH MAIN IDEA IN BOLDFACE:** Pope flattered tyrants too much when he said, "For forms of government let fools contest, That which is best administered is best."

Nothing can be more fallacious than this. But poets read history to collect flowers, not fruits; they attend to fanciful images, not the effects of social institutions. Nothing is more certain from the history of nations and nature of man than that **some forms of government are better fitted for being well administered than others.**

Metaphor

A **metaphor** is a direct comparison of two apparently unlike things, stating that A is B. In an **implied metaphor,** the author does not say "A is B," but describes A as if it were B. An **extended metaphor** is one that the author continues to develop through several lines of prose or verse.

EXAMPLES:

METAPHOR (STATED)	EXTENDED METAPHOR (IMPLIED)
But soft! what light through yonder window breaks? It is the East, and Juliet is the sun.	The yellow fog that rubs its back upon the window-panes,
	The yellow smoke that rubs its muzzle on the window-panes
	Licked its tongue into the corners of the evening,
	Lingered upon the pools that stand in drains,
	Let fall upon its back the soot that falls from chimneys,
	Slipped by the terrace, made a sudden leap,
	And seeing that it was a soft October night,
	Curled once about the house, and fell asleep.

(In the example on the right, instead of saying "The fog is a cat," the poet describes the fog as if it were a cat.)

Meter

In poetry, **meter** refers to the number of times a rhythmic pattern occurs in a line of verse. Meter is measured in **metric feet.** Each repetition of a rhythmic pattern represents one metric foot. The most common meters in English-language poetry are **tetrameter** (four metric feet per line), **pentameter** (five), and **hexameter** (six).

> **EXAMPLE:** In placid hours well-pleased we dream
> Of many a brave unbodied scheme;
> But form to lend, pulsed life create,
> What unlike things must meet and mate.

(This excerpt is written in tetrameter, with each metric foot containing a weak beat followed by a strong one.)

Mood

In a literary sense, the word **mood** is used to refer to the overall emotional impact of a work on the reader. The mood of a work might be suspenseful, ironic, funny—there are many possibilities. The term *mood* can also be used in its everyday sense to describe how a character feels about something.

EXAMPLE: "Is matchmaking at all in your line?"

Hugo Peterby asked the question with a certain amount of personal interest.

"I don't specialize in it," said Clovis; "it's all right while you're doing it, but the after-effects are sometimes so disconcerting—the mute reproachful looks of the people you've aided and abetted in matrimonial experiments. It's as bad as selling a man a horse with half a dozen latent vices and watching him discover them piecemeal in the course of the hunting season."

(The author uses the witty dialogue to establish a mood of frivolous humor.)

Narrator

The **narrator** is the character from whose point of view a work of prose fiction is told. The narrator refers to him- or herself as *I* and *me* and may play either a major or a minor role in the plot. The word *narrator* is NOT used in discussing nonfiction; the "narrator" of a nonfiction work is the author. (See also **perspective/point of view,** below.)

EXAMPLE: Call me Ishmael. Some years ago—never mind how long precisely—having little or no money in my purse, and nothing particular to interest me on shore, I thought I would sail about a little and see the watery part of the world.

Paraphrase

To **paraphrase** a text means to restate it in different words. A paraphrase should restate all the ideas in the original.

Personification

To **personify** an inanimate object means to endow it with the abilities, qualities, or emotions of living creatures. Animals can also be personified, such as in folk or fantasy literature, where they converse, dress up, walk on two legs, and live in houses like human beings.

EXAMPLE: Besides, the Kettle was aggravating and obstinate. It wouldn't allow itself to be adjusted on the top bar; it wouldn't hear of accommodating itself kindly to the knobs of coal; it would lean forward with a drunken air, and dribble, a very Idiot of a Kettle, on the hearth. It was quarrelsome; and hissed and spluttered morosely at the fire.

Plot

The **plot** is the series of events that make up a prose narrative or a narrative poem. A plot contains five stages:

- **Exposition,** in which the characters and conflicts are introduced
- **Rising action,** in which the conflicts begin to play out

- **Climax,** the point of highest interest, excitement, and suspense
- **Falling action,** in which the characters begin to resolve their conflicts
- **Resolution,** at which point the narrative ends

Point of View/Perspective

An author tells a story from a specific **point of view,** or **perspective.** The narrative point of view determines how the reader will experience and understand the story.

A **limited** point of view means the reader can only see into the thoughts and feelings of one character. Both first-person and third-person narrators can tell a story from a limited point of view.

An **omniscient** point of view means that the reader can see into the thoughts and feelings of all the characters in turn. This is typical of a story narrated in the third person.

EXAMPLE OF OMNISCIENT POINT OF VIEW/PERSPECTIVE:

Ray … was thinking of that afternoon and how it had affected his whole life when a spirit of protest awoke in him. He had forgotten about Hal and muttered words. "Tricked by Gad, that's what I was, tricked by life and made a fool of," he said in a low voice.

As though understanding his thoughts, Hal Winters spoke up. "Well, has it been worth while? What about it, eh? What about marriage and all that?" he asked and then laughed. Hal tried to keep on laughing but he too was in an earnest mood.

Purpose

An author's **purpose** is his or her reason for writing a particular text. There are four main purposes:

- Expository: to inform or teach the reader
- Narrative: to relate a story or recount events
- Entertaining: to amuse or entertain the reader
- Persuasive: to convince the reader to believe an idea or to take a course of action

EXAMPLE: O, when she's angry, she is keen and shrewd!
She was a vixen when she went to school;
And though she be but little, she is fierce.

(*The purpose of Shakespeare's* A Midsummer Night's Dream *is to entertain.*)

Rhyme—Exact Rhyme and Slant Rhyme

To form **exact rhymes,** words must have the same vowel sound on the stressed syllable and the same final consonant. **Slant rhyme** (also called near rhyme or off rhyme) is achieved when the words share beginning and/or final consonants but have different vowel sounds.

EXAMPLE: 1 Now all the truth is out,
  Be secret and take defeat
  From any brazen throat,
  For how can you compete,
 5 Being honor bred, with one
  Who, were it proved he lies,
  Were neither shamed in his own
  Nor in his neighbor's eyes?

(The odd-numbered lines form slant rhymes: out/throat *and* one/own. *The even-numbered lines are exact rhymes:* defeat/compete *and* lies/eyes.)

Rhythm

Rhythm refers to the pattern of stressed and unstressed syllables in verse. Common rhythmic patterns include the following:

- **Spondaic** STRONG / STRONG / STRONG
- **Anapestic** weak weak STRONG / weak weak STRONG
- **Trochaic** STRONG weak / STRONG weak / STRONG weak
- **Iambic** weak STRONG / weak STRONG / weak STRONG

Setting

The **setting** of a literary work is the time and place in which the events occur. An author's description of a setting can contribute to mood, tone, and character. The setting can also affect the events of the plot.

EXAMPLE: The few houses which seemed to be securely wedged and tree-nailed in among the ledges by the Landing ... made the most of their seaward view, and there was a gayety and determined floweriness in their bits of garden ground; the small-paned high windows in the peaks of their steep gables were like knowing eyes that watched the harbor and the far sea-line beyond, or looked northward all along the shore and its background of spruces and balsam firs.

Simile

A **simile** is a comparison between two apparently unlike things, stating that A is like/as B.

EXAMPLES: She raised her head from her arms and dried her eyes with the back of her hand like a child.

Like distant music these words that he had written years before were borne towards him from the past.

Sonnet

A **sonnet** is a fourteen-line poem in **iambic pentameter** (see above). There are two standard rhyme schemes for sonnets:

- An **Italian** or **Petrarchan sonnet** describes a problem or conflict in its first eight lines (the octave). With the final six lines (the sestet), the speaker's thoughts usually take a turn toward some kind of resolution of the conflict. The sestet is set off from the octave by a change in rhyme scheme.
- A **Shakespearean sonnet** asks a question or describes a problem in three quatrains of four lines each, rhymed either ABBA or ABAB, then sums up and resolves the situation in a final rhymed couplet.

Many sonnets deviate from these two patterns. A sonnet can be entirely or partly unrhymed, or it can have a rhyme scheme all its own. As long as it consists of fourteen lines of iambic pentameter, it is still a sonnet.

EXAMPLE OF AN ITALIAN SONNET:

Oh soft embalmer of the still midnight!
   Shutting with careful fingers and benign
Our gloom-pleased eyes, embower'd from the light
   Enshaded in forgetfulness divine;
O soothest Sleep! If so it please thee, close
   In midst of this thine hymn, my willing eyes,
Or wait the amen, ere my poppy throws
   Around my bed its lulling charities;
Then save me, or the passèd day will shine
   Upon my pillow, breeding many woes;
Save me from curious conscience, that still lords
   In strength for darkness, burrowing like a mole;
Turn the key deftly in the oiled wards
   And seal the hushèd casket of my soul.

Speaker

The **speaker** is the first-person narrator of a poem, who refers to him- or herself as *I* and *me*. In a **lyric poem,** the speaker may or may not represent the author's views, experiences, and emotions. In a **narrative poem,** the speaker is NOT to be identified with the author, but is simply a character in the poem's story.

EXAMPLE: SPEAKER OF A NARRATIVE POEM

Once upon a midnight dreary, while I pondered, weak and weary,
Over many a quaint and curious volume of forgotten lore,
While I nodded, nearly napping, suddenly there came a tapping
As of someone gently rapping, rapping at my chamber door.
"'Tis some visitor," I muttered, "tapping at my chamber door—
         Only this, and nothing more."

Stanza

A **stanza** is a grouped set of lines within a poem. Multiple stanzas are usually separated by blank lines.

> **EXAMPLE:** Because I could not stop for Death –
> He kindly stopped for me –
> The Carriage held but just Ourselves –
> And Immortality.
>
> We slowly drove – He knew no haste
> And I had put away
> My labor and my leisure too,
> For His Civility –

Summary

Unlike a **paraphrase** (see above), a **summary** does not rephrase the original text. A summary briefly recapitulates the major themes or main ideas and the most important supporting details of a literary work.

Symbolism

When an author gives a character, place, or thing in a story or poem a meaning beyond its face value, this is referred to as **symbolism.** In the following example, the city of Christminster has both literal and symbolic meaning. Literally, it is a city of buildings, streets, and people. Symbolically, it represents the main character's fondest dream—his desire to acquire learning and wisdom.

> **EXAMPLE:** The air increased in transparency with the lapse of minutes, till
> the topaz points showed themselves to be the vanes, windows,
> wet roof slates, and other shining spots upon the spires, domes,
> freestone-work, and varied outlines that faintly revealed it. It was
> Christminster, unquestionably; either directly seen, or miraged in
> the peculiar atmosphere … And the city acquired a tangibility, a
> permanence, a hold on his life, mainly from the one nucleus of fact
> that the man for whose knowledge and purposes he had so much
> reverence was actually living there.

Theme

The **theme** is the overall meaning of a literary work. The theme encompasses the most important concept or idea that the author wants the reader to take away and think about. A theme must usually be **inferred** (see above) from details in the text. A theme is usually spoken of as being **universal**—common to human experience in all times, places, and cultures.

EXAMPLE: If I should die, think only this of me:
> That there's some corner of a foreign field,
> That is forever England. There shall be
> In that rich earth a richer dust concealed;
> A dust whom England bore, shaped, made aware,
> Gave, once, her flowers to love, her ways to roam,
> A body of England's breathing English air,
> Washed by the rivers, blest by suns of home.

(The theme of this excerpt is patriotism, or love for one's country.)

Tone

In a literary sense, **tone** refers to the author's attitude toward the subject. An author might write with a nostalgic, humorous, or sarcastic tone, to name only a few possibilities.

EXAMPLE: "What do we talk of marks and brands, whether on the bodice of her gown, or the flesh of her forehead?" cried another female, the ugliest as well as the most pitiless of these self-constituted judges. "This woman has brought shame upon us all, and ought to die. Is there not law for it? Truly, there is, both in the Scripture and the statute-book. Then let the magistrates, who have made it of no effect, thank themselves if their own wives and daughters go astray!"

(The author's tone is condemnatory; he shows his sympathy for the criminal by painting a harsh and unflattering portrait of her "self-constituted judge.")

Voice

The author's **voice** is his or her individual writing style. It is developed through the use of syntax, diction, dialogue, punctuation, tone, pacing, and character development.

REVIEW QUESTIONS

Questions 1–5. Read the following passage carefully before you choose your answers.

"I want to know what I should do—Today, Edgar Linton has asked me to marry him, and I've given him an answer ... I accepted him, Nelly. Be quick, and say whether I was wrong!"

"You accepted him? then, what good is it discussing the matter? You have pledged your
5 word, and cannot retract."

"But, say whether I should have done so—do!" she exclaimed in an irritated tone, chafing her hands together, and frowning.

"There are many things to be considered, before that question can be answered properly," I said sententiously. "First and foremost, do you love Mr. Edgar?"

10 "Who can help it? Of course I do," she answered.

Then I put her through the following catechism—for a girl of twenty-two, it was not injudicious.

"Why do you love him, Miss Cathy?"

"Nonsense, I do—that's sufficient."

15 "By no means; you must say why."

"Well, because he is handsome, and pleasant to be with."

"Bad," was my commentary.

"And because he is young and cheerful."

"Bad, still."

20 "And because he loves me."

"Indifferent, coming there."

"And he will be rich, and I shall like to be the greatest woman of the neighborhood, and I shall be proud of having such a husband."

"Worst of all! And now, you say how you love him?"

25 "As everybody loves—You're silly, Nelly."

"Not at all—Answer."

"I love the ground under his feet, and the air over his head, and everything he touches, and every word he says—I love all his looks, and all his actions, and him entirely, and altogether. There now!"

30 "… And now, let us hear what you are unhappy about. Your brother will be pleased … the old lady and gentleman will not object, I think—you will escape from a disorderly, comfortless home into a wealthy, respectable one; and you love Edgar, and Edgar loves you. All seems smooth and easy—where is the obstacle?"

"*Here*! and *here*!" replied Catherine, striking one hand on her forehead, and the other 35 on her breast: "In whichever place the soul lives—in my soul, and in my heart, I'm convinced I'm wrong! … I've no more business to marry Edgar Linton than I have to be in heaven; and if the wicked man in there[1] had not brought Heathcliff so low, I shouldn't have thought of it. It would degrade me to marry Heathcliff, now; so he shall never know how I love him: and that, not because he's handsome, Nelly, but because he's more myself 40 than I am. Whatever our souls are made of, his and mine are the same, and Linton's is as different as a moonbeam from lightning, or frost from fire … I want to cheat my uncomfortable conscience, and be convinced that Heathcliff has no notion of these things—he has not, has he? He does not know what being in love is?"

[1]Catherine refers to her older brother Hindley, who abuses Heathcliff and treats him like a servant.

"I see no reason that he should not know, as well as you," I returned; "and if *you* are his choice, he'll be the most unfortunate creature that ever was born! As soon as you become Mrs Linton, he loses friend, and love, and all! Have you considered how you'll bear the separation, and how he'll bear to be quite deserted in the world? Because, Miss Catherine—"

"He quite deserted! we separated!" she exclaimed, with an accent of indignation. "Who is to separate us, pray? They'll meet the fate of Milo! Not as long as I live, Ellen—for no mortal creature. Every Linton on the face of the earth might melt into nothing, before I could consent to forsake Heathcliff! ... I cannot express it; but surely you and everybody have a notion that there is, or should be, an existence of yours beyond you. What were the use of my creation if I were entirely contained here? My great miseries in this world have been Heathcliff's miseries, and I watched and felt each from the beginning; my great thought in living is himself. If all else perished, and *he* remained, I should still continue to be; and if all else remained, and he were annihilated, the universe would turn to a mighty stranger. I should not seem a part of it. My love for Linton is like the foliage in the woods. Time will change it, I'm well aware, as winter changes the trees. My love for Heathcliff resembles the eternal rocks beneath—a source of little visible delight, but necessary. Nelly, I *am* Heathcliff—he's always, always in my mind—not as a pleasure, any more than I am always a pleasure to myself—but as my own being."

(1847)

1. From the way they speak to one another, you can infer that Nelly is Catherine's
(A) friend
(B) mother
(C) servant
(D) sister
(E) employer

2. Which of the following does NOT represent a use of figurative language, but is meant literally only?
(A) "I love the ground under his feet, and the air over his head, and everything he touches, and every word he says."
(B) "Whatever our souls are made of, his and mine are the same, and Linton's is as different as a moonbeam from lightning, or frost from fire."
(C) "Every Linton on the face of the earth might melt into nothing, before I could consent to forsake Heathcliff!"
(D) "My great miseries in this world have been Heathcliff's miseries, and I watched and felt each from the beginning; my great thought in living is himself."
(E) "I love all his looks, and all his actions, and him entirely, and altogether."

3. Catherine's statement "Nelly, I *am* Heathcliff" might be paraphrased as which of the following?

   (A) Heathcliff and I are, in fact, the same person.
   (B) Heathcliff is my twin brother.
   (C) Heathcliff is my best friend.
   (D) Heathcliff and I love each other very much.
   (E) Heathcliff and I are kindred spirits.

4. Catherine's character is best described as

   (A) impulsive and rash
   (B) cautious and prudent
   (C) sensible and reasonable
   (D) good natured and kind
   (E) charming and lively

5. Which of the following lines from the passage contains a simile?

   (A) "I shall like to be the greatest woman of the neighborhood, and I shall be proud of having such a husband."
   (B) "My love for Linton is like the foliage in the woods."
   (C) "All seems smooth and easy—where is the obstacle?"
   (D) "Every Linton on the face of the earth might melt into nothing, before I could consent to forsake Heathcliff!"
   (E) "Whatever our souls are made of, his and mine are the same …"

ANSWERS AND EXPLANATIONS

1. **(C)** Although they speak to one another frankly and bluntly, as if they were equals, Nelly addressed Catherine as "Miss Cathy" and "Miss Catherine," while Catherine calls Nelly by her first name. This supports choice C—that Nelly is Catherine's servant.

2. **(D)** Choices A, C, and E are hyperbole—an exaggeration of the love Catherine feels for Linton. (In this case, the hyperbole is made for dramatic rather than comic effect.) Choice B contains a simile, or imaginative comparison. This leaves choice D, which Catherine means literally—she has watched Heathcliff suffer; she has herself suffered because she loves and sympathizes with him; and he is the central person in her life.

3. **(E)** Catherine's earlier statement that "his (soul) and mine are the same" helps explain her meaning. She believes that she and Healthcliff are spiritually akin; that they think and feel the same way about everything; and that they understand one another perfectly and completely. Choice E, "kindred spirits," matches this analysis. Catherine and Heathcliff are obviously two separate individuals, not one. Because Catherine has evidently considered marrying Heathcliff, he cannot be her twin. Details in the passage show that choices C and D are true statements; but Catherine speaks of a bond stronger than friendship or even love when she says, "I *am* Heathcliff."

4. **(A)** It is fair to use choice A, "impulsive and rash," to describe Catherine. She acts first on the spur of the moment, and only afterward does she think about the consequences of her hasty decision. A cautious or sensible person would have thought things through before acting; a good-natured, kind person would never say something like, "It would degrade me to marry Heathcliff"; and in this passage, Catherine is too serious and earnest to be described as charming or lively.

5. **(B)** Choice B compares Catherine's love for Linton to the foliage in the woods.

Questions 6–10. Read the following poem carefully before you choose your answers.

"Upon the Heights" by Yone Noguchi, 1875–1947

And victor of life and silence,
I stood upon the Heights; triumphant,
With upturned eyes, I stood,
And smiled unto the sun, and sang
5 A beautifully sad farewell unto the dying day.

And my thoughts and the eve gathered
Their serpentine mysteries around me,
My thoughts like alien breezes,
The eve like a fragrant legend.
10 My feeling was that I stood as one
Serenely poised for flight, as a muse
Of golden melody and lofty grace.

Yea, I stood as one scorning the swords
And wanton menace of the cities.

15 The sun had heavily sunk into the seas beyond,
And left me a tempting sweet and twilight.

The eve with trailing shadows westward
Swept on, and the lengthened shadows of trees
Disappeared: how silently the songs of silence
20 Steal into my soul! And still I stood
Among the crickets, in the beauteous profundity
Sung by stars; and I saw me
Softly melted into the eve. The moon
Slowly rose: my shadow on the ground
25 Dreamily began a dreamy roam,
And I upward smiled silent welcome.

6. Which of the following lines from the poem best states the overall theme?

   (A) "And still I stood / Among the crickets,"
   (B) "My feeling was that I stood as one / Serenely poised for flight,"
   (C) "… and sang / A beautifully sad farewell unto the dying day."
   (D) "Yea, I stood as one scorning the swords / And wanton menace of the cities."
   (E) "With upturned eyes, I stood, / And smiled unto the sun,"

7. "… silently the songs of silence / Steal into my soul" is an example of

   (A) dialect
   (B) simile
   (C) allusion
   (D) irony
   (E) alliteration

8. The poet uses the word *profundity* (line 21) to emphasize

   (A) the intensity of the emotions brought about by the moment
   (B) how immense the moon appeared as it rose
   (C) the totality of the silence around the narrator
   (D) the importance of a dream the narrator had
   (E) the coolness of the breeze on the hilltop

9. What style of narration is used in the poem?

   (A) an unreliable narrator
   (B) a first-person narrator
   (C) a third-person limited narrator
   (D) a third-person omniscient narrator
   (E) a second-person narrator

10. What does the narrator mean when he says, "My thoughts like alien breezes" (line 8)?

    (A) He is imagining what other people would think of the sunset.
    (B) He is emphasizing the difficulty of an immigrant fitting in to English society.
    (C) He acknowledges that his thoughts may seem strange to other people.
    (D) He draws a parallel between dreamlike changes brought by the sunset and his gently wandering thoughts.
    (E) He creates a metaphor comparing his disjointed thoughts to the sections of a strange serpent.

ANSWERS AND EXPLANATIONS

6. **(C)** The poem centers on a narrator watching the dreamlike change from day to night. The poet frequently uses language about songs and singing, and the tone is both pensive and sweet. Choice C best captures both the theme and the tone.

7. **(E)** The poet uses alliteration in this line, as well as elsewhere in the poem, with the repetition of the beginning *s* sound.

8. **(A)** The complete line is, "And still I stood / Among the crickets, in the beauteous profundity / Sung by stars." Since *profound* means very great or intense, you can conclude that the narrator is overwhelmed by the beauty of the oncoming night. Choice A best reflects the intense emotion the narrator feels.

9. **(B)** The poem has a first-person narrator, as evidenced by the use of *I* throughout the poem. While an unreliable narrator may also be first-person style, there is no reason to distrust this narrator.

10. **(D)** This line does not use the word *alien* to refer to foreigners or other people. It simply means strange. The poet uses this phrase to emphasize the dreamlike qualities of the scene and how the narrator's thoughts mirror the flow from day to evening. Choice D best describes this use of the phrase.

CHAPTER 2

Fiction

Prose Fiction

The key word in the definition of **prose fiction** is *imagination*. Fiction consists of imagined stories. Although authors often base works of fiction on their own experiences or on historical events, these stories are considered fiction because they recount actual experiences in an imaginative way.

This chapter contains a brief overview of prose fiction: its forms, structure, and history. Use the sample passages and questions to test your ability to read and understand works of prose fiction.

Forms of Prose Fiction

Prose fiction comes in three forms: the **novel,** the **novella,** and the **short story.**

The Novel and the Novella

A **novel** is a full-length work of prose fiction; a **novella** is a short novel. Roughly speaking, a narrative of about 80 to 150 pages is called a novella; any narrative longer than that is called a novel. The typical novel runs 200 to 350 pages, but there is no outside limit to its length. The longest novels, such as *War and Peace* (Leo Tolstoy, 1865–1869), *In Search of Lost Time* (Marcel Proust, 1913–1927), and *Les Miserables* (Victor Hugo, 1862) run well over 1,000 pages.

Some authors imagine stories of such scope that they must be told over the course of an entire series of novels. In a series of novels, each novel can be read as one long chapter of the extended story. Examples include the Palliser and Barchester novels by Anthony Trollope (6 novels in each series), *The Raj Quartet* by Paul Scott (4 novels), the Rougon-Macquart novels of Emile Zola (20 novels), *A Dance to the Music of Time* by Anthony Powell (12 novels), *Strangers and Brothers* by C. P. Snow (11 novels), and the Aubrey-Maturin novels of Patrick O'Brian (20 novels, plus one left half-finished at the author's death).

Structure of the Novel

A novel employs a full range of literary techniques to tell a story in an imaginative way. In a novel, the author can take all the time he or she wants to describe and develop characters and conflicts.

A novel is rooted in four major elements: **plot, character, setting,** and **theme.** (See Chapter 1 for definitions and examples of these terms). The author imagines people, sets them in a specific time and place, and gives them actions to carry out. The overall story is written to illustrate a meaning beyond itself, something that can be phrased as a statement that readers will recognize as a universal human truth. The only distinction between a novel and a novella is one of length; the author of a novella must deal with these four elements somewhat more concisely.

Because of its length, a novel can cover these four elements in great detail. For example, a novel may have more than one plot. It may have two major plot lines linked in some important way, or one main plot line and one or more **subplots**—chains of events that usually involve minor characters and relate to the central plot line.

In its hundreds of pages, a novel can portray dozens of characters. Some make only brief appearances, while others play major roles in the plot. Novels generally present a variety of settings, as the characters enact the events of the plot in different places. Many novels cover the activities of months or years in the characters' lives; others concentrate on a much shorter period of time. *Ulysses* (James Joyce, 1922) takes nearly 800 pages to recount only one day in the life of its protagonist, Leopold Bloom. A long novel can address a variety of major and minor themes.

Although novels are by definition prose works, authors often play with this convention, borrowing from other forms. For example, *Moby-Dick* (Herman Melville, 1851), *Ulysses,* and *This Side of Paradise* (F. Scott Fitzgerald, 1920) contain sections that are composed entirely of dialogue and stage directions, like play scripts. **Epistolary novels,** such as *Clarissa* (Samuel Richardson, 1748) and *The Ides of March* (Thornton Wilder, 1948) are made up of letters exchanged among the characters. *Dracula* (Bram Stoker, 1897) and *The Moonstone* (Wilkie Collins, 1868) tell their stories in whole or in part by means of journal entries. *Eugene Onegin* (Alexander Pushkin, 1833) is an eight-part story described by its author not as a modern epic poem but as "a novel in verse."

History of the Novel's Development

Literary historians generally agree that the world's first important novel was written in 1022 C.E. by Murasaki Shikibu of Japan. *The Tale of Genji* is a romance set in the Japanese royal palace.

The technological breakthrough that allowed and encouraged the development of long works of fiction was the invention of the printing press that used movable type. This technology was invented in Korea; in the West, it was perfected in Germany around 1450. For the first time, the mass production of books and other printed material was possible. The demand for literature rose along with the supply, as more and more western Europeans learned to read and write.

The first European novels began to appear in the 1500s: *Gargantua and Pantagruel* (François Rabelais, France, 1532) and *Don Quixote* (Miguel de Cervantes, Spain, 1605). *Don Quixote* owes a great deal to the form of the linked short-story collection (see **short story,** below). The novel has been an extraordinarily popular form of entertainment ever since.

The Eighteenth Century

Daniel Defoe, Samuel Richardson, Henry Fielding, and Laurence Sterne are the fathers of the English novel. They were among the first of their era to write long prose narratives that were wildly popular among the reading public. Their works were set in a recognizable, realistic time and place—the present-day England in which their readers lived. The characters were prone to be types rather than distinct individuals, but their motivations and actions were believable within that limitation. The plots often bordered on the improbable. Many of these novels were coming-of-age tales, in which the protagonist begins as an immature young person, learns important lessons about life in the course of the plot, and ends as a mature adult. Although these early novels may seem stilted and artificial today, they laid a foundation for a marvelous flowering of the form in the next century.

The Nineteenth Century

The novel was maturing as a form. In the nineteenth century, characters became three-dimensional individuals with strong personalities. Plots became more realistic, often dealing with everyday events. Novelists explored universal human themes. When people read novels, they often found themselves in a realistic and recognizable world. Many nineteenth-century writers devoted dozens of pages to descriptive writing, portraying settings in great detail. A novel's setting added to its atmosphere, and readers in the nineteenth century were not in a hurry to finish a book.

The nineteenth century is generally considered to be the high point of the full-length novel. The English population was highly literate, and the middle and upper classes had enough leisure time to enjoy reading. Major English novelists included Jane Austen, George Eliot, the Brontë sisters, and Charles Dickens.

With the nation established and expanding, and with an educated population of its own, American authors began experimenting with the novel. James Fenimore Cooper found huge popular success with his historical novels of the American frontier. Other important American novelists of this century included Herman Melville, Mark Twain, Nathaniel Hawthorne, and Harriet Beecher Stowe, whose *Uncle Tom's Cabin* (1852) outsold every book except the Bible in the years leading up to the American Civil War.

Nineteenth-century writers wrote not only to entertain their readers but also to educate them about society. In this era before broadcast media existed, popular novelists were major celebrities, and they used their power to sway the public on important issues of the day. In novels such as *Oliver Twist* and *Hard Times,* Dickens wrote with such passion about the terrible conditions in prisons and boys' schools that he convinced his readers to support reform. *Uncle Tom's Cabin,* a detailed look at American slavery, painted an unsparing picture of a system that corrupted everyone it touched. Stowe's novel was so widely read and discussed that it played a major role in committing Northerners to the cause of abolition. When President Abraham Lincoln met Stowe at the White House in the 1860s, he is reported to have greeted her with the words, "So you're the little lady who started this great war!"

The Twentieth Century and Beyond

American prose fiction came into its own in the twentieth century with such authors as Henry James, Edith Wharton, Willa Cather, Ernest Hemingway, F. Scott Fitzgerald, and John Steinbeck. Notable British novelists of the era included Graham Greene, Evelyn Waugh, E. M. Forster, and D. H. Lawrence. Irish novelists included Elizabeth Bowen, and James Joyce—one of the greatest fiction writers of the modern era. Authors from other lands also wrote great works of English-language fiction. Joseph Conrad of Poland and Vladimir Nabokov of Russia wrote numerous novels in English. Nabokov is best known for the notorious *Lolita*; Conrad, for the short novel *Heart of Darkness* and other tales of Southeast Asia.

Modern and contemporary novels have less of an emphasis on descriptive writing, and their prose is often more spare than that of their nineteenth-century counterparts. The novel was affected by the rise of technology, as other forms of entertainment (such as movies, professional sports, and eventually television and the Internet) competed for people's attention. Modern novels are perhaps more prone to imply important information about characters, rather than to state it directly. They are also more likely than earlier novels to have open-ended or ambiguous resolutions.

Two highly popular forms of the novel that first appeared in the nineteenth century became enormously popular in the twentieth—the detective story and the science-fiction novel. Both are written almost solely for entertainment purposes; however, detective novelists such as John le Carré and Raymond Chandler produced works of very high literary merit.

The Short Story

A **short story** is like a miniature novel. Short stories generally run from two or three to about 50 pages. Some stories run as long as 80 pages. When stories become much longer than this, they are usually considered novellas. Short stories are usually published in collections of 10 or 15—sometimes all by one author, sometimes by various authors. A novella may be published on its own or together with a few shorter stories by the same author.

Structure of the Short Story

The major differences between novels and short stories are dictated by their comparative length. In a short story, an author must use the same literary techniques to tell a story more concisely. There is much less time to develop a character or a conflict. A short story generally aims to produce a single effect on the reader. It has a much narrower focus than a novel.

Whereas a novel may have multiple plots and subplots, a short story usually has only one plot. A short story will develop only a few characters in detail. Although a novel constantly shifts its physical setting, a short story usually takes place entirely in one setting, or in a very few settings at most. A short story usually concentrates on only one major theme.

History of the Short Story's Development

The Ancient World

The world's first written short stories included the fables of Aesop (Greece, sixth century B.C.E.) and Chuang-Tzu (China, fourth century B.C.E.). Aesop's brief tales feature animal and sometimes human characters who, in the course of the story, learn lessons that the author sums up as morals, or good advice to the reader. Chuang-Tzu's fables feature peasants, artisans, and scholars debating the meaning of the natural phenomena they observe in the world around them.

The Middle Ages

As the ancient world gave way to the modern, authors began to imagine more sophisticated and complex plots featuring individual personalities. One of the earliest and most famous short-story collections dates to about 950 C.E. *The Thousand and One Nights,* also known as *The Arabian Nights,* appeared in Persia (modern-day Iran) at this time. *The Arabian Nights* begins with a frame story: the account of a sultan who is convinced that all women are faithless. He therefore makes love to a different woman every night, only to order her executed in the morning. When Scheherazade is brought in to spend the night with him, she tells him the beginning of an exciting tale. Wanting to hear the end of the story, the sultan decides to keep her alive for one more night. As the nights pass, Scheherazade breaks off each new story at some exciting point, and the sultan continues to postpone her execution until the whole idea of killing her is long forgotten. Each of Scheherazade's tales is a self-contained short story, but the overall framing device unifies the entire work.

Two famous fourteenth-century short-story collections, *The Decameron* and *The Canterbury Tales,* employ a similar structure. In *The Decameron* (1353), Giovanni Boccaccio created the story of ten young men and women fleeing the city of Florence to escape the plague. They settle in a country villa and pass the time by telling stories. Each character tells one story every day for 10 days, making a total of 100 tales. *The Decameron* is an unforgettable collection of tales of romance, comedy, tragedy, and farce.

In England, Geoffrey Chaucer published *The Canterbury Tales* (c. 1386). Like *The Thousand and One Nights* and *The Decameron,* it is a collection of self-contained short stories linked by an overall framing device. Several religious pilgrims on their way to Canterbury Cathedral meet en route at the Tabard Inn. They agree to hold a storytelling contest to while away the tedium of the journey. Although all but two tales in the collection are written in verse, *The Canterbury Tales* is considered a short-story collection because of the length of each tale and its strong basis in the major elements of prose fiction: plot, character, setting, and theme.

The Nineteenth Century

The world's first literary and popular magazines began appearing in the early 1800s. The magazine was a perfect medium for publishing individual short stories. Many novelists of the era were also short-story writers. An author who took many months to finish a novel was glad to be able to earn money in the meantime by tossing off short stories for the magazines. To this day, magazines such as *The New Yorker* continue to publish short stories by the best-known writers.

The Twentieth Century

In the twentieth century, the best-known American short-story writers included O. Henry, Henry James, Edith Wharton, Ernest Hemingway, F. Scott Fitzgerald, Sherwood Anderson, and William Faulkner. Notable British short-story writers of the era included Graham Greene, D. H. Lawrence, and Elizabeth Bowen.

Collections of linked short stories remained popular. Sherwood Anderson's *Winesburg, Ohio* portrays an entire town by focusing each story in the collection on a different character, with several characters appearing in more than one story. In 1914, James Joyce published *Dubliners,* stories that provide a portrait of a city and its people by showing various aspects of contemporary Dublin.

Some writers create a popular character and write a series of self-contained short stories linked only by the fact that they feature this character. Saki (the pen name of H. H. Munro) wrote a collection of satirical stories about Reginald and another about Clovis. Sir Arthur Conan Doyle stumbled on an enormous success with his stories of Sherlock Holmes, who may be the best-known literary character ever created.

REVIEW QUESTIONS

Questions 1–5. Read the following passage carefully before you choose your answers.

While the mate was getting the hammer, Ahab, without speaking, was slowly rubbing the gold piece against the skirts of his jacket, as if to heighten its lustre, and without using any words was meanwhile lowly humming to himself, producing a sound so strangely muffled and inarticulate that it seemed the mechanical humming of the wheels
5 of his vitality in him.

Receiving the top-maul from Starbuck, he advanced towards the main-mast with the hammer uplifted in one hand, exhibiting the gold with the other, and with a high raised voice exclaiming: "Whosoever of ye raises me a white-headed whale with a wrinkled brow and a crooked jaw; whosoever of ye raises me that white-headed whale, with three

10 holes punctured in his starboard fluke—look ye, whosoever of ye raises me that same white whale, he shall have this gold ounce, my boys!"

"Huzza! huzza!" cried the seamen, as with swinging tarpaulins they hailed the act of nailing the gold to the mast.

"It's a white whale, I say," resumed Ahab, as he threw down the top-maul: "a white whale.

15 Skin your eyes for him, men; look sharp for white water; if ye see but a bubble, sing out."

All this while Tashtego, Daggoo, and Queequeg had looked on with even more intense interest and surprise than the rest, and at the mention of the wrinkled brow and crooked jaw they had started as if each was separately touched by some specific recollection.

"Captain Ahab," said Tashtego, "that white whale must be the same that some call

20 Moby Dick."

. . . "Captain Ahab," said Starbuck, who, with Stubb and Flask, had thus far been eyeing his superior with increasing surprise, but at last seemed struck with a thought which somewhat explained all the wonder. "Captain Ahab, I have heard of Moby Dick—but it was not Moby Dick that took off thy leg?"

25 "Who told thee that?" cried Ahab; then pausing, "Aye, Starbuck; aye, my hearties all round; it was Moby Dick that dismasted me; Moby Dick that brought me to this dead stump I stand on now. Aye, aye," he shouted with a terrific, loud, animal sob, like that of a heart-stricken moose; "Aye, aye! it was that accursed white whale that razeed me; made a poor pegging lubber of me for ever and a day!" Then tossing both arms, with measureless

30 imprecations he shouted out: "Aye, aye! and I'll chase him round Good Hope, and round the Horn, and round the Norway Maelstrom, and round perdition's flames before I give him up. And this is what ye have shipped for, men! to chase that white whale on both sides of land, and over all sides of earth, till he spouts black blood and rolls fin out. What say ye, men, will ye splice hands on it, now? I think ye do look brave."

35 "Aye, aye!" shouted the harpooners and seamen, running closer to the excited old man: "A sharp eye for the White Whale; a sharp lance for Moby Dick!"

"God bless ye," he seemed to half sob and half shout. "God bless ye, men. Steward! go draw the great measure of grog. But what's this long face about, Mr. Starbuck; wilt thou not chase the white whale? art not game for Moby Dick?"

40 "I am game for his crooked jaw, and for the jaws of Death too, Captain Ahab, if it fairly comes in the way of the business we follow; but I came here to hunt whales, not my commander's vengeance. How many barrels will thy vengeance yield thee even if thou gettest it, Captain Ahab? it will not fetch thee much in our Nantucket market."

"Nantucket market! Hoot! But come closer, Starbuck; thou requirest a little lower layer.

45 If money's to be the measurer, man, and the accountants have computed their great counting-house the globe, by girdling it with guineas, one to every three parts of an inch; then, let me tell thee, that my vengeance will fetch a great premium *here*!"

"He smites his chest," whispered Stubb, "what's that for? methinks it rings most vast, but hollow."

50 "Vengeance on a dumb brute!" cried Starbuck, "that simply smote thee from blindest instinct! Madness! To be enraged with a dumb thing, Captain Ahab, seems blasphemous."

"Hark ye yet again,—the little lower layer. All visible objects, man, are but as pasteboard masks. But in each event—in the living act, the undoubted deed—there, some unknown 55 but still reasoning thing puts forth the mouldings of its features from behind the unreasoning mask. If man will strike, strike though the mask! How can the prisoner reach outside except by thrusting through the wall? To me, the white whale is that wall, shoved near to me. Sometimes I think there's naught beyond. But 'tis enough. He tasks me; he heaps me; I see in him outrageous strength, with an inscrutable malice sinewing 60 it. That inscrutable thing is chiefly what I hate; and be the white whale agent, or be the white whale principal, I will wreak that hate upon him."

(1851)

1. Why does Starbuck question Ahab's plan to hunt down Moby Dick?

(A) He is afraid Moby Dick will attack Ahab again.

(B) He does not believe that they can catch Moby Dick.

(C) He believes it is a sin to hunt down and kill an animal for revenge.

(D) He does not want to chase whales because that is not the purpose of the ship's voyage.

(E) He believes that Ahab is insane to hunt whales.

2. Given Ahab's statements in this excerpt, Moby Dick appears to symbolize for him

(A) his own desire for revenge against an evil force

(B) a malicious and tyrannical God

(C) an elusive love who cannot be caught and held

(D) his own mysterious destiny or fate

(E) freedom from authority and fear

3. How does the shipboard setting affect the relationships among the characters?

(A) The ship is a setting that no one can escape except in death.

(B) The setting gives Ahab supreme authority, which the crew will not question except in an extreme situation.

(C) The crew members are packed together in a small space, so they all get along well.

(D) Captain Ahab would not be able to pursue Moby Dick except in a ship.

(E) The characters feel lost and uncertain on a ship, when they would be strong and sure of themselves on land.

4. Based on this excerpt, the novel deals with all of the following universal themes EXCEPT

   (A) the conflict between conscience and professional duties
   (B) the obsession with revenge against an enemy
   (C) the battle between man and nature
   (D) the temptation to sin in spite of warnings
   (E) the pursuit of an unattainable love

5. Which of the following best describes Captain Ahab's mood in this excerpt?

   (A) obsessed
   (B) grateful
   (C) reverent
   (D) surprised
   (E) amused

ANSWERS AND EXPLANATIONS

1. **(C)** Dialogue in the passage shows that the ship's business is to hunt and kill whales for their oil. Therefore, Starbuck would find it perfectly appropriate to kill Moby Dick if they came across him in the natural course of the voyage. However, Starbuck sees a tremendous difference between killing whales as a profession and chasing one particular whale to kill him for personal revenge. Starbuck describes this as "blasphemy." This makes choice C correct.

2. **(B)** Ahab seems to believe that life is unknowable, consisting of mysterious enemy forces that wear masks. God has created these enemy forces and given them their masks, and humankind must constantly struggle to survive in this hostile environment. Moby Dick is a symbol of what Ahab sees as God's tyranny and his arbitrary creation of a dangerous world. This best matches choice B.

3. **(B)** A nineteenth-century ship is a small world, floating by itself in an ocean. The captain is the ruler of this small universe, in which a chain of command is highly important. The setting gives Ahab a measure of authority and absolute power that he would not possess anywhere else. Starbuck does question him, but only in an extreme situation—because he believes the captain's plan is endangering the voyage. Ahab's word is law on the ship, and the other characters will have to obey him. This makes choice B correct. The other four choices are either untrue statements or they do not really address the question of character relationships.

4. **(E)** Note the word EXCEPT in the question. Choice E is correct because Moby Dick does not represent love. Ahab is chasing him because of entirely different motives.

5. **(A)** Throughout the excerpt, Ahab demonstrates his obsession with hunting Moby Dick. He shows gratitude for his sailors' support, but this emotion is brief. He does not show amusement, surprise, or reverence.

Questions 6–10. Read the following passage carefully before you choose your answers.

I did it—I should have known better. I persuaded Reginald to go to the McKillops' garden-party against his will.

We all make mistakes occasionally. "They know you're here, and they'll think it so funny if you don't go. And I want particularly to be in with Mrs. McKillop just now."

5   "I know, you want one of her smoke Persian kittens as a prospective wife for Wumples— or a husband, is it?" (Reginald has a magnificent scorn for details, other than sartorial.) "And I am expected to undergo social martyrdom to suit the connubial exigencies—"

"Reginald! It's nothing of the kind, only I'm sure Mrs. McKillop would be pleased if I brought you. Young men of your brilliant attractions are rather at a premium at her
10   garden-parties."

"Should be at a premium in heaven," remarked Reginald complacently.

"There will be very few of you there, if that is what you mean. But seriously, there won't be any great strain upon your powers of endurance; I promise you that you shan't have to play croquet, or talk to the Archdeacon's wife, or do anything that is likely to bring on
15   physical prostration. You can just wear your sweetest clothes and a moderately amiable expression, and eat chocolate-creams with the appetite of a *blasé* parrot. Nothing more is demanded of you."

Reginald shut his eyes. "There will be the exhaustingly up-to-date young women who will ask me if I have seen *San Toy*: a less progressive grade who will yearn to hear about
20   the Diamond Jubilee—the historic event, not the horse. With a little encouragement, they will inquire if I saw the Allies march into Paris. Why are women so fond of raking up the past? They're as bad as tailors, who invariably remember what you owe them for a suit long after you've ceased to wear it."

"I'll order lunch for one o'clock; that will give you two and a half hours to dress in."

25   Reginald puckered his brow into a tortured frown, and I knew that my point was gained. He was debating what tie would go with which waistcoat.

Even then I had my misgivings.

(1904)

6. Which best describes the author's purpose in writing this passage?

   (A) to entertain readers with an amusing tale
   (B) to persuade readers not to pressure their friends into accepting
       invitations against their wills
   (C) to inform readers what happens at a garden-party
   (D) to describe the modern up-to-date young society woman
   (E) to intrigue readers with a challenging puzzle

7. Based on this passage, what is the major conflict in the story?

    (A) Reginald's desire to remain in his comfortable chair versus his desire to go to the party

    (B) the narrator's desire that Reginald attend the party versus Reginald's desire to avoid it

    (C) Reginald's desire to dress well for the party versus the lack of time to get ready

    (D) the young women's desire to talk to Reginald versus his desire to keep to himself

    (E) Reginald's desire to behave well at the party versus the narrator's desire to make mischief

8. What literary technique does the writer use to describe the garden-party setting?

    (A) He lets readers imagine the setting from the simple term *garden-party*.

    (B) He has his two main characters discuss the party in detail in the dialogue.

    (C) He writes a detailed descriptive passage that allows the reader to experience the party through the five senses.

    (D) He indicates the social rank of the character who is hosting the party.

    (E) He has one character describe the garden to the other in detail.

9. The sentences "I did it—I should have known better" and "Even then I had my misgivings" can best be described as examples of

    (A) imagery

    (B) flashbacks

    (C) characterization

    (D) foreshadowing

    (E) verbal irony

10. During which time period does this story most likely take place?

    (A) just before the American Revolutionary War

    (B) in the early 1900s

    (C) during the Italian Renaissance

    (D) during the Victorian period

    (E) in the years following World War II

ANSWERS AND EXPLANATIONS

6. **(A)** The tone of the story is light, the subject matter is frivolous, and there is plenty of sarcastic humor in the dialogue. The story was clearly written mainly to entertain the reader, choice A.

7. **(B)** The dialogue shows that the narrator wants Reginald to go to the party, and Reginald wants to stay away. This describes choice B—a basic literary conflict, in which one character pushes and the other one resists. The lines "I should have known better" and "We all make mistakes occasionally" further support this choice, showing that because Reginald does not want to go to the party, he will not behave well there.

8. **(B)** In the dialogue, the narrator and Reginald discuss many details of the party. The reader knows there will be croquet and refreshments, that people will be well dressed, and that there will be pleasant conversation. This supports choice B.

9. **(D)** Foreshadowing means hinting to the reader about what is to come next. This matches choice D. Imagery is language that appeals to the five senses, a flashback occurs when the narration shifts to an earlier time, characterization helps to develop an individual's personality, and verbal irony is the difference between what is stated and what is meant.

10. **(E)** Reginald imagines that the ladies at the party will ask him if he saw the Allies march into Paris. This indicates that World War II took place during Reginald's lifetime.

CHAPTER 3

Nonfiction

Nonfiction

Nonfiction is the opposite of fiction—it is not imagined stories, but true ones. Nonfiction comes in two varieties: **narrative nonfiction** and **expository nonfiction.**

Narrative nonfiction resembles narrative fiction in its structure and its use of literary elements. Narrative **history, biography,** or **autobiography,** like narrative fiction, consist of characters acting out events in a specific setting. The difference is that in nonfiction, the **characters** are real people, the **settings** are the real times and places in which those people lived, and the **plot** consists of events that actually took place. **Historical novels** are outside the category of narrative nonfiction; they are based on real people and events, but they are works of fiction because the author retells the events in an imaginative way.

Expository nonfiction includes prose works written by authors who want to persuade, inform, and/or entertain readers by writing about their thoughts, ideas, and observations. **Essays** and **speeches** are the primary forms of expository nonfiction.

This chapter gives a brief overview of the three types of nonfiction you are most likely to see excerpted on the SAT Literature Test: the autobiography or memoir, the essay, and the speech. Use the sample passages and questions to test your ability to read and understand literary nonfiction.

The Autobiography

An **autobiography** or **memoir** is the story of the author's life. Autobiographies are usually written in the form of journal entries or prose narratives; a notable exception to this rule is the free-verse autobiography *Leaves of Grass* (Walt Whitman, United States, 1855). Writing about this work more than 30 years later, Whitman explained,

> *Leaves of Grass* indeed (I cannot too often reiterate) has mainly been the outcropping of my own emotional and other personal nature—an attempt, from first to last, to put *a Person*, a human being (myself, in the latter half of the Nineteenth Century, in America), freely, fully, and truly on record.

When studying or analyzing an autobiography, the reader must consider what is termed in fiction the **unreliable narrator**—a first-person narrator whose account of events the reader should accept only with caution. There are three reasons that autobiographies may be unreliable accounts, despite the fact that their authors were (obviously) eyewitnesses to everything they describe.

First, many autobiographers rely on their memories rather than looking up dates, names, and facts. This often leads to major and minor errors, because no one has a perfect memory of recent events, let alone those that happened many years ago. Second, few people are objective about themselves and their own motives. Like anyone else, the authors of autobiographies have the natural human temptation to portray themselves in the best possible light. Before the nineteenth century, authors often acknowledged their own bias by including the word *Apologia* (meaning "self-justification") in the titles of their memoirs.

Third, an autobiography represents only one point of view—the author's. A biographer is likely to consult numerous sources, all of which will give slightly different points of view about the subject. An autobiographer usually does not consult any sources, but instead writes from his or her memory.

Both ordinary and extraordinary individuals have been writing autobiographies since the beginning of recorded history. Notable literary autobiographies include *Confessions* (Saint Augustine, North Africa, 397–398 C.E.), *The Autobiography of Benvenuto Cellini* (Italy, 1556–1558), *Autobiography* (Benjamin Franklin, United States, 1771–1790), and *Narrative of the Life of Frederick Douglass* (United States, 1845). Douglass's autobiography is an example of a **slave narrative**—an autobiography that recounts the author's experiences as a slave in the United States. Many escaped slaves wrote and published slave narratives in the years between the American Revolution and the Civil War.

Two of the most famous twentieth-century autobiographies are *Good-bye to All That* (Robert Graves, England, 1929) and *The Autobiography of Alice B. Toklas* (Gertrude Stein, United States, 1933). Graves's memoir concentrates on his youth, particularly his combat experiences during World War I. It is a notable example of antiwar literature. Stein's work is typical of her delight in confounding readers' expectations; it may well be the only autobiography ever written from a point of view other than the author's. Despite its title, *The Autobiography of Alice B. Toklas* is the story of Stein's life, written by Stein from the point of view of her life's companion.

The Essay

An **essay** is a short piece of writing, from several paragraphs to several pages in length. It may defend an opinion, express a point of view, or discuss and describe ideas and observations. An essay is generally built around an **argument,** also called a **thesis statement** or a statement of the author's main idea. The argument or thesis is the focus of the essay. It is generally stated directly, rather than implied. The essayist then defends his or her opinion with facts and evidence.

The literary essay was first identified as such in 1580, when Michel de Montaigne published his *Les Essais* in France. The French verb *essayer* means "to attempt." Montaigne used this name for his short prose discussions to indicate that they were only attempts to explore certain subjects and ideas—that they bore the same relationship to finished works of philosophy that rough sketches would bear to a completed oil painting. Nearly 20 years later, Francis Bacon of England wrote a volume of *Essays* of his own, adopting Montaigne's title, style, and format. These two works are the fathers of the essay form.

The first literary magazines appeared in the early eighteenth century. The magazine provided a perfect opportunity for essay writers to publish their short works. Rather than having to write enough essays to fill a book, an author could submit each one to a magazine as soon as it was finished, thus earning a steady income. Because magazines were intended as light entertainment, essays published in them began to diverge somewhat from their serious philosophical beginnings. They became lighter, more humorous, and less formal.

In the late eighteenth century, the essay pendulum swung back again toward the more serious and substantial. One of the best-known collections of essays of this era is the *Federalist Papers*, which appeared serially in print from 1787 to 1788 and were later collected as a book. Written under the pseudonym "Publius" by Alexander Hamilton, James Madison, and John Jay, these 85 essays argue for the passage of the U.S. Constitution. The most famous of the essays, "Federalist No. 10," discusses the dangers of faction in a democratic government.

Serious essays continued to appear through the nineteenth century. The best-known American essayists of the time were Ralph Waldo Emerson and Henry David Thoreau. Emerson's essays are lengthy and thoughtful explorations of the human character, with such titles as "On Friendship" and "On Love." Thoreau's "Civil Disobedience" examines human motivations and what he saw as the evils of society.

In modern and contemporary times, essays are everywhere in print. The essay category is broad enough to include introductions and prefaces to literary works; movie, theater, and concert reviews; art criticism; newspaper editorials—in fact, almost any short piece of writing that proposes and defends a particular argument or point of view.

When analyzing or studying an essay, the reader should always ask, "Do I believe the thesis?" In an essay, the author's purpose is, above all, to persuade. The reader should consider whether the thesis seems reasonable and whether it is adequately supported with details and facts.

The Speech

A **speech** is a prose work delivered orally to a listening audience. Most speeches are written down first, so that the speaker can be sure to include all the necessary points and express him- or herself as memorably and clearly as possible. Most speeches are made by politicians and government officials or by candidates for government. In the past, public figures wrote their own speeches; today, most hire speechwriters to do it for them.

The purposes of a speech are to explain, inform, and persuade. To accomplish these purposes, a speech employs many **rhetorical devices**, such as **parallelism** (the repetition of a grammatical pattern) and **repetition** of words and phrases. Speechwriters use rhetorical devices so that their words and ideas will linger in a listener's memory.

A speech can be as brief as a few paragraphs or as long as several pages. One of the most effective speeches in history, Abraham Lincoln's Gettysburg Address, is only 10 sentences long.

When analyzing or studying a speech, the reader should first identify the speaker's purpose, then pay close attention to the literary devices the writer uses to accomplish that purpose.

REVIEW QUESTIONS

Questions 1–3. Read the following passage carefully before you choose your answers.

As I journeyed across France to Marseilles, and made thence a terribly rough voyage to Alexandria, I wrote my allotted number of pages every day … When I have commenced a new book, I have always prepared a diary, divided into weeks, and carried it on for the period which I have allowed myself for the completion of the work. In this I have entered,
5   day by day, the number of pages I have written, so that if at any time I have slipped into idleness for a day or two, the record of that idleness has been there, staring me in the face, and demanding of me increased labor, so that the deficiency might be supplied. According to the circumstances of the time,—whether my other business might be then heavy or light, or whether the book which I was writing was or was not wanted with
10   speed,—I have allotted myself so many pages a week …

I have been told that such appliances are beneath the notice of a man of genius. I have never fancied myself to be a man of genius, but had I been so I think I might well have subjected myself to these trammels …

I have known authors whose lives have always been troublesome and painful because
15   their tasks have never been done in time. They have ever been as boys struggling to learn their lessons as they entered the school gates. Publishers have distrusted them, and they have failed to write their best because they have seldom written at ease. I have done double their work—though burdened with another profession,—and have done it almost without an effort. I have not once, through all my literary career, felt myself even
20   in danger of being late with my task. I have known no anxiety as to "copy." The needed pages far ahead—very far ahead—have almost always been in the drawer beside me. And that little diary, with its dates and ruled spaces, its record that must be seen, its daily, weekly demand upon my industry, has done all that for me.

There are those who would be ashamed to subject themselves to such a taskmaster, and
25 who think that the man who works with his imagination should allow himself to wait
till—inspiration moves him. When I have heard such doctrine preached, I have hardly
been able to repress my scorn. To me it would not be more absurd if the shoemaker were
to wait for inspiration, or the tallow-chandler for the divine moment of melting. If the
man whose business it is to write has eaten too many good things, or has drunk too
30 much, or smoked too many cigars,—as men who write sometimes will do,—then his
condition may be unfavorable for work; but so will be the condition of a shoemaker who
has been similarly imprudent. I have sometimes thought that the inspiration wanted
has been the remedy which time will give to the evil results of such imprudence.—*Mens
sana in corpore sano.*[1] The author wants that as does every other workman,—that and a
35 habit of industry. I was once told that the surest aid to the writing of a book was a piece
of cobbler's wax on my chair. I certainly believe in the cobbler's wax much more than the
inspiration.

It will be said, perhaps, that a man whose work has risen to no higher pitch than mine
has attained, has no right to speak of the strains and impulses to which real genius is
40 exposed. I am ready to admit the great variations in brain power which are exhibited by
the products of different men, and am not disposed to rank my own very high; but my
own experience tells me that a man can always do the work for which his brain is fitted if
he will give himself the habit of regarding his work as a normal condition of his life.

(1883)

1. Why is the author "hardly able to repress his scorn" when he hears people say
   that an artist should only write when "inspiration moves him" (lines 26–27)?

   (A) He feels that he himself is an uninspired writer and cannot wait for such
       inspiration.
   (B) He looks upon writing as a job that should be done on schedule like any
       other job.
   (C) He is jealous of greater writers' bursts of creative imagination, knowing
       that he has little imagination of his own.
   (D) He has worked as a publisher and knows how exasperating it is when an
       author does not deliver manuscript on time.
   (E) He believes that there is no such thing as creative inspiration in literature.

2. The author feels that other authors he knows "have ever been as boys
   struggling to learn their lessons as they entered the school gates" (lines
   15–16) because

   (A) they do not know how to write well
   (B) they have no imagination
   (C) they use their writing time inefficiently
   (D) they never get through their research on time
   (E) they do not keep daily diaries of their progress

[1] A sound mind in a healthy body.

3. All these aspects of this passage suggest that the author is a reliable narrator EXCEPT

(A) he draws reasonable conclusions that are based on personal observation and experience

(B) his description of his approach to writing is not intended to make him look glamorous or "artistic"

(C) he is not describing personal or emotional matters on which he is likely to write with a strong bias

(D) he does not claim to be a genius or an extraordinary talent

(E) he assumes that his approach to writing as a career is the best possible system

ANSWERS AND EXPLANATIONS

1. **(B)** The author compares writing to two other jobs, shoemaker and chandler (maker of candles). He approaches his own writing not so much as a creative art but as a job that should be done in a professional manner, according to contracts made by businessmen. This matches choice B.

2. **(C)** The schoolboys the author describes did not do their homework at a reasonable pace the night before and now have to cram an evening's study into a few minutes. Naturally, this is not a good way to learn a lesson thoroughly or well. By the same token, a writer should produce his work at an even, steady pace. He or she should not waste time for days or weeks, then frantically try to catch up in order to meet a looming deadline. Choice C summarizes the fault the author finds with other authors.

3. **(E)** In the final paragraph, the author acknowledges that there may be other ways of working than his own, but he still feels that there is no author who could not profit by using his system. This describes choice E, which is the only item that might make a reader question the author's reliability. Anyone who is convinced his or her own view is best is not necessarily making an objective evaluation.

Questions 4–7. Read the following passage carefully before you choose your answers.

The ways by which you may get money almost without exception lead downward. To have done anything by which you earned money *merely* is to have been truly idle or worse. If the laborer gets no more than the wages which his employer pays him, he is cheated, he cheats himself. If you would get money as a writer or lecturer, you must be popular, which is to go
5 down perpendicularly. Those services which the community will most readily pay for it is most disagreeable to render. You are paid for being something less than a man. The State does not commonly reward a genius any more wisely. Even the poet-laureate would rather not have to celebrate the accidents of royalty. He must be bribed with a pipe of wine; and perhaps another poet is called away from his muse to gauge that very pipe. As for my own
10 business, even that kind of surveying which I could do with most satisfaction my employers do not want. They would prefer that I should do my work coarsely and not too well, ay, not well enough. When I observe that there are different ways of surveying, my employer commonly asks which will give him the most land, not which is most correct. I once invented a rule for measuring cord-wood, and tried to introduce it in Boston; but the measurer there
15 told me that the sellers did not wish to have their wood measured correctly,—that he was already too accurate for them, and therefore they commonly got their wood measured in Charlestown before crossing the bridge.

The aim of the laborer should be, not to get his living, to get "a good job," but to perform well a certain work; and, even in a pecuniary sense, it would be economy for a town to
20 pay its laborers so well that they would not feel that they were working for low ends, as for a livelihood merely, but for scientific, or even moral ends. Do not hire a man who does your work for money, but him who does it for love of it.

It is remarkable that there are few men so well employed, so much to their minds, but that a little money or fame would commonly buy them off from their present pursuit. I
25 see advertisements for *active* young men, as if activity were the whole of a young man's capital. Yet I have been surprised when one has with confidence proposed to me, a grown man, to embark in some enterprise of his, as if I had absolutely nothing to do, my life having been a complete failure hitherto. What a doubtful compliment this is to pay me! As if he had met me half-way across the ocean beating up against the wind, but
30 bound nowhere, and proposed to me to go along with him! If I did, what do you think the underwriters would say? No, no! I am not without employment at this stage of the voyage. To tell the truth, I saw an advertisement for able-bodied seamen, when I was a boy, sauntering in my native port, and as soon as I came of age I embarked.

The community has no bribe that will tempt a wise man. You may raise money enough to
35 tunnel a mountain, but you cannot raise money enough to hire a man who is minding *his own* business. An efficient and valuable man does what he can, whether the community pay him for it or not. The inefficient offer their inefficiency to the highest bidder, and are forever expecting to be put into office. One would suppose that they were rarely disappointed.

(1863)

4. Which of the following best encompasses the author's thesis or argument?

   (A) "The ways by which you may get money almost without exception lead downward." (line 1)
   (B) "Those services which the community will most readily pay for it is most disagreeable to render." (lines 5–6)
   (C) "The aim of the laborer should be, not to get his living, to get 'a good job,' but to perform well a certain work." (lines 18–19)
   (D) "An efficient and valuable man does what he can, whether the community pay him for it or not." (lines 36–37)
   (E) "The inefficient offer their inefficiency to the highest bidder, and are forever expecting to be put into office." (lines 37–38)

5. When the author says "To have done anything by which you earned money *merely* is to have been truly idle or worse" (lines 1–2), he means

   (A) you never have to work hard to earn a lot of money
   (B) you should earn enough money to be able to retire and live idly
   (C) there is nothing more important in life than earning enough money
   (D) if you earn only money, not inner satisfaction, you have wasted your time
   (E) earning money is a waste of time because money is not essential for any reason

6. Why does the author believe that his employers do not want him to do his work too well?

   (A) They do not want his efficiency to make them look lazy by contrast.
   (B) They do not want to pay him as much as a better worker would demand.
   (C) They do not want to have to fire him for incompetence or laziness.
   (D) They do not want to lose his services to a better company.
   (E) They do not want him to impress their clients too much.

7. What is the meaning of the word *pecuniary* (line 19)?

   (A) hard-working
   (B) relating to money
   (C) unnecessarily expensive
   (D) of good moral character
   (E) pointless labor

ANSWERS AND EXPLANATIONS

4. **(C)** The author's main point is that people should choose the job they love for its own sake, not the job that pays the most money, because loving your job enriches your life. Choice C most closely expresses this idea.

5. **(D)** The author believes that the true goal of work is, or should be, to acquire wisdom and experience while doing something you love. Money, in his view, is simply a by-product or a bonus; as long as you are earning what you need for self-support, you should be content with that. If you want to earn the most money possible simply for its own sake, you are wasting your time; given the number of hours most adults work, you are in fact wasting your life. Choice D best expresses the author's definition of "earning money *merely*."

6. **(A)** The author observes that his employers are comfortable with their system exactly as it is. When he thinks he can make improvements, they discourage him. He realizes that they do not want to make the effort that would be involved in having everyone work more efficiently; they prefer to muddle along as they are, doing the least possible work for the maximum amount of money. If the author were allowed to be efficient, he would make everyone else look bad. This approximates choice A.

7. **(B)** The word *pecuniary* means relating to money. The context of the paragraph shows that this word relates to money because it discusses the economic benefits to a town of paying its workers well.

Questions 8–10. Read the following speech carefully before you choose your answers.

First of all, let me assert my firm belief that the only thing we have to fear is fear itself—nameless, unreasoning, unjustified terror which paralyzes needed efforts to convert retreat into advance. In every dark hour of our national life, a leadership of frankness and vigor has met with that understanding and support of the people them-
5 selves which is essential to victory. I am convinced that you will again give that support to leadership in these critical days.

In such a spirit on my part and on yours we face our common difficulties. They concern, thank God, only material things. Values have shrunken to fantastic levels; taxes have risen; our ability to pay has fallen; government of all kinds is faced by serious curtailment of
10 income; the means of exchange are frozen in the currents of trade; the withered leaves of industrial enterprise lie on every side; farmers find no markets for their produce; the savings of many years in thousands of families are gone.

More important, a host of unemployed citizens face the grim problem of existence, and an equally great number toil with little return. Only a foolish optimist can deny the dark
15 realities of the moment.

Yet our distress comes from no failure of substance. We are stricken by no plague of locusts. Compared with the perils which our forefathers conquered because they believed and were not afraid, we have still much to be thankful for. Nature still offers her bounty and human efforts have multiplied it. Plenty is at our doorstep, but a generous
20 use of it languishes in the very sight of the supply. Primarily this is because the rulers of the exchange of mankind's goods have failed, through their own stubbornness and their own incompetence, have admitted their failure, and abdicated. Practices of the unscrupulous moneychangers stand indicted in the court of public opinion, rejected by the hearts and minds of men.

25 True, they have tried, but their efforts have been cast in the pattern of an outworn tradition. Faced by failure of credit they have proposed only the lending of more money. Stripped of the lure of profit by which to induce our people to follow their false leadership, they have resorted to exhortations, pleading tearfully for restored confidence. They know only the rules of a generation of self-seekers. They have no vision, and when
30 there is no vision the people perish.

The moneychangers have fled from their high seats in the temple of our civilization. We may now restore that temple to the ancient truths. The measure of the restoration lies in the extent to which we apply social values more noble than mere monetary profit.

Happiness lies not in the mere possession of money; it lies in the joy of achievement, in
35 the thrill of creative effort. The joy and moral stimulation of work no longer must be forgotten in the mad chase of evanescent profits. These dark days will be worth all they cost us if they teach us that our true destiny is not to be ministered unto, but to minister to ourselves and to our fellow men.

Recognition of the falsity of material wealth as the standard of success goes hand in hand
40 with the abandonment of the false belief that public office and high political position are to be valued only by the standards of pride of place and personal profit; and there

must be an end to a conduct in banking and in business which too often has given to a sacred trust the likeness of callous and selfish wrongdoing. Small wonder that confidence languishes, for it thrives only on honesty, on honor, on the sacredness of obligations, on

45 faithful protection, on unselfish performance; without them it cannot live.

(1933)

8. Which line(s) does the speaker use to imply that his listeners must play a major role in the struggle that is to come?

   I. I am convinced that you will again give that support to leadership in these critical days.
   II. In such a spirit on my part and on yours we face our common difficulties.
   III. Practices of the unscrupulous moneychangers stand indicted in the court of public opinion, rejected by the hearts and minds of men.

   (A) I and II only
   (B) II only
   (C) II and III only
   (D) III only
   (E) I, II, and III

9. Which period of American history is the speaker describing in paragraphs 2 and 3?

   (A) World War I
   (B) World War II
   (C) the Great Depression
   (D) the Civil Rights era
   (E) the Oklahoma land rush

10. The speaker uses the words in each pair to convey the same or nearly the same idea EXCEPT

   (A) frankness and vigor (line 4)
   (B) understanding and support (line 4)
   (C) failure and substance (line 16)
   (D) stubbornness and incompetence (lines 21–22)
   (E) hearts and minds (line 24)

ANSWERS AND EXPLANATIONS

8. **(E)** Option I suggests that the leader alone cannot end the financial crisis; the people must lend him their support. Option II mentions facing "our common difficulties" together with a determination to overcome them. Option III suggests that "the hearts and minds of men"—in other words, the hearts and minds of the listeners—are the opposite of the "unscrupulous moneychangers." All three options satisfy the question. Therefore choice E is correct.

9. **(C)** The speaker refers to a financial crisis, a failure of credit, and the idea that financial profit should not be the basis of a society. The only choice that matches these references to an economic issue is choice C, the Great Depression. The fact that the speech is dated 1933 is another clue to the correct answer; the Great Depression began in 1929, when the stock market crashed, and continued through the 1930s.

10. **(C)** The two words in choice C are opposite or nearly opposite in meaning. Therefore C is the correct answer.

CHAPTER 4

Poetry

Poetry

Poetry stands out from other forms of writing because it is written in verse, not prose. Of all forms of literature, poetry is most closely allied to music, because so much of poetry is dictated by consideration of sound effects. **Meter, rhyme,** and **rhythm** are the three major elements of verse (see Chapter 1 for definitions and examples).

This chapter gives a brief overview of poetry: its history, structural elements, and forms. Use the sample poems and questions in this chapter to test your ability to read and understand poetry.

Poetic Structure

The one thing all poems have in common is that they are written in verse. Poetry is written in rhymed or unrhymed lines in patterns of stressed and unstressed syllables, with a certain number of syllables per line. This gives poetry a unique appearance on a page; a poem takes up a block of space rather than reaching all the way to the right margin like prose. Free verse lacks the rhythm and meter of other poetry, but you can still identify it as poetry simply by the way it looks on the page. It does not look like prose.

The basic unit of prose is the paragraph; the basic unit of poetry is the line. Just as a new paragraph always begins on a new line of the page, so does a new line of poetry. A line of poetry may or may not equal a complete phrase, sentence, or thought. The ends of lines in poetry are dictated by sound, not by sense—the demands of the meter and rhythm, not the completion of the thought, mark the end of a line of verse. If a poet is writing in iambic pentameter, with ten syllables per line, each line will end with the tenth syllable, no matter where this occurs in the sentence or complete thought. A group of lines in a poem is called a **stanza**; you can identify the end of a stanza because there will be a blank space on the page between one stanza and the next.

Poets employ a great variety of meters and rhythms. Until modern times, most (not all) English and American poetry rhymed. This began to change in the mid-nineteenth century with the appearance of free verse. By the end of the twentieth century, unrhymed poetry and free verse were quite common, although rhyme had by no means disappeared altogether.

Types of Poems

Poems come in three varieties: **narrative, epic,** and **lyric.** The purpose of a **narrative poem** is to tell a story; like any work of fiction, it is built on the four elements of plot, character, setting, and theme. An **epic poem** is a book-length narrative poem focusing on the life of the **epic hero,** a man of extraordinary strength and courage. He is a leader of his people and undergoes a series of adventures that test his moral and physical strength. Like other types of mythology, an epic was considered by the listening audience to be something between fiction and nonfiction. People believed that the heroes existed and that their adventures were true, although they conceded that the tales told by poets were exaggerated versions of what really happened.

Although **lyric poems** can describe characters performing actions and can suggest or imply stories, their main purpose is to evoke a specific emotional reaction in the reader. Lyric poems capture a mood or feeling rather than recounting a plot. Although not all lyric poems are short, most short poems are lyric poems.

Lyric poems are much shorter than epics. A lyric poem aims at producing a single effect on the reader. It is usually a highly personal expression of the speaker's (and possibly also the poet's) emotions and experiences. The speaker and the poet are not necessarily the same person; they may be, but this should only be assumed based on factual knowledge of the poet's life. In general, it is best to assume that the speaker of a lyric poem is a first-person narrator, like any other fictional character, and does not necessarily represent the author.

Literary Elements in Poetry

Because lyric and narrative poems are more concise than most prose fiction, each word in the poem must be chosen with extra care. There is no room for anything extra or unnecessary. Because each individual word has to carry extra freight, poems are rich in **figurative language** and **imagery.** Poets use **similes, metaphors,** and other **figures of speech** with greater frequency than do prose writers.

Two other major elements for the poetry reader to consider are **speaker** and **mood.** The speaker is the poem's first-person narrator, a fictional character like any prose narrator. Comprehending the speaker's personality and character are of central importance to understanding a lyric poem. **Mood,** the total effect the poem has on the reader, is equally important. The reader must identify the poem's mood and analyze how the poet used language and literary elements to create this mood.

History of Poetry's Development

Ancient Times

In the ancient world, most poems were epics that were told or sung aloud. The earliest epics come from Iraq. *The Descent of Inanna* was first written down about 2000 B.C.E., although versions of the story go back another 1500 years before that. *The Epic of Gilgamesh,* though unknown to modern scholars until the mid-1800s, may date back equally far; the first written version dates to the seventh century B.C.E. Parts of the Bible, some of which (such as the story of David) can be considered epic poetry, first appeared as early as 1000 B.C.E.

The most ancient poetic works in Western literature are Homer's *Iliad* and *Odyssey* (Greece, c. 700 B.C.E.), two epics of the Trojan War and its heroes. In the Roman world, the *Aeneid* (Virgil, Italy, 19 C.E.) continued the epic tradition with its tales of Aeneas, the hero who founded Italy.

Lyric poetry dates back at least to the Bible, written between approximately 1000 B.C.E. and 200 C.E. The works of Sappho of Lesbos (c. 550 B.C.E.) are considered the greatest of all Greek lyrics, though only a few examples of her poetry have survived. Lyric poetry later enjoyed great success in Rome, with poets such as Catullus and Ovid.

The Middle Ages to the Seventeenth Century

Epic poetry began to appear in northern Europe by the 700s C.E., with *Beowulf* (Anglo-Saxon, c. 750) and a variety of Irish sagas. In 1321, the Italian poet Dante Alighieri published *The Divine Comedy,* in which the spirit of Virgil guides the speaker through hell, purgatory, and paradise. *The Divine Comedy* can be regarded as the first modern epic, because it does not tell the story of a traditional epic hero. Instead, its central figure is a contemporary man—the poet himself—who is a cultural hero rather than a warrior, chieftain, or king.

Dante was not the only major Italian poet of the era. His contemporary Francesco Petrarch invented the **sonnet,** which quickly became a favorite form among poets of other countries as well. Sir Thomas Wyatt, Petrarch's translator and a poet in his own right, wrote the first English-language sonnets. English poets modified the **Petrarchan sonnet** by changing its rhyme scheme; this English sonnet form is called the **Shakespearean sonnet.** (See **sonnet,** Chapter 1.)

It was around the late 1500s that the English language achieved the form that we speak and read today. Apart from differences in spelling and in the use of the informal pronoun *thou/thee* and its verb forms, Elizabethan English is perfectly comprehensible to a modern English speaker—with a little practice to get used to the differences in writing style.

The Renaissance (the period between approximately 1400 and 1600 C.E.) was a true high point of English poetry. William Shakespeare, widely considered the greatest of all English-language writers, produced the world's most famous sonnet sequence and some longer narrative poems, in addition to his plays (see Chapter 5).

Other great English poets of the era include John Milton, author of the epic *Paradise Lost* and many shorter poems; Christopher Marlowe, who like Shakespeare is also famous for his plays; Sir Philip Sidney; and John Donne.

Most British poetry of the era concentrated on one of four themes: love, religion, abstract philosophy, or descriptions of nature. Donne, for example, is famous for his secular love poems and also for a deeply religious series of sonnets called the *Holy Sonnets*. Plays on words, puns, and the use of words with double meanings are characteristic of Elizabethan poetry.

The first English-speaking American poets began writing in the seventeenth century. Many of their poems were religious in nature, due in part to the central importance of worship in their communities and, in part to the harsh realities of life in the original thirteen British colonies. Americans had to conquer a wilderness, combat extremes of weather, build or make everything they needed, and either make friends with the Indians or fight them off. Life was a struggle for survival, and Americans did what they could to make sure God was on their side, including dedicating much of their literature to Him. Americans also wrote poems about love and nature. Anne Bradstreet is one of the best-known American poets of this early colonial era.

The Nineteenth Century

The nineteenth century ushered in the Romantic era in poetry. William Wordsworth, Samuel Taylor Coleridge, Percy Bysshe Shelley, John Keats, and Lord Byron are the best-known of the British Romantics. Later in the century came Elizabeth Barrett Browning, Robert Browning, and Alfred Lord Tennyson. All of these authors produced both lyric and narrative poetry.

Epic poetry continued as a form. Byron wrote the modern epics *Childe Harold's Pilgrimage* and *Don Juan*. Tennyson wrote several book-length narrative poems, including *Idylls of the King* (tales of King Arthur and his knights), *The Princess*, and *Maud*.

American poets of the era included Walt Whitman, Herman Melville, Henry Wadsworth Longfellow, Emily Dickinson, and Edgar Allan Poe. Longfellow is dismissed as an artist by modern scholars but holds the distinction of being the first American to earn his living by writing poetry. Dickinson is almost as famous for her reclusive lifestyle as for her highly unusual poems. It was only in 1955 that readers finally saw Dickinson's work as she wrote it, with its unconventional capitalization, punctuation, and use of dashes; the few poems published during her lifetime and immediately after her death were heavily edited to bring them into line with accepted usage.

The nineteenth century saw the first **free-verse poems** (see Chapter 1). Whitman, unconventional and ahead of his time in many ways, published the free-verse collection *Leaves of Grass* in 1855. He continued to put out new editions until the 1890s, adding to the collection until it contained more than 400 poems, including the highly unconventional autobiographical epic *Song of Myself*. In 1894, Stephen Crane followed Whitman's example by publishing his own free-verse collection, *The Black Riders*.

The Romantic era is characterized by a new interest in expressing one's self. This was true across all forms of the creative arts. Poems were more likely to deal openly with, and even exaggerate, the speaker's emotions. There was less formal wordplay than in the Elizabethan era and less reliance on clever rhyme than in the eighteenth century. Romantic poetry was above all about emotion and individualism.

The Twentieth Century and Beyond

The first major twentieth-century event to affect the development of poetry was the outbreak of World War I in 1914. Several British soldiers and officers, known to history as the World War I poets, won immortality by publishing lyric poems about their experiences in the trenches. Siegfried Sassoon, Wilfred Owen, and Rupert Brooke are among them; neither Owen nor Brooke survived the war.

Irish poets came into their own in the twentieth century, including William Butler Yeats, Dylan Thomas, and Seamus Heaney. Intensity and a kind of wild ecstasy of language characterize their works.

American lyric poets include T. S. Eliot, Carl Sandburg, E. E. Cummings, and Sylvia Plath. Eliot is best known for *The Waste Land*, a set of four free-form dramatic lyrics filled with so many obscure literary allusions that Eliot included a list of endnotes so that readers could track them down and "decode" his work for themselves. Sandburg echoed Whitman's style and subject matter—the glorification of the common working man. Cummings developed a style all his own, dispensing with capital letters and punctuation and playing with rhythm and rhyme in ways that made his lyrics appear to dance right off the page. Plath wrote a highly praised, savage collection of lyrics called *Ariel* before she committed suicide at an early age, following the breakup of her marriage to fellow poet Ted Hughes.

Twentieth-century poets, like other writers and artists of their time, had few illusions left. Apart from light verse written strictly to amuse (such as the works of Ogden Nash), their poems tend to be darker in outlook, more ambiguous in tone, and more spare in imagery than verse of earlier times.

Questions 1–3. Read the following poem carefully before you choose your answers.

Some lovers speak when they their muses entertain,
Of hopes begot by fear, of wot not what desires,
Of force of heav'nly beams, infusing hellish pain,
   Of living deaths, dear wounds, fair storms and freezing fires.
5   Some one his song in Jove, and Jove's strange tales, attires,
Broidered with bulls and swans, powdered with golden rain.
Another, humbler, wit to shepherd's pipe retires,
Yet hiding royal blood full oft in rural vein.
   To some a sweetest plaint a sweetest style affords,
10   While tears pour out his ink, and sighs breathe out his words,
His paper, pale despair, and pain his pen doth move.
   I can speak what I feel, and feel as much as they,
   But think that all the map of my state I display,
When trembling voice brings forth, that I do Stella love.

(c. 1581)

1. This poem meets all the usual standards for a sonnet EXCEPT

   (A) meter
   (B) number of lines
   (C) subject matter
   (D) rhythm
   (E) imagery

2. Which best sums up the speaker's main point?

   (A) Others write long poems and use a lot of figurative language to express their feelings; I express just as much feeling when I say simply "I love Stella."
   (B) I wish that I could express my love as others do, by writing beautiful and elaborate poems about Stella whom I love so much.
   (C) Since my muse is paying so much attention to other lovers, who spend all their time writing poems to their ladies, I can only say "I love Stella."
   (D) I cannot compare my love for Stella to the love felt by poets who write beautiful poetry, because I can only say directly that I love Stella.
   (E) I think it is much better to say directly "I love Stella" than to cry because I am unable to write beautiful poetry about her.

3. When the speaker says "Another, humbler, wit to shepherd's pipe retires, / Yet hiding royal blood full oft in rural vein" (lines 7–8), he means

(A) A humble shepherd may write a love poem pretending that he is really a prince in disguise.

(B) If a prince is clever and witty, he may ask a shepherd to change places with him.

(C) A royal prince may write a love poem suggesting that he is a humble shepherd.

(D) A poet may give up writing altogether, and serenade his beloved with the music of a shepherd's pipe.

(E) When a prince goes into the country, he often amuses himself by pretending he is a common shepherd.

ANSWERS AND EXPLANATIONS

1. **(D)** The meter is iambic, which is standard for sonnets. The number of lines is 14, which is standard. A sonnet can address almost any topic, but love is certainly one of the most common. This sonnet is full of imagery, like most sonnets. The correct answer is D; most sonnets have five iambic feet (10 syllables) per line, while this sonnet has six feet (12 syllables).

2. **(A)** The speaker spends the first 11 lines of the sonnet describing all the elaborate poems that other lovers write about their ladies. In the last 3 lines, he explains that in order to show the same feeling, all he has to say is "I love Stella." A simple "I love you" is as good as bushels of carefully written poetry. This best matches choice A.

3. **(D)** "Hiding royal blood" is the key phrase. It shows that the prince is disguising his royal rank by pretending to be a shepherd. This eliminates choice A. Choice B is wrong because there is nothing here about the shepherd pretending to be the prince. Choice C is wrong because the phrase "to shepherd's pipe retires" means that the prince has given up on poetry altogether; his wit is too humble to write. He has turned to music instead. Choice E leaves out the reason for the prince's disguise: to win the love of the lady. Choice D is the correct explanation: the prince's wit is too humble to write clever poetry, so he gives up the attempt and plays music to his lady instead.

Questions 4-6. Read the following poem carefully before you choose your answers.

Ode to Memory

I

Thou who stealest fire,
From the fountains of the past,
To glorify the present; oh, haste,
   Visit my low desire!
5 Strengthen me, enlighten me!
I faint in this obscurity,
Thou dewy dawn of memory.

II

   Come not as thou camest of late,
   Flinging the gloom of yesternight
10 On the white day; but robed in soften'd light
      Of orient state.
Whilome thou camest with the morning mist,
   Even as a maid, whose stately brow
The dew-impearled winds of dawn have kiss'd,
15   When she, as thou,
Stays on her floating locks the lovely freight
Of overflowing blooms, and earliest shoots
Of orient green, giving safe pledge of fruits,
Which in wintertide shall star
20 The black earth with brilliance rare.

(1830)

4. The lines "Thou who stealest fire, / From the fountains of the past, / To glorify the present" (lines 1–3) are an example of

   (A) personification
   (B) verbal irony
   (C) simile
   (D) theme
   (E) slant rhyme

5. The imagery throughout the poem appeals most strongly to the sense of

   (A) hearing
   (B) sight
   (C) taste
   (D) touch
   (E) smell

6. What does the speaker mean by "obscurity" (line 6)?

    (A) He cannot see in the dark.

    (B) He is desperately ill and afraid to die.

    (C) He cannot remember something important.

    (D) He cannot understand something.

    (E) He is angry about something.

ANSWERS AND EXPLANATIONS

4. **(A)** The lines are an example of personification. The speaker endows memory, an abstract concept, with the human ability to steal. Choice A is the correct answer.

5. **(B)** Most of the sensory details in the poem are visual. There are several references to light and dark and a physical description of memory as a beautiful young girl. Choice B is the correct answer.

6. **(C)** The speaker pleads for memory to visit him because he is "fainting in obscurity"—in other words, he has lost his memories of the past and needs to find them again for the sake of their comfort. Choice C is correct.

Questions 7–10. Read the following poem carefully before you choose your answers.

The Leaders of the Crowd

They must to keep their certainty accuse
All that are different of a base intent;
Pull down established honor; hawk for news
Whatever their loose phantasy invent
5 And murmur it with bated breath, as though
The abounding gutter had been Helicon
Or calumny a song. How can they know
Truth flourishes where the student's lamp has shone,
And there alone, that have no solitude?
10 So the crowd come they care not what may come.
They have loud music, hope every day renewed
And heartier loves; that lamp is from the tomb.

                                        (1921)

7. Who are the "they" the poet mentions in line 1?

    (A) journalists
    (B) politicians
    (C) poets
    (D) lovers
    (E) entertainers

8. By saying that "they" "have no solitude" (line 9), the poet implies that "they"

        I. avoid spending any time by themselves
        II. never sit quietly alone thinking about anything serious
        III. would feel frightened and nervous if they found themselves alone

    (A) I and II only
    (B) I and III only
    (C) II and III only
    (D) II only
    (E) I, II, and III

9. The word "calumny" (line 7) is best defined as

    (A) music
    (B) slander
    (C) insult
    (D) noise
    (E) information

10. Which of the following is an example of allusion?

    (A) "How can they know / Truth flourishes where the student's lamp has shone,"
    (B) "So the crowd come they care not what may come."
    (C) "They must to keep their certainty accuse / All that are different of a base intent;"
    (D) "hawk for news / Whatever their loose phantasy invent"
    (E) ". . . murmur it with bated breath, as though / The abounding gutter had been Helicon"

ANSWERS AND EXPLANATIONS

7. **(B)** The poem's title suggests that choice B, politicians, is the correct answer. This is supported by a careful reading of the poem's long first sentence (lines 1–7).

8. **(E)** In the first half of the poem, the poet describes a group of people who are so insecure that they attack everyone who disagrees with them; people who make things up and pass them off to journalists as news; people who do not care what happens as long as the crowd follows them. People like this avoid spending time alone because they only feel important if surrounded by a cheering crowd. They do not want any time to think quietly, because they do not know how to think in a serious way. They would be frightened if they were alone, because they do not know who they are. All three options are reasonable answers, so choice E is correct.

9. **(B)** The poet uses *song* in contrast to *calumny*, so A is wrong. "They" are making stories up and selling them to the press as news, which suggests that *calumny* is something false. You can therefore eliminate choices D and E. *Slander* and *insult* are relatively close in meaning—they are both malicious statements about others—but while an insult may be true, slander is by definition false. This is the closest in meaning to *calumny*, which means "a false accusation" (it comes from a Latin root meaning "to deceive"). Choice B is correct.

10. **(E)** The poet mentions "Helicon," which is an allusion to Mt. Helicon. In Greek mythology, Mt. Helicon was sacred to the Muses.

CHAPTER 5

Drama

Drama

Drama is a special kind of literature that is written to be performed by actors. Once a **play** has been produced on stage for the first time, it is published in book form as a play or a **playscript**.

This chapter contains a brief overview of the structural elements and history of drama. Use the sample dramatic excerpt and questions at the end of the chapter to test your ability to read and interpret drama.

Structural Elements of Drama

Playscripts consist primarily of two structural elements: **dialogue** and **stage directions**. A playwright may also include a **foreword** or **preface, introduction, afterword,** or **notes.**

Dialogue refers to the words the actors speak. This is the part of the play the audience members hear when they go to the theater. Dialogue in a play contains a full range of literary elements: **figurative language, imagery, irony, humor,** and so on. Dialogue may be written in verse or in prose. The entire story of the play is told solely through the dialogue.

Dialogue is written by the playwright, but unlike prose writers and poets, a playwright has a group of collaborators. Since the Elizabethan era, playwrights have been, and continue to be, a central part of the production process, in which the play is prepared for its first performance. During rehearsals, as they see the effects of their work on stage for the first time, playwrights make both substantial and minor changes to their scripts. Depending on the historical period and the individuals involved, the director and the leading actors involved in the first production may have considerable input into the final version of the script.

Stage directions note the following information:

1. when the characters enter and exit the stage, and how they move about during the scene
2. the location and appearance of each scene
3. the tone of voice in which the actor is to read the line or speech
4. any details or information the playwright wishes to share with readers

The audience in the theater does not hear, read, or see stage directions. These are provided in published scripts primarily to help the reader visualize the way the play would look on stage.

Playwrights do not write stage directions in categories 1 and 2 in the list above. In most cases, these stage directions are simply the stage manager's record of how the actors moved about the stage during the play's first production. When the play was published in print, the stage directions were included as a record of the first production and as a guide to actors and directors of future productions.

Stage directions in categories 3 and 4 in the list above did not begin to appear in playscripts until the late nineteenth century. These stage directions are written by the playwright.

A play may also include a preface, introduction, afterword, or notes. Again, these materials are not part of the audience's experience of seeing the play performed. The playwright includes these elements for the reader.

Plays are written primarily to entertain, but many playwrights also write to comment on and reform society. George Bernard Shaw (Ireland), Henrik Ibsen (Norway), and Bertolt Brecht (Germany) are examples of major playwrights who believed that social reform was an important part of their task as writers.

History of the Drama's Development

Ancient Times

The earliest Western dramas were religious ceremonies held in honor of the god Dionysus. Ceremonies dealing with life, death, and resurrection led to the development of **tragedy,** while **comedy** has its roots in fertility rites.

A comedy is a play written to make people laugh; a tragedy is more likely to make them cry, although it may be uplifting. Comedies often feature mistaken identities, disguised characters, misunderstandings, and a variety of silly plot complications. In a comedy, the characters generally straighten out all misunderstandings in the final scene, and a happy ending is achieved.

A tragedy generally features a **tragic hero** or **heroine,** usually someone who occupies a high place at the beginning of the story and is brought down by a central flaw in his or her own character.

The drama as we understand it today—that is, an imagined or historical story acted out on a stage—dates back to the fifth century B.C.E. The playwrights Aeschylus, Euripides, and Sophocles were the pillars of Greek tragedy, and their works are still performed today. Aristophanes was the outstanding comic writer of the ancient era. Plautus was an important Roman writer of comedy; one of his works, as adapted into the book of the musical *A Funny Thing Happened on the Way to the Forum,* continues to amuse today's audiences.

The Middle Ages

Medieval drama began to develop around the ninth century and reached its pinnacle around the fourteenth century. Like ancient drama, its roots were religious—in this case, Christian. Strolling troops of players performed miracle, passion, and morality plays that grew directly from the text of the church service. Miracle plays dramatized the lives of Christ, his mother Mary, and the saints. Passion plays depicted the story of Christ's death. Morality plays were allegories that dramatized the consequences of sin and the rewards of virtue. Morality plays were the direct precursors of Elizabethan drama.

The Renaissance

The Renaissance was one of the great eras for English drama. At this point, drama moved away from its medieval basis in religion and once again became a medium for telling secular stories. Elizabethan playwrights made up their own original stories or borrowed them from earlier sources. Audiences could choose among comedies, tragedies, romances, and histories. Plays were generally presented in five acts that corresponded to the five stages of a plot: Act I introduced the characters and conflicts; in Act II, the action rose to the Act III climax; Acts IV and V contained the falling action that led to the Act V resolution.

Elizabethan plays are written in a mix of **blank verse** (see Chapter 1), rhymed verse, and prose. In general, upper-class characters speak in verse, and commoners speak in prose; blank verse is allied with tragedy, whereas other verse forms and prose are associated with comedy. However, authors often played with these conventions to create dramatic interest. For example, in Shakespeare's *Henry V,* the king speaks in prose during a scene when he is disguised as a common soldier.

In Renaissance era scripts, stage directions are the bare minimum; they specify a location and give the characters' entrances and exits. Shakespeare and his contemporaries did not write these stage directions; they were added at the time of publication. Their purpose is simply to help the reader follow the action on the page.

Elizabethan dialogue, in contrast to the stage directions, is extraordinarily elaborate, making full use of poetic techniques such as figurative language, imagery, and rhetorical devices. Imagery was especially important on the Elizabethan stage, because there were no theatrical illusions such as we have today. Plays were performed outdoors in the daylight; costumes were hastily thrown together, often consisting of contemporary street clothes; and there were no sets, apart from an occasional bench, bed, or table if needed. The power of language helped the audiences imagine a great variety of exotic and elaborate settings.

William Shakespeare was the most important playwright of the English Renaissance (he can safely be called the most important English-language writer in history). His colleagues included Christopher Marlowe, Ben Jonson, John Webster, and John Ford.

The most important element of a Shakespearean play is **character.** Every generation has marveled at Shakespeare's ability to create believable human individuals with whom audiences can empathize and identify. Even the minor characters are so strong and individual that they are great favorites with both actors and audiences.

The Seventeenth and Eighteenth Centuries

The years 1642 to 1666 are known in English history as the Interregnum (meaning "between monarchs"). As the result of a civil war, commoner Oliver Cromwell deposed the hereditary monarch and took over the throne in 1642. Cromwell, a Puritan, thought theater was sinful and banned it altogether. In 1666, the monarchy was restored to the throne, and the theaters were reopened.

During this period, known as the Restoration, plays became much more artificial. Light comedy and farce were the order of the day. Shakespeare's plays were still performed, but they were substantially rewritten to reflect the current taste for lighter fare. Irishman Richard Brinsley Sheridan is the best-known British playwright of the era.

The plots of Restoration and eighteenth-century comedies and dramas were elaborate and full of improbable twists and coincidences. Characters were archetypes—the frivolous young girl, the cantankerous older man, and the bawdy serving maid. The purpose of these plays was strictly to amuse the audiences and to poke fun at social customs without having any serious reforming spirit.

The Nineteenth Century to the Present

Since the late nineteenth century, plays have usually been written in speech appropriate to what the characters might say in reality. Dialogue no longer needs to fill in visual details for the audience; designers provide lighting, sound effects, costumes, and scenery to help create the theatrical illusion.

During this era, stage directions became much more detailed, often describing sets, giving an idea of a character's physical appearance, and specifying how the actors were to read their lines (i.e., happily, with a puzzled expression, angrily). Irish playwright George Bernard Shaw is known for extraordinarily meticulous stage directions. Shaw also wrote long prefaces to his plays, discussing the social and political issues treated in each play. These prefaces were not part of the performance in the theater; Shaw wrote them for the reading public.

Two of the most important playwrights of the modern era, Henrik Ibsen and Bertolt Brecht, were not English-language writers, but their work had an enormous influence on their British and American colleagues. Norwegian playwright Ibsen is considered the father of modern drama. His plays feature middle-class and working-class characters in ordinary settings, dealing with serious personal problems such as infidelity, old family grievances, lost love, and similar conflicts. When audiences went to see an Ibsen play, they were watching characters like themselves and their neighbors in dramatic situations that might well occur in real life. Major English-language playwrights of the time followed Ibsen's lead, bringing a welcome new realism to the stage.

Like Ibsen and Shaw, German writer Brecht was a passionate social critic. Brecht believed that the primary purpose of a play was to hold up a mirror to the audience and shake them out of their complacency. He not only wrote many plays but also created an entirely new style of design and production known as *Brechtian*, loosely meaning "detached." Most people believed that theater's purpose was to create an illusion of reality; Brecht believed it was his job always to remind the audience that they were watching actors performing on a stage. He did not want audiences to identify with his characters as though they were real individuals; he wanted people to think about the overall social message of the piece. Brecht is the father of all political theater.

Important English-language playwrights of the era included Eugene O'Neill, Tennessee Williams, Arthur Miller, and Thornton Wilder in the United States; and Shaw, T. S. Eliot, Oscar Wilde, William Butler Yeats, and John Millington Synge in Britain.

Verse plays had not entirely disappeared; major authors of verse plays in this era include Yeats (*The Land of Heart's Desire,* 1894), W. H. Auden (*The Dance of Death,* 1933), Eliot (*Murder in the Cathedral,* 1935), and Archibald MacLeish (*J.B.,* 1956).

After World War II, a movement called **theater of the absurd** arose. Its two best-known practitioners are Harold Pinter and Samuel Beckett. Beckett's *Waiting for Godot* (1952), originally written in French and translated into English by Beckett himself, is the best-known play of this school; many people believe it to be the most influential play of its time. In a typical theater-of-the-absurd play, the characters exchange short and banal lines of dialogue, and nothing much happens. Theater of the absurd is intended to emphasize the meaninglessness, banality, and random cruelty of everyday life.

The most important English-language playwright of the present day is probably Tom Stoppard. Born in Czechoslovakia and raised in India and England, Stoppard is classified as a British playwright. His works range from a theater-of-the-absurd retelling of Shakespeare's *Hamlet* (*Rosencrantz and Guildenstern Are Dead,* 1966) to a somber trilogy about nineteenth-century Russian philosophers (*The Coast of Utopia,* 2002). Other major contemporary playwrights include David Mamet, Tony Kushner, Edward Albee, Peter Shaffer, and August Wilson. Wilson's plays portray the African American experience in the twentieth century, with one play set in each decade.

REVIEW QUESTIONS

Questions 1–5. Read the following dramatic excerpt carefully before you choose your answers.

(In Act I, Serbians and Bulgarians are fighting in the streets. A soldier [Captain Bluntschli] in enemy uniform appears at Raina Petkoff's window, demanding refuge. Raina takes pity on him, gives him a night's shelter, and lends him an old coat of her father's in which to escape. Soon after, peace is declared. In Act II, Bluntschli comes by to return the borrowed coat. In the Act III excerpt below, he and Raina find themselves alone for the first time since their encounter in Act I.)

RAINA *[going to the table, and leaning over it towards him]*. It must have made a lovely story for them: all that about me and my room.

BLUNTSCHLI. Capital story. But I only told it to one of them: a particular friend.

RAINA. On whose discretion you could absolutely rely?

5 BLUNTSCHLI. Absolutely.

RAINA. Hmm! He told it all to my father and Sergius[1] the day you exchanged the prisoners. *[She turns away and strolls carelessly across to the other side of the room.]*

BLUNTSCHLI *[deeply concerned, and half incredulous]*. No! you don't mean that, do you?

10 RAINA *[turning, with sudden earnestness]*. I do indeed. But they don't know that it was in this house you took refuge. If Sergius knew, he would challenge you and kill you in a duel.

BLUNTSCHLI. Bless me! then don't tell him.

RAINA. Please be serious, Captain Bluntschli. Can you realize what it is to me to deceive

15 him? I want to be quite perfect with Sergius: no meanness, no smallness, no deceit. My relation to him is the one really beautiful and noble part of my life. I hope you can understand that.

BLUNTSCHLI *[skeptically]*. You mean that you wouldn't like him to find out that the story about the ice pudding was a—a—a—You know.

20 RAINA *[wincing]*. Ah, don't talk of it in that flippant way. I lied: I know it. But I did it to save your life. He would have killed you. That was the second time I ever uttered a falsehood . . .

BLUNTSCHLI *[dubiously]*. There's reason in everything. You said you'd told only two lies in your whole life. Dear young lady: isn't that rather a short allowance? I'm quite a

25 straightforward man myself; but it wouldn't last me a whole morning.

RAINA *[staring haughtily at him]*. Do you know, sir, that you are insulting me?

BLUNTSCHLI. I can't help it. When you strike that noble attitude and speak in that thrilling voice, I admire you; but I find it impossible to believe a single word you say.

RAINA *[superbly]*. Captain Bluntschli!

30 BLUNTSCHLI *[unmoved]*. Yes?

RAINA *[standing over him, as if she could not believe her senses]*. Do you mean what you said just now? Do you *know* what you said just now?

BLUNTSCHLI. I do.

[1] Raina's fiancé

RAINA *[gasping]*. I! I!!! *[She points to herself incredulously, meaning "I, Raina Petkoff, tell*
35 *lies!" He meets her gaze unflinchingly. She suddenly sits down beside him, and adds, with*
a complete change of manner from the heroic to a babyish familiarity.] How did you find
me out?

BLUNTSCHLI *[promptly]*. Instinct, dear young lady. Instinct, and experience of
the world.

40 RAINA *[wonderingly]*. Do you know, you are the first man I ever met who did not take me
seriously?

BLUNTSCHLI. You mean, don't you, that I am the first man that has ever taken you quite
seriously?

RAINA. Yes: I suppose I do mean that. *[Cosily, quite at her ease with him]* How strange
45 it is to be talked to in such a way! You know, I've always gone on like that . . . I mean the
noble attitude and the thrilling voice. *[They laugh together]* I did it when I was a tiny
child to my nurse. *She* believed in it. I do it before my parents. *They* believe in it. I do it
before Sergius. *He* believes in it.

BLUNTSCHLI. Yes: he's a little in that line himself, isn't he?

50 RAINA *[startled]*. Oh! Do you think so?

BLUNTSCHLI. You know him better than I do.

RAINA. I wonder—I wonder, is he? If I thought that—! *[Discouraged]* Ah, well, what
does it matter? I suppose, now that you've found me out, you despise me.

BLUNTSCHLI *[warmly, rising]*. No, my dear young lady, no, no, no a thousand times.
55 It's part of your youth: part of your charm. I'm like all the rest of them: the nurse, your
parents, Sergius: I'm your infatuated admirer.

RAINA *[pleased]*. Really?

BLUNTSCHLI *[slapping his breast smartly with his hand, German fashion]*. *Hand aufs
Herz!*[2] Really and truly.

60 RAINA *[very happy]*. But what did you think of me for giving you my portrait?

BLUNTSCHLI *[astonished]*. Your portrait! You never gave me your portrait.

RAINA *[quickly]*. Do you mean to say you never got it?

BLUNTSCHLI. No. *[He sits down beside her, with renewed interest, and says, with some
complacency]* When did you send it to me?

65 RAINA *[indignantly]*. I did not send it to you. *[She turns her head away, and adds,
reluctantly]* It was in the pocket of that coat.

(1898)

---

[2] Cross my heart!

1. What does Bluntschli mean by telling Raina he is "the first person who has ever taken you quite seriously" (lines 42–43)?

   (A) He admires her grand manner and the ideals she expresses.
   (B) He appreciates the real person beneath the act she puts on.
   (C) He finds her beautiful, attractive, and charming.
   (D) He is very grateful to her for saving his life in Act I.
   (E) He is intrigued by her confession that she gave him her portrait.

2. Why has Raina "always gone on like that . . . I mean, the noble attitude and the thrilling voice" (lines 45–46)?

   (A) She acts like the person she wishes she truly were.
   (B) She is a liar and a faker by nature.
   (C) She enjoys the admiration and attention she gets.
   (D) She does not trust any of the people around her.
   (E) She wants to make Sergius fall in love with her.

3. What does Bluntschli's statement, "I'm quite a straightforward man, myself; but [two lies] wouldn't last me a whole morning" (lines 24–25) imply about him?

   (A) He thinks he is honest, but his frequent lies show that he is really dishonest.
   (B) He is only careful to tell the truth in certain situations.
   (C) He wants to make Raina feel better about having told a lie.
   (D) He is horrified by any evidence that another person is a liar.
   (E) He often tells polite lies, but does not regard this as true dishonesty.

4. What is the meaning of the word *flippant* (line 20)?

   (A) frivolous
   (B) hateful
   (C) dishonest
   (D) vulgar
   (E) serious

5. Which of the following is the most likely reason Raina is able to be more honestly herself with Bluntschli than with her nurse, parents, or Sergius?

   (A) She does not care what Bluntschli thinks of her.
   (B) She likes Bluntschli more than anyone else and wants to pay him respect.
   (C) She hopes it will make Bluntschli love her.
   (D) She is tired of acting and will now be herself with everyone.
   (E) Bluntschli is outside her circle of family and friends, and she will probably never see him again.

ANSWERS AND EXPLANATIONS

1. **(B)** Bluntschli tells Raina frankly that he does not believe in her "noble attitude and thrilling voice"; that he doesn't mind her telling lies because it is "part of your youth, part of your charm." He sees through her pose, and he likes her anyway. This best matches choice B. Choice C does not go far enough, because by "taking you quite seriously," Bluntschli means "liking you for who you really are." It is not just that he finds her charming, but that he sees through her act and still finds her charming.

2. **(C)** Choice A is wrong because Raina does not genuinely wish to be as noble as the act she puts on; some of her dialogue in this scene shows she finds the act rather tiresome. Choice B is wrong because she seems to be quite frank when she drops the act. Choice C fits best; she sees that people admire and look up to her when she puts on the "noble attitude and thrilling voice," and naturally she enjoys the attention. Choice D is wrong because distrust of others does not seem to be an issue. Choice E is wrong because she has been putting on this act all her life, since long before she met Sergius.

3. **(E)** The dialogue in this scene shows clearly that Bluntschli is blunt by nature as well as by name. Therefore you can eliminate any choices that suggest that he is dishonest. If Bluntschli is really in the habit of telling more than two lies every morning, it suggests that he spends a lot of time in business or social situations where one always utters certain polite lies, such as saying automatically, "Fine, thank you," when someone asks how you are. Bluntschli regards such polite lies as social necessities and does not blame himself for them. This best fits choice E.

4. **(A)** Bluntschli is making fun of Raina a bit, trying to get her to admit that she is putting on an act. *Flippant* means frivolous or not serious.

5. **(E)** Raina has a moment when she decides to abandon her pretense, and her manner and voice change completely. She most likely has decided that she has nothing to lose and that her act isn't worth the effort with this man. He will soon depart, and she will never see him again. He will not expose her to her friends and family, so she can be at ease with him.

PART III
Practice Tests

Practice Test 1

The following practice test is designed to be just like the real SAT Literature Test. It matches the actual test in content coverage and degree of difficulty.

Once you finish the practice test, determine your score. Carefully read the answer explanations of the questions you answered incorrectly. Identify any weaknesses in your literature skills by determining the areas in which you made the most errors. Review those sections of this book first. Then, as time permits, go back and review your strengths.

Allow one hour to take the test. Time yourself and work uninterrupted. If you run out of time, take note of where you stopped when time ran out. Remember that you lose a quarter point for each incorrect answer, but you do not lose points for questions you leave blank. Therefore, unless you can eliminate one or more of the five choices, it is best to leave a question unanswered.

Use the following formula to calculate your score:

(number of correct answers) – ¼ (number of incorrect answers)

If you treat this practice test just like the actual exam, it will accurately reflect how you are likely to perform on test day. Here are some hints on how to create test-taking conditions similar to those of the actual exam:

- Complete the test in one sitting. On test day, you will not be allowed to take a break.
- Tear out the answer sheet and fill in the ovals just as you will on the actual test day.
- Have a good eraser and more than one sharp pencil handy. On test day, you will not be able to go get a new pencil if yours breaks.
- Do not allow yourself any extra time; put down your pencil after exactly one hour, no matter how many questions are left to answer.
- Become familiar with the directions on the test. If you go in knowing what the directions say, you will not have to waste time reading and thinking about them on the actual test day.

Answer Sheet

Tear out this answer sheet and use it to mark your answers.

1. Ⓐ Ⓑ Ⓒ Ⓓ Ⓔ	16. Ⓐ Ⓑ Ⓒ Ⓓ Ⓔ	31. Ⓐ Ⓑ Ⓒ Ⓓ Ⓔ	46. Ⓐ Ⓑ Ⓒ Ⓓ Ⓔ
2. Ⓐ Ⓑ Ⓒ Ⓓ Ⓔ	17. Ⓐ Ⓑ Ⓒ Ⓓ Ⓔ	32. Ⓐ Ⓑ Ⓒ Ⓓ Ⓔ	47. Ⓐ Ⓑ Ⓒ Ⓓ Ⓔ
3. Ⓐ Ⓑ Ⓒ Ⓓ Ⓔ	18. Ⓐ Ⓑ Ⓒ Ⓓ Ⓔ	33. Ⓐ Ⓑ Ⓒ Ⓓ Ⓔ	48. Ⓐ Ⓑ Ⓒ Ⓓ Ⓔ
4. Ⓐ Ⓑ Ⓒ Ⓓ Ⓔ	19. Ⓐ Ⓑ Ⓒ Ⓓ Ⓔ	34. Ⓐ Ⓑ Ⓒ Ⓓ Ⓔ	49. Ⓐ Ⓑ Ⓒ Ⓓ Ⓔ
5. Ⓐ Ⓑ Ⓒ Ⓓ Ⓔ	20. Ⓐ Ⓑ Ⓒ Ⓓ Ⓔ	35. Ⓐ Ⓑ Ⓒ Ⓓ Ⓔ	50. Ⓐ Ⓑ Ⓒ Ⓓ Ⓔ
6. Ⓐ Ⓑ Ⓒ Ⓓ Ⓔ	21. Ⓐ Ⓑ Ⓒ Ⓓ Ⓔ	36. Ⓐ Ⓑ Ⓒ Ⓓ Ⓔ	51. Ⓐ Ⓑ Ⓒ Ⓓ Ⓔ
7. Ⓐ Ⓑ Ⓒ Ⓓ Ⓔ	22. Ⓐ Ⓑ Ⓒ Ⓓ Ⓔ	37. Ⓐ Ⓑ Ⓒ Ⓓ Ⓔ	52. Ⓐ Ⓑ Ⓒ Ⓓ Ⓔ
8. Ⓐ Ⓑ Ⓒ Ⓓ Ⓔ	23. Ⓐ Ⓑ Ⓒ Ⓓ Ⓔ	38. Ⓐ Ⓑ Ⓒ Ⓓ Ⓔ	53. Ⓐ Ⓑ Ⓒ Ⓓ Ⓔ
9. Ⓐ Ⓑ Ⓒ Ⓓ Ⓔ	24. Ⓐ Ⓑ Ⓒ Ⓓ Ⓔ	39. Ⓐ Ⓑ Ⓒ Ⓓ Ⓔ	54. Ⓐ Ⓑ Ⓒ Ⓓ Ⓔ
10. Ⓐ Ⓑ Ⓒ Ⓓ Ⓔ	25. Ⓐ Ⓑ Ⓒ Ⓓ Ⓔ	40. Ⓐ Ⓑ Ⓒ Ⓓ Ⓔ	55. Ⓐ Ⓑ Ⓒ Ⓓ Ⓔ
11. Ⓐ Ⓑ Ⓒ Ⓓ Ⓔ	26. Ⓐ Ⓑ Ⓒ Ⓓ Ⓔ	41. Ⓐ Ⓑ Ⓒ Ⓓ Ⓔ	56. Ⓐ Ⓑ Ⓒ Ⓓ Ⓔ
12. Ⓐ Ⓑ Ⓒ Ⓓ Ⓔ	27. Ⓐ Ⓑ Ⓒ Ⓓ Ⓔ	42. Ⓐ Ⓑ Ⓒ Ⓓ Ⓔ	57. Ⓐ Ⓑ Ⓒ Ⓓ Ⓔ
13. Ⓐ Ⓑ Ⓒ Ⓓ Ⓔ	28. Ⓐ Ⓑ Ⓒ Ⓓ Ⓔ	43. Ⓐ Ⓑ Ⓒ Ⓓ Ⓔ	58. Ⓐ Ⓑ Ⓒ Ⓓ Ⓔ
14. Ⓐ Ⓑ Ⓒ Ⓓ Ⓔ	29. Ⓐ Ⓑ Ⓒ Ⓓ Ⓔ	44. Ⓐ Ⓑ Ⓒ Ⓓ Ⓔ	59. Ⓐ Ⓑ Ⓒ Ⓓ Ⓔ
15. Ⓐ Ⓑ Ⓒ Ⓓ Ⓔ	30. Ⓐ Ⓑ Ⓒ Ⓓ Ⓔ	45. Ⓐ Ⓑ Ⓒ Ⓓ Ⓔ	60. Ⓐ Ⓑ Ⓒ Ⓓ Ⓔ

PRACTICE TEST 1
Time: 60 Minutes

Directions: This test consists of selections from literary works and questions on their content, form, and style. After reading each passage or poem, choose the best answer to each question and then fill in the corresponding oval on the answer sheet.

Note: Pay particular attention to the requirements of questions that contain the words NOT or EXCEPT.

Questions 1–9. Read the following poem carefully before you choose your answers.

I died for Beauty—but was scarce
Adjusted in the Tomb
When One who died for Truth, was lain
In an adjoining Room—

5 He questioned softly "Why I failed"?
"For Beauty," I replied—
"And I—for truth—Themself are One—
We Bretheren, are," He said—

And so, as Kinsmen, met a Night—
10 We talked between the Rooms—
Until the Moss had reached our lips—
And covered up—our names—

                    (1862)

1. The word "Themself" (line 7) refers to

   (A) the dead man and the other character
   (B) truth and beauty
   (C) beauty and failure
   (D) kinsmen and bretheren
   (E) truth and bretheren

2. Which of the following might the speaker mean by saying "I died for Beauty" (line 1)?

   (A) I died fighting for a cause in whose beauty and justice I believed.
   (B) I died because I was a woman of great physical beauty.
   (C) I died because I knew I would be beautiful to look at only in death.
   (D) I died of a disease that disfigured me and destroyed my beauty.
   (E) I died of old age, having lost the beauty of my youth.

3. What does the statement "We Bretheren are" (line 8) suggest?

   (A) that lonely people should turn to one another for companionship
   (B) that the two characters in the poem loved the same person
   (C) that the two characters in the poem died at the same time
   (D) that the speaker and the dead man are brothers
   (E) that people who believe in the same things are kindred spirits

GO ON TO THE NEXT PAGE ⟼

4. The mood of the poem is best described as

   (A) philosophical
   (B) melancholy
   (C) eerie
   (D) bitter
   (E) passionate

5. The word "softly" (line 5) implies which of the following about the dead man?

   (A) He died for Truth.
   (B) His voice is beautiful.
   (C) He knew the other character in life.
   (D) His manner is gentle.
   (E) He is delighted not to be buried alone.

6. Lines 11–12 suggest that the speaker and the dead man

   (A) continued talking for many years
   (B) talked throughout the night
   (C) talked together until they died
   (D) could not talk because they were dead
   (E) had nothing to say to one another

7. All of the following words are used metaphorically in this poem EXCEPT

   (A) Beauty (line 1)
   (B) Tomb (line 2)
   (C) Truth (line 3)
   (D) Bretheren (line 8)
   (E) Kinsmen (line 9)

8. The poem is an example of which of the following?

   (A) ballad
   (B) free verse
   (C) quatrain
   (D) couplet
   (E) narrative poem

9. Why do the two characters feel that they are "Kinsmen" and "Bretheren"?

   I. They are both dead.
   II. They died for similar reasons.
   III. They care about the same things.

   (A) I and III
   (B) II only
   (C) II and III only
   (D) III only
   (E) I, II, and III

Questions 10–17. Read the following poem carefully before you choose your answers.

Mamie

Mamie beat her head against the bars of a little Indiana
                                                            town and
dreamed of romance and big things off somewhere the
    way the railroad trains all ran.
She could see the smoke of the engines get lost down
                                            where the
5   streaks of steel flashed in the sun and when the
    newspapers came in on the morning mail she knew
                                                        there
was a big Chicago far off, where all the trains ran.
She got tired of the barber shop boys and the post office
                                                        chatter
and the church gossip and the old pieces the band
                                                        played
10 on the Fourth of July and Decoration Day
And sobbed at her fate and beat her head against the
                                            bars and
    was going to kill herself
When the thought came to her that if she was going to
                                            die she
    might as well die struggling for a clutch of romance
15 among the streets of Chicago.
She has a job now at six dollars a week in the basement
                                            of the
    Boston Store
And even now she beats her head against the bars in the
                                            same old
    way and wonders if there is a bigger place the railroads
20 run to from Chicago where maybe there is
                    romance
                    and big things
                    and real dreams
                    that never go smash.

                                    (1916)

10. Which best describes the poet's attitude
    toward Mamie?

(A) He pities her for her unhappiness.
(B) He thinks she is silly.
(C) He loves and admires her.
(D) Her behavior amuses him.
(E) She reminds him of himself.

11. The repetition of the phrase "beat(s) her head
    against the bars" accomplishes which of the
    following?

　I. emphasizes the strength of Mamie's
    despair and helplessness
　II. suggests that Mamie will never get
    through the "bars," no matter how far
    she travels
　III. makes the reader feel that Mamie is
    ridiculous and contemptible

(A) I only
(B) I and II only
(C) II only
(D) III only
(E) I, II, and III

12. The poet includes the list of things Mamie
    is tired of (lines 8–10) for all the following
    reasons EXCEPT

(A) to give the reader a picture of her
    everyday life
(B) to help the reader understand why she wants
    to escape
(C) to contrast the life she has with the romance
    she longs for
(D) to show his own impatience with small-
    town life
(E) to help the reader get a mental picture of her
    character

13. Which best defines the word "romance" as it is
    used in this poem?

(A) lies and exaggerations
(B) a love affair
(C) exciting adventures
(D) everyday reality
(E) a work of unrealistic fiction

14. For Mamie, Chicago symbolizes

    (A) excitement and glamour
    (B) sin and wickedness
    (C) noise and confusion
    (D) anonymity and solitude
    (E) community and home

15. The phrase "Mamie beat her head against the bars" means that Mamie

    (A) is in reform school because she ran away
    (B) is in a mental hospital because she tried to kill herself
    (C) feels like an animal in a zoo because people always stare at her
    (D) feels trapped and confined like a caged animal
    (E) has to be locked in her room because she can't be trusted

16. Why does the poet set off the final four lines of the poem, both by their brevity and their visual placement on the page?

    (A) to show that what Mamie wants from life is permanently beyond her reach
    (B) to reveal what made Mamie unhappy enough to leave Indiana
    (C) to keep the last stanza of the poem from being too long
    (D) to emphasize the intangibles that Mamie longs for
    (E) to leave the reader with some hope that Mamie will find happiness

17. Why is Mamie no happier in Chicago than she was in the little Indiana town?

    (A) She misses her home town in a way she did not anticipate.
    (B) She is unable to earn any money in Chicago.
    (C) She has discovered that life in a big city is as routine as in a small town.
    (D) She does not know where the Chicago trains might take her.
    (E) She has no one to talk to or spend her free time with.

Questions 18–25. Read the following passage carefully before you choose your answers.

In my preceding chapters I have tried, by going into the minutiae of the science of piloting, to carry the reader step by step to a comprehension of what the science consists of; and at the same time I have tried to show him that it is a
5 very curious and wonderful science, too, and very worthy of his attention. If I have seemed to love my subject, it is no surprising thing, for I loved the profession far better than any I have followed since, and I took a measureless pride in it. The reason is plain: a pilot, in those days, was the only
10 unfettered and entirely independent human being that lived in the earth. Kings are but the hampered servants of parliament and people; parliaments sit in chains forged by their constituency; the editor of a newspaper cannot be independent, but must work with one hand tied behind
15 him by party and patrons, and be content to utter only half or two-thirds of his mind; no clergyman is a free man and may speak the whole truth, regardless of his parish's opinions; writers of all kinds are manacled servants of the public. We write frankly and fearlessly, but then we
20 "modify" before we print. In truth, every man and woman and child has a master, and worries and frets in servitude; but in the day I write of, the Mississippi pilot had *none*. The captain could stand upon the hurricane-deck, in the pomp of a very brief authority, and give him five or six
25 orders while the vessel backed into the stream, and then that skipper's reign was over. The moment that the boat was under way in the river, she was under the sole and unquestioned control of the pilot. He could do with her exactly as he pleased, run her when and whither he chose,
30 and tie her up to the bank whenever his judgment said that that course was best. His movements were entirely free; he consulted no one, he received commands from nobody, he promptly resented even the merest suggestions. Indeed, the law of the United States forbade him to listen
35 to commands or suggestions, rightly considering that the pilot necessarily knew better how to handle the boat than anybody could tell him. So here was the novelty of a king without a keeper, an absolute monarch who was absolute in sober truth and not by a fiction of words. I have seen a
40 boy of eighteen taking a great steamer serenely into what seemed almost certain destruction, and the aged captain standing mutely by, filled with apprehension but powerless to interfere. His interference, in that particular instance, might have been an excellent thing, but to permit it would

45 have been to establish a most pernicious precedent. It will easily be guessed, considering the pilot's boundless authority, that he was a great personage in the old steamboating days. He was treated with marked courtesy by the captain and with marked deference by all the
50 officers and servants; and this deferential spirit was quickly communicated to the passengers, too. I think pilots were about the only people I ever knew who failed to show, in some degree, embarrassment in the presence of traveling foreign princes. But then, people in one's own grade of life
55 are not usually embarrassing objects.

(1896)

18. The metaphor "parliaments sit in chains forged by their constituency" (lines 12–13) is best paraphrased as

(A) Only the voters can decide who will hold elective office.

(B) Parliament must convene for a specific number of months each year.

(C) Voters are always eager to catch politicians behaving dishonestly.

(D) Government representatives must obey the will of the voters.

(E) Members of government are often jailed for improper behavior.

19. The author compares the steamboat pilot to a king, an absolute monarch, and a traveling foreign prince in order to

(A) explain why he wanted so badly to become a pilot

(B) show how much he loved piloting a steamboat professionally

(C) demonstrate his bias in favor of republicanism over monarchy

(D) make the reader understand the extent of the pilot's authority

(E) emphasize the glamour of a steamboat pilot's life on the river

20. The word "pernicious" (line 45) is best defined as

    (A) unwise
    (B) calming
    (C) irritating
    (D) important
    (E) destructive

21. All these details support the author's statement that the Mississippi pilot had no master EXCEPT

    (A) "I loved the profession far better than any I have followed since"
    (B) "the boat . . . was under the sole and unquestioned control of the pilot"
    (C) "the law of the United States forbade him to listen to commands"
    (D) "he consulted no one, he received commands from nobody"
    (E) "He could do with her exactly as he pleased . . . when and whither he chose"

22. The writer suggests that he prefers the profession of steamboat pilot to that of writer because

    (A) pilots make more money than writers
    (B) a pilot is his own boss, while a writer must please his employers
    (C) pilots work outdoors and writers work indoors
    (D) pilots work in dangerous situations, while writers are always safe
    (E) a pilot need not obey the laws, but a writer must obey them

23. The tone of the last two sentences of the passage is best described as

    (A) earnest
    (B) satirical
    (C) thoughtful
    (D) humorous
    (E) serious

24. The phrase "marked deference" (line 49) means that the crew showed the pilot

    (A) nervous fear
    (B) warm friendliness
    (C) unquestioning obedience
    (D) sullen anger
    (E) kindness and compassion

25. The fact that a pilot's authority is determined by law implies which of the following?

    I. Steamboat pilots are government employees.
    II. River traffic is a matter of national importance.
    III. There are many steamboat accidents every year.

    (A) I only
    (B) II only
    (C) I and II only
    (D) I and III only
    (E) II and III only

GO ON TO THE NEXT PAGE ⟼

Questions 26–34. Read the following poem carefully before you choose your answers.

On Time

Fly envious Time, till thou run out thy race,
Call on the lazy leaden-stepping hours,
Whose speed is but the heavy Plummet's[1] pace;
And glut thyself with what thy womb devours,
5   Which is no more than what is false and vain,
And merely mortal dross;
So little is our loss,
So little is thy gain.
For when as each thing bad thou hast entomb'd,
10 And, last of all, thy greedy self consum'd,
Then long Eternity shall greet our bliss
With an individual kiss;
And Joy shall overtake us as a flood,
When every thing that is sincerely good
15 And perfectly divine,
With Truth, and Peace, and Love, shall ever shine
About the supreme Throne
Of him, t'whose happy-making sight alone,
When once our heav'nly-guided soul shall clime,
20 Then all this Earthy grossness quit,
Attir'd with Stars, we shall for ever sit,
    Triumphing over Death, and Chance, and thee
    O Time.

                        (1633)

[1] A weight regulating the movement of a clock's hands.

26. Why does the speaker call Time "envious" (line 1)?

(A) Time resents the poet's dismissive attitude toward it.
(B) Time wants to be able to pass more quickly.
(C) Time wants to become a creative, not a destructive, force.
(D) Time wants human beings to pay more attention to it.
(E) Time resents its lack of real power over human beings.

27. When the poet says Time devours "what is false and vain, / And merely mortal dross" (lines 5–6), you can conclude that he means

(A) the passage of time cannot destroy anything of real importance
(B) time can only be measured at the pace of the Plummet
(C) living people do not worry about the passage of time
(D) time can only destroy life; it cannot create or build anything
(E) no harm can come to anyone solely because of the passage of time

28. The speaker implies that people triumph over Death, Chance, and Time by

(A) being extraordinarily lucky throughout their mortal lives
(B) achieving salvation and eternal life after death
(C) saving their material goods for a comfortable old age
(D) "living" forever in one's children, grandchildren, and descendants
(E) dying when they are young, healthy, and beautiful

29. "Attir'd with Stars, we shall for ever sit" (line 21) is best paraphrased as

(A) we shall wear robes decorated with the stars of heaven
(B) we shall sit under the stars and await eternal life
(C) our bodies will be wrapped in star-spangled shrouds
(D) our souls shall live in heaven, among the stars
(E) we shall be buried under a starry sky

30. "The supreme Throne / Of him" (lines 17–18) refers to

    (A) the seat of God in heaven
    (B) the throne of the King of England
    (C) the poet's chair in his study or library
    (D) the clock in which Time is "enthroned"
    (E) the tomb in which the dead lie in state

31. Which of the following best states the argument of the poem?

    (A) Time will eventually take the poet's life, but his poems are immortal.
    (B) The poet has the power to create, but time can only destroy.
    (C) Things that are truly worth having come only with the passage of time.
    (D) Human beings should spend their time preparing for life after death.
    (E) Time can kill the mortal body, but the soul achieves eternal life in heaven.

32. Which of the following is NOT personified in the poem?

    (A) Time (line 1)
    (B) Plummet (line 3)
    (C) Eternity (line 11)
    (D) Truth (line 16)
    (E) Peace (line 16)

33. The poet employs an irregular meter in order to emphasize which of the following?

    I. the mystery of eternal life
    II. the powerlessness of time
    III. his pleasure in his own creative powers

    (A) I only
    (B) I and II only
    (C) II only
    (D) II and III only
    (E) I and III only

34. The phrase "our heav'nly guided soul" (line 19) is best paraphrased as

    (A) a dead person who is resurrected to life
    (B) the soul we have helped guide to heaven
    (C) our soul that has been guided to heaven
    (D) our soul that heaven has guided to eternity
    (E) the way that guides help our soul to heaven

Questions 35–42. Read the following speech carefully before you choose your answers.

Two thousand years ago the proudest boast was "Civis Romanus sum."[1] Today, in the world of freedom, the proudest boast is "Ich bin ein Berliner."[2]

I appreciate my interpreter translating my German!

5 There are many people in the world who really don't understand, or say they don't, what is the great issue between the free world and the Communist world. Let them come to Berlin. There are some who say that communism is the wave of the future. Let them come to Berlin. And there are
10 some who say in Europe and elsewhere we can work with the Communists. Let them come to Berlin. And there are even a few who say that it is true that communism is an evil system, but it permits us to make economic progress. Lass' sie nach Berlin kommen.[3] Let them come to Berlin.

15 Freedom has many difficulties and democracy is not perfect, but we have never had to put a wall up to keep our people in, to prevent them from leaving us. I want to say, on behalf of my countrymen, who live many miles away on the other side of the Atlantic, who are far distant from
20 you, that they take the greatest pride that they have been able to share with you, even from a distance, the story of the last 18 years. I know of no town, no city, that has been besieged for 18 years that still lives with the vitality and the force, and the hope and the determination of the city of
25 West Berlin. While the wall is the most obvious and vivid demonstration of the failures of the Communist system, for all the world to see, we take no satisfaction in it, for it is, as your Mayor has said, an offense not only against history but an offense against humanity, separating families,
30 dividing husbands and wives and brothers and sisters, and dividing a people who wish to be joined together . . .

Freedom is indivisible, and when one man is enslaved, all are not free. When all are free, then we can look forward to that day when this city will be joined as one and this
35 country and this great Continent of Europe in a peaceful and hopeful globe. When that day finally comes, as it will,

the people of West Berlin can take sober satisfaction in the fact that they were in the front lines for almost two decades.

40 All free men, wherever they may live, are citizens of Berlin, and, therefore, as a free man, I take pride in the words "Ich bin ein Berliner."

(1963)

[1] I am Roman citizen.
[2] I am from Berlin.
[3] Let them come to Berlin.

35. The speaker uses two German phrases in an otherwise largely English-language speech in order to
   (A) refer to his early life and education in Germany
   (B) show his German audience that he identifies with them
   (C) ensure that his audience understands what he is saying
   (D) prove to his audience that he speaks fluent German
   (E) explain to his audience that he is of German descent

36. The comment "I appreciate my interpreter translating my German!" (line 4) shows the speaker's
   (A) sense of humor
   (B) impatience
   (C) discourtesy
   (D) uncertainty
   (E) intensity

37. What does the speaker mean when he says "All free men, wherever they may live, are citizens of Berlin" (lines 40–41)?

   (A) that all people in the world were born in Berlin
   (B) that Germany rules an empire of many nations
   (C) that all free people support a free Berlin and a free Germany
   (D) that it is easy for anyone to acquire German citizenship
   (E) that the United States and West Germany are permanent allies

38. The speaker's tone is best described as

   (A) pensive, introspective, and dreamy
   (B) neutral, objective, and matter-of-fact
   (C) intense, scholarly, and thoughtful
   (D) excited, hysterical, and passionate
   (E) forceful, determined, and confident

39. The metaphor "in the front lines" (line 38) suggests that the speaker regards the people of Berlin as

   (A) free men and women
   (B) soldiers
   (C) citizens
   (D) Communists
   (E) victims

40. Why does the speaker believe that "Ich bin ein Berliner" is "the proudest boast" of the day?

   (A) The fact that West Berlin maintains a free society shows the moral courage of its people.
   (B) West Berlin's existence is proof that a Communist system will succeed.
   (C) The Berlin Wall isolates West Berlin in the middle of Communist East Germany.
   (D) West Berliners are permitted to travel freely between West and East Berlin.
   (E) Although West Berlin is an occupied city, it is one of the wealthiest cities in Europe.

41. What does the speaker imply will happen if the people he describes in the third paragraph take up his challenge and "come to Berlin"?

   (A) They will realize they were right to support Communism.
   (B) They will learn to speak German.
   (C) They will try to find a way to combine Communism with freedom.
   (D) They will see that democracy is a better system than Communism.
   (E) They will become citizens of Berlin.

42. The speaker uses both words in each pair to emphasize the same idea, EXCEPT

   (A) "Europe and elsewhere" (line 10)
   (B) "Freedom . . . and democracy" (line 15)
   (C) "the vitality and the force" (lines 23–24)
   (D) "the hope and the determination" (line 24)
   (E) "peaceful and hopeful" (lines 35–36)

(Earlier in the play, Macbeth and Lady Macbeth murdered the King of Scotland and seized his throne. Guilt has driven Lady Macbeth insane. In this scene, Macbeth prepares to face the army who is coming to avenge Duncan's death.)

Macbeth
        Seyton!—I am sick at heart,
When I behold—Seyton, I say!—This push
Will cheer me ever, or disseat me now.
I have lived long enough: my way of life
5 Is fall'n into the sere, the yellow leaf;
And that which should accompany old age,
As honor, love, obedience, troops of friends,
I must not look to have; but, in their stead,
Curses, not loud but deep, mouth-honor, breath,
10 Which the poor heart would fain deny, and dare not.
Seyton!

(Enter Seyton)

Seyton
What is your gracious pleasure?

Macbeth
               What news more?

Seyton
All is confirm'd, my lord, which was reported.

Macbeth
I'll fight till from my bones my flesh be hack'd.
15 Give me my armor.

Seyton
'Tis not needed yet.

Macbeth
        I'll put it on.
Send out more horses; skirr the country round;
Hang those that talk of fear. Give me mine armor.
How does your patient,[1] doctor?

[1] Lady Macbeth

Doctor
20 Not so sick, my lord,
As she is troubled with thick coming fancies,
That keep her from her rest.

Macbeth
           Cure her of that.
Canst thou not minister to a mind diseas'd,
Pluck from the memory a rooted sorrow,
25 Raze out the written troubles of the brain
And with some sweet oblivious antidote
Cleanse the stuff'd bosom of that perilous stuff
Which weighs upon the heart?

Doctor
           Therein the patient
Must minister to himself.

Macbeth
30 Throw physic to the dogs; I'll none of it.
Come, put mine armor on; give me my staff.
Seyton, send out. Doctor, the thanes fly from me.—
Come, sir, dispatch.—If thou couldst, doctor, cast
The water of my land, find her disease,
35 And purge it to a sound and pristine health,
I would applaud thee to the very echo,
That should applaud again.

               (C. 1607)

43. In this context, the word "oblivious" (line 26) means
(A) unaware of
(B) causing forgetfulness
(C) bitter-tasting
(D) long-lasting
(E) insensitive

GO ON TO THE NEXT PAGE

44. The statement "I'll fight till from my flesh my bones be hack'd" (line 14) shows that Macbeth is

(A) afraid
(B) resigned
(C) courageous
(D) enraged
(E) brutal

45. The questions Macbeth asks the Doctor show that he feels which of the following for Lady Macbeth?

   I. love and concern
  II. guilt and shame
 III. pity and sorrow

(A) I and II only
(B) II and III only
(C) I and III only
(D) I only
(E) III only

46. "This push / Will cheer me ever, or disseat me now" (lines 2–3) is best paraphrased as

(A) If the army marching toward me does not cheer me up, it will take my throne away from me.
(B) If Lady Macbeth does not soon recover her health and good cheer, I will have to give up the throne.
(C) I have been so unhappy since taking the throne that I think I should allow the army to defeat me.
(D) If the Doctor brings good news of Lady Macbeth, it will cheer me up enough to win the battle.
(E) The coming attack will fail and leave me permanently safe, or succeed and seize my throne from me.

47. You can infer from Seyton's words and the way Macbeth speaks to him that Seyton is a

(A) doctor
(B) prince
(C) warrior
(D) servant
(E) priest

48. When Macbeth says he will receive "mouth-honor" (line 9), he means

(A) people will address him by the title "Your Majesty"
(B) the Scots will think and speak well of him
(C) his subjects will give him only an outward show of respect
(D) he will be honored for being a brave soldier
(E) he will say what he pleases to anyone in his kingdom

49. Which of the following is NOT a reasonable inference to make about the Doctor?

(A) He is adequate, no more, as a physician.
(B) He feels little sympathy for Lady Macbeth's suffering.
(C) He does not like Macbeth, nor want to serve him.
(D) He is afraid he may be killed in the coming battle.
(E) He is not qualified or able to treat mental illness.

Questions 50–60. Read the following passage carefully before you choose your answers.

She was fast asleep.

Gabriel, leaning on his elbow, looked for a few moments unresentfully on her tangled hair and half-open mouth, listening to her deep-drawn breath. So she had had that
5   romance in her life: a man had died for her sake. It hardly pained him now to think how poor a part he, her husband, had played in her life. He watched her while she slept as though he and she had never lived together as man and wife. His curious eyes rested long upon her face and on her hair:
10 and, as he thought of what she must have been then, in that time of her first girlish beauty, a strange friendly pity for her entered his soul. He did not like to say even to himself that her face was no longer beautiful but he knew that it was no longer the face for which Michael Furey had braved death.

15 Perhaps she had not told him all the story. His eyes moved to the chair over which she had thrown some of her clothes. A petticoat string dangled to the floor. One boot stood upright, its limp upper fallen down: the fellow of it lay upon its side. He wondered at his riot of emotions of an
20 hour before. From what had it proceeded? From his aunt's supper, from his own foolish speech, from the wine and dancing, the merry-making when saying good-night in the hall, the pleasure of the walk along the river in the snow. Poor Aunt Julia! She, too, would soon be a shade with the
25 shade of Patrick Morkan and his horse. He had caught that haggard look upon her face for a moment when she was singing *Arrayed for the Bridal*. Soon, perhaps, he would be sitting in that same drawing-room, dressed in black, his silk hat on his knees. The blinds would be drawn down and
30 Aunt Kate would be sitting beside him, crying and blowing her nose and telling him how Julia had died. He would cast about in his mind for some words that might console her, and would find only lame and useless ones. Yes, yes: that would happen very soon.

35 The air of the room chilled his shoulders. He stretched himself cautiously along under the sheets and lay down beside his wife. One by one they were all becoming shades. Better pass boldly into that other world, in the full glory of some passion, than fade and wither dismally
40 with age. He thought of how she who lay beside him had locked in her heart for so many years that image of her lover's eyes when he had told her that he did not wish to live.

Generous tears filled Gabriel's eyes. He had never felt like
45 that himself towards any woman but he knew that such a feeling must be love. The tears gathered more thickly in his eyes and in the partial darkness he imagined he saw the form of a young man standing under a dripping tree. Other forms were near. His soul had approached
50 that region where dwell the vast hosts of the dead. He was conscious of, but could not apprehend, their wayward and flickering existence. His own identity was fading out into a grey impalpable world: the solid world itself which these dead had one time reared and lived in was dissolving and
55 dwindling.

A few light taps upon the pane made him turn to the window. It had begun to snow again. He watched sleepily the flakes, silver and dark, falling obliquely against the lamplight. The time had come for him to set out on his
60 journey westward. Yes, the newspapers were right: snow was general all over Ireland. It was falling on every part of the dark central plain, on the treeless hills, falling softly upon the Bog of Allen and, farther westward, softly falling into the dark mutinous Shannon waves. It was falling,
65 too, upon every part of the lonely churchyard on the hill where Michael Furey lay buried. It lay thickly drifted on the crooked crosses and headstones, on the spears of the little gate, on the barren thorns. His soul swooned slowly as he heard the snow falling faintly through the universe and
70 faintly falling, like the descent of their last end, upon all the living and the dead.

(1916)

50. The word "shade" as used in this passage means

(A) shadow
(B) ghost
(C) snowfall
(D) death
(E) curtain

51. Which of the following best describes Gabriel's feeling toward his wife in these paragraphs?

    (A) sympathetic
    (B) romantic
    (C) jealous
    (D) angry
    (E) amused

52. Which of the following best describes the tone of the passage?

    (A) merry
    (B) hopeless
    (C) ominous
    (D) resigned
    (E) elegiac

53. What happens to Gabriel in the final paragraph?

    (A) He dies of a broken heart.
    (B) He ponders the meaning of his existence.
    (C) He decides to ask his wife for a divorce.
    (D) He falls asleep while watching the snow fall.
    (E) He resolves to be a better person hereafter.

54. Which of the following literary elements appears in the final sentence?

    (A) rhyme
    (B) alliteration
    (C) hyperbole
    (D) comedy
    (E) allusion

55. The author uses snow throughout the passage to symbolize

    (A) death
    (B) winter
    (C) passion
    (D) sleep
    (E) cold

56. The writer describes Gabriel's tears as "generous" (line 44) in order to

    (A) show that Gabriel's wife has never loved him
    (B) reveal Gabriel's sorrow at the death of his friend Michael Furey
    (C) foreshadow Gabriel's grief over the death of Aunt Julia
    (D) emphasize Gabriel's sympathy with his wife's grief over her loss
    (E) underline Gabriel's bitterness over his wife's deception

57. Gabriel's thoughts and emotions in this passage enable the reader to characterize him as

    (A) intellectual and detached
    (B) credulous and naive
    (C) petty and jealous
    (D) kind and unselfish
    (E) stodgy and dull

58. The sentence beginning "It lay thickly drifted" in the final paragraph (lines 66–68) contains three images that allude to the

    (A) death of Michael Furey
    (B) poetry of Shakespeare
    (C) history of Ireland
    (D) cycle of seasons
    (E) crucifixion of Jesus

59. In the paragraph beginning "The air of the room chilled his shoulders," Gabriel concludes that it is better to

(A) die young than to live a long life
(B) die of a broken heart than to live with one
(C) experience both passion and pain than to experience neither
(D) live without love than to die of love
(E) kill oneself rather than to wait for a natural death

60. Which of the following does the author achieve with the repetition of the word "falling" in the final paragraph?

   I. lulls the reader to sleep with the repetition
  II. helps the reader visualize the gently falling snow
 III. emphasizes the warmth of the room

(A) I only
(B) I and II only
(C) II only
(D) II and III only
(E) III only

STOP

If you finish before time is called, you may check your work on this test only.

Do not turn to any other test in this book.

Answer Key

1. B	16. D	31. E	46. E
2. A	17. C	32. B	47. D
3. E	18. D	33. D	48. C
4. A	19. D	34. C	49. D
5. D	20. E	35. B	50. B
6. A	21. A	36. A	51. A
7. B	22. B	37. C	52. E
8. E	23. D	38. E	53. D
9. C	24. C	39. B	54. B
10. A	25. B	40. A	55. A
11. B	26. E	41. D	56. D
12. D	27. A	42. A	57. D
13. C	28. B	43. B	58. E
14. A	29. D	44. C	59. C
15. D	30. A	45. C	60. B

Answers and Explanations

1. **(B)** The two characters say the following: "Why did you fail?" "For Beauty." "And I for truth; Themself are one." The pronoun clearly refers to "truth and beauty."

2. **(A)** "I died for Beauty" is a metaphor. Beauty in this context is not a reference to the speaker's own literal, physical beauty or lack thereof. If a person fights and dies for a glorious cause, that person might say he or she "died for Beauty."

3. **(E)** Since Truth and Beauty "are One," both characters died for the same thing. They both believed in the same cause and shared the same values. This makes them kindred spirits. D is wrong because the word "bretheren" is used metaphorically.

4. **(A)** The mood is one of mystery because the atmosphere is hushed and still, and the poet leaves the reader wondering about many questions. The two characters seem calm, safe, and happy, which makes the other four choices wrong.

5. **(D)** The dead man speaks softly because he feels gentle and compassionate toward the other character. By itself, speaking softly does not imply any of the other four choices.

6. **(A)** If they talked until the moss grew up the sides of their coffins, they talked for many years. Moss grows slowly. D is obviously wrong; although they are dead, they still have the power of speech. C is wrong because they only meet and talk after death.

7. **(B)** The tomb appears to be a literal tomb—a place in which dead people are buried. The other four words are not used literally. Beauty and Truth might mean any number of things; and the two characters are kinsmen or brothers only in the metaphorical sense of being alike in character.

8. **(E)** Although this is very short for a narrative poem, it has the necessary elements of characters, a setting, and a plot. A sonnet is a 14-line poem in iambic pentameter, free verse lacks a rhyme scheme and metric structure, a quatrain has only four lines, and a couplet has only two.

9. **(C)** The fact of being dead, by itself, would not make the two characters feel that they share a common bond of sympathy, so option I is wrong. They are drawn to each other because they died for truth and beauty, which they believe are the same thing, and their values are alike.

10. **(A)** The poet seems to feel a gentle pity for Mamie, without any expectation that she will find what she wants.

11. **(B)** The phrase is repeated three times in a short poem. The author's focus is on Mamie's feeling of being trapped, her unhappiness, and her desire to escape the metaphorical "bars" of her situation. Option III is incorrect because the author shows no contempt for Mamie; he regards her as an object of compassion.

12. **(D)** The poet does not give his own opinion of life in the little Indiana town. He understands that Mamie hates it, and he shows compassion for her, but he gives no hint of his own feelings about places like this town.

13. **(C)** Choices A, B, C, and E are all accurate definitions of *romance*, but only choice C makes sense in this context. Mamie is looking for an exciting life in which adventures will happen. Choice D is wrong because it means the opposite of romance.

14. **(A)** Mamie is looking for a place more exciting than her little home town in Indiana—a place of romance and adventure.

15. **(D)** Mamie is not literally beating her head against actual bars. She is not physically locked up anywhere. The "bars" are the lack of opportunity, the conventions, and a lack of money that keep her in a certain socioeconomic situation. She feels trapped, like an animal in a cage at the zoo who wants his freedom.

16. **(D)** Repeating Mamie's desires and setting them off visually emphasizes them so that the reader will remember them.

17. **(C)** Mamie went to Chicago to escape a dreary everyday routine. All she finds in Chicago is a different dreary routine—this time a full-time job in a basement where she can't even look out a window.

18. **(D)** *Constituency* means "voters." In a representative government like the parliamentary system, the representatives are bound to pass laws supported by the people who voted for them. The chains are not literal.

19. **(D)** The main idea of the entire passage is that the pilot has total authority over his boat, in the same way that an absolute monarch has total command of his kingdom.

20. **(E)** *Pernicious* is derived from a French word meaning "destruction." The other choices are inaccurate definitions.

21. **(A)** Choices B, C, D, and E all give specific examples of a steamboat pilot's authority. Choice A is not relevant.

22. **(B)** The writer says that writers have to modify what they write. By contrast, a pilot has unquestioned authority and can always do exactly what he wants. Choices A, C, and D might be true statements, but the writer does not suggest they are why he loves the profession of pilot the most. Choice E is a false statement.

23. **(D)** In any literal sense, a steamboat pilot is many social grades below a foreign prince; the comparison is exaggerated for humor. There is humor in the mental image of a common working man like a pilot greeting a prince with perfect unconcern, as if they were of the same rank.

24. **(C)** To defer to someone means to yield to his wishes or commands.

25. **(B)** Because the government regulates traffic on the river, it must be a matter of importance to the nation. Option I is wrong because all citizens, not just government employees, must obey laws. Option III is wrong because a rise in steamboat accidents would likely lead to laws that lessened the pilot's authority.

26. **(E)** The main idea of the poem is that Time can only destroy what has no value. Time is "envious" because it wants more power.

27. **(A)** The poet states that one's mortal, physical life is of no importance compared to the eternal life of the soul. Time can only destroy "mortal dross," meaning youth, health, wealth, and physical beauty; it has no power over the immortal soul.

28. **(B)** The argument of the poem is that Time is "envious" because it has no power over the eternal life of the soul. What is true of Time is also true of Death and Chance; they can kill the body but not the soul.

29. **(D)** Renaissance-era Christians believed that heaven was in the sky; therefore the souls of the dead will live among the stars. The other choices are either too literal in meaning or they miss the point of the line.

30. **(A)** Christians believe that Heaven is God's kingdom, where He sits on a throne just as an earthly king would. The context makes it clear that the poet is describing the soul's eternal life in God's kingdom.

31. (E) The first sentence of the poem (lines 1–8) states that Time can only kill "mortal dross" for "little gain." The rest of the poem explains that the soul escapes Time's power when it achieves eternal life.

32. (B) The poet does not give the Plummet any human attributes. The other four words are given human attributes: Time is characterized throughout the poem, Eternity "shall greet our bliss / With a kiss," Truth and Peace "shall ever shine / About the supreme Throne."

33. (D) Time itself is characterized by a regular rhythm, *tick tock, tick tock,* and an unchanging pace. The poet's decision NOT to use a fixed meter and rhythm underscores how little power Time has over anything of value in life. Therefore option II is correct. The poet's choice of an irregular meter was conscious, and he most likely enjoyed defying Time in this witty way; therefore option III is also correct.

34. (C) The poet refers to the soul that has been guided to heaven.

35. (B) The speaker is clearly addressing a German-speaking audience. He speaks to them in their own language to underline his fellow-feeling with them, which he discusses in detail in the text of the speech. If he spoke fluent German, he would need no interpreter; and since he has an interpreter, he need not speak German to be sure his audience understands him.

36. (A) The speech is evidently being simultaneously translated into German, and the interpreter repeated the phrase "Ich bin ein Berliner." The speaker is amused, perhaps at his own possibly faulty pronunciation, or perhaps because it was not necessary for the interpreter to repeat German words in German.

37. (C) The speaker does not mean this statement literally. He is telling the people of West Berlin "the rest of the free world is behind you, supports you, and identifies with you."

38. (E) The speaker uses many short declarative and imperative sentences, which contribute to the forceful and confident tone. He also says "When all are free" rather than "If all ever become free," showing his firm belief that this will happen.

39. (B) The "front lines" is a metaphor drawn from battle, referring to the troops who are positioned closest to the enemy. The speaker refers to the people of Berlin, his audience, as soldiers in the front lines because they are the people most directly and nearly threatened by the Communist enemy.

40. (A) The speaker admires West Berliners for insisting on maintaining a free and democratic society in spite of the fact that they face serious threats from Communist East Germany. Choice C is a true statement, but not in itself a reason for pride.

41. (D) The speaker addresses those people who believe that Communism is a good system. He challenges them to come to Berlin so they can see what a terrible system it is, by looking at the wall that physically prevents East Germans from choosing to leave.

42. (A) Both words in each pair have similar meaning and connotations, except "Europe and elsewhere." This pair shows a contrast—it lists two opposite ideas.

43. (B) *Oblivious* usually means *unaware,* but in this case Shakespeare uses it to mean "causing oblivion" or "causing forgetfulness." The lines "pluck from the memory a rooted sorrow" and "raze out the written troubles of the brain" show that the only antidote that will cure Lady Macbeth is to forget the horrors of the past. Therefore choice B is the only one that makes sense.

44. (C) Anyone who refuses to give in, no matter how high the odds are against him, is brave.

45. (C) Macbeth does not show any sense of guilt for his wife's sad condition. He does show pity, love, concern, and a great desire for her to be cured.

46. (E) Macbeth knows that the coming battle will mean either a final victory or a final defeat for him.

47. (D) Seyton addresses Macbeth by his title, while Macbeth calls Seyton by his name. This shows that Macbeth is of higher rank. Macbeth asks Seyton to help him with his armor and to carry out other orders. All these things show that Seyton is a servant. Seyton and the Doctor are two separate characters, so choice A is wrong.

48. (C) The expression "mouth-honor" means the same as the contemporary "lip service." Macbeth has just stated that he will receive only the outward show of the respect due to his position as king; this outward show will not reflect what his subjects truly feel about him.

49. (D) The Doctor's tone in speaking to Macbeth is almost curt; his brief answers make it reasonable to infer that he does not like Macbeth. He expresses little concern or sympathy for Lady Macbeth. He says that a mentally ill patient "must minister to himself," showing that he is not capable of treating such a patient. A dedicated doctor would try to be of more help. This leaves choice D, which is NOT a reasonable inference because the Doctor expresses no fear of the battle and because as a doctor, he would not be likely to take any part in the fighting.

50. (B) This definition of *shade* is no longer common usage, but the context of the passage makes it clear that Gabriel is referring to ghosts.

51. (A) The phrase "a strange friendly pity for her entered his soul" makes it clear that he feels sympathy rather than any of the other choices.

52. (E) An elegy is a speech made over the dead. Gabriel is pondering the subject of death, of those who have died and those who will soon die, and he thinks of his marriage and his life and being "dead" because they both lack intense emotion. The tenderness Gabriel expresses throughout the passage make "hopeless" and "resigned" inappropriate answers.

53. (D) "His soul swooned slowly" is a poetical, metaphorical way of saying he has fallen asleep. Although writers commonly compare sleep metaphorically to death, it is only a metaphor; Gabriel has not actually died; and although he is moved by his wife's story and shares her grief, he is not heartbroken.

54. (B) "Soul swooned slowly," "faintly falling," and "falling faintly" are examples of alliteration, a series of words beginning with the same sound.

55. (A) Throughout the passage, Gabriel is preoccupied with thoughts of death, of those who are dead and are soon to die, and of the living death of people who feel no intense emotions. Snow and winter are common symbols for death because they represent the "death" or sleep of plants and animals during the cycle of the seasons.

56. (D) Sympathy and generosity go together better than any of the other choices. Gabriel is described as feeling "a strange friendly pity" for his wife.

57. (D) The writer applies the words "generous" and "friendly" to Gabriel and makes it clear that he thinks only of his wife's grief as she shares her memories of the boy who died for love of her. Many people would be jealous, petty, or bitter in this situation, but Gabriel is sympathetic.

58. (E) The crooked cross, the spears, and the thorns all allude to the Crucifixion. Jesus was crowned with thorns and nailed to a crooked cross; soldiers poked spears in his side to see if he was dead.

59. (C) Michael Furey experienced the glory of passionate love and also the anguish of losing his beloved. The pain of the separation is what killed him. Gabriel feels it is better to have felt the passion, in spite of the pain it can bring, than to live a quiet, uneventful life that contains neither a great passion nor any anguish.

60. (B) Gabriel is falling asleep during the last paragraph, and the repetition helps the reader "become" Gabriel as he or she too is lulled. Option I is correct. Option II is also correct because the word repeatedly draws attention to the falling snow, reminding the reader of it and helping the reader to picture it. Option III is incorrect: the repetition of "falling" does not evoke feelings of the cold weather or the warmth of the room.

How To Calculate Your Score

Count the number of correct answers and enter the total below.

Count the number of wrong answers. Do NOT include any questions you did not answer.

Multiply the number of wrong answers by 0.25 and enter the total below.

Do the subtraction. The answer is your raw score. Use the scoring scale to find your scaled score.

$$\overline{\text{(number of correct answers)}} - \overline{\text{(number of wrong answers} \times 0.25)} = \overline{\text{(raw score)}}$$

RAW SCORE	SCALED SCORE	RAW SCORE	SCALED SCORE	RAW SCORE	SCALED SCORE	RAW SCORE	SCALED SCORE	RAW SCORE	SCALED SCORE
60	800	44	710	28	560	12	420	–4	260
59	800	43	700	27	550	11	410	–5	250
58	800	42	690	26	540	10	400	–6	240
57	800	41	690	25	530	9	390	–7	230
56	800	40	680	24	520	8	380	–8	220
55	800	39	670	23	510	7	370	–9	210
54	790	38	660	22	500	6	360	–10	200
53	790	37	650	21	500	5	350	–11	200
52	780	36	640	20	490	4	340	–12	200
51	770	35	630	19	490	3	330	–13	200
50	760	34	620	18	480	2	320	–14	200
49	750	33	610	17	470	1	310	–15	200
48	740	32	600	16	460	0	300		
47	740	31	590	15	450	–1	290		
46	730	30	580	14	440	–2	280		
45	720	29	570	13	430	–3	270		

Note: This is only a sample scoring scale. Scoring scales differ from exam to exam.

Practice Test 2

The following practice test is designed to be just like the real SAT Literature Test. It matches the actual test in content coverage and degree of difficulty.

Once you finish the practice test, determine your score. Carefully read the answer explanations of the questions you answered incorrectly. Identify any weaknesses in your literature skills by determining the areas in which you made the most errors. Review those sections of this book first. Then, as time permits, go back and review your strengths.

Allow one hour to take the test. Time yourself and work uninterrupted. If you run out of time, take note of where you stopped when time ran out. Remember that you lose a quarter point for each incorrect answer, but you do not lose points for questions you leave blank. Therefore, unless you can eliminate one or more of the five choices, it's best to leave a question unanswered.

Use the following formula to calculate your score:

(number of correct answers) – ¼ (number of incorrect answers)

If you treat this practice test just like the actual exam, it will accurately reflect how you are likely to perform on test day. Here are some hints on how to create test-taking conditions similar to those of the actual exam:

- Complete the test in one sitting. On test day, you will not be allowed to take a break.
- Tear out the answer sheet and fill in the ovals just as you will on the actual test day.
- Have a good eraser and more than one sharp pencil handy. On test day, you will not be able to go get a new pencil if yours breaks.
- Do not allow yourself any extra time; put down your pencil after exactly one hour, no matter how many questions are left to answer.
- Become familiar with the directions on the test. If you go in knowing what the directions say, you will not have to waste time reading and thinking about them on the actual test day.

Practice Test 2

Answer Sheet

Tear out this answer sheet and use it to mark your answers.

1. Ⓐ Ⓑ Ⓒ Ⓓ Ⓔ	16. Ⓐ Ⓑ Ⓒ Ⓓ Ⓔ	31. Ⓐ Ⓑ Ⓒ Ⓓ Ⓔ	46. Ⓐ Ⓑ Ⓒ Ⓓ Ⓔ
2. Ⓐ Ⓑ Ⓒ Ⓓ Ⓔ	17. Ⓐ Ⓑ Ⓒ Ⓓ Ⓔ	32. Ⓐ Ⓑ Ⓒ Ⓓ Ⓔ	47. Ⓐ Ⓑ Ⓒ Ⓓ Ⓔ
3. Ⓐ Ⓑ Ⓒ Ⓓ Ⓔ	18. Ⓐ Ⓑ Ⓒ Ⓓ Ⓔ	33. Ⓐ Ⓑ Ⓒ Ⓓ Ⓔ	48. Ⓐ Ⓑ Ⓒ Ⓓ Ⓔ
4. Ⓐ Ⓑ Ⓒ Ⓓ Ⓔ	19. Ⓐ Ⓑ Ⓒ Ⓓ Ⓔ	34. Ⓐ Ⓑ Ⓒ Ⓓ Ⓔ	49. Ⓐ Ⓑ Ⓒ Ⓓ Ⓔ
5. Ⓐ Ⓑ Ⓒ Ⓓ Ⓔ	20. Ⓐ Ⓑ Ⓒ Ⓓ Ⓔ	35. Ⓐ Ⓑ Ⓒ Ⓓ Ⓔ	50. Ⓐ Ⓑ Ⓒ Ⓓ Ⓔ
6. Ⓐ Ⓑ Ⓒ Ⓓ Ⓔ	21. Ⓐ Ⓑ Ⓒ Ⓓ Ⓔ	36. Ⓐ Ⓑ Ⓒ Ⓓ Ⓔ	51. Ⓐ Ⓑ Ⓒ Ⓓ Ⓔ
7. Ⓐ Ⓑ Ⓒ Ⓓ Ⓔ	22. Ⓐ Ⓑ Ⓒ Ⓓ Ⓔ	37. Ⓐ Ⓑ Ⓒ Ⓓ Ⓔ	52. Ⓐ Ⓑ Ⓒ Ⓓ Ⓔ
8. Ⓐ Ⓑ Ⓒ Ⓓ Ⓔ	23. Ⓐ Ⓑ Ⓒ Ⓓ Ⓔ	38. Ⓐ Ⓑ Ⓒ Ⓓ Ⓔ	53. Ⓐ Ⓑ Ⓒ Ⓓ Ⓔ
9. Ⓐ Ⓑ Ⓒ Ⓓ Ⓔ	24. Ⓐ Ⓑ Ⓒ Ⓓ Ⓔ	39. Ⓐ Ⓑ Ⓒ Ⓓ Ⓔ	54. Ⓐ Ⓑ Ⓒ Ⓓ Ⓔ
10. Ⓐ Ⓑ Ⓒ Ⓓ Ⓔ	25. Ⓐ Ⓑ Ⓒ Ⓓ Ⓔ	40. Ⓐ Ⓑ Ⓒ Ⓓ Ⓔ	55. Ⓐ Ⓑ Ⓒ Ⓓ Ⓔ
11. Ⓐ Ⓑ Ⓒ Ⓓ Ⓔ	26. Ⓐ Ⓑ Ⓒ Ⓓ Ⓔ	41. Ⓐ Ⓑ Ⓒ Ⓓ Ⓔ	56. Ⓐ Ⓑ Ⓒ Ⓓ Ⓔ
12. Ⓐ Ⓑ Ⓒ Ⓓ Ⓔ	27. Ⓐ Ⓑ Ⓒ Ⓓ Ⓔ	42. Ⓐ Ⓑ Ⓒ Ⓓ Ⓔ	57. Ⓐ Ⓑ Ⓒ Ⓓ Ⓔ
13. Ⓐ Ⓑ Ⓒ Ⓓ Ⓔ	28. Ⓐ Ⓑ Ⓒ Ⓓ Ⓔ	43. Ⓐ Ⓑ Ⓒ Ⓓ Ⓔ	58. Ⓐ Ⓑ Ⓒ Ⓓ Ⓔ
14. Ⓐ Ⓑ Ⓒ Ⓓ Ⓔ	29. Ⓐ Ⓑ Ⓒ Ⓓ Ⓔ	44. Ⓐ Ⓑ Ⓒ Ⓓ Ⓔ	59. Ⓐ Ⓑ Ⓒ Ⓓ Ⓔ
15. Ⓐ Ⓑ Ⓒ Ⓓ Ⓔ	30. Ⓐ Ⓑ Ⓒ Ⓓ Ⓔ	45. Ⓐ Ⓑ Ⓒ Ⓓ Ⓔ	60. Ⓐ Ⓑ Ⓒ Ⓓ Ⓔ

PRACTICE TEST 2
Time: 60 Minutes

Directions: This test consists of selections from literary works and questions on their content, form, and style. After reading each passage or poem, choose the best answer to each question and then fill in the corresponding oval on the answer sheet.

Note: Pay particular attention to the requirements of questions that contain the words NOT or EXCEPT.

Questions 1–9. Read the following speech carefully before you choose your answers.

My loving people, we have been persuaded by some, that are careful of our safety, to take heed how we commit ourselves to armed multitudes, for fear of treachery; but I assure you, I do not desire to live to
5   distrust my faithful and loving people. Let tyrants fear; I have always so behaved myself that, under God, I have placed my chiefest strength and safeguard in the loyal hearts and good will of my subjects. And therefore I am come amongst you at this time, not as
10 for my recreation or sport, but being resolved, in the midst and heat of the battle, to live or die amongst you all; to lay down, for my God, and for my kingdom, and for my people, my honor and my blood, even the dust. I know I have but the body of a weak
15 and feeble woman; but I have the heart of a king, and of a king of England, too; and think foul scorn that Parma or Spain, or any prince of Europe, should dare to invade the borders of my realms: to which, rather than any dishonor should grow by me, I myself will
20 take up arms; I myself will be your general, judge, and rewarder of every one of your virtues in the field. I know already, by your forwardness, that you have deserved rewards and crowns; and we do assure you, on the word of a prince, they shall be duly paid you.
25 In the mean my lieutenant general shall be in my stead, than whom never prince commanded a more noble and worthy subject; not doubting by your obedience to my general, by your concord in the camp, and by your valor in the field, we shall shortly have

30 a famous victory over the enemies of my God, of my kingdom, and of my people.

(1588)

1. The speaker uses the word "forwardness" (line 22) to mean

   (A) demonstration of bravery on the battlefield
   (B) promptness in volunteering for military duty
   (C) disrespectful, familiar, or brazen behavior
   (D) high rank in the nobility or aristocracy
   (E) eagerness among the crowd to get close enough to hear

2. The tone of the speech is best described as

   (A) ironic
   (B) anguished
   (C) solemn
   (D) ominous
   (E) inspiring

3. What is the source of the potential treachery the speaker refers to in the opening sentence?

   (A) her close advisers
   (B) her family members
   (C) her volunteer soldiers
   (D) the enemy army
   (E) the opposing political party

4. By saying "Let tyrants fear" (lines 5–6), the speaker implies which of the following?

   (A) that her enemies are tyrants
   (B) that she is not a tyrant
   (C) that subjects fear a tyrant
   (D) that tyrants cannot be trusted
   (E) that she is abdicating the throne

5. In which sense does the speaker use the word "mean" (line 25)?

   (A) interval
   (B) average
   (C) miserly
   (D) spiteful
   (E) intend

6. Why does the speaker repeat the phrase "for/of my God, my kingdom, and my people" (lines 12–13 and 30–31)?

   I. to lull her audience into a calmer mood
   II. to emphasize the rightness of her cause
   III. to arouse her listeners' patriotism

   (A) I only
   (B) II only
   (C) II and III only
   (D) III only
   (E) I, II, and III

7. Which best describes the character of the speaker?

   (A) determined and courageous
   (B) cautious and prudent
   (C) cynical and bitter
   (D) manipulative and dishonest
   (E) brutal and fierce

8. The final sentence of the speech contains two examples of which literary technique?

   (A) rhetoric
   (B) parallelism
   (C) enjambment
   (D) simile
   (E) hyperbole

9. The word "crowns" (line 23) is a metaphor for

   (A) coin of the realm
   (B) rewards
   (C) medals and honors
   (D) royal headgear
   (E) ceremonies

Questions 10–17. Read the following poem carefully before you choose your answers.

Remembrance

Cold in the earth—and the deep snow piledabove thee—
Far, far removed, cold in the dreary grave!
Have I forgot, my only love, to love thee,
Severed at last by time's all-severing wave?

5 Now, when alone, do my thoughts no longer hover
Over the mountains on that northern shore;
Resting their wings where heath and fern-leaves cover
Thy noble heart for ever, ever more?

Cold in the earth—and fifteen wild Decembers
10 From those brown hills have melted into spring—
Faithful, indeed, is the spirit that remembers
After such years of change and suffering!
Sweet love of youth, forgive if I forget thee
While the world's tide is bearing me along—
15 Other desires and other hopes beset me,
Hopes which obscure but cannot do thee wrong.

No later light has lightened up my heaven,
No second morn has ever shone for me:

All my life's bliss from thy dear life was given—
20 All my life's bliss is in the grave with thee.

But when the days of golden dreams had perished
And even despair was powerless to destroy,
Then did I learn how existence could be cherished,
Strengthened and fed without the aid of joy.

25 Then did I check my tears of useless passion—
Weaned my young soul from yearning after thine—
Sternly denied its burning wish to hasten
Down to that tomb already more than mine!

And even yet I dare not let it languish,
30 Dare not indulge in memory's rapturous pain—
Once drinking deep of that divinest anguish,
How could I seek the empty world again?

(1845)

10. In the second stanza, the speaker compares her thoughts to

(A) a faithful dog
(B) a bird
(C) the sun
(D) a clock
(E) the darkness

11. Which best sums up the speaker's message to the beloved?

(A) She has moved on from her loss and achieved peace and serenity.
(B) Her greatest wish is to be buried by the side of her beloved.
(C) She refuses to think about her lost love because if she does she will lose her will to live.
(D) She is grateful to have known happiness with her lost love, even though it was brief.
(E) She has found another love, but promises always to remember the beloved who has died.

12. By "Severed at last by time's all-severing wave" (line 4), the speaker implies that

(A) in time, she will forget her beloved
(B) her lover died of old age
(C) the passage of time can destroy love
(D) her beloved drowned in the ocean
(E) her lover has been away for a long time

13. What consequences does the speaker anticipate from the act of writing/narrating this poem?

(A) She will cease to care about living.
(B) The act of expressing her feelings will lessen them.
(C) The world will learn her most precious secret.
(D) She will be reunited with her lover in heaven.
(E) She will make her love immortal in a work of art.

14. Remembering her beloved causes the speaker to feel all of the following EXCEPT

(A) dread
(B) anguish
(C) passion
(D) serenity
(E) emptiness

15. Which line from the poem seems to contradict the fact of the poem's existence?

(A) "Faithful, indeed, is the spirit that remembers" (line 11)
(B) "Other desires and other hopes beset me" (line 15)
(C) "No later light has lightened up my heaven" (line 17)
(D) "All my life's bliss is in the grave with thee" (line 20)
(E) "[I] Dare not indulge in memory's rapturous pain" (line 30)

16. Which of the following has NOT happened to the speaker since the death of the beloved?

   (A) She has found another lover.

   (B) She has tried to forget her dead lover.

   (C) She has been tempted to commit suicide.

   (D) She has found reasons besides love to go on living.

   (E) She has lost all her happiness.

17. The fact that the speaker decided to go on living despite her loss implies that she is

   (A) frustrated and angry

   (B) listless and apathetic

   (C) disciplined and determined

   (D) romantic and dreamy

   (E) haughty and proud

Questions 18–24. Read the following passage carefully before you choose your answers.

Mrs. Ballinger was one of the ladies who pursue Culture in bands, as though it were dangerous to meet alone. To this end she had founded the Lunch Club, an association composed of herself and several other indomitable
5 huntresses of erudition. The Lunch Club, after three or four winters of lunching and debate, had acquired such local distinction that the entertainment of distinguished strangers became one of its accepted functions; in recognition of which it duly extended to the celebrated
10 "Osric Dane," on the day of her arrival in Hillbridge, an invitation to be present at the next meeting.

The Club was to meet at Mrs. Ballinger's. The other members, behind her back, were of one voice in deploring her unwillingness to cede her rights in favor of
15 Mrs. Plinth, whose house made a more impressive setting for the entertainment of celebrities; while, as Mrs. Leveret observed, there was always the picture-gallery to fall back on.

Mrs. Plinth made no secret of sharing this view. She had
20 always regarded it as one of her obligations to entertain the Lunch Club's distinguished guests. Mrs. Plinth was almost as proud of her obligations as she was of her picture-gallery; she was in fact fond of implying that the one possession implied the other, and that only a
25 woman of her wealth could afford to live up to a standard as high as that which she had set herself. An all-round sense of duty, roughly adaptable to various ends, was, in her opinion, all that Providence exacted of the more

humbly stationed; but the power which had predestined
30 Mrs. Plinth to keep footmen clearly intended her to maintain an equally specialized staff of responsibilities. It was the more to be regretted that Mrs. Ballinger, whose obligations to society were bounded by the narrow scope of two parlor-maids, should have been so tenacious of the
35 right to entertain Osric Dane.

The question of that lady's reception had for a month past profoundly moved the members of the Lunch Club. It was not that they felt themselves unequal to the task, but that their sense of the opportunity plunged them
40 into the agreeable uncertainty of the lady who weighs the alternatives of a well-stocked wardrobe. If such subsidiary members as Mrs. Leveret were fluttered by the thought of exchanging ideas with the author of "The Wings of Death," no forebodings of the kind disturbed the
45 conscious adequacy of Mrs. Plinth, Mrs. Ballinger and Miss Van Vluyck. "The Wings of Death" had, in fact, at Miss Van Vluyck's suggestion, been chosen as the subject of discussion at the last club meeting, and each member had thus been enabled to express her own opinion or to
50 appropriate whatever seemed most likely to be of use in the comments of the others.

                                       (1911)

18. The author of the passage thinks the Lunch Club members are

    I. pretentious
    II. insincere
    III. intellectual

    (A) I only
    (B) I and II only
    (C) II only
    (D) III only
    (E) I, II, and III

19. The fact that Mrs. Plinth owns the most impressive of the club members' houses is an example of

    (A) enjambment
    (B) verbal irony
    (C) metaphor
    (D) hyperbole
    (E) foreshadowing

20. The LEAST powerful and important member of the Lunch Club is

    (A) Mrs. Ballinger
    (B) Mrs. Plinth
    (C) Miss Van Vluyck
    (D) Osric Dane
    (E) Mrs. Leveret

21. The phrase "indomitable huntresses of erudition" (lines 4–5) is striking because

    (A) it suggests that the ladies would rather hunt than read books
    (B) the Lunch Club members have become famous in Hillbridge
    (C) literature is meant to be enjoyed, not conquered with weapons
    (D) hunting is an outdoor activity and reading an indoor one
    (E) Osric Dane has written a novel about hunting

22. The name of "Osric Dane" (line 10), is an allusion to a character in which of the following?

    (A) *Hamlet*
    (B) *Othello*
    (C) *King Lear*
    (D) *Romeo and Juliet*
    (E) *A Midsummer Night's Dream*

23. The author implies that the Lunch Club's true purpose is

    (A) to read and discuss interesting new books
    (B) to meet and talk to famous authors
    (C) to enjoy exploring Mrs. Plinth's picture gallery
    (D) to make its members more important in their own eyes
    (E) to find out whose cook can provide the best lunch

24. The phrase "deploring her unwillingness to cede her rights" (line 14) means

    (A) laughing at her for thinking she has any rights
    (B) thinking worse of her for sacrificing her rights
    (C) praying that she will hold fast to her rights
    (D) criticizing her for wanting to give up her rights
    (E) regretting her refusal to give up her rights

Questions 25–34. Read the following poem carefully before you choose your answers.

In Cabin'd Ships at Sea

In cabin'd ships at sea,
The boundless blue on every side expanding,
With whistling winds and music of the waves, the
                                large imperious waves,
Or some lone bark buoy'd on the dense marine,
5 Where joyous full of faith, spreading white sails,
She cleaves the ether, mid the sparkle and the foam of day,
        or under many a star at night,
By sailors young and old haply will I, a reminiscence of
                                the land, be read,
In full rapport at last.

10 Here are our thoughts, voyagers' thoughts,
Here not the land, firm land, alone appears, may then by
                                them be said,
The sky o'erarches here, we feel the undulating deck
                                beneath our feet,
We feel the long pulsation, ebb and flow of endless motion,
The tones of unseen mystery, the vague and vast suggestions
15   of the briny world, the liquid-flowing syllables,
The perfume, the faint creaking of the cordage, the
                                melancholy rhythm,
The boundless vista and the horizon far and dim are all here,
And this is ocean's poem.

Then falter not O book, fulfil your destiny,
20 You not a reminiscence of the land alone,
You too as a lone bark cleaving the ether, purpos'd I know
                                not whither,
        yet ever full of faith,
Consort to every ship that sails, sail you!
Bear forth to them folded my love, (dear mariners, for
                                you I fold it here in every leaf;)
25 Speed on my book! spread your white sails my little bark
        athwart the imperious waves,
Chant on, sail on, bear o'er the boundless blue from me
                                to every sea,
This song for mariners and all their ships.

(c. 1892)

25. The speaker of this poem is
(A) an author
(B) a traveler
(C) a sailor
(D) a voyager
(E) a ship's captain

26. What is the effect of the alliteration in the line "With whistling winds and music of the waves, the large imperious waves" (line 3)?
    I. It echoes the wash of the ocean water.
    II. It suggests the ocean water because so many words begin with *w*.
    III. It shows how much the speaker loves the sound of the ocean.
(A) I only
(B) I and II only
(C) II only
(D) III only
(E) I, II, and III

27. What does the speaker hope the mariners will find in his book?
(A) happy memories of their lives on shore
(B) religious inspiration and guidance
(C) a sense of fellowship with a poet who understands them
(D) blank pages on which they can write their own poems
(E) entertainment that will help them pass the time

28. Which pair of words does the poet use to create a contrast?
(A) winds and music (line 3)
(B) sparkle and foam (line 6)
(C) ebb and flow (line 13)
(D) vague and vast (line 14)
(E) far and dim (line 17)

29. The metaphor "white sails" (line 25) refers to

(A) the sails of the "cabin'd ships"
(B) the pages of the speaker's book
(C) the white caps on the waves
(D) the clouds in the sky
(E) the mariners' letters to their families

30. This poem is an example of which of the following?

(A) sonnet
(B) elegy
(C) epic
(D) free verse
(E) limerick

31. The speaker directly addresses his book in which of the following stanzas?

    I. stanza 1
    II. stanza 2
    III. stanza 3

(A) I only
(B) I and III only
(C) II only
(D) II and III only
(E) III only

32. The word "haply" (line 8) means

(A) happily
(B) eagerly
(C) perhaps
(D) easily
(E) aloud

33. Which of the following is personified in the poem?

(A) "the boundless blue" (line 2)
(B) "some lone bark" (line 4)
(C) "many a star" (line 4)
(D) "the undulating deck" (line 12)
(E) "the briny world" (line 15)

34. What quality does the speaker believe the mariners will respond to when they read his book?

(A) the rhythm, rhymes, and meter
(B) the allusions to mythology
(C) the speaker's love for the ocean
(D) the visual images
(E) the practical advice

Questions 35–41. Read the following passage carefully before you choose your answers.

I have had to work hard; I have been often cheated, insulted, abused and injured; yet a black man, if he will be industrious and honest, can get along here as well as any one who is poor and in a situation to be imposed
5 on. I have been very unfortunate in life in this respect. Notwithstanding all my struggles, and sufferings, and injuries, I have been an honest man. There is no one who can come forward and say he knows anything against Grimes. This I know, that I have been punished for being
10 suspected of things of which some of those who were loudest against me were actually guilty . . .

I have forebore to mention names in my history where it might give the least pain; in this I have made it less interesting, and injured myself.

15 I may sometimes be a little mistaken, as I have to write from memory, and there is a great deal I have omitted from want of recollection at the time of writing. I cannot speak as I feel on some subjects. If those who read my history think I have not led a life of trial, I have failed
20 to give a correct representation. I think I must be forty years of age, but don't know; I could not tell my wife my age. I have learned to read and write pretty well; if I had an opportunity I could learn very fast. My wife has had a tolerable good education, which has been a help to me.

25 I hope some will buy my books from charity; but I am no beggar. I am now entirely destitute of property; where and how I shall live I don't know; where and how I shall die I don't know; but I hope I may be prepared. If it were not for the stripes on my back which were made while I
30 was a slave, I would in my will leave my skin as a legacy to the government, desiring that it might be taken off and made into parchment, and then bind the Constitution of glorious, happy and *free* America. Let the skin of an American slave bind the charter of American liberty!

(1824)

35. The information in the second paragraph allows you to conclude that Grimes

(A) cares more for the facts than for anyone's feelings
(B) hates everyone from his past life
(C) does not want to praise anyone too highly
(D) is a person of ethics and integrity
(E) cannot remember the names of his enemies

36. The tone of the sentence beginning "If it were not for the stripes on my back" (line 28) is best described as

(A) bitter and angry
(B) resigned and weary
(C) neutral and calm
(D) noble and majestic
(E) proud and confident

37. Why does Grimes include the final sentence when its ideas were already expressed one sentence earlier?

(A) to demonstrate that he is a free citizen
(B) to support his claim that he is an honest man
(C) to emphasize his rage at his past treatment
(D) to make sure his readers remember his words
(E) to urge the government to free all slaves

38. Which is NOT a likely reason for Grimes to have written and published his life story?

(A) to earn enough money to support himself and his family
(B) to avenge himself on those who treated him badly
(C) to persuade his readers to oppose slavery and support abolition
(D) to make his readers aware of the evils of slavery
(E) to put his true story on record so that he will be remembered accurately

39. This passage is an example of which of the
following?

(A) political satire
(B) editorial
(C) confession
(D) slave narrative
(E) biography

40. All of the following seem to characterize Grimes
accurately EXCEPT

(A) bitterness
(B) cynicism
(C) impatience
(D) rage
(E) self-pity

41. Which of the following suggest that Grimes is a
reliable narrator?

(A) He is writing about experiences he lived
through.
(B) He provides supporting details from other
eyewitnesses.
(C) His poverty and suffering are the common
lot of a slave.
(D) He is unable to remember all the events of
his past.
(E) He refuses to give the names of many people
from his past.

Questions 42–49. Read the following poem carefully before you choose your answers.

The Dream

Dear love, for nothing less than thee
Would I have broke this happy dream;
   It was a theme
For reason, much too strong for fantasy.
5 Therefore thou wakd'st me wisely; yet
My dream thou brok'st not, but continued'st it.
Thou art so true that thoughts of thee suffice
To make dreams truths, and fables histories;
Enter these arms, for since thou thought'st it best
10 Not to dream all my dream, let's do the rest.

As lightning, or a taper's light,
Thine eyes, and not thy noise, waked me;
   Yet I thought thee
(For thou lov'st truth) an angel, at first sight,
15 But when I saw thou sawest my heart,
And knew'st my thoughts, beyond an angel's art,
When thou knew'st what I dreamt, when thou knew'st when
Excess of joy would wake me, and cam'st then,
I must confess it could not choose but be
20 Profane to think thee anything but thee.

Coming and staying show'd thee, thee,
But rising makes me doubt, that now
   Thou art not thou.
That love is weak, where Fear's as strong as he;
25 'Tis not all spirit, pure, and brave
If mixture it of *fear, shame, honor* have.
Perchance, as torches, which must ready be,
Men light and put out, so thou deal'st with me.
Thou cam'st to kindle, goest to come: then I
30 Will dream that hope again, but else would die.

                  (1633)

42. What happened just before the beginning of
this poem?

(A) The speaker was awakened from a nightmare.
(B) The speaker received a visit from his lover.
(C) The speaker's lover woke him up from
a dream.
(D) The speaker was unable to get his lover to
wake up.
(E) The speaker dropped something on the floor
and broke it.

43. What causes the speaker to wake up?

    (A) a glance from his beloved's eyes
    (B) the thought of his beloved
    (C) being shaken awake by his beloved
    (D) the light of the bedside candles
    (E) his beloved's whisper in his ear

44. The lines "Thou art so true that thoughts of thee suffice / To make dreams truths, and fables histories" (lines 7 and 8) represent or include all of the following EXCEPT

    (A) slant rhyme
    (B) hyperbole
    (C) allusion
    (D) enjambment
    (E) heroic couplet

45. Why does the speaker say he is "profane" (line 20) for mistaking his beloved for an angel?

    (A) because comparing a mortal to an angel is blasphemy
    (B) because his beloved is higher and better than an angel
    (C) because he does not believe in angels, God, or heaven
    (D) because he saw an angel in his dream before he woke up
    (E) because only a dead mortal can join the ranks of the angels

46. By "It was a theme / For reason, much too strong for fantasy" (lines 3 and 4), the speaker means

    (A) the reason for his dream was his desire to escape into a fantasy
    (B) in the morning, he will write a logical argument about his dream
    (C) only in a dream could he understand this topic so clearly
    (D) he cannot explain the subject of his dream to his beloved
    (E) he was dreaming about a topic that required serious, conscious thought

47. Which quality does the speaker seem to value most in his beloved?

    (A) her beauty
    (B) her humor
    (C) her intelligence
    (D) her perceptiveness
    (E) her loyalty

48. Which is the best paraphrase of the phrase "Coming and staying show'd thee, thee" (line 21)?

    (A) Coming and staying shows you to yourself.
    (B) Your coming to me and staying proved to me that it really was you.
    (C) I know that only you would ever come to me and stay with me.
    (D) You saw your reflection when you came to me and looked into my eyes.
    (E) When I first woke up I knew right away that it was you.

49. Which is the best explanation of the comparison in the poem's last four lines?

    (A) The beloved kindles the speaker's desire just as a man lights a torch.
    (B) The beloved's eyes are like a torch that lights up a room.
    (C) The love of the two characters is as bright as a torch.
    (D) The lovers are so happy they don't notice when the torch goes out.
    (E) The speaker would recognize his lover even without the light of the torch.

Questions 50–60. Read the following passage carefully before you choose your answers.

The one opened the door with a latch-key and went in, followed by a young fellow who awkwardly removed his cap. He wore rough clothes that smacked of the sea, and he was manifestly out of place in the spacious hall
5 in which he found himself. He did not know what to do with his cap, and was stuffing it into his coat pocket when the other took it from him. The act was done quietly and naturally, and the awkward young fellow appreciated it. "He understands," was his thought. "He'll see me through
10 all right."

He walked at the other's heels with a swing to his shoulders, and his legs spread unwittingly, as if the level floors were tilting up and sinking down to the heave and lunge of the sea. The wide rooms seemed too narrow for
15 his rolling gait, and to himself he was in terror lest his broad shoulders should collide with the doorways or sweep the bric-a-brac from the low mantel. He recoiled from side to side between the various objects and multiplied the hazards that in reality lodged only in his
20 mind. Between a grand piano and a centre-table piled high with books was space for a half a dozen to walk abreast, yet he essayed it with trepidation. His heavy arms hung loosely at his sides. He did not know what to do with those arms and hands, and when, to his excited
25 vision, one arm seemed liable to brush against the books on the table, he lurched away like a frightened horse, barely missing the piano stool. He watched the easy walk of the other in front of him, and for the first time realized that his walk was different from that of other men. He
30 experienced a momentary pang of shame that he should walk so uncouthly. The sweat burst through the skin of his forehead in tiny beads, and he paused and mopped his bronzed face with his handkerchief.

"Hold on, Arthur, my boy," he said, attempting to mask
35 his anxiety with facetious utterance. "This is too much all at once for yours truly. Give me a chance to get my nerve. You know I didn't want to come, an' I guess your fam'ly ain't hankerin' to see me neither."

"That's all right," was the reassuring answer. "You mustn't
40 be frightened at us. We're just homely people—Hello, there's a letter for me."

He stepped back to the table, tore open the envelope, and began to read, giving the stranger an opportunity to recover himself. And the stranger understood and
45 appreciated. His was the gift of sympathy, understanding; and beneath his alarmed exterior that sympathetic process went on. He mopped his forehead dry and glanced about him with a controlled face, though in the eyes there was an expression such as wild animals
50 betray when they fear the trap. He was surrounded by the unknown, apprehensive of what might happen, ignorant of what he should do, aware that he walked and bore himself awkwardly, fearful that every attribue and power of him was similarly afflicted. He was keenly sensitive,
55 hopelessly self-conscious, and the amused glance that the other stole privily at him over the top of the letter burned into him like a dagger-thrust. He saw the glance, but he gave no sign, for among the things he had learned was discipline. Also, that dagger-thrust went to his pride.
60 He cursed himself for having come, and at the same time resolved that, happen what would, having come, he would carry it through. The lines of his face hardened, and into his eyes came a fighting light. He looked about more unconcernedly, sharply observant, every detail of
65 the pretty interior registering itself on his brain. His eyes were wide apart; nothing in their field of vision escaped; and as they drank in the beauty before them the fighting light died out and a warm glow took its place. He was responsive to beauty, and here was cause to respond.

(1909)

50. Arthur is an example of which of the following?

(A) a protagonist
(B) a foil
(C) a main character
(D) an anti-hero
(E) a narrator

51. Which of the following can you conclude about Arthur's guest?

    (A) He has been at sea for a very long time.
    (B) He is clumsy and awkward by nature.
    (C) He tries too hard to impress other people.
    (D) He resents Arthur's attempts to set him at ease.
    (E) He is from an intellectual and artistically inclined family.

52. The guest's response to the "amused glance that the other stole at him" (lines 55–56) shows that the guest is

    (A) cowardly
    (B) good-natured
    (C) unselfconscious
    (D) courageous
    (E) temperamental

53. The author compares the guest to "wild animals" (line 49) and "a frightened horse" (line 26) for all of the following reasons EXCEPT

    (A) to show that he reacts by instinct alone
    (B) to emphasize how out of place he feels
    (C) to describe the strength of his uncertainty
    (D) to demonstrate his awkwardness
    (E) to show that he has no self-control

54. In which respect are Arthur and his guest alike?

    (A) Each wants to reassure the other.
    (B) Each is secretly amused at the other's behavior.
    (C) Each is aware of how the other one feels.
    (D) Each feels awkward in a strange setting.
    (E) Each wants to be a good host.

55. Which line from the passage suggests that in the end, the guest will overcome his discomfort?

    (A) "The wide rooms seemed too narrow for his rolling gait" (lines 14–15)
    (B) "He did not know what to do with those arms and hands" (lines 23–24)
    (C) "[He] realized that his walk was different from that of other men" (lines 28–29)
    (D) "[He] resolved that, happen what would, having come, he would carry it through" (lines 61–62)
    (E) "His eyes were wide apart; nothing in their field of vision escaped" (lines 65–66)

56. In this passage, the author concentrates on

    (A) describing a character
    (B) developing a conflict
    (C) introducing his plot
    (D) foreshadowing the resolution
    (E) analyzing the main theme

57. Why does the author have the guest speak in dialect at the end of the third paragraph?

    (A) to arouse the reader's contempt for him
    (B) to suggest that he is not very smart
    (C) to show that he has not been formally educated
    (D) to indicate where he comes from
    (E) to show that he is a foreigner

58. When Arthur says "We're just homely people" (line 40), he means

    (A) We are plain in appearance.
    (B) Welcome to our home.
    (C) We are rude and unrefined.
    (D) We are simple and ordinary.
    (E) Our home is a nice place.

59. The phrase "facetious utterance" (line 35) means

(A) a joking comment
(B) a cry for help
(C) a shout
(D) a speech in dialect
(E) a plea

60. The description of his home suggests that Arthur is

(A) extremely wealthy
(B) cultured and educated
(C) careless and untidy
(D) sociable and fun-loving
(E) active and athletic

STOP

If you finish before time is called, you may check your work on this test only.

Do not turn to any other test in this book.

Answer Key

1. B	16. A	31. E	46. E
2. E	17. C	32. C	47. D
3. C	18. B	33. B	48. B
4. B	19. B	34. C	49. A
5. A	20. E	35. D	50. B
6. C	21. C	36. A	51. A
7. A	22. A	37. C	52. D
8. B	23. D	38. B	53. E
9. C	24. E	39. D	54. C
10. B	25. A	40. C	55. D
11. C	26. E	41. C	56. A
12. C	27. C	42. C	57. C
13. A	28. C	43. A	58. D
14. D	29. B	44. C	59. A
15. E	30. D	45. B	60. B

Answers and Explanations

1. (B) The context shows that this is a speech to the troops before a major battle. The speaker praises her troops for being so ready and eager to fight; "forwardness" means they have come forward to volunteer.

2. (E) The speaker says she has complete faith in her subjects' loyalty and the rightness of their cause, and she vows to lead the troops herself if need be. These words are intended to instill courage and determination in her hearers.

3. (C) The speaker's advisers warn her against "armed multitudes," which refers to her own soldiers. They believe that if she gives weapons to a citizen army, the citizens may turn against the government.

4. (B) The speaker contrasts herself with a tyrant, saying in effect "Let tyrants fear; I need not fear because I am not a tyrant."

5. (A) The phrase "in the mean" refers to the interval of time between the delivery of this speech and the end of the battle, when the soldiers will receive "rewards and crowns." All five choices define *mean* accurately, but only choice A makes sense in the context.

6. (C) Option I is wrong because the intent of the speech is not to lull, but to call soldiers to action. The mention of kingdom and people is likely to arouse the listeners' patriotic instincts, and the mention of God suggests that the speaker is fighting on the side of justice and right.

7. (A) The speaker shows her determination to protect her kingdom. Her decision to lead her troops herself, if necessary, shows great courage, particularly as she is a woman and thus lacks military experience.

8. (B) "By your obedience / by your concord / by your valor" and "of my God / of my kingdom / of my people" are examples of parallelism or parallel structure—a repetition of a given grammatical pattern for emphasis.

9. (C) The speaker says "rewards and crowns," which suggests that they are two different things. The most likely meaning is "medals and honors," because these are what a monarch would most likely give soldiers after a battle.

10. (B) Of the five choices, only birds have the ability to hover and rest their wings.

11. (C) The speaker explains that she has chosen to "cherish, strengthen and feed" her existence, even though her whole happiness is dead in the lover's grave. She dare not look back at her memories, because if she does, she will not want to "seek the empty world again."

12. (C) The speaker asks her beloved if her love for him has finally been destroyed by time. The phrase "all-severing" implies that time has unlimited power to destroy.

13. (A) The speaker thinks along these lines: "It is dangerous to remember you, because the act of remembering shows me how empty my life is now compared to how rich and full it was when you were alive." By narrating/writing this poem about her lover, she is remembering him. Therefore, this act will make her lose interest in life.

14. (D) The speaker's memories do *not* bring her peace, calm, or serenity. They bring the opposite—violent, unsettling feelings that she describes throughout the poem.

15. (E) The act of narrating and/or writing this poem shows that the speaker *does* dare to "indulge in memory's rapturous pain."

16. **(A)** When the speaker says "No later light has lightened up my heaven, / No second morn has ever shone for me," she means that she has not fallen in love again. The phrase "my only love" (line 3) also supports this answer.

17. **(C)** Stanzas 6 and 7 show that the speaker has made a conscious decision to move forward. Phrases like "sternly denied" and "check the tears of passion" show that it takes both self-control and determination to conquer a great sorrow like hers.

18. **(B)** The author pokes fun at the Lunch Club throughout the passage, showing that the ladies are both pretentious and insincere for pretending that they love books, when all they really want to do is impress themselves and others with a show of interest in literature.

19. **(B)** It is ironic that the lady who owns the finest house is named for an architectural element; a *plinth* is a block used to support the decorative molding over a door or arch.

20. **(E)** Mrs. Leveret is described as being a "subsidiary" member, which means she is of less importance than the others. Osric Dane is not a member at all, but the author who is to be the next guest of honor.

21. **(C)** The image of huntresses, along with the phrase "ladies who pursue Culture in bands," suggests that the Lunch Club members have a basically hostile attitude toward reading; that it is a battle they are determined to win. The image is striking because one expects people who form a book club to do it because they enjoy reading. *Indomitable* means "unconquerable," and *erudition* means "learning."

22. **(A)** Allusion is the correct answer because the author's mention of a character, Osric the Dane, in the play *Hamlet* is a literary reference that the reader is expected to recognize.

23. **(D)** What the ladies truly care about is impressing each other, themselves, and Hillbridge society with their pretensions to being well-read and intellectual. Choices A and B are wrong because these are only the ostensible purposes of the club; these ladies are not genuinely interested in reading and thinking about interesting new books, nor in hearing what the authors have to say. Their interest in literature is a sham.

24. **(E)** *Deploring* means "lamenting or sorrowing over." To *cede* means "to give up." Choice E closely matches these definitions.

25. **(A)** The speaker has written a book that he hopes sailors will read on their voyages.

26. **(E)** Option I is correct because the repeated *w* sound in the line does echo the wash of the ocean waves. Option II is correct because the repetition of the word *waves* and the *w* sound does remind the reader of water, which also begins with *w*. Option III is correct because the speaker echoes the sound of the ocean so successfully it is clear that he has listened to it and loves it.

27. **(C)** In stanza 2, the mariners are looking at the book and saying it reflects not only the lives and experiences of the landsman but also the experiences and images of the ocean. Therefore, they feel that the book's author is a kindred spirit. The poet's belief that he and the mariners will achieve "full rapport" (line 9) through his book also supports this answer choice.

28. **(C)** When the ocean *ebbs,* it retreats from the shore. When it *flows,* it washes up on the shore. The other pairs of words are not opposites.

29. **(B)** The line "Speed on my book!" (line 25) shows that the speaker is directly addressing his book. The book is his "little bark," and its paper pages are the "white sails" that will carry it over the ocean.

30. (D) The lack of regular rhyme, meter, and rhythmic structure make this a free-verse poem.

31. (E) The line "Then falter not O book" shows that the speaker is addressing the book in stanza 3. In stanza 1, the speaker is talking to himself; in stanza 2, he is imagining what the mariners will say when they read his book.

32. (C) *Haply* is an archaic way of saying "perhaps." *Haply will I* means "perhaps I will." The speaker is imagining what *may* happen when "sailors young and old" read his book.

33. (B) The phrase "joyous full of faith" attributes human emotions to the bark.

34. (C) In every line of the poem, the sound effects, alliteration, imagery, and word choice reflect the speaker's deep love for the ocean's power, mystery, and beauty. He is sure the sailors will respond to this because they share the feeling.

35. (D) Grimes protects his enemies by not naming them, and he does this at some cost to himself. Only an ethical, honorable man would make this choice.

36. (A) There is an almost palpable sneer in the words "a glorious, happy and *free* America"— deeply ironic words when written by a former slave.

37. (C) The deeply angry tone of the two sentences shows that choice C is the best response. For choice D to be true, Grimes should have used the same words twice, rather than repeating the same idea in different words.

38. (B) The line "I have forbore to mention names in my history where it might give the least pain" suggests that Grimes is not seeking revenge. Details in the passage and a general knowledge of slave narratives and their contents show that the other four choices are likely reasons for publication.

39. (D) A slave narrative is an autobiography dealing with the writer's life as a slave. The final sentence of the passage proves that Grimes was once a slave, and the first-person point of view shows that the selection is an autobiography.

40. (C) Grimes displays self-pity in his frequent allusions to his troubles—for example, "I am now entirely destitute of property." The final two sentences show both cynicism and open rage; bitterness appears in many references to past injuries. The only quality of the five that he does not display is impatience.

41. (C) It is a given that a slave narrative will describe terrible abuse and suffering. Choice A is wrong because people frequently rewrite their lives inaccurately (in the passage, Grimes refers to his faulty memory). Choice B is wrong because Grimes does not provide any evidence for his statements. Choice D is wrong because an inability to remember does not suggest that he is reliable. Choice E is wrong because Grimes says he is concealing names to protect people, not because he cannot remember them.

42. (C) The lines "Dear love, for nothing less than thee / Would I have broke this happy dream" (lines 1 and 2) make it clear that he was dreaming and his lover woke him up. Because it was a "happy dream," choice A is wrong.

43. (A) The speaker says "Thine eyes, and not thy noise, waked me" (line 12). He compares her eyes to the light of a taper, or candle, but this is only a simile; the actual bedside taper did not wake him.

44. (C) *Suffice / histories* is a slant rhyme, not an exact rhyme. The idea that thoughts of someone can make true histories out of fables is hyperbole, or exaggeration. Line 7 continues without pause into line 8, an example of enjambment. Two rhymed lines of iambic pentameter make a heroic couplet. The lines contain no allusions to any outside source, so choice C is the only one that does not apply.

45. (B) In lines 15–18, the speaker explains that an angel would not be able to see his heart, know his thoughts, know what he was dreaming, or know when to wake him up. Because his lover *does* know all these things, she is a higher form of creation than any angel, and he was *profaning*, or insulting, her by thinking she was "only" an angel.

46. (E) The theme, or subject, of the dream deserves the logical reasoning that the speaker might bring to it awake. It is less appropriate for the fleeting, sensory impressions he feels when he is asleep and dreaming.

47. (D) The speaker praises his beloved at length for her perceptiveness; she is better than an angel because unlike an angel, she can see into his heart and know what he is thinking. The other choices are wrong because he only implies that she has beauty and loyalty, and he says nothing about her humor or intelligence.

48. (B) The action in the poem can be described as follows: The speaker awakens. Confused for a moment, he thinks an angel has awakened him. When his beloved embraces him and remains by his side, he realizes that she is not an angel, but herself. In effect he says to her, "The fact that you came to me and stayed with me showed me that you were indeed you."

49. (A) The speaker says that just as a man can light or douse a torch, his lover can kindle or quench his desire by entering or leaving the room.

50. (B) A foil is a character who serves as a contrast to the main character of a literary work, as Arthur and his guest are contrasted in this passage. The guest, not Arthur, is apparently the main character or protagonist, since his actions and thoughts are described in detail and Arthur's are not.

51. (A) The fact that the guest's clothes "smacked of the sea" and that he walks as if he were on the heaving deck of a ship suggest that he has been away at sea for a very long time. Choice B is wrong because it takes considerable physical grace to be a successful sailor, and the guest seems only afraid of awkwardness because he doesn't yet have his "land legs."

52. (D) When the guest sees that Arthur is laughing at him, it pricks his pride and puts a "fighting light" into his eyes. His feelings are hurt, but he conceals this and determines not to run away. This response shows courage.

53. (E) The guest's fears of breaking something are instinctive, not logical. The guest feels out of place on land in a nice house, because he is so accustomed to being on a ship. He is almost as unsure of himself in this setting as an animal would be. The guest's fear of breaking something emphasizes his awkwardness in his surroundings. Only choice E is untrue; the final paragraph shows that the guest does have self-control and self-discipline.

54. (C) Choices A, B, and E are only true of Arthur. Choice D is only true of the guest. Choice C is true of both; the guest is aware of Arthur's understanding, and observes Arthur's "amused glance." Arthur knows how awkward his guest feels, and he tries to reassure him and give him time to recover.

55. **(D)** The guest's resolve and his vow to "carry it through" suggest, with other details in the passage that show his determination, that he will not give in to his desire to run away.

56. **(A)** This passage concentrates almost exclusively on introducing the reader to the character of Arthur's guest.

57. **(C)** The author indicates that the guest is a "young fellow" who has nonetheless been at sea for several years. This suggests, along with the dialect, that he has had little formal schooling. The author shows sympathy and respect for the guest throughout the passage, so choice A is wrong. Details in the last paragraph show that the guest is observant and aware, so choice B is wrong. Readers could not identify a region from such a short dialogue, so choice D is wrong. A foreigner would speak much more formal English, so choice E is wrong.

58. **(D)** Arthur tries to put his guest at ease with the word *homely*, meaning that he and his family are "just plain folks," simple, friendly, nothing to be alarmed about. Choices A and C are both accurate definitions of *homely,* but they do not fit this context.

59. **(A)** The word *facetious* means "witty." The guest is trying to be clever in a funny way, so that Arthur won't see how scared he feels underneath.

60. **(B)** The presence of the piano and the table "piled high with books," plus the visual beauty that the guest responds to, suggest that Arthur and his family appreciate literature and music. Because Arthur says "we're just homely people" and there are no servants in evidence, they are probably not extremely wealthy. Nothing in the passage supports the other three choices.

How To Calculate Your Score

Count the number of correct answers and enter the total below.

Count the number of wrong answers. Do NOT include any questions you did not answer.

Multiply the number of wrong answers by 0.25 and enter the total below.

Do the subtraction. The answer is your raw score. Use the scoring scale to find your scaled score.

$$\overline{\text{(number of correct answers)}} - \overline{\text{(number of wrong answers} \times 0.25)} = \overline{\text{(raw score)}}$$

RAW SCORE	SCALED SCORE	RAW SCORE	SCALED SCORE	RAW SCORE	SCALED SCORE	RAW SCORE	SCALED SCORE	RAW SCORE	SCALED SCORE
60	800	44	710	28	560	12	420	-4	260
59	800	43	700	27	550	11	410	-5	250
58	800	42	690	26	540	10	400	-6	240
57	800	41	690	25	530	9	390	-7	230
56	800	40	680	24	520	8	380	-8	220
55	800	39	670	23	510	7	370	-9	210
54	790	38	660	22	500	6	360	-10	200
53	790	37	650	21	500	5	350	-11	200
52	780	36	640	20	490	4	340	-12	200
51	770	35	630	19	490	3	330	-13	200
50	760	34	620	18	480	2	320	-14	200
49	750	33	610	17	470	1	310	-15	200
48	740	32	600	16	460	0	300		
47	740	31	590	15	450	-1	290		
46	730	30	580	14	440	-2	280		
45	720	29	570	13	430	-3	270		

Note: This is only a sample scoring scale. Scoring scales differ from exam to exam.

Practice Test 3

The following practice test is designed to be just like the real SAT Literature Test. It matches the actual test in content coverage and degree of difficulty.

Once you finish the practice test, determine your score. Carefully read the answer explanations of the questions you answered incorrectly. Identify any weaknesses in your literature skills by determining the areas in which you made the most errors. Review those sections of this book first. Then, as time permits, go back and review your strengths.

Allow one hour to take the test. Time yourself and work uninterrupted. If you run out of time, take note of where you stopped when time ran out. Remember that you lose a quarter point for each incorrect answer, but you do not lose points for questions you leave blank. Therefore, unless you can eliminate one or more of the five choices, it is best to leave a question unanswered.

Use the following formula to calculate your score:

(number of correct answers) – ¼ (number of incorrect answers)

If you treat this practice test just like the actual exam, it will accurately reflect how you are likely to perform on test day. Here are some hints on how to create test-taking conditions similar to those of the actual exam:

- Complete the test in one sitting. On test day, you will not be allowed to take a break.
- Tear out the answer sheet and fill in the ovals just as you will on the actual test day.
- Have a good eraser and more than one sharp pencil handy. On test day, you will not be able to go get a new pencil if yours breaks.
- Do not allow yourself any extra time; put down your pencil after exactly one hour, no matter how many questions are left to answer.
- Become familiar with the directions on the test. If you go in knowing what the directions say, you will not have to waste time reading and thinking about them on the actual test day.

Answer Sheet

Tear out this answer sheet and use it to mark your answers.

1. Ⓐ Ⓑ Ⓒ Ⓓ Ⓔ	16. Ⓐ Ⓑ Ⓒ Ⓓ Ⓔ	31. Ⓐ Ⓑ Ⓒ Ⓓ Ⓔ	46. Ⓐ Ⓑ Ⓒ Ⓓ Ⓔ
2. Ⓐ Ⓑ Ⓒ Ⓓ Ⓔ	17. Ⓐ Ⓑ Ⓒ Ⓓ Ⓔ	32. Ⓐ Ⓑ Ⓒ Ⓓ Ⓔ	47. Ⓐ Ⓑ Ⓒ Ⓓ Ⓔ
3. Ⓐ Ⓑ Ⓒ Ⓓ Ⓔ	18. Ⓐ Ⓑ Ⓒ Ⓓ Ⓔ	33. Ⓐ Ⓑ Ⓒ Ⓓ Ⓔ	48. Ⓐ Ⓑ Ⓒ Ⓓ Ⓔ
4. Ⓐ Ⓑ Ⓒ Ⓓ Ⓔ	19. Ⓐ Ⓑ Ⓒ Ⓓ Ⓔ	34. Ⓐ Ⓑ Ⓒ Ⓓ Ⓔ	49. Ⓐ Ⓑ Ⓒ Ⓓ Ⓔ
5. Ⓐ Ⓑ Ⓒ Ⓓ Ⓔ	20. Ⓐ Ⓑ Ⓒ Ⓓ Ⓔ	35. Ⓐ Ⓑ Ⓒ Ⓓ Ⓔ	50. Ⓐ Ⓑ Ⓒ Ⓓ Ⓔ
6. Ⓐ Ⓑ Ⓒ Ⓓ Ⓔ	21. Ⓐ Ⓑ Ⓒ Ⓓ Ⓔ	36. Ⓐ Ⓑ Ⓒ Ⓓ Ⓔ	51. Ⓐ Ⓑ Ⓒ Ⓓ Ⓔ
7. Ⓐ Ⓑ Ⓒ Ⓓ Ⓔ	22. Ⓐ Ⓑ Ⓒ Ⓓ Ⓔ	37. Ⓐ Ⓑ Ⓒ Ⓓ Ⓔ	52. Ⓐ Ⓑ Ⓒ Ⓓ Ⓔ
8. Ⓐ Ⓑ Ⓒ Ⓓ Ⓔ	23. Ⓐ Ⓑ Ⓒ Ⓓ Ⓔ	38. Ⓐ Ⓑ Ⓒ Ⓓ Ⓔ	53. Ⓐ Ⓑ Ⓒ Ⓓ Ⓔ
9. Ⓐ Ⓑ Ⓒ Ⓓ Ⓔ	24. Ⓐ Ⓑ Ⓒ Ⓓ Ⓔ	39. Ⓐ Ⓑ Ⓒ Ⓓ Ⓔ	54. Ⓐ Ⓑ Ⓒ Ⓓ Ⓔ
10. Ⓐ Ⓑ Ⓒ Ⓓ Ⓔ	25. Ⓐ Ⓑ Ⓒ Ⓓ Ⓔ	40. Ⓐ Ⓑ Ⓒ Ⓓ Ⓔ	55. Ⓐ Ⓑ Ⓒ Ⓓ Ⓔ
11. Ⓐ Ⓑ Ⓒ Ⓓ Ⓔ	26. Ⓐ Ⓑ Ⓒ Ⓓ Ⓔ	41. Ⓐ Ⓑ Ⓒ Ⓓ Ⓔ	56. Ⓐ Ⓑ Ⓒ Ⓓ Ⓔ
12. Ⓐ Ⓑ Ⓒ Ⓓ Ⓔ	27. Ⓐ Ⓑ Ⓒ Ⓓ Ⓔ	42. Ⓐ Ⓑ Ⓒ Ⓓ Ⓔ	57. Ⓐ Ⓑ Ⓒ Ⓓ Ⓔ
13. Ⓐ Ⓑ Ⓒ Ⓓ Ⓔ	28. Ⓐ Ⓑ Ⓒ Ⓓ Ⓔ	43. Ⓐ Ⓑ Ⓒ Ⓓ Ⓔ	58. Ⓐ Ⓑ Ⓒ Ⓓ Ⓔ
14. Ⓐ Ⓑ Ⓒ Ⓓ Ⓔ	29. Ⓐ Ⓑ Ⓒ Ⓓ Ⓔ	44. Ⓐ Ⓑ Ⓒ Ⓓ Ⓔ	59. Ⓐ Ⓑ Ⓒ Ⓓ Ⓔ
15. Ⓐ Ⓑ Ⓒ Ⓓ Ⓔ	30. Ⓐ Ⓑ Ⓒ Ⓓ Ⓔ	45. Ⓐ Ⓑ Ⓒ Ⓓ Ⓔ	60. Ⓐ Ⓑ Ⓒ Ⓓ Ⓔ

PRACTICE TEST 3

Time: 60 Minutes

Directions: This test consists of selections from literary works and questions on their content, form, and style. After reading each passage or poem, choose the best answer to each question and then fill in the corresponding oval on the answer sheet.

Note: Pay particular attention to the requirements of questions that contain the words NOT or EXCEPT.

Questions 1–9. Read the following poem carefully before you choose your answers.

When most I wink, then do mine eyes best see,
For all the day they view things unrespected;
But when I sleep, in dreams they look on thee,
And darkly bright are bright in dark directed.
5 Then thou, whose shadow shadows doth make bright,
How would thy shadow's form form happy show
To the clear day with thy much clearer light,
When to unseeing eyes thy shade shines so!
How would, I say, mine eyes be blessed made
10 By looking on thee in the living day,
When in dead night thy fair imperfect shade
Through heavy sleep on sightless eyes doth stay!
　　All days are nights to see till I see thee,
　　And nights bright days when dreams do show thee me.

　　　　　　　　　　　　　(1609)

1. Metaphorically, the speaker sees his beloved as a source of
   (A) inspiration
   (B) strength
   (C) light
   (D) love
   (E) shadow

2. When the speaker says that his eyes "view things unrespected" (line 2), he means
   (A) he sees without noticing or observing
   (B) he feels contempt for what he sees
   (C) he cannot see because his eyes are closed
   (D) his love has robbed him of the ability to see
   (E) he feels that he is invisible to others

3. Which of the following can you conclude about the relationship between the speaker and the beloved?
   　I. They are in love with each other and happy together.
   　II. They were in love long ago but no longer see one another.
   　III. They have not seen one another for some time.

   (A) I only
   (B) I and II only
   (C) II only
   (D) III only
   (E) II and III only

4. Which is the best paraphrase of the lines "How would thy shadow's form form happy show / To the clear day with thy much clearer light, / When to unseeing eyes thy shade shines so!" (lines 6–8)?

(A) You were very beautiful when alive, but your ghost that I see in the darkness is even more beautiful.

(B) Given how beautiful your image looks to me in my sleep, think how much more beautiful you would be in the light of day!

(C) How beautiful you would look in the light of day, if people were not too blind to recognize your beauty!

(D) You would look so beautiful in the light of day that you should not be afraid to show yourself.

(E) Even though you have never thought you were beautiful, the admiring stares you draw prove that you are.

5. Which literary element does the poet use most extensively in this sonnet?

(A) contrast
(B) hyperbole
(C) parody
(D) simile
(E) allusion

6. The phrase "thy fair imperfect shade" (line 11) implies which of the following about the beloved?

(A) The speaker does not find her truly beautiful to look at.

(B) She has no existence outside the speaker's imagination.

(C) The beloved is dead and her ghost haunts the speaker.

(D) She is under a magic spell that makes her hard to see.

(E) Her image is hazy because he sees her only in his mind's eye.

7. How do lines 13–14 differ from the first 12 lines?

    I. They form a rhymed couplet.

    II. They restate and summarize the main idea of the poem.

    III. They do not rhyme with any of the other lines.

(A) I only
(B) I and III only
(C) II and III only
(D) I and II only
(E) III only

8. The imagery in this poem appeals most directly to the sense of

(A) sight
(B) hearing
(C) touch
(D) smell
(E) taste

9. By saying "All days are nights" (line 14), the speaker means

(A) days and nights are the same to him
(B) days are dark and overcast
(C) days offer him no pleasure or fun
(D) he can see nothing during the day
(E) he does not like to see people during the day

GO ON TO THE NEXT PAGE ⟼

Questions 10–17. Read the following passage carefully before you choose your answers.

At the upper end of the Fair Ground, in Winesburg, there is a half decayed old grand-stand. It has never been painted and the boards are all warped out of shape. The Fair Ground stands on top of a low hill rising out of the
5 valley of Wine Creek and from the grand-stand one can see at night, over a cornfield, the lights of the town reflected against the sky.

George and Helen climbed the hill to the Fair Ground, coming by the path past Waterworks Pond. The feeling
10 of loneliness and isolation that had come to the young man in the crowded streets of his town was both broken and intensified by the presence of Helen. What he felt was reflected in her.

In youth there are always two forces fighting in people.
15 The warm unthinking little animal struggles against the thing that reflects and remembers, and the older, the more sophisticated thing had possession of George Willard. Sensing his mood, Helen walked beside him filled with respect. When they got to the grand-stand
20 they climbed up under the roof and sat down on one of the long bench-like seats.

There is something memorable in the experience to be had by going into a fair ground that stands at the edge of a Middle Western town on a night after the annual fair
25 has been held. The sensation is one never to be forgotten. On all sides are ghosts, not of the dead, but of living people. Here, during the day just passed, have come the people pouring in from the town and the country around. Farmers with their wives and children and all the people
30 from the hundreds of little frame houses have gathered within these board walls. Young girls have laughed and men with beards have talked of the affairs of their lives. The place has been filled to overflowing with life. It has itched and squirmed with life and now it is night and the
35 life has all gone away. The silence is almost terrifying. One conceals oneself standing silently beside the trunk of a tree and what there is of a reflective tendency in his nature is intensified. One shudders at the thought of the meaninglessness of life while at the same instant, and

40 if the people of the town are his people, one loves life so intensely that tears come into the eyes.

In the darkness under the roof of the grand-stand, George Willard sat beside Helen White and felt very keenly his own insignificance in the scheme of existence.
45 Now that he had come out of town where the presence of the people stirring about, busy with a multitude of affairs, had been so irritating, the irritation was all gone. The presence of Helen renewed and refreshed him. It was as though her woman's hand was assisting him to make
50 some minute readjustment of the machinery of his life. He began to think of the people in the town where he had always lived with something like reverence. He had reverence for Helen. He wanted to love and to be loved by her, but he did not want at the moment to be confused
55 by her womanhood. In the darkness he took hold of her hand and when she crept close put a hand on her shoulder. A wind began to blow and he shivered. With all his strength he tried to hold and to understand the mood that had come upon him. In that high place in the
60 darkness the two oddly sensitive human atoms held each other tightly and waited. In the mind of each was the same thought. "I have come to this lonely place and here is this other," was the substance of the thing felt.

(1919)

10. Which quality in this setting brings out the "reflective tendency" in a person's character?

(A) the silence and stillness
(B) the ghosts of the people who have gone home
(C) the moon lighting up the darkness
(D) the decay of the grand-stand's board seats
(E) the company of another person

11. The "two forces" that "are always fighting in people" (line 14) might be identified as

    (A) youth and age
    (B) temptation and discipline
    (C) the heart and the brain
    (D) courage and fear
    (E) happiness and sorrow

12. From whose point of view is this passage written?

    (A) George's
    (B) Helen's
    (C) a first-person narrator's
    (D) an omniscient narrator's
    (E) a limited third-person narrator's

13. What is the effect of setting this scene at the top of the grand-stand?

    (A) It physically isolates George and Helen from the town, mirroring their emotional isolation from it.
    (B) It explains why George and Helen are so unhappy with each other and the town they live in.
    (C) It intensifies the romance of the scene and foreshadows what is to come.
    (D) It helps the reader identify with George, Helen, and their hopes for romance.
    (E) It allows the reader to understand what kind of town George and Helen come from.

14. The emotion Helen and George feel for each other in the passage is best described as

    (A) romance
    (B) comradeship
    (C) desire
    (D) wariness
    (E) curiosity

15. The phrase "he did not want at the moment to be confused by her womanhood" (lines 54–55) implies that George

    (A) does not like Helen and wants her to leave him alone
    (B) would be more comfortable with Helen if she were a boy
    (C) does not want to kiss Helen or talk to her of love
    (D) regrets bringing Helen to the Fair Ground with him
    (E) does not know what to say to Helen and hopes she will help him

16. Which major theme does the passage address?

    (A) the pain of loving a person who does not respond
    (B) the conformity of small-town society
    (C) the reawakening of nature in spring
    (D) the transition from youth to maturity
    (E) the struggle between temptation and discipline

17. Which of the following can you conclude about the narrator of the passage?

    I. He has been through experiences similar to George and Helen's.
    II. He lives in Winesburg and has often been to the Fair Ground.
    III. He is a close friend of George and Helen's.

    (A) I only
    (B) II only
    (C) I and III only
    (D) II and III only
    (E) III only

Questions 18–24. Read the following poem carefully before you choose your answers.

The Wild Swans at Coole

The trees are in their autumn beauty,
The woodland paths are dry,
Under the October twilight the water
Mirrors a still sky;
5 Upon the brimming water among the stones
Are nine-and-fifty swans.

The nineteenth autumn has come upon me
Since I first made my count;
I saw, before I had well finished,
10 All suddenly mount
And scatter wheeling in great broken rings
Upon their clamorous wings.

I have looked upon those brilliant creatures,
And now my heart is sore.
15 All's changed since I, hearing at twilight,
The first time on this shore,
The bell-beat of their wings above my head,
Trod with a lighter tread.

Unwearied still, lover by lover,
20 They paddle in the cold
Companionable streams or climb the air;
Their hearts have not grown old;
Passion or conquest, wander where they will,
Attend upon them still.

25 But now they drift on the still water,
Mysterious, beautiful;
Among what rushes will they build,
By what lake's edge or pool
Delight men's eyes when I awake some day
30 To find they have flown away?

(1919)

18. The image "their clamorous wings" (line 12) appeals to which of the five senses?

   (A) sight
   (B) hearing
   (C) taste
   (D) touch
   (E) smell

19. In which sense does the speaker use the phrase "attend upon" (line 24)?

   (A) to pay attention to
   (B) to wait for
   (C) to be present at
   (D) to accompany
   (E) to assist; to wait on

20. For the speaker, the swans symbolize

   (A) love
   (B) nature
   (C) grace
   (D) strength
   (E) serenity

21. This poem is best described as

   (A) a ballad
   (B) a sonnet
   (C) a lyric poem
   (D) a narrative poem
   (E) a dramatic monologue

22. Which of the following is an example of slant rhyme?

   (A) stones/swans (lines 5 and 6)
   (B) creatures/twilight (lines 13 and 15)
   (C) head/tread (lines 17 and 18)
   (D) passion/conquest (line 23)
   (E) day/away (lines 29 and 30)

GO ON TO THE NEXT PAGE ⟹

23. What does the speaker mean by saying that the swans' hearts "have not grown old" (line 22)?

(A) They are not the same swans he first saw.
(B) They have made his heart sore.
(C) They are healthy and strong.
(D) They are still capable of feeling emotion.
(E) They show no physical signs of aging.

24. Which best captures the swans' effect on the speaker?

(A) They cause his heart to ache.
(B) They fill him with elation.
(C) They distract him from writing.
(D) They inspire him with awe.
(E) They comfort him with their friendliness.

Questions 25–33. Read the following speech carefully before you choose your answers.

Friends and fellow citizens: I stand before you tonight under indictment for the alleged crime of having voted at the last presidential election, without having a lawful right to vote. It shall be my work this evening to prove
5 to you that in thus voting, I not only committed no crime, but, instead, simply exercised my citizen's rights, guaranteed to me and all United States citizens by the National Constitution, beyond the power of any state to deny.

10 The preamble of the Federal Constitution says:

"We, the people of the United States, in order to form a more perfect union, establish justice, insure domestic tranquility, provide for the common defense, promote the general welfare, and secure the blessings of liberty to
15 ourselves and our posterity, do ordain and establish this Constitution for the United States of America."

It was we, the people; not we, the white male citizens; nor yet we, the male citizens; but we, the whole people, who formed the Union. And we formed it, not to
20 give the blessings of liberty, but to secure them; not to the half of ourselves and the half of our posterity, but to the whole people—women as well as men. And it is a downright mockery to talk to women of their enjoyment of the blessings of liberty while they are
25 denied the use of the only means of securing them provided by this democratic-republican government— the ballot.

For any state to make sex a qualification that must ever result in the disfranchisement of one entire half of the
30 people, is to pass a bill of attainder, or, an ex post facto law, and is therefore a violation of the supreme law of the land. By it the blessings of liberty are forever withheld from women and their female posterity.

To them this government has no just powers derived from
35 the consent of the governed. To them this government is not a democracy. It is not a republic. It is an odious aristocracy; a hateful oligarchy of sex; the most hateful aristocracy ever established on the face of the globe; an oligarchy of wealth, where the rich govern the poor.
40 An oligarchy of learning, where the educated govern the ignorant, or even an oligarchy of race, where the Saxon rules the African, might be endured; but this oligarchy of sex, which makes father, brothers, husband, sons, the oligarchs over the mother and sisters, the wife
45 and daughters, of every household—which ordains all men sovereigns, all women subjects, carries dissension, discord, and rebellion into every home of the nation.

Webster, Worcester, and Bouvier all define a citizen to be a person in the United States, entitled to vote and hold
50 office.

The only question left to be settled now is: Are women persons? And I hardly believe any of our opponents will have the hardihood to say they are not. Being persons, then, women are citizens; and no state has a right to make

GO ON TO THE NEXT PAGE ⟹

55 any law, or to enforce any old law, that shall abridge their privileges or immunities. Hence, every discrimination against women in the constitutions and laws of the several states is today null and void, precisely as is every one against Negroes.

(1873)

25. Which of the following states the main idea of the speech?

   (A) "I stand before you tonight under indictment for the alleged crime of having voted at the last presidential election, without having a lawful right to vote." (lines 1–4)

   (B) "We formed it, not to give the blessings of liberty, but to secure them; not to the half of ourselves and the half of our posterity, but to the whole people—women as well as men." (lines 19–22)

   (C) "To them this government is not a democracy. It is not a republic. It is an odious aristocracy; a hateful oligarchy of sex; the most hateful aristocracy ever established on the face of the globe." (lines 35–38)

   (D) "This oligarchy of sex, which . . . ordains all men sovereigns, all women subjects, carries dissension, discord, and rebellion into every home of the nation." (lines 42–47)

   (E) "Being persons, then, women are citizens; and no state has a right to make any law, or to enforce any old law, that shall abridge their privileges or immunities." (lines 53–56)

26. What is the effect of the repetition of the word "oligarchy" throughout the fifth paragraph?

   (A) to explain why the speaker was arrested

   (B) to identify the speaker's cause with democracy and freedom

   (C) to convince the women in the audience to defy their husbands

   (D) to persuade the speaker's opponents that she is right

   (E) to support the speaker's main idea

27. Why does the speaker cite Webster, Worcester, and Bouvier (line 48)?

   (A) to show that their published writings support her argument

   (B) to suggest that everyone should go home and read their works

   (C) to explain why they accuse her of committing a crime

   (D) to demonstrate that she is an educated citizen

   (E) to emphasize that in the United States, men have more rights than women

28. Why does the speaker address her audience as "fellow citizens" (line 1)?

   I. to draw attention to the subject and main idea of her speech

   II. to remind both male and female listeners that they are citizens

   III. to show that she is a patriotic American

   (A) I only

   (B) II only

   (C) I and III only

   (D) II and III only

   (E) I, II, and III

29. The word "posterity" (line 21) is best defined as

    (A) slaves
    (B) citizens
    (C) representatives
    (D) descendants
    (E) voters

30. Which best characterizes the speaker?

    (A) wistful, dreamy, unrealistic
    (B) emotional, upset, irrational
    (C) satirical, cynical, humorous
    (D) enraged, prejudiced, biased
    (E) stubborn, intelligent, defiant

31. What is meant by the phrase "abridge their privileges or immunities" (lines 55–56)?

    (A) curtail their rights and protections under the law
    (B) make them less able to protect themselves
    (C) allow them to read only shortened versions of important documents
    (D) abolish their right to run for state or national office
    (E) amend the Constitution to grant them the right to vote

32. To which historical event does the speaker allude in the final sentence?

    (A) the American victory over Great Britain in the Revolutionary War
    (B) the national adoption of the Constitution by the individual states
    (C) the passage of the Reconstruction Amendments to the Constitution
    (D) the Union victory at the Battle of Gettysburg during the Civil War
    (E) the start of the Civil War at Fort Sumter, South Carolina, in 1861

33. The speech addresses all of the following universal themes EXCEPT

    (A) love
    (B) equality
    (C) freedom
    (D) progress
    (E) justice

Questions 34–41. Read the following passage carefully before you choose your answers.

And first, truly, to all them that, professing learning, inveigh against poetry, may justly be objected that they go very near to ungratefulness, to seek to deface that which, in the noblest nations and languages that are
5   known, hath been the first light-giver to ignorance, and first nurse, whose milk by little and little enabled them to feed afterwards of tougher knowledges. And will they now play the hedgehog that, being received into the den, drave out his host? Or rather the vipers, that with their
10 birth kill their parents?

Let learned Greece in any of his manifold sciences be able to show me one book before Musaeus, Homer, and Hesiod, all three nothing else but poets. Nay, let any history be brought that can say any writers were there
15 before them, if they were not men of the same skill, as Orpheus, Linus, and some others are named, who, having been the first of that country that made pens deliverers of their knowledge to their posterity, may justly challenge to be called their fathers in learning; for
20 not only in time they had this priority (although in itself antiquity be venerable) but went before them, as causes to draw with their charming sweetness the wild untamed wits to an admiration of knowledge. So, as Amphion was said to move stones with his poetry to build Thebes,
25 and Orpheus to be listened to by beasts, indeed, stony and beastly people; so among the Romans were Livius Andronicus and Ennius. So in the Italian language the first that made it aspire to be a treasure-house of science were the poets Dante, Boccaccio, and Petrarch. So in
30 our English were Gower and Chaucer, after whom, encouraged and delighted with their excellent fore-going, others have followed, to beautify our mother tongue, as well in the same kind as in other arts.

(1595)

34. To "inveigh against poetry" (line 2) means

   (A) to enjoy reading it
   (B) to write it badly
   (C) to express contempt for it
   (D) to teach it in schools
   (E) to refuse to publish it

35. What is the author's main purpose in writing this passage?

   (A) to list great poets of many different nations and cultures
   (B) to praise the great poets of earlier ages
   (C) to complain about the quality of scientific and historical writing
   (D) to persuade people to read more poetry
   (E) to prove that poetry is the greatest of all the arts

36. To support his main argument, the author uses all of the following EXCEPT

   (A) specific examples
   (B) literary and historical allusions
   (C) logical reasoning
   (D) loaded language
   (E) scientific proofs

37. When the author says that "Orpheus, Linus, and some others . . . made pens deliverers of their knowledge to their posterity" (lines 16–18), he means that

   (A) they wrote down their life stories for their descendants to read
   (B) they left their pens to their descendants in their wills
   (C) they passed on to their descendants the ability to write poetry
   (D) their descendants can find out what they knew by reading their written work
   (E) all living poets are descendants of the poets of ancient Greece

GO ON TO THE NEXT PAGE ▸

38. What claim does the author make for poetry in the statement "for not only in time they had this priority . . . but went before them, as causes to draw with their charming sweetness the wild untamed wits to an admiration of knowledge" (lines 19–23)?

    (A) It was developed later than any of the other arts.
    (B) Its beauty attracted listeners and made them want to acquire learning.
    (C) It is superior to science because it is a product of the human imagination.
    (D) It has inspired great writers in every age and culture.
    (E) It was created by the greatest and most famous of the Greek philosophers.

39. To what does the author compare poetry in the opening paragraph?

    (A) light and nourishment
    (B) nations and languages
    (C) hedgehogs and vipers
    (D) history and science
    (E) nobility and toughness

40. In what way does the author suggest that poetry is like the "first nurse" (line 6)?

    (A) It feeds the heart and soul with its beauty.
    (B) It entertains the listener or reader.
    (C) It enriches and nourishes the mind.
    (D) It provides rhymes with which nurses sing babies to sleep.
    (E) It enlightens and teaches ignorant people.

41. To what does the author compare those who criticize poetry in the opening paragraph?

    (A) ungratefulness and ignorance
    (B) first nurse and tougher knowledges
    (C) ignorance and hedgehogs
    (D) ignorance and tougher knowledges
    (E) hedgehogs and vipers

Questions 42–48. Read the following poem carefully before you choose your answers.

Bird-spirit

I am the nearest nightingale
That singeth in Eden after you;
And I am singing loud and true,
And sweet,—I do not fail.
5   I sit upon a cypress bough,
Close to the gate, and I fling my song
Over the gate and through the mail
Of the warden angels marshall'd strong,—
      Over the gate and after you!
10 And the warden angels let it pass,
Because the poor brown bird, alas,
      Sings in the garden, sweet and true.
And I build my song of high pure notes,
      Note over note, height over height,
15   Till I strike the arch of the Infinite,
And I bridge abysmal agonies
With strong, clear calms of harmonies,—
And something abides, and something floats,
In the song which I sing after you.
20   Fare ye well, farewell!
The creature-sounds, no longer audible,
      Expire at Eden's door.
      Each footstep of your treading
Treads out some cadence which ye heard before
25   Farewell! the birds of Eden
      Ye shall hear nevermore!

                                        (c. 1840)

42. For whom is the nightingale singing?

(A) the warden angels
(B) someone who lives in Eden
(C) a poor brown bird
(D) the arch of the Infinite
(E) someone who is leaving Eden

43. What does the author mean in the use of the word "marshall'd" (line 8)?

(A) dispersed
(B) arranged in an orderly manner
(C) arrayed for battle
(D) led ceremoniously
(E) scattered

44. Which is the best definition of "abysmal agonies" (line 16)?

(A) profound suffering
(B) intense physical pain
(C) total ignorance
(D) deep caverns
(E) endless sorrow

45. What can you conclude about the "warden angels" (line 8)?

(A) They do not let anyone out through the gate of Eden.
(B) They are there to protect Eden from intruders or enemies.
(C) They cannot hear the song of the nightingale.
(D) They do not want the nightingale to sing.
(E) They pass judgment on those who live in Eden.

46. The nightingale's chief characteristic is

(A) passion
(B) courage
(C) loyalty
(D) bitterness
(E) timidity

47. The nightingale believes that her song may affect the listener by

(A) charming him

(B) comforting him and easing his sorrow

(C) transforming him into another creature

(D) making him fall in love with her

(E) making him return to her

48. "Farewell! The birds of Eden / Ye shall hear nevermore!" (lines 25–26) is an example of

(A) a couplet

(B) personification

(C) enjambment

(D) free verse

(E) iambic pentameter

Questions 49–60. Read the following passage carefully before you choose your answers.

It was about this time I conceived the bold and arduous project of arriving at moral perfection. I wished to live without committing any fault at any time; I would conquer all that either natural inclination, custom, or
5 company might lead me into. As I knew, or thought I knew, what was right and wrong, I did not see why I might not *always* do the one and avoid the other. But I soon found I had undertaken a task of more difficulty than I had imagined . . .

10 My list of virtues contained at first but twelve. But a Quaker friend having kindly informed me that I was generally thought proud, that my pride showed itself frequently in conversation, that I was not content with being in the right when discussing any point, but was
15 overbearing and rather insolent—of which he convinced me by mentioning several instances—I determined endeavouring to cure myself if I could of this vice or folly among the rest, and I added *Humility* to my list, giving an extensive meaning to the word. I cannot boast
20 of much success in acquiring the *reality* of this virtue, but I had a good deal with regard to the *appearance* of it. I made it a rule to forbear all direct contradiction to the sentiments of others and all positive assertion of my own. I even forbid myself agreeable to the old
25 laws of our Junto,[1] the use of every word or expression in the language that imported a fixed opinion, such as *certainly, undoubtedly,* etc.; and I adopted instead of them, *I conceive, I apprehend,* or *I imagine* a thing to be

so or so, or *It so appears to me at present.* When another
30 asserted something that I thought an error, I denied myself the pleasure of contradicting him abruptly and of showing immediately some absurdity in his proposition; and in answering I began by observing that in certain cases or circumstances his opinion would be right, but
35 in the present case there *appeared* or *seemed to me* some difference, etc. I soon found the advantage of this change in my manners: The conversations I engaged in went on more pleasantly; the modest way in which I proposed my opinions procured them a readier reception and less
40 contradiction; I had less mortification when I was found to be in the wrong, and I more easily prevailed with others to give up their mistakes and join with me when I happened to be in the right. And this mode, which I at first put on with some violence to natural inclination,
45 became at length so easy and so habitual to me that perhaps for these fifty years past no one has ever heard a dogmatical expression escape me. And to this habit (after my character of integrity) I think it principally owing that I had early so much weight with my fellow citizens
50 when I proposed new institutions or alterations in the old, and so much influence in public councils when I became a member. For I was but a bad speaker, never eloquent, subject to much hesitation in my choice of words, hardly correct in language, and yet I generally carried my point.

55 In reality there is perhaps no one of our natural passions so hard to subdue as *pride*; disguise it, struggle with it,

[1] An informal debating and essay-writing club to which the author belonged

GO ON TO THE NEXT PAGE ⟹

beat it down, stifle it, mortify it as much as one pleases, it is still alive, and will every now and then peep out and show itself. You will see it perhaps often in this
60 history. For even if I could conceive that I had completely overcome it, I should probably be proud of my humility.

(1784)

49. In what sense is the Quaker friend "kind" to the author?

      I. in helping him see himself more accurately than before

      II. in refraining from offering any criticism of his character

      III. in helping him to identify the virtues he wants to adopt

(A) I only
(B) II only
(C) III only
(D) I and II only
(E) I and III only

50. The phrase "I had less mortification when I was found to be in the wrong" (lines 40–41) is best paraphrased as

(A) I hated to be proved mistaken, because it was so humiliating.
(B) I was so embarrassed to be proved wrong that I wanted to die.
(C) I never felt the embarrassment of being wrong, because I was always right.
(D) It was no longer so humiliating to have to admit to a mistake.
(E) Other people were more eager than before to prove that I was wrong.

51. The phrase "I should probably be proud of my humility" (line 61) is an example of

(A) a paradox
(B) a metaphor
(C) personification
(D) an allusion
(E) a play on words

52. In the third paragraph, what effect does the series of verbs beginning "disguise it" have?

(A) demonstrates how easy it is to behave humbly
(B) encourages the reader to follow the author's example
(C) supports the point made in the previous clause of the sentence
(D) proves the author's statement that he is a bad speaker
(E) explains why it is important to appear humble

53. Which best characterizes the author of the passage?

(A) self-aware and humorous
(B) haughty and arrogant
(C) mild and humble
(D) temperamental and emotional
(E) gracious and kind

54. The author uses the word "pride" to mean

(A) temperament
(B) intellect
(C) snobbery
(D) arrogance
(E) haughtiness

55. The passage is an example of

(A) an oral history
(B) a persuasive essay
(C) an autobiography
(D) a character analysis
(E) an instruction manual

GO ON TO THE NEXT PAGE ⟹

Practice Test

56. Why does the author find the task of "arriving at moral perfection" to be so difficult?

    (A) because he does not really know right from wrong
    (B) because he is often tempted to do something wrong
    (C) because other people make fun of his attempts to do right
    (D) because there are too many virtues on his list
    (E) because the idea of arriving at moral perfection is unrealistic

57. In which pair do the two words NOT convey the same, or approximately the same, idea?

    (A) bold and arduous (line 1)
    (B) overbearing and insolent (line 15)
    (C) vice or folly (lines 17–18)
    (D) contradiction and assertion (lines 22–23)
    (E) conceive and imagine (line 28)

58. Which line from the passage best supports the writer's claim to have achieved the appearance of humility?

    (A) "I wished to live without committing any fault at any time" (lines 2–3)
    (B) "I was not content with being in the right when discussing any point" (lines 13–14)
    (C) "I soon found the advantage to this change in my manners" (lines 36–37)
    (D) "I was but a bad speaker, never eloquent . . . hardly correct in language" (lines 52–54)
    (E) "In reality there is perhaps no one of our natural passions so hard to subdue as *pride*" (lines 55–56)

59. For the author, the concept of humility encompasses all of the following EXCEPT

    (A) diplomacy
    (B) humor
    (C) modesty
    (D) politeness
    (E) tact

60. The first sentence of the last paragraph includes an example of which literary technique?

    (A) personification
    (B) alliteration
    (C) exposition
    (D) resolution
    (E) prediction

STOP

If you finish before time is called, you may check your work on this test only.

Do not turn to any other test in this book.

Answer Key

1. C	16. D	31. A	46. C
2. A	17. A	32. C	47. B
3. D	18. B	33. A	48. C
4. B	19. B	34. C	49. E
5. A	20. E	35. E	50. D
6. E	21. C	36. E	51. A
7. D	22. A	37. D	52. C
8. A	23. D	38. B	53. A
9. C	24. D	39. A	54. D
10. A	25. E	40. C	55. C
11. C	26. B	41. E	56. B
12. D	27. A	42. E	57. D
13. A	28. E	43. B	58. D
14. B	29. D	44. A	59. B
15. C	30. E	45. B	60. A

Answers and Explanations

1. (C) Throughout the poem, the speaker associates his beloved with images of light.

2. (A) The speaker explains that he pays no attention to what he sees during the day, when his eyes are open. The only image he cares for is that of his beloved, which he only sees at night when his eyes are closed.

3. (D) The speaker says that he never sees his beloved except in his imagination and in his dreams. Therefore option III must be true. Option II cannot be true because the speaker is clearly still in love. Because the two people do not meet, and the speaker never suggests that his love is returned, option I is unlikely to be true.

4. (B) In modern terms, *form happy show* means "make an attractive picture" or "make a lovely sight." The speaker says, in effect, "How lovely your form would appear in the clear light of day, since your image shines so brightly to my unseeing eyes at night!"

5. (A) The poet contrasts images of darkness/light and night/day in almost every line of the sonnet.

6. (E) *Shade* is used here to mean "image." The speaker cannot see the beloved clearly because she is only an image or shadow in his memory; therefore she appears *imperfect*, like an out-of-focus picture.

7. (D) Option I is true; like all Shakespearean sonnets, this poem has three quatrains with an ABAB rhyme scheme, followed by a rhymed couplet. Option II is true because the purpose of a Shakespearean sonnet's final couplet is to sum up, resolve, and/or restate the main ideas set forth in the four quatrains. Option III is not true because lines 13 and 14 rhyme with lines 1 and 3.

8. (A) The images are all about darkness and light and what the speaker can and cannot see.

9. (C) The speaker's only pleasure is seeing his beloved's image, and he can only see her in his dreams at night. Therefore the days are nothing to look forward to or enjoy. Choice B is only correct in a metaphorical sense; choice C is a better description of what the speaker actually means.

10. (A) The narrator suggests that the Fair Ground inspires reflection because it is quiet and deserted, when its normal state is to be crowded, busy, and noisy. The fact that everyone has gone home contributes to this, but it is the place itself, not the people who have gone home, that puts George and Helen in a thoughtful mood.

11. (C) The narrator describes the two forces as animal warmth and a quality that "reflects and remembers." These can readily be identified with the brain and the emotions, or the heart.

12. (D) *Omniscient* means "all-knowing." An omniscient narrator may share any or all the characters' thoughts and feelings with the reader. The narrator of this passage describes both George's and Helen's thoughts. A limited third-person narrator could only describe one character's thoughts. A first-person narrator would use the pronouns *I* and *me*.

13. (A) The top of the grand-stand is as far as George and Helen can get from the rest of the town without leaving it. Their physical isolation up there echoes the loneliness and isolation of their mood.

14. (B) The boy and girl achieve true mutual understanding in the passage, without having to say anything. They are united in thought and feeling. This makes them kindred spirits, comrades, or true friends. *Romance* and *desire* are inappropriate choices because George specifically does not want "to be confused by Helen's womanhood" at this moment.

15. **(C)** George's feelings for Helen are intense, but they are not romantic or physical. In this scene, they respond to one another as two human beings, not as a boy and girl. For the moment, George wants to experience this deep human communication, rather than turning it into a conventional romantic or physical situation.

16. **(D)** The passage describes a crucial moment in George's life (and to a lesser extent in Helen's)—the moment when he begins to leave his boyhood behind to become a mature adult.

17. **(A)** The narrator never identifies himself, so there is no way to know whether he knows George and Helen or comes from the same town. He does know from his own knowledge what it is like to go to a Midwestern fair ground at night, and he describes doing much the same thing that George and Helen do; in his case, "standing silently beside the trunk of a tree" and reflecting on life and on the people in his community.

18. **(B)** *Clamorous* means "noisy." Swans are very large birds, and when they take off in flight, their wings make a tremendous noise.

19. **(B)** All five are correct definitions of *attend upon*, but the context makes it clear that the speaker uses the archaic meaning "wait for." No matter where the swans go, high adventures and strong emotions wait for them.

20. **(E)** The speaker comments that the swans' "hearts have not grown old," contrasting this to his own heart, which is "sore." He characterizes them as being untroubled and "unwearied," wishing he were the same. Serenity best captures what he sees and longs for in the swans.

21. **(C)** A lyric poem has a single speaker who describes his or her personal thoughts and feelings. It does not tell a story so much as it evokes an emotion in the reader.

22. **(A)** Slant rhyme (or off rhyme) refers to two words that have the same consonant sounds, but different vowel sounds. *Stones/swans* is thus an example of slant rhyme. Choices C and E are exact rhymes, and choices B and D are words that do not rhyme at all.

23. **(D)** In spite of the passage of years, the swans are "unwearied." "Their hearts have not grown old" means that their emotions are still those of youth—strong and passionate.

24. **(D)** The speaker describes the swans as *brilliant, beautiful,* and *mysterious.* Choice D best captures the thrill that their beauty, strength, and majesty give him. Since he is unhappy, choice B must be wrong. Choice A is wrong because, if anything, the sight of the swans' beauty seems to comfort him.

25. **(E)** The speaker's main purpose is to prove to her audience that women are citizens and therefore have the right to vote.

26. **(B)** By stating that her opponents support oligarchy, or government by the few, the speaker implies that those who agree with her support democracy. By repeating *oligarchy* so many times in a few sentences, she implies that her opponents and their beliefs are undemocratic, therefore un-American and wrong.

27. **(A)** The speaker cites respected works of reference to prove that important writers agree with her main point.

28. **(E)** Options I and II are true because the opening address emphasizes the main point; everyone born in the United States is a citizen and is thus entitled to certain rights, such as the right to vote when old enough. Option III is true because anyone who exercises the right to vote is doing his or her civic duty, taking an active part in government, and is by that very act a patriotic American.

29. **(D)** The context shows that *posterity* refers to future generations of a family or society.

30. **(E)** The first three choices are clearly wrong. Choice D is an overstatement; the speaker is too reasonable and logical in her argument to be labeled *biased* or *prejudiced*. Choice E fairly sums her up as someone who is so determined to fight for her rights that she is even willing to risk arrest.

31. **(A)** To *abridge* means to make less, to curtail, to shorten. A *privilege*, in this context, is a legal right. An *immunity* is a legal protection.

32. **(C)** The reference to "Negroes," the post–Civil War date of the passage (1873), and the fact that the topic is constitutional rights are the clues that tell you she is referring to the passage of the amendments that abolished slavery and granted African Americans the right to vote (Amendments 13–15, passed between 1865 and 1870).

33. **(A)** The speech deals with *equality* of the sexes, *freedom* for women, the *progress* of society toward the ideals of democracy, and the *justice* of giving equal rights to all citizens. Only choice A is not addressed in this speech.

34. **(C)** The context makes it clear that the speaker is defending poetry against those who criticize or sneer at it.

35. **(E)** Almost every sentence in the passage is written to show that poetry is the earliest and greatest of the arts. Choices A and B are secondary purposes used to support the primary purpose described in choice E. Choice D might be an effect of reading the passage but is not part of the author's purpose.

36. **(E)** The poets' names and descriptions of their activities account for choices A and B. The general tone of the passage and the specific supporting details account for choice C. The comparison to hedgehogs and vipers accounts for choice D. The only type of persuasion that does NOT appear is choice E.

37. **(D)** Pens deliver knowledge by writing it down on paper, so that it can be passed on to future generations. The author is saying that Orpheus, Linus, and the others wrote down what they knew, and thus passed on their knowledge to those who came after them.

38. **(B)** The author states that poetry is so charming and enticing that it made people enjoy reading and learning; because studying poetry is so delightful, people begin to seek other kinds of knowledge.

39. **(A)** The author states that poetry is a "light-giver to ignorance" and humankind's "first nurse."

40. **(C)** The nurse's milk feeds and nourishes the baby, making it strong enough to eat and digest solid food. In the same way, poetry enriches and nourishes the mind, stretching it and opening it up so that it can understand more difficult subjects, such as science or philosophy.

41. **(E)** The author compares those who criticize poetry to hedgehogs that drive their hosts out of the den and vipers who kill their parents at birth. Ungratefulness is mentioned, but those who criticize poetry are not compared to it. Ignorance is mentioned in the context of poetry being the first light-giver. "Tougher knowledges" are the disciplines that developed from poetry.

42. **(E)** The line "I fling my song / Over the gate and after you" makes it clear that the bird is in Eden, but the one for whom she sings is outside the gate. The repeated "Farewell" and the reference to "each footstep of your treading" suggest that the listener started out in Eden but is moving away.

43. **(B)** The angels are the wardens of heaven and are placed in a formation as guards at the entrance. The best match is choice B. Choices A and E are wrong because "dispersed" and "scattered" mean the opposite of orderly. These choices are also synonyms, which should indicate to you that they are wrong. Even though "marshall'd" has a military tone, choice C is wrong because the angels are not preparing for battle. Choice D is wrong because the angels are not going anywhere.

44. **(A)** *Abysmal* means "like an abyss," therefore "profound, deep." *Agonies* in this context means "suffering."

45. **(B)** The word "warden" shows that the angels are guards at the gate. It is a guard's job either to keep enemies from entering an enclosed place or to prevent prisoners from leaving. The best match to this is choice B. Because the exile is leaving Eden, choice A is wrong.

46. **(C)** You can conclude that the exile from Eden must have committed a sin or crime, or he would not be sent away. The nightingale's concern for the exile, and her attempt to reach him in song, prove that she is loyal to him in spite of his transgression.

47. **(B)** The line "And I bridge abysmal agonies" suggests that the nightingale sings in order to give comfort to one who is suffering.

48. **(C)** A line of verse that has a punctuation mark at the end is referred to as *end-stopped*. If the line has no punctuation mark at the end, the thought continues without pause to the next line. This technique is called *enjambment*.

49. **(E)** The Quaker pointed out a serious character flaw to the author, thus helping him to overcome it. Once the author sees his own flaw, he can complete his list of virtues. Option II is wrong because the Quaker did exactly the opposite of this.

50. **(D)** *Mortification* is a somewhat more intense synonym for "humiliation"—if you are *mortified,* you literally "wish you were dead." The author explains that it was much more humiliating to be proved wrong when he was overly insistent in the first place on being right. Now that he is less insistent, he is less embarrassed when he turns out to be mistaken.

51. **(A)** A paradox is a statement that includes a contradiction. A truly humble person cannot be proud, because humility means the absence of pride. Yet, the possession of such a great virtue as humility is something to be proud of.

52. **(C)** The sentence's opening clause states that "there is . . . no one of our natural passions so hard to subdue as pride." The series of verbs supports this point by describing this as a physical effort: "struggle with it, beat it down, stifle it" all describe hard physical work.

53. **(A)** The author's open avowal that he is not really humble, but only appears so, shows how aware he is of his true character. The general tone of the passage is humorous, especially the final sentence.

54. **(D)** To the author, *pride* seems to mean an unswerving belief in the rightness of his own opinions and an insistence on proving wrong anyone who disagrees with him. *Righteousness*—a firm belief that one is always right—is the best match for this kind of pride. *Haughtiness* and *snobbery* refer to pride in one's social superiority; because the author discusses only his sense of intellectual superiority, these are not accurate definitions of *pride* as described in this passage.

55. **(C)** The passage describes certain experiences in the author's life. He makes some comments about his own character, but this is not the primary purpose of the passage. A reader wishing to follow the author's example might use the text as an instructional manual, but the author's primary purpose was to write the story of his life.

56. (B) The author says that speaking humbly is against his natural inclinations and that contradicting people and making them look foolish was a pleasure to him. In other words, he is accustomed to doing the wrong thing because of strong temptation. Although moral perfection sounds like an unrealistic goal, the speaker apparently did achieve it.

57. (D) A *contradiction* is a denial; an *assertion* is the opposite, a positive statement.

58. (D) This statement is the most self-deprecating, or humble, of the five choices, and thus provides the best evidence that the author has succeeded in his goal of at least appearing humble.

59. (B) The author has a sense of humor but does not suggest that humor is an essential part of being humble. He does explain and demonstrate that if a person wishes not to appear proud, he or she must master tact, modesty, diplomacy, and politeness.

60. (A) Pride is personified throughout the entire sentence as an entity that can be struggled with, beaten down, stifled and mortified.

How To Calculate Your Score

Count the number of correct answers and enter the total below.

Count the number of wrong answers. Do NOT include any questions you did not answer.

Multiply the number of wrong answers by 0.25 and enter the total below.

Do the subtraction. The answer is your raw score. Use the scoring scale to find your scaled score.

$$\overline{\text{(number of correct answers)}} - \overline{\text{(number of wrong answers} \times 0.25)} = \overline{\text{(raw score)}}$$

RAW SCORE	SCALED SCORE	RAW SCORE	SCALED SCORE	RAW SCORE	SCALED SCORE	RAW SCORE	SCALED SCORE	RAW SCORE	SCALED SCORE
60	800	44	710	28	560	12	420	-4	260
59	800	43	700	27	550	11	410	-5	250
58	800	42	690	26	540	10	400	-6	240
57	800	41	690	25	530	9	390	-7	230
56	800	40	680	24	520	8	380	-8	220
55	800	39	670	23	510	7	370	-9	210
54	790	38	660	22	500	6	360	-10	200
53	790	37	650	21	500	5	350	-11	200
52	780	36	640	20	490	4	340	-12	200
51	770	35	630	19	490	3	330	-13	200
50	760	34	620	18	480	2	320	-14	200
49	750	33	610	17	470	1	310	-15	200
48	740	32	600	16	460	0	300		
47	740	31	590	15	450	-1	290		
46	730	30	580	14	440	-2	280		
45	720	29	570	13	430	-3	270		

Note: This is only a sample scoring scale. Scoring scales differ from exam to exam.

Practice Test 4

The following practice test is designed to be just like the real SAT Literature Test. It matches the actual test in content coverage and degree of difficulty.

Once you finish the practice test, determine your score. Carefully read the answer explanations of the questions you answered incorrectly. Identify any weaknesses in your literature skills by determining the areas in which you made the most errors. Review those sections of this book first. Then, as time permits, go back and review your strengths.

Allow one hour to take the test. Time yourself and work uninterrupted. If you run out of time, take note of where you stopped when time ran out. Remember that you lose a quarter point for each incorrect answer, but you do not lose points for questions you leave blank. Therefore, unless you can eliminate one or more of the five choices, it is best to leave a question unanswered.

Use the following formula to calculate your score:

(number of correct answers) – ¼ (number of incorrect answers)

If you treat this practice test just like the actual exam, it will accurately reflect how you are likely to perform on test day. Here are some hints on how to create test-taking conditions similar to those of the actual exam:

- Complete the test in one sitting. On test day, you will not be allowed to take a break.
- Tear out the answer sheet and fill in the ovals just as you will on the actual test day.
- Have a good eraser and more than one sharp pencil handy. On test day, you will not be able to go get a new pencil if yours breaks.
- Do not allow yourself any extra time; put down your pencil after exactly one hour, no matter how many questions are left to answer.
- Become familiar with the directions on the test. If you go in knowing what the directions say, you will not have to waste time reading and thinking about them on the actual test day.

Answer Sheet

Tear out this answer sheet and use it to mark your answers.

1. (A) (B) (C) (D) (E)	16. (A) (B) (C) (D) (E)	31. (A) (B) (C) (D) (E)	46. (A) (B) (C) (D) (E)
2. (A) (B) (C) (D) (E)	17. (A) (B) (C) (D) (E)	32. (A) (B) (C) (D) (E)	47. (A) (B) (C) (D) (E)
3. (A) (B) (C) (D) (E)	18. (A) (B) (C) (D) (E)	33. (A) (B) (C) (D) (E)	48. (A) (B) (C) (D) (E)
4. (A) (B) (C) (D) (E)	19. (A) (B) (C) (D) (E)	34. (A) (B) (C) (D) (E)	49. (A) (B) (C) (D) (E)
5. (A) (B) (C) (D) (E)	20. (A) (B) (C) (D) (E)	35. (A) (B) (C) (D) (E)	50. (A) (B) (C) (D) (E)
6. (A) (B) (C) (D) (E)	21. (A) (B) (C) (D) (E)	36. (A) (B) (C) (D) (E)	51. (A) (B) (C) (D) (E)
7. (A) (B) (C) (D) (E)	22. (A) (B) (C) (D) (E)	37. (A) (B) (C) (D) (E)	52. (A) (B) (C) (D) (E)
8. (A) (B) (C) (D) (E)	23. (A) (B) (C) (D) (E)	38. (A) (B) (C) (D) (E)	53. (A) (B) (C) (D) (E)
9. (A) (B) (C) (D) (E)	24. (A) (B) (C) (D) (E)	39. (A) (B) (C) (D) (E)	54. (A) (B) (C) (D) (E)
10. (A) (B) (C) (D) (E)	25. (A) (B) (C) (D) (E)	40. (A) (B) (C) (D) (E)	55. (A) (B) (C) (D) (E)
11. (A) (B) (C) (D) (E)	26. (A) (B) (C) (D) (E)	41. (A) (B) (C) (D) (E)	56. (A) (B) (C) (D) (E)
12. (A) (B) (C) (D) (E)	27. (A) (B) (C) (D) (E)	42. (A) (B) (C) (D) (E)	57. (A) (B) (C) (D) (E)
13. (A) (B) (C) (D) (E)	28. (A) (B) (C) (D) (E)	43. (A) (B) (C) (D) (E)	58. (A) (B) (C) (D) (E)
14. (A) (B) (C) (D) (E)	29. (A) (B) (C) (D) (E)	44. (A) (B) (C) (D) (E)	59. (A) (B) (C) (D) (E)
15. (A) (B) (C) (D) (E)	30. (A) (B) (C) (D) (E)	45. (A) (B) (C) (D) (E)	60. (A) (B) (C) (D) (E)

PRACTICE TEST 4

Time: 60 Minutes

Directions: This test consists of selections from literary works and questions on their content, form, and style. After reading each passage or poem, choose the best answer to each question and then fill in the corresponding oval on the answer sheet.

Note: Pay particular attention to the requirements of questions that contain the words NOT or EXCEPT.

Questions 1–9. Read the following dramatic excerpt carefully before you choose your answers.

ACT I SCENE 2
A room in Sir Peter Teazle's house.
(Enter Sir Peter.)

SIR PETER. When an old bachelor marries a young wife, what is he to expect? 'Tis now six months since Lady Teazle made me the happiest of men—and I have been the most miserable dog ever since! We tiffed a little going
5 to church, and fairly quarreled before the bells had done ringing. I was more than once nearly choked with gall during the honeymoon, and had lost all comfort in life before my friends had done wishing me joy. Yet I chose with caution—a girl bred wholly in the country, who
10 never knew luxury beyond one silk gown, nor dissipation above the annual gala of a race ball. Yet she now plays her part in all the extravagant fopperies of fashion and the town, with as ready a grace as if she never had seen a bush or a grass-plot out of Grosvenor Square! I am sneered
15 at by all my acquaintance, and paragraphed in the newspapers. She dissipates my fortune, and contradicts all my humors; yet the worst of it is, I doubt I love her, or I should never bear all this. However, I'll never be weak enough to own it.

(Enter Rowley.)

20 ROWLEY. Oh! Sir Peter, your servant: how is it with you, sir?
SIR PETER. Very bad, Master Rowley, very bad. I meet with nothing but crosses and vexations.
ROWLEY. What can have happened since yesterday?
25 SIR PETER. A good question to a married man!

ROWLEY. Nay, I'm sure, Sir Peter, your lady can't be the cause of your uneasiness.
SIR PETER. Why, has anybody told you she was dead?
ROWLEY. Come, come, Sir Peter, you love her,
30 notwithstanding your tempers don't exactly agree.
SIR PETER. But the fault is entirely hers, Master Rowley. I am, myself, the sweetest-tempered man alive, and hate a teasing temper; and so I tell her a hundred times a day.
ROWLEY. Indeed!
35 SIR PETER. Ay; and what is very extraordinary, in all our disputes she is always in the wrong!

(1777)

1. When Sir Peter says he was "nearly choked with gall" (line 6), he means he felt

   (A) angry
   (B) bitter
   (C) foolish
   (D) upset
   (E) jealous

2. Which of the following is closest in meaning to "tiffed" (line 4)?

   (A) argued
   (B) kissed
   (C) ate
   (D) prayed
   (E) delayed

3. Why is Sir Peter surprised that Lady Teazle enjoys "the extravagant fopperies of fashion and the town"?

   (A) When he met her, she was living simply, quietly, and modestly.
   (B) He thought she was too much in love with him to want to go out all the time.
   (C) He knows that she is a quarrelsome person who does not enjoy society.
   (D) Before their marriage, she had promised to be a thrifty and frugal wife.
   (E) She married him in order to have children as soon as possible.

4. In which sense does Sir Peter use the word "doubt" (line 17)?

   (A) state
   (B) wish
   (C) hate
   (D) question
   (E) believe

5. This play is best described as

   (A) a tragedy
   (B) a comedy
   (C) a morality play
   (D) theater of the absurd
   (E) a romance

6. "She dissipates my fortune" (line 16) means

   (A) It is my bad luck that she likes to spend money.
   (B) She has brought me bad luck.
   (C) She spends my money too freely.
   (D) She takes money from me to send home to her parents.
   (E) I always argue with her about money.

7. The frequent use of hyperbole in Sir Peter's long opening speech allows the reader to conclude that he

   (A) wishes he had married an older woman
   (B) gets irritated and annoyed over every little thing
   (C) has an optimistic view of his situation
   (D) enjoys feeling sorry for himself
   (E) has a poetic streak in his nature

8. From the comment "I'll never be weak enough to own it" (lines 18–19), you can conclude that

   (A) Sir Peter is not a strong or forceful man
   (B) Sir Peter sees marriage as a battle that he is determined to win
   (C) Lady Teazle has no power over Sir Peter
   (D) Lady Teazle knows how much Sir Peter loves her
   (E) Sir Peter is a generous husband

9. Which best describes Rowley's main function in this excerpt?

   (A) to set up funny lines spoken by Sir Peter
   (B) to win the audience's sympathy and interest
   (C) to defend Lady Teazle from Sir Peter's attacks
   (D) to act as a go-between for Sir Peter and Lady Teazle
   (E) to show the audience that Sir Peter is a wealthy man

GO ON TO THE NEXT PAGE ➡

Questions 10–18. Read the following poem carefully before you choose your answers.

Dover Beach

The sea is calm to-night,
The tide is full, the moon lies fair
Upon the Straits;—on the French coast, the light
Gleams, and is gone; the cliffs of England stand,
5   Glimmering and vast, out in the tranquil bay.
Come to the window, sweet is the night air!
Only, from the long line of spray
Where the ebb meets the moon-blanch'd sand,
Listen! you hear the grating roar
10 Of pebbles which the waves suck back, and fling,
At their return, up the high strand,
Begin, and cease, and then again begin,
With tremulous cadence slow, and bring
The eternal note of sadness in.

15   Sophocles long ago
Heard it on the Aegean, and it brought
Into his mind the turbid ebb and flow
Of human misery; we
Find also in the sound a thought,
20 Hearing it by this distant northern sea.

The sea of faith
Was once, too, at the full, and round earth's shore
Lay like the folds of a bright girdle furl'd;
But now I only hear
25 Its melancholy, long, withdrawing roar,
Retreating to the breath
Of the night-wind down the vast edges drear
And naked shingles of the world.

Ah, love, let us be true
30 To one another! for the world, which seems
To lie before us like a land of dreams,
So various, so beautiful, so new,
Hath really neither joy, nor love, nor light,
Nor certitude, nor peace, nor help for pain;
35 And we here as on a darkling plain
Swept with confused alarms of struggle and flight,
Where ignorant armies clash by night.

(1867)

10. "Certitude" (line 34) is best defined as

(A) facts and statistics
(B) insanity or lack of reason
(C) equality under the law
(D) sense of right and wrong
(E) unarguable belief or faith

11. "The moon-blanch'd sand" (line 8) appears to be which color?

(A) black
(B) white
(C) gold
(D) tan
(E) red

12. Which experience does the speaker share with Sophocles?

(A) hearing the sea waves wash pebbles up on the shore
(B) having a serious talk with a lover late one night
(C) realizing that the world is a place without hope or faith
(D) looking at the Aegean Sea by the light of the moon
(E) viewing the French coast and the English cliffs by night

13. What is the source of the speaker's perception of the world as a joyless and dark place?

(A) the prevalence of wars between nations
(B) the decline of religious faith
(C) the extent of human misery
(D) his memories of Sophocles
(E) the tone of his lover's remarks

14. In the lines "And we here as on a darkling plain /
Swept with confused alarms of struggle and
flight, / Where ignorant armies clash by night"
(lines 35–37), the speaker compares himself and
his lover to

   (A) soldiers
   (B) prisoners of war
   (C) criminals
   (D) refugees
   (E) survivors

15. To the speaker, the sound of the "grating roar /
Of pebbles which the waves suck back"
(lines 9–10) seems

   (A) eerie
   (B) calming
   (C) ominous
   (D) terrifying
   (E) painful

16. During the course of the poem, the speaker's
mood changes from

   (A) pensive to alert
   (B) serene to apprehensive
   (C) anxious to calm
   (D) romantic to sensible
   (E) amused to outraged

17. How does the speaker contradict his own
statement that the world "Hath really neither joy,
nor love, nor light / Nor certitude, nor peace, nor
help for pain (lines 33–34)?

   (A) by perceiving the "eternal note of sadness"
       in the sound of the sea
   (B) by recalling Sophocles' meditations on
       human misery
   (C) by appealing to his lover to remain true
   (D) by comparing the "sea of faith" to "a bright
       girdle"
   (E) by comparing the faithless to "ignorant
       armies"

18. The word "turbid" (line 17) means

   (A) evil, wicked
   (B) raucous, noisy
   (C) nonstop, endless
   (D) spinning, dizzy
   (E) muddy, unclear

GO ON TO THE NEXT PAGE ⟼

Questions 19–24. Read the following poem carefully before you choose your answers.

E'en like two little bank-dividing brooks,
  That wash the pebbles with their wanton streams,
And having ranged and search'd a thousand nooks,
  Meet both at length in silver-breasted Thames,
5   Where in a greater current they conjoin:
So I my Best-belovèd's am; so He is mine.

E'en so we met; and after long pursuit,
  E'en so we joined; we both became entire;
No need for either to renew a suit,
10   For I was flax, and He was flames of fire:
    Our firm-united souls did more than twine;
So I my Best-belovèd's am; so He is mine.

If all those glittering Monarchs, that command
  The servile quarters of this earthly ball,
15 Should tender in exchange their shares of land,
  I would not change my fortunes for them all:
    Their wealth is but a counter to my coin:
    The world's but theirs; but my Belovèd's mine.

                                                    (1635)

19. In what sense does the poet use the word "counter" (line 17)?

(A) one who adds up items to find a total
(B) a chip or token used in place of actual money
(C) a weight used to balance a scale
(D) a response that disagrees with a statement
(E) a long, hard, table-like surface

20. The poet uses the extended comparison to "two little bank-dividing brooks" (line 1) to show the speaker's

(A) appreciation of the beauties of nature
(B) understanding of natural science
(C) sense of profound unity with the Beloved
(D) dwelling-place by the riverbank
(E) passionate desire for the Beloved

21. In the third stanza, the speaker will not "change my fortunes" for which of the following?

(A) a gala ball given in the speaker's honor
(B) the riches of all the local merchants
(C) a promise of eternal life in heaven
(D) the kingdoms of the earth
(E) a beautiful new house with rich furnishings

22. The Beloved might be identified with which of the following?

  I. God
  II. the speaker's spouse or lover
  III. the speaker's favorite child

(A) I and II only
(B) II only
(C) II and III only
(D) III only
(E) I, II, and III

23. The repetition of the line "So I my Best-belovèd's am; so He is mine"

(A) stresses the speaker's belief that the union with the Beloved is eternal
(B) explains why the speaker is attached to the Beloved
(C) emphasizes the strength of the speaker's attachment to the Beloved
(D) clarifies that the Beloved dominates the speaker in their relationship
(E) reveals the meaning of the figurative language in lines 10 and 17

24. The phrase "their wanton streams" (line 2) means

(A) the speaker and the Beloved desire one another
(B) the water in the brooks tumbles playfully over the pebbles
(C) the speaker treats the Beloved with willful cruelty
(D) the stream is a popular meeting place for lovers
(E) the speaker and the Beloved feel merry when they see the water

GO ON TO THE NEXT PAGE ⟼

Questions 25–32. Read the following passage carefully before you choose your answers.

Into the First National Bank of San Rosario the newcomer walked, never slowing his brisk step until he stood at the cashier's window. The bank opened for business at nine, and the working force was already
5 assembled, each member preparing his department for the day's business. The cashier was examining the mail when he noticed the stranger standing at his window.

"Bank doesn't open 'til nine," he remarked, curtly, but without feeling. He had had to make that statement
10 so often to early birds since San Rosario adopted city banking hours.

"I am well aware of that," said the other man, in cool, brittle tones. "Will you kindly receive my card?"

J. F. C. NETTLEWICK

National Bank Examiner

"Oh—er—will you walk around inside, Mr.—er—
15 Nettlewick. Your first visit—didn't know your business, of course. Walk right around, please."

The examiner was quickly inside the sacred precincts of the bank, where he was ponderously introduced to each employee in turn by Mr. Edlinger, the cashier—a middle-
20 aged gentleman of deliberation, discretion, and method.

"I was kind of expecting Sam Turner round again, pretty soon," said Mr. Edlinger. "Sam's been examining us now for about four years. I guess you'll find us all right, though, considering the tightness in business. Not overly
25 much money on hand, but able to stand the storms, sir, stand the storms."

"Mr. Turner and I have been ordered by the Comptroller to exchange districts," said the examiner, in his decisive, formal tones. "He is covering my old territory in southern
30 Illinois and Indiana. I will take the cash first, please."

Perry Dorsey, the teller, was already arranging his cash on the counter for the examiner's inspection. He knew

it was right to a cent, and he had nothing to fear, but he was nervous and flustered. So was every man in the bank.
35 There was something so icy and swift, so impersonal and uncompromising about this man that his very presence seemed an accusation. He looked to be a man who would never make nor overlook an error.

Mr. Nettlewick first seized the currency, and with a rapid,
40 almost juggling motion, counted it by packages. Then he spun the sponge cup toward him and verified the count by bills. His thin, white fingers flew like some expert musician's upon the keys of a piano. He dumped the gold upon the counter with a crash, and the coins whined and
45 sang as they skimmed across the marble slab from the tips of his nimble digits. The air was full of fractional currency when he came to the halves and quarters. He counted the last nickel and dime. He had the scales brought, and he weighed every sack of silver in the vault. He questioned
50 Dorsey concerning each of the cash memoranda—certain checks, charge slips, etc., carried over from the previous day's work—with unimpeachable courtesy, yet with something so mysteriously momentous in his frigid manner, that the teller was reduced to pink cheeks and a
55 stammering tongue.

This newly imported examiner was so different from Sam Turner. It had been Sam's way to enter the bank with a shout, pass the cigars, and tell the latest stories he had picked up on his rounds. His customary greeting to
60 Dorsey had been, "Hello, Perry! Haven't skipped out with the boodle yet, I see." Turner's way of counting the cash had been different, too. He would finger the packages of bills in a tired kind of way, and then go into the vault and kick over a few sacks of silver, and the thing was done.
65 Halves and quarters and dimes? Not for Sam Turner. "No chicken feed for me," he would say when they were set before him. "I'm not in the agricultural department." But then, Turner was a Texan, an old friend of the bank's president, and had known Dorsey since he was a baby.

(c. 1905)

25. Which detail suggests the cause for the Comptroller's order that Nettlewick and Turner exchange districts?

    (A) "Into the First National Bank of San Rosario the newcomer walked, never slowing his brisk step until he stood at the cashier's window." (lines 1–3)
    (B) "He knew it was right to a cent, and he had nothing to fear, but he was nervous and flustered. So was every man in the bank." (lines 32–34)
    (C) "There was something so icy and swift, so impersonal and uncompromising about this man that his very presence seemed an accusation." (lines 35–37)
    (D) "He dumped the gold upon the counter with a crash, and the coins whined and sang as they skimmed across the marble slab from the tips of his nimble digits." (lines 43–46)
    (E) "He would finger the packages of bills in a tired kind of way, and then go into the vault and kick over a few sacks of silver, and the thing was done." (lines 62–64)

26. The author uses all of the following to characterize Mr. Nettlewick EXCEPT

    (A) his manner of speaking
    (B) his effect on the other characters
    (C) his approach to his job
    (D) his physical appearance
    (E) his differences from Sam Turner

27. "His thin, white fingers flew like some expert musician's upon the keys of a piano" (lines 42–43) shows that Mr. Nettlewick

    (A) is a fine musician
    (B) enjoys listening to music
    (C) is highly skilled at his job
    (D) likes to do magic tricks with money
    (E) is eager to impress the staff of the bank

28. Why is Sam Turner's approach to examining the bank's assets so different from Mr. Nettlewick's?

    (A) Turner is less competent at the job.
    (B) Turner prefers to avoid his friends during business hours.
    (C) Turner is older and slower than Nettlewick.
    (D) Turner knows and trusts the bank's employees.
    (E) Turner hopes to be transferred to another district.

29. What about Mr. Nettlewick makes the bank's staff feel "nervous and flustered"?

    (A) his early-morning arrival
    (B) the courtesy in his manner
    (C) his high degree of efficiency
    (D) the fact that he has come to examine the bank
    (E) the fact that he is a stranger to them

30. Mr. Nettlewick treats the bank employees formally and without warmth for which of the following reasons?

    I. He has never met any of them before.
    II. He must maintain objectivity in order to do his job properly.
    III. His is formal, precise, and cool by nature.

    (A) I only
    (B) I and II only
    (C) II only
    (D) III only
    (E) I, II, and III

31. By saying that Mr. Edlinger is a "gentleman of deliberation" (line 20), the author means that

    (A) he is slow and unhurried in his actions
    (B) he means exactly what he says at all times
    (C) he has a habit of debating issues with others
    (D) he can be trusted to keep a secret
    (E) he is prone to using colorful figures of speech

32. The word "ponderously" (line 18) is best defined as

    (A) cautiously
    (B) weightily
    (C) cordially
    (D) quickly
    (E) nervously

Questions 33–40. Read the following poem carefully before you choose your answers.

The Poetess' Hasty Resolution

Reading my verses, I liked them so well,
Self-love did make my judgment to rebel.
Thinking them so good, I thought more to write;
Considering not how others would them like.
5 I writ so fast, I thought, if I lived long,
A pyramid of fame to build thereon.
Reason observing which way I was bent,
Did stay my hand, and asked me what I meant;
Will you, said she, thus waste your time in vain,
10 On that which in the world small praise shall gain?
For shame leave off, said she, the Printer spare,
He'll lose by your ill poetry, I fear.
Besides the world hath already such a weight
Of useless books, as it is over fraught.
15 Then pity take, do the world a good turn,
And all you write cast in the fire, and burn.
Angry I was, and Reason struck away,
When I did hear, what she to me did say.
Then all in haste I to the press it sent,
20 Fearing persuasion might my book prevent:
But now 'tis done, with grief repent do I,
Hang down my head with shame, blush, sigh, and cry.
Take pity, and my drooping spirits raise,
Wipe off my tears with handkerchiefs of praise.

(1653)

33. Who is the "she" who speaks in lines 9–16?

    (A) the poetess
    (B) Reason
    (C) Self-love
    (D) the Printer
    (E) persuasion

34. Whom does the speaker address in the last two lines?

    (A) her readers
    (B) her friends
    (C) her parents
    (D) her husband
    (E) her doctor

35. "Angry I was, and Reason struck away" (line 17) is best paraphrased as

    (A) Listening to Reason always made me angry.
    (B) It struck me that Reason was getting angry with me.
    (C) Reason knocked my poems off the desk, which made me angry.
    (D) When Reason saw she had made me angry, she went away.
    (E) I was angry at Reason, so I pushed her away.

36. Which two forces are in conflict in this poem?

    (A) the printer and the speaker
    (B) the poet and the speaker
    (C) the speaker and the critics
    (D) the speaker's heart and brain
    (E) the speaker and the readers

37. Which of the following best characterizes the speaker?

    (A) emotional and impulsive
    (B) tough and determined
    (C) cheerful and easygoing
    (D) deliberate and cautious
    (E) violent and fierce

38. Why does the speaker repent having sent her poems to the press?

    (A) She is afraid that people will not like her poems.
    (B) She knows in her heart that her poems are not good.
    (C) She knows she cannot afford to pay for the poems to be printed.
    (D) She hopes that her poems will please the critics.
    (E) She realizes that it is too late to stop publication.

39. The speaker gets angry at Reason because

    (A) Reason is responsible for the speaker's failure
    (B) Reason has right on her side
    (C) Reason is unsympathetic and critical
    (D) Reason refuses to print the speaker's poems
    (E) Reason does not like to read poetry

40. Which of the following motivates the speaker to write poetry?

    I. She wants to become a famous author.
    II. She is pleased with the evidence of her own talent.
    III. She needs to write in order to earn money.

    (A) I only
    (B) I and II only
    (C) III only
    (D) II and III only
    (E) I, II, and III

Questions 41–50. Read the following passage carefully before you choose your answers.

None of them knew the color of the sky. Their eyes glanced level, and were fastened upon the waves that swept toward them. These waves were of the hue of slate, save for the tops, which were of foaming white, and
5 all of the men knew the colors of the sea. The horizon narrowed and widened, and dipped and rose, and at all times its edge was jagged with waves that seemed thrust up in points like rocks.

Many a man ought to have a bathtub larger than the boat
10 which here rode upon the sea. These waves were most wrongfully and barbarously abrupt and tall, and each froth-top was a problem in small boat navigation.

The cook squatted in the bottom and looked with both eyes at the six inches of gunwale which separated
15 him from the ocean. His sleeves were rolled over his fat forearms, and the two flaps of his unbuttoned vest dangled as he bent to bail out the boat. Often he said: "Gawd! That was a narrow clip." As he remarked it, he invariably gazed eastward over the broken sea.

20 The oiler, steering with one of the two oars in the boat, sometimes raised himself suddenly to keep clear of water that swirled in over the stern. It was a thin little oar, and it seemed often ready to snap.

The correspondent, pulling at the other oar, watched the
25 waves and wondered why he was there.

The injured captain, lying in the bow, was at this time buried in that profound dejection and indifference which comes, temporarily at least, to even the bravest and most enduring when, willy-nilly, the firm fails, the army loses,
30 the ship goes down. The mind of the master of a vessel is rooted deep in the timbers of her, though he command for a day or a decade; and this captain had on him the stern impression of a scene in the grays of dawn of seven turned faces, and later a stump of a topmast with a white
35 ball on it, that slashed to and fro at the waves, went low and lower, and down. Thereafter there was something strange in his voice. Although steady, it was deep with mourning, and of a quality beyond oration or tears.

"Keep 'er a little more south, Billie," said he.

40 "A little more south, sir," said the oiler in the stern.

A seat in this boat was not unlike a seat upon a bucking bronco, and, by the same token, a bronco is not much smaller. The craft pranced and reared and plunged like an animal. As each wave came, and she rose for it, she
45 seemed like a horse making at a fence outrageously high. The manner of her scramble over these walls of water is a mystic thing, and, moreover, at the top of them were ordinarily these problems in white water, the foam racing down from the summit of each wave requiring a
50 new leap, and a leap from the air. Then, after scornfully bumping a crest, she would slide and race and splash down a long incline, and arrive bobbing and nodding in front of the next menace.

A singular disadvantage of the sea lies in the fact that
55 after successfully surmounting one wave, you discover that there is another behind it just as important and just as nervously anxious to do something effective in the way of swamping boats. In a ten-foot dinghy one can get an idea of the resources of the sea in the line of waves that is
60 not probable to the average experience which is never at sea in a dinghy. As each slaty wall of water approached, it shut all else from the view of the men in the boat, and it was not difficult to imagine that this particular wave was the final outburst of the ocean, the last effort of the
65 grim water. There was a terrible grace in the move of the waves, and they came in silence, save for the snarling of the crests.

(1897)

41. Why does none of the men know the color of the sky?

    (A) They are too busy maintaining their boat to look up.
    (B) It is too dark to see the color of the sky.
    (C) Their eyes are dazzled by the light of the sun.
    (D) The sky is the same color as the sea.
    (E) The bulk of the boat hides the sky from their view.

42. Why are the four men in the dinghy?

    (A) Their ship had an accident and sank.
    (B) They are traveling for business.
    (C) They are escaping from a mutiny.
    (D) They are going for help to save the ship.
    (E) They are trying to get the captain to a doctor.

43. The statement "Many a man ought to have a bathtub larger than the boat which here rode upon the sea" (lines 9–10) exaggerates

    (A) the danger the men are in
    (B) the small size of the dinghy
    (C) the safety of being in a bathtub
    (D) the amount of water washing into the boat
    (E) the sailing skills of the four men

44. The four men perceive the ocean as all of the following EXCEPT

    (A) tireless
    (B) endless
    (C) threatening
    (D) powerful
    (E) magical

45. Which is NOT a reasonable conclusion to draw about the captain?

    (A) He feels responsible for the loss of his ship.
    (B) He was injured during the shipwreck.
    (C) He is an experienced sailor.
    (D) He is too proud to row or bail water.
    (E) He is not in the habit of showing much emotion.

46. What is the effect of the extended comparison of the boat to a bucking bronco?

    (A) It shows that the dinghy has a mind of its own.
    (B) It demonstrates that the captain is a poor navigator.
    (C) It helps the reader feel the unsteady motion of the boat.
    (D) It proves that the men can easily control the dinghy.
    (E) It shows that the characters know more about horses than boats.

47. Why do the characters have so little to say to each other?

    (A) They blame one another for the shipwreck.
    (B) They do not all speak the same language.
    (C) They are all strangers to each other.
    (D) They put all their energy into keeping the dinghy afloat.
    (E) They feel no interest in or sympathy with one another.

48. The tone of the passage is best described as

    (A) mournful
    (B) suspenseful
    (C) melancholy
    (D) serene
    (E) satirical

Practice Test

49. Which major theme(s) does the passage address?

    I. the struggle between man and nature
    II. the unpredictability of existence
    III. the importance of courage in the face of impossible odds

(A) I only
(B) II only
(C) I and II only
(D) II and III only
(E) I, II, and III

50. From whose perspective or point of view does the reader experience the events in the passage?

(A) the captain's
(B) the cook's
(C) the correspondent's
(D) the oiler's
(E) the author's or narrator's

Questions 51–60. Read the following passage carefully before you choose your answers.

She conceived a true estimate of Drouet. To her, and indeed to all the world, he was a nice, good-hearted man. There was nothing evil in the fellow. He gave her the money out of a good heart—out of a realization of
5 her want. He would not have given the same amount to a poor young man, but we must not forget that a poor young man could not, in the nature of things, have appealed to him like a poor young girl. Femininity affected his feelings. He was the creature of an inborn
10 desire. Yet no beggar could have caught his eye and said, "My God, mister, I'm starving," but he would gladly have handed out what was considered the proper portion to give beggars and thought no more about it. There would have been no speculation, no philosophising. He had no
15 mental process in him worthy the dignity of either of those terms. In his good clothes and fine health, he was a merry, unthinking moth of the lamp. Deprived of his position, and struck by a few of the involved and baffling forces which sometimes play upon man, he would
20 have been as helpless as Carrie—as helpless, as non-understanding, as pitiable, if you will, as she.

Now, in regard to his pursuit of women, he meant them no harm, because he did not conceive of the relation which he hoped to hold with them as being harmful.
25 He loved to make advances to women, to have them succumb to his charms, not because he was a cold-blooded, dark, scheming villain, but because his inborn desire urged him to that as a chief delight. He was vain, he was boastful, he was as deluded by fine clothes as any
30 silly-headed girl. A truly deep-dyed villain could have hornswaggled him as readily as he could have flattered a pretty shop-girl. His fine success as a salesman lay in his geniality and the thoroughly reputable standing of his house. He bobbed about among men, a veritable bundle
35 of enthusiasm—no power worthy the name of intellect, no thoughts worthy the adjective noble, no feelings long continued in one strain. A Madame Sappho would have called him a pig; a Shakespeare would have said "my merry child"; old, drinking Caryoe[1] thought him a clever,
40 successful businessman. In short, he was as good as his intellect conceived.

The best proof that there was something open and commendable about the man was the fact that Carrie took the money. No deep, sinister soul with ulterior
45 motives could have given her fifteen cents under the guise of friendship. The unintellectual are not so helpless. Nature has taught the beasts of the field to fly when some unheralded danger threatens. She has put into the small, unwise head of the chipmunk the untutored fear of
50 poisons. "He keepeth His creatures whole," was not written of beasts alone. Carrie was unwise, and, therefore, like the sheep in its unwisdom, strong in feeling. The instinct of self-protection, strong in all such natures, was roused but feebly, if at all, by the overtures of Drouet.

(1900)

---

[1] Co-owner of the firm, or "house," for which Drouet works

51. The word "hornswaggled" (line 31) is best defined as

    (A) befriended
    (B) insulted
    (C) conned
    (D) hired
    (E) fought

52. Which of the following does NOT characterize Drouet?

    (A) generosity
    (B) kindness
    (C) subtlety
    (D) honesty
    (E) friendliness

53. The metaphor "he was a merry, unthinking moth of the lamp" (line 17) implies which of the following about Drouet?

    (A) He does what he likes without thinking about possible consequences.
    (B) His ready interest in other people often gets him into trouble.
    (C) He impresses Carrie with his warmth of personality and enthusiasm.
    (D) He is so successful at his job that he can afford to enjoy himself in his free time.
    (E) He is especially cheerful in the bright lights of a restaurant or theater at night.

54. Which best describes the author's attitude toward Drouet?

    (A) condescending
    (B) respectful
    (C) compassionate
    (D) wary
    (E) affectionate

55. The author suggests that the difference between Drouet and "a cold-blooded, dark, scheming villain" (lines 26–27) is that

    (A) Drouet is an unrefined man of the world.
    (B) Drouet does not intend or wish to harm or injure anyone.
    (C) Drouet's behavior is guided largely by selfishness.
    (D) Drouet chases after women and often tells them lies.
    (E) Drouet has no sensitivity toward other people.

56. The author suggests that Carrie trusts Drouet because

    (A) his offer of money is a generous one
    (B) his boss has assured her that he is a good man
    (C) she has no experience of evil men
    (D) her instincts tell her that he can be trusted
    (E) she finds him handsome and attractive

57. Drouet hopes that Carrie will eventually become his

    (A) friend
    (B) wife
    (C) lover
    (D) colleague
    (E) employee

58. What is the author's main purpose in this passage?

    (A) to examine the relationship between Drouet and Carrie
    (B) to analyze Drouet's personality for the reader
    (C) to explain why Carrie finds Drouet attractive
    (D) to show the reader how Carrie and Drouet are alike
    (E) to portray a successful salesman of the period

GO ON TO THE NEXT PAGE ⟼

59. Which of the following supports the author's suggestion that Carrie will come to no harm by trusting Drouet?

    (A) "...to all the world, he was a nice, good-hearted man" (lines 2–3)
    (B) "He would not have given the same amount to a poor young man" (lines 5–6)
    (C) "He was the creature of an inborn desire" (lines 9–10)
    (D) "He loved to make advances to women, to have them succumb to his charms" (lines 25–26)
    (E) "He bobbed about among men, a veritable bundle of enthusiasm" (lines 34–35)

60. The author suggests that Drouet's main motive for helping Carrie is

    (A) his concern for her plight
    (B) his understanding of her character
    (C) his desire to think well of himself
    (D) his true nobility of character
    (E) his physical desire for her

STOP

If you finish before time is called, you may check your work on this test only.

Do not turn to any other test in this book.

Answer Key

1. B	16. B	31. A	46. C
2. A	17. D	32. B	47. D
3. A	18. E	33. B	48. B
4. E	19. B	34. A	49. E
5. B	20. C	35. E	50. E
6. C	21. D	36. D	51. C
7. D	22. A	37. A	52. C
8. B	23. C	38. B	53. A
9. A	24. B	39. C	54. E
10. E	25. E	40. B	55. B
11. B	26. D	41. A	56. D
12. A	27. C	42. A	57. C
13. B	28. D	43. B	58. B
14. D	29. C	44. E	59. A
15. C	30. E	45. D	60. E

Answers and Explanations

1. **(B)** *Gall,* also called *bile,* is a fluid secreted by the liver. *Gall* has been a literary synonym for bitterness of spirit since the Middle Ages.

2. **(A)** The context makes it clear that Sir Peter and his lady had a spat followed by a more serious quarrel.

3. **(A)** Sir Peter is surprised at his wife's behavior because he thought she would want to continue living in the modest style she was accustomed to.

4. **(E)** Today, to *doubt* means to question or disbelieve. However, in the late eighteenth century, English people used the word in ordinary conversation to mean just the opposite. As the context shows, "I doubt I love her" means "I believe I love her."

5. **(B)** The tried-and-true comic staple of a marriage between an old bachelor and a young girl, the wordplay, and the funny lines make it clear that this play is a comedy.

6. **(C)** *Dissipates* means "scatters." *Fortune,* in this context, refers to wealth rather than luck. Lady Teazle is spending money far more freely than Sir Peter had anticipated she would.

7. **(D)** Sir Peter would not express his discontent with so much wit and style if he were not enjoying wallowing in self-pity. He is perfectly well aware that things are not as bad as he suggests; the point of humorous exaggeration is that you know you are exaggerating for effect. Choice A is wrong because he confesses that he loves his wife; choice B is wrong because he is complaining about a major difference of views between himself and his wife, not a series of little things.

8. **(B)** If a person is worried about showing weakness, that implies he considers the other person to be his enemy. Sir Peter sees his marriage as a power struggle in which Lady Teazle will gain more power if he admits that he loves her.

9. **(A)** Rowley acts as a "straight man"; four of his five lines set up laugh lines spoken by Sir Peter.

10. **(E)** *Certitude* means much the same as "certainty." It implies an unshakable belief or faith in something, not so much because there is factual proof of it, but because one is completely convinced of its existence or rightness.

11. **(B)** *Blanch'd* is derived from the Latin for "white." The strong, bright light of the moon makes the sand appear white.

12. **(A)** The speaker comments that "Sophocles long ago / Heard it on the Aegean." *It* refers to the same sound he hears himself—the waves breaking on the shore.

13. **(B)** The sound of the sea retreating from the shore inspires the speaker to think about the widespread loss of religious faith.

14. **(D)** The speaker suggests that he and his love will be caught up in the middle of a war, not as participants on either side, but rather trapped between armies. "Refugees" most closely matches this comparison.

15. **(C)** When the speaker hears this sound, it directs his thoughts toward the future and suggests that the world is a terrible place. *Ominous,* which means "portending or predicting evil," is the best match to the sound's effect on him.

16. **(B)** In the first six lines of the poem, the words *calm, full, fair, light, tranquil,* and *sweet* convey the speaker's serene mood. The word *Only* (line 7) begins the transition to a mood of apprehension, as he meditates on the terrors that lie ahead in a faithless and hopeless society.

17. **(D)** Since the speaker has a lover, and he says "Let us be true / To one another," there *is* still love and hope in the world, even though he asserts there is not.

18. **(E)** *Turbid* waters have been stirred up, disturbing the sediment on the bottom and making the water cloudy and dark. *Turbid* and *disturbed* come from the same root.

19. **(B)** All five are accurate definitions of *counter*. In this context, the speaker contrasts *counter* with *coin*, showing that choice B is correct. The speaker has the true wealth—love—while the "glittering Monarchs" can offer only a counter—fake money—in exchange.

20. **(C)** The comparison shows that the two brooks become one, inseparable and indivisible, when they meet in the river. In the same way, the speaker considers herself so close to the beloved that they form one entity.

21. **(D)** "Those glittering Monarchs, that command / The servile quarters of this earthly ball" can be paraphrased "The kings who rule the nations of the earth." The speaker would not exchange the Beloved even for this.

22. **(A)** The Beloved is male, and the nouns and pronouns which refer to him are capitalized; this supports option I. The central importance of the love in the speaker's life, its intensity, and the metaphors of indivisible union support option II. Parents do not normally express love for their children in terms like those used in this poem, so option III is unlikely.

23. **(C)** Writers often use repetition for emphasis. In this case, line 12's exact repetition of line 6 (and the partial repetition again in line 18) underscores the speaker's profound sense of union with the Beloved and the enormous importance of the relationship.

24. **(B)** The phrase describes the brooks, not the speaker and the Beloved. The word *wanton* can mean "playful and lively," which fits the context of water rushing over pebbles.

25. **(E)** Nettlewick's actions in the bank show that Turner has not been doing the job thoroughly or properly. The Comptroller probably reasons that Turner will be more thorough and less friendly and trusting with people who are strangers to him.

26. **(D)** The passage does not describe Nettlewick's appearance except to say that he has thin fingers, which does not reveal anything about his character.

27. **(C)** The statement is an imaginative comparison; Nettlewick is not himself a musician. The word *expert* and the description of his quick, accurate, and thorough actions show that choice C is correct.

28. **(D)** The author states that Turner has known Dorsey "since he was a baby" and is an old friend of the bank's president. Knowing and trusting the staff for many years, Turner feels no need to check up on every small detail.

29. **(C)** The men are nervous because Nettlewick is so efficient that they think he "would neither make nor overlook an error." His efficiency shows both in the way he does his job and in his refusal to waste any words.

30. (E) All three options are reasonable possibilities. Many people are stiff and formal with strangers, especially in professional situations. Nettlewick's whole manner is in keeping with his formal and precise diction, so it may be that he is always this way. And if the bank employees are the examiner's friends, he might find it awkward to check up on them in detail, as the job requires. Nettlewick probably finds that his job is easier if he keeps his distance.

31. (A) A *deliberate* person does not like to be rushed. The author indicates that Mr. Erdlinger is the opposite of an *impulsive* person. He moves at his own slow pace, not letting anyone hurry him.

32. (B) *Ponderously* is derived from the Latin word for "weight." The author means that Mr. Erdlinger carried out the introductions in a slow, heavy, plodding way, without haste.

33. (B) Lines 7–8 show that Reason is the speaker of lines 9–16.

34. (A) The speaker pleads with her readers to be kinder than Reason. She hopes they will like her poems so much that she can stop repenting having sent them to the printer.

35. (E) The speaker is made angry by Reason's criticism of her verse. "Reason struck away" means literally that she "put these thoughts out of my mind."

36. (D) The conflict is between the speaker and "Reason": in other words, between what her brain tells her (don't try to publish your work) and what her heart tells her (I want to publish my work).

37. (A) The speaker's refusal to listen to Reason and her rush to deliver her poems before she thinks better of it, plus the anger she feels toward Reason, show that she is emotional and impulsive.

38. (B) The speaker behaves as though she thinks Reason was right after all and that she feels certain her work will not be well received. The title "The Poetess' Hasty Resolution" also supports the idea that sending the manuscript out was not a wise decision, because the work is not really very good.

39. (C) Reason refers to the speaker's "ill poetry" and tells her that it will make a "useless" book. Reason is both critical and unkind.

40. (B) The speaker says she likes her verses so well that she wants to write more and that she hopes, if she writes enough, to become famous. She does not say anything about needing to earn money.

41. (A) The author says that the men's "eyes glanced level, and were fastened upon the waves."

42. (A) The sixth paragraph describes the sinking of the ship. The men are in the lifeboat trying to reach the shore.

43. (B) The dingy is ten feet long, so it is quite a bit larger than a bathtub. The author exaggerates to contrast the tiny boat with the huge ocean and to emphasize how little shelter it gives the men.

44. (E) Tireless: There is always another wave coming along and washing over the boat. Endless: They can see nothing but the ocean in every direction. Threatening: The waves are trying to swamp the boat. Powerful: The waves are strong and they toss the boat about without mercy.

45. (D) The captain's failure to take an oar or bail is not due to pride but necessity. He is injured, and he is the only man in the boat with enough skill and experience to navigate. The other four choices are supported by various details in the passage.

46. (C) Phrases like "pranced and reared and plunged" and "scramble over these walls of water" draws the reader in with a vivid description of the way the waves toss the little boat about.

47. **(D)** The men are so busy rowing, bailing, and watching the sea that they do not even take time to look up at the sky; clearly, then, they have no energy or attention to waste on unnecessary conversation.

48. **(B)** The author puts his characters in a life-threatening situation that they may or may not survive. The reader keeps reading in order to find out whether they will reach the shore or be rescued.

49. **(E)** The passage addresses all three themes. Option I: The characters are in a life-and-death struggle against the sea. Option II: None of the men ever dreamed he would find himself fighting for his life in a leaky ten-foot boat. Option III: The men greatly improve their chances of survival by following the captain's orders and not giving in to panic or fear.

50. **(E)** The passage allows the reader to know the thoughts of two characters: the correspondent, who "wondered why he was there," and the captain, who still has the impression of the sinking ship before his eyes. Only an outside narrator, or the author, can see into the thoughts of more than one character.

51. **(C)** The author describes Drouet as unsuspicious—someone who would be helpless if faced with a schemer who wanted to harm him. *Hornswaggled* is an American dialect word that means "deliberately made a fool of" or "took advantage of"—that is, conned.

52. **(C)** Drouet is described as someone who is exactly what he appears to be on the surface; someone who has no secrets and no hidden depths.

53. **(A)** A moth flies into a lamp because the lamplight is an irresistible lure. Similarly, Drouet finds women irresistible. Whenever he meets an attractive woman, he succumbs to the attraction just as the moth succumbs to the glow of the light.

54. **(E)** The author emphasizes Drouet's good qualities—generosity, warmth, friendliness—and points out that he is harmless. The tone is affectionate.

55. **(B)** A scheming villain would have offered Carrie money in order to get her into his power, most probably to seduce and then abandon her. Drouet has no such harmful intentions toward Carrie; he is genuinely attracted to her and behaves accordingly.

56. **(D)** The author compares Carrie to animals who rely on their instincts to protect them from predators. She knows nothing about Drouet except what she can perceive for herself; her trust is not based on information, but on what her instincts tell her about him.

57. **(C)** Drouet wants Carrie "to succumb to his charms" and he feels an "inborn desire" for her. The passage is dated 1900; at that time, it was highly improper for a young woman to accept money from a man. It was understood that he expected to become her lover in return for it.

58. **(B)** Almost every line of the passage describes Drouet's unique personality. The author drops only a few hints and statements about Drouet's relationship with Carrie, so this is not his main purpose. Choice E is wrong because the author is interested in Drouet as an individual, not a representative type.

59. **(A)** Carrie is not likely to come to great harm with a "nice, good-hearted man" whose intentions are generous and kind, if partly selfish.

60. **(E)** Drouet's main motive is his own appetite. His concern for Carrie's plight is only a secondary motive; as the author notes, he would not have felt the same concern if Carrie had been a boy instead of a pretty girl.

How To Calculate Your Score

Count the number of correct answers and enter the total below.

Count the number of wrong answers. Do NOT include any questions you did not answer.

Multiply the number of wrong answers by 0.25 and enter the total below.

Do the subtraction. The answer is your raw score. Use the scoring scale to find your scaled score.

$$\overline{\text{(number of correct answers)}} - \overline{\text{(number of wrong answers} \times 0.25)} = \overline{\text{(raw score)}}$$

RAW SCORE	SCALED SCORE	RAW SCORE	SCALED SCORE	RAW SCORE	SCALED SCORE	RAW SCORE	SCALED SCORE	RAW SCORE	SCALED SCORE
60	800	44	710	28	560	12	420	−4	260
59	800	43	700	27	550	11	410	−5	250
58	800	42	690	26	540	10	400	−6	240
57	800	41	690	25	530	9	390	−7	230
56	800	40	680	24	520	8	380	−8	220
55	800	39	670	23	510	7	370	−9	210
54	790	38	660	22	500	6	360	−10	200
53	790	37	650	21	500	5	350	−11	200
52	780	36	640	20	490	4	340	−12	200
51	770	35	630	19	490	3	330	−13	200
50	760	34	620	18	480	2	320	−14	200
49	750	33	610	17	470	1	310	−15	200
48	740	32	600	16	460	0	300		
47	740	31	590	15	450	−1	290		
46	730	30	580	14	440	−2	280		
45	720	29	570	13	430	−3	270		

Note: This is only a sample scoring scale. Scoring scales differ from exam to exam.

Practice Test 5

The following practice test is designed to be just like the real SAT Literature Test. It matches the actual test in content coverage and degree of difficulty.

Once you finish the practice test, determine your score. Carefully read the answer explanations of the questions you answered incorrectly. Identify any weaknesses in your literature skills by determining the areas in which you made the most errors. Review those sections of this book first. Then, as time permits, go back and review your strengths.

Allow one hour to take the test. Time yourself and work uninterrupted. If you run out of time, take note of where you stopped when time ran out. Remember that you lose a quarter point for each incorrect answer, but you do not lose points for questions you leave blank. Therefore, unless you can eliminate one or more of the five choices, it is best to leave a question unanswered.

Use the following formula to calculate your score:

(number of correct answers) – ¼ (number of incorrect answers)

If you treat this practice test just like the actual exam, it will accurately reflect how you are likely to perform on test day. Here are some hints on how to create test-taking conditions similar to those of the actual exam:

- Complete the test in one sitting. On test day, you will not be allowed to take a break.
- Tear out the answer sheet and fill in the ovals just as you will on the actual test day.
- Have a good eraser and more than one sharp pencil handy. On test day, you will not be able to go get a new pencil if yours breaks.
- Do not allow yourself any extra time; put down your pencil after exactly one hour, no matter how many questions are left to answer.
- Become familiar with the directions on the test. If you go in knowing what the directions say, you will not have to waste time reading and thinking about them on the actual test day.

Answer Sheet

Tear out this answer sheet and use it to mark your answers.

1. (A) (B) (C) (D) (E)	16. (A) (B) (C) (D) (E)	31. (A) (B) (C) (D) (E)	46. (A) (B) (C) (D) (E)
2. (A) (B) (C) (D) (E)	17. (A) (B) (C) (D) (E)	32. (A) (B) (C) (D) (E)	47. (A) (B) (C) (D) (E)
3. (A) (B) (C) (D) (E)	18. (A) (B) (C) (D) (E)	33. (A) (B) (C) (D) (E)	48. (A) (B) (C) (D) (E)
4. (A) (B) (C) (D) (E)	19. (A) (B) (C) (D) (E)	34. (A) (B) (C) (D) (E)	49. (A) (B) (C) (D) (E)
5. (A) (B) (C) (D) (E)	20. (A) (B) (C) (D) (E)	35. (A) (B) (C) (D) (E)	50. (A) (B) (C) (D) (E)
6. (A) (B) (C) (D) (E)	21. (A) (B) (C) (D) (E)	36. (A) (B) (C) (D) (E)	51. (A) (B) (C) (D) (E)
7. (A) (B) (C) (D) (E)	22. (A) (B) (C) (D) (E)	37. (A) (B) (C) (D) (E)	52. (A) (B) (C) (D) (E)
8. (A) (B) (C) (D) (E)	23. (A) (B) (C) (D) (E)	38. (A) (B) (C) (D) (E)	53. (A) (B) (C) (D) (E)
9. (A) (B) (C) (D) (E)	24. (A) (B) (C) (D) (E)	39. (A) (B) (C) (D) (E)	54. (A) (B) (C) (D) (E)
10. (A) (B) (C) (D) (E)	25. (A) (B) (C) (D) (E)	40. (A) (B) (C) (D) (E)	55. (A) (B) (C) (D) (E)
11. (A) (B) (C) (D) (E)	26. (A) (B) (C) (D) (E)	41. (A) (B) (C) (D) (E)	56. (A) (B) (C) (D) (E)
12. (A) (B) (C) (D) (E)	27. (A) (B) (C) (D) (E)	42. (A) (B) (C) (D) (E)	57. (A) (B) (C) (D) (E)
13. (A) (B) (C) (D) (E)	28. (A) (B) (C) (D) (E)	43. (A) (B) (C) (D) (E)	58. (A) (B) (C) (D) (E)
14. (A) (B) (C) (D) (E)	29. (A) (B) (C) (D) (E)	44. (A) (B) (C) (D) (E)	59. (A) (B) (C) (D) (E)
15. (A) (B) (C) (D) (E)	30. (A) (B) (C) (D) (E)	45. (A) (B) (C) (D) (E)	60. (A) (B) (C) (D) (E)

PRACTICE TEST 5
Time: 60 Minutes

Directions: This test consists of selections from literary works and questions on their content, form, and style. After reading each passage or poem, choose the best answer to each question and then fill in the corresponding oval on the answer sheet.

Note: Pay particular attention to the requirements of questions that contain the words NOT or EXCEPT.

Questions 1–9. Read the following passage carefully before you choose your answers.

The slaves selected to go to the Great House Farm, for the monthly allowance for themselves and their fellow-slaves, were peculiarly enthusiastic. While on their way, they would make the dense old woods, for miles around,
5   reverberate with their wild songs, revealing at once the highest joy and the deepest sadness. They would compose and sing as they went along, consulting neither time nor tune. The thought that came up, came out—if not in the word, in the sound;—and as frequently in the one as in
10 the other. They would sometimes sing the most pathetic sentiment in the most rapturous tone, and the most rapturous sentiment in the most pathetic tone. Into all of their songs they would manage to weave something of the Great House Farm. Especially would they do this, when
15 leaving home. They would then sing most exultingly the following words:

I am going away to the Great House Farm!
O, yea! O, yea! O!

This they would sing, as a chorus, to words which
20 to many would seem unmeaning jargon, but which, nevertheless, were full of meaning to themselves. I have sometimes thought that the mere hearing of those songs would do more to impress some minds with the horrible character of slavery, than the reading of whole volumes of
25 philosophy on the subject could do.

I did not, when a slave, understand the deep meaning of those rude and apparently incoherent songs. I was myself within the circle; so that I neither saw nor heard as those without might see and hear. They told a tale
30 of woe which was then altogether beyond my feeble

comprehension; they were tones loud, long, and deep; they breathed the prayer and complaint of souls boiling over with the bitterest anguish. Every tone was a testimony against slavery, and a prayer to God for deliverance from
35 chains. The hearing of those wild notes always depressed my spirit, and filled me with ineffable sadness. I have frequently found myself in tears while hearing them. The mere recurrence to those songs, even now, afflicts me; and while I am writing these lines, an expression
40 of feeling has already found its way down my cheek. To those songs I trace my first glimmering conception of the dehumanizing character of slavery. I can never get rid of that conception. Those songs still follow me, to deepen my hatred of slavery, and quicken my sympathies for my
45 brethren in bonds. If anyone wishes to be impressed with the soul-killing effects of slavery, let him go to Colonel Lloyd's plantation, and, on allowance-day, place himself in the deep pine woods, and there let him, in silence, analyze the sounds that shall pass through the chambers
50 of his soul,—and if he is not thus impressed, it will only be because "there is no flesh in his obdurate heart."

I have often been utterly astonished, since I came to the north, to find persons who could speak of the singing, among slaves, as evidence of their contentment and
55 happiness. It is impossible to conceive of a greater mistake. Slaves sing most when they are most unhappy. The songs of the slave represent the sorrows of his heart; and he is relieved by them, only as an aching heart is relieved by its tears. At least, such is my experience. I have
60 often sung to drown my sorrow, but seldom to express my happiness. Crying for joy, and singing for joy, were alike

GO ON TO THE NEXT PAGE ⟩⟩

uncommon to me while in the jaws of slavery. The singing of a man cast away upon a desolate island might be as appropriately considered as evidence of contentment and
65 happiness, as the singing of a slave; the songs of the one and of the other are prompted by the same emotion.

(1845)

1. "An expression of feeling has already found its way down my cheek" (lines 39–40) is the author's way of saying that

   (A) his reflection in the mirror reminds him of his days as a slave
   (B) thinking about the past affects his emotions
   (C) he does not like to write about unpleasant topics
   (D) a tear is running down his face
   (E) his story will upset many readers

2. The author uses the phrase "his obdurate heart" (line 51) to show that those who are not moved by the slaves' songs are

   (A) brutal and cruel
   (B) ignorant and stupid
   (C) selfish and greedy
   (D) unfeeling and harsh
   (E) just and upright

3. In what sense does the author use the word "rude" (line 27)?

   (A) ill-mannered
   (B) incomplete
   (C) rough and unrefined
   (D) rugged and strong
   (E) violent and savage

4. According to the author, slaves sing in order to

   (A) release their pent-up emotions
   (B) communicate with each other
   (C) celebrate joyous occasions
   (D) make their working hours seem shorter
   (E) persuade people that slavery is a cruel system

5. The slaves are "peculiarly enthusiastic" (line 3) about the trip to the Great House Farm because

   I. it provides a brief holiday from their usual labors
   II. they receive food and supplies at the end of the journey
   III. taking a journey gives them the sense of being free

   (A) I and II only
   (B) II and III only
   (C) I and III only
   (D) III only
   (E) I, II, and III

6. The author uses the words "wild" (line 5), "rapturous" (line 12), and "exultingly" (line 15) to show that the slaves' songs are characterized by

   (A) beautiful melodies and harmonies
   (B) strong passions and emotions
   (C) catchy tunes and clever lyrics
   (D) a loud volume of sound
   (E) primitive and exotic rhythms

7. Phrases such as "the dehumanizing character of slavery" (line 42), "my hatred of slavery" (line 44), and "the soul-killing effects of slavery" (line 46) suggest that the author's main purpose is to

   (A) describe his feelings and emotions
   (B) show readers what it is like to live as a slave
   (C) persuade readers to oppose and abolish slavery
   (D) place the details of his past life on record
   (E) reminisce about important events in his early youth

GO ON TO THE NEXT PAGE ⟶

8. Why does the author believe that hearing slaves sing "would do more to impress some minds with the horrible character of slavery, than the reading of whole volumes of philosophy on the subject" (lines 23–25)?

   (A) Music has a more immediate and direct emotional impact than words.
   (B) Songs come from the slaves themselves, while books are written by outside observers.
   (C) The same piece of music can mean different things to different listeners.
   (D) It is easier to learn by listening than it is to learn by reading.
   (E) Music is a universal language that can be understood by any listener.

9. The author uses the word "glimmering" (line 41) to explain

   (A) how abominable he finds the system of human slavery
   (B) how fragmentary his original grasp of the evils of slavery was
   (C) how slowly and gradually he comprehended the evils of slavery
   (D) how bitter he felt when he first realized he was a slave
   (E) how eager he is to make others understand his views on slavery

Questions 10–18. Read the following poem carefully before you choose your answers.

If by dull rhymes our English must be chained,
And, like Andromeda, the Sonnet sweet
Fettered, in spite of pained loveliness;
Let us find out, if we must be constrained,
5 Sandals more interwoven and complete
To fit the naked foot of poesy;
Let us inspect the lyre, and weigh the stress
Of every chord, and see what may be gained
By ear industrous, and attention meet;
10 Misers of sound and syllable, no less
Than Midas of his coinage, let us be
Jealous of dead leaves in the bay wreath crown;
So, if we may not let the Muse be free,
She will be bound with garlands of her own.

(1819)

10. When the poet writes, "Misers of sound and syllable, no less / Than Midas of his coinage" (lines 10–11), he means that

   (A) his fellow poets are misers with words because they fail to adhere to the traditional rhyme schemes
   (B) his fellow poets should be restrictive with their words the way Midas was with his gold
   (C) his fellow poets are restrictive with their words the way Midas was with his gold because of their insistence to adhering to traditional rhyme schemes
   (D) his fellow poets fail to be misers with words because they love elaborate language the way that Midas loved large quantities of gold
   (E) his fellow poets should not be misers just because writing poetry does not pay well

11. This poem meets all the usual standards for a sonnet EXCEPT in which category?

    (A) meter
    (B) line length
    (C) rhyme scheme
    (D) number of lines
    (E) rhythm

12. Which best sums up the argument of the poem?

    (A) We must find more truly poetic and meaningful ways to use rhyme in poetry.
    (B) We must stop allowing the Muse to force us to use rhymes in poetry.
    (C) We must do away with rhyme altogether if poetry is to survive as a form.
    (D) We must recite our poems aloud to be sure of their quality before we publish.
    (E) We will destroy poetry as a form of writing if we continue to write in the old ways.

13. By "Sandals more interwoven and complete / To fit the naked foot of poesy" (lines 5–6), the poet means

    (A) end rhymes that will make every new poem complete
    (B) new schemes of internal rhyme that will improve the art of writing poetry
    (C) metric feet that suit the content of each individual poem
    (D) shoes and clothing that fit properly for greater ease in writing
    (E) rhyme schemes that relate more closely to the meaning of a poem

14. Which best describes the relationship between the content and structure of the poem?

    (A) The content describes the poet's inability to write, and the irregular structure proves his point.
    (B) The content alludes to ancient tales, and the structure is borrowed from ancient forms of poetry.
    (C) The content laments the scarcity of great love poetry, and the structure echoes that of great love poems of the past.
    (D) The content argues for new poetic forms and demonstrates their worth by employing an irregular structure.
    (E) The content suggests that rhyme should be eliminated from poetry, and the structure is unrhymed.

15. The phrase "Jealous of dead leaves in the bay wreath crown" (line 12) is best paraphrased as

    (A) envious of the works of ancient, long-dead poets
    (B) distrustful of old, outworn rules for writing poetry
    (C) suspicious of time-honored poetic forms
    (D) competitive with other poets for high honors
    (E) strictly observant of ancient methods of artistic creation

16. Which best describes the poet's attitude toward rhyme in poetry?

    (A) He believes that poems should not have to rhyme.
    (B) He enjoys the challenge of making his ideas fit the accepted rhyme schemes.
    (C) He feels that a poet should adapt a rhyme scheme to fit the content of the poem.
    (D) He respects and honors the rhyme schemes that poets have always used.
    (E) He finds it very difficult to rhyme English words.

17. The poet uses the word "meet" (line 9) to mean

(A) encounter
(B) assemble
(C) fulfill
(D) confront
(E) appropriate

18. "Let us inspect the lyre, and weigh the stress / Of every chord, and see what may be gained, / By ear industrous, and attention meet" (lines 7–9) means that poets should

(A) take great care to choose words that sound exactly right
(B) spend more time listening to music
(C) read their work aloud as they write and revise
(D) take care that their poems are neither too long nor too short
(E) pay more attention to the structure of their poems

Questions 19–25. Read the following poem carefully before you choose your answers.

The Lake

In youth's spring, it was my lot
To haunt of the wide earth a spot
The which I could not love the less;
So lovely was the loneliness
5 Of a wild lake, with black rock bound.
And the tall pines that tower'd around.
But when the night had thrown her pall
Upon that spot—as upon all,
And the wind would pass me by
10 In its stilly melody,
My infant spirit would awake
To the terror of the lone lake.
Yet that terror was not fright—
But a tremulous delight,
15 And a feeling undefin'd,
Springing from a darken'd mind.
Death was in that poison'd wave
And in its gulf a fitting grave
For him who thence could solace bring
20 To his dark imagining;
Whose wild'ring thought could even make
An Eden of that dim lake.

(1827)

19. Which quality most strongly attracts the speaker to the lake?

(A) its isolated setting
(B) its border of black rocks
(C) its appearance at night
(D) the taste of its water
(E) the nearby graves

20. Which best explains the speaker's meaning when he says "Yet that terror was not fright" (line 13)?

(A) Terror and fear are similar emotions.
(B) Terror attracts me rather than making me want to run away.
(C) I concealed my terror so that no one would know I was frightened.
(D) Something terrible happened to me at the lake.
(E) The lake made me feel both terror and fear.

21. Why does the speaker describe his mind as "darken'd" (line 16)?

    (A) He is enthralled by images of death and terror.
    (B) He likes wandering in the woods at night.
    (C) He would rather be alone than with other people.
    (D) He is attracted by water even though he cannot swim.
    (E) He likes the nighttime better than the day.

22. The "feeling undefin'd" (line 15) in the speaker's mind can best be described as

    (A) idle curiosity
    (B) painful anxiety
    (C) wondering awe
    (D) morbid fascination
    (E) ignorant bliss

23. The word "Eden" (line 22) is particularly effective because it shows that the speaker

    (A) is worried by the attraction he feels for the lake
    (B) is determined to make the lake a more beautiful place
    (C) is a person of profound gloom who takes pleasure in desolation
    (D) is imaginative enough to pretend that the lake is beautiful
    (E) is a deeply religious person who prefers to worship in isolation

24. The word "haunt" (line 2) contributes to the poem's mood of

    (A) mysteriousness
    (B) suspense
    (C) horror
    (D) decay
    (E) ominousness

25. The rhythmic irregularities in the poem contribute which of the following to the overall effect?

    I. They mirror the disturbed state of the speaker's mind.
    II. They help to portray the lake as a strange and eerie place.
    III. They create an unsettled feeling in the reader.

    (A) I and II only
    (B) I and III only
    (C) II only
    (D) II and III only
    (E) I, II, and III

Questions 26–35. Read the following passage carefully before you choose your answers.

"What a splendid night it is!"

"You like this weather?"

"It suits my purpose. Watson, I mean to burgle Milverton's house tonight."

5   I had a catching of the breath, and my skin went cold at the words, which were slowly uttered in a tone of concentrated resolution. As a flash of lightning in the night shows up in an instant every detail of a wide landscape, so at one glance I seemed to see every possible
10 result of such an action—the detection, the capture, the honored career ending in irreparable failure and disgrace, my friend himself lying at the mercy of the odious Milverton.

  "For Heaven's sake, Holmes, think what you are doing," I
15 cried.

  "My dear fellow, I have given it every consideration. I am never precipitate in my actions, nor would I adopt so energetic and indeed dangerous a course if any other were possible. Let us look at the matter clearly and fairly.
20 I suppose that you will admit that the action is morally justifiable, though technically criminal. To burgle his house is no more than to forcibly take his pocket-book—an action in which you were prepared to aid me."

  I turned it over in my mind.

25   "Yes," I said; "it is morally justifiable so long as our object is to take no articles save those which are used for an illegal purpose."

  "Exactly. Since it is morally justifiable I have only to consider the question of personal risk. Surely a gentleman
30 should not lay much stress upon this when a lady is in most desperate need of his help?"

  "You will be in such a false position."

  "Well, that is part of the risk. There is no other possible way of regaining these letters. The unfortunate lady has
35 not the money, and there are none of her people in whom she could confide. Tomorrow is the last day of grace,

and unless we can get the letters tonight this villain will be as good as his word and will bring about her ruin. I must, therefore, abandon my client to her fate or I must
40 play this last card. Between ourselves, Watson, it's a sporting duel between this fellow Milverton and me. He had, as you saw, the best of the first exchanges; but my self-respect and my reputation are concerned to fight it to a finish."

45   "Well, I don't like it; but I suppose it must be," said I. "When do we start?"

  "You are not coming."

  "Then you are not going," said I. "I give you my word of honor—and I never broke it in my life—that I will take a
50 cab straight to the police station and give you away unless you let me share this adventure with you."

  "You can't help me."

  "How do you know that? You can't tell what may happen. Anyway, my resolution is taken. Other people besides you
55 have self-respect and even reputations."

  Holmes had looked annoyed, but his brow cleared, and he clapped me on the shoulder.

  "Well, well, my dear fellow, be it so. We have shared the same room for some years, and it would be amusing
60 if we ended up sharing the same cell . . . We shall have some cold supper before we start. It is now nine-thirty. At eleven we shall drive as far as Church Row. It is a quarter of an hour's walk from there to Appledore Towers. We shall be at work before midnight. Milverton is a heavy sleeper
65 and retires punctually at ten-thirty. With any luck we should be back here by two, with the Lady Eva's letters in my pocket."

(c. 1904)

26. The author uses the phrase "my skin went cold at the words" (lines 5–6) to show that Watson

    (A) is shocked to learn that Holmes is a criminal
    (B) knows that Holmes is walking into a trap
    (C) has a strict sense of right and wrong
    (D) is cautious and prudent by nature
    (E) is dismayed by the consequences Holmes may suffer

27. Why does Watson threaten to give Holmes up to the police "unless you let me share this adventure with you" (lines 50–51)?

    (A) He wants to be on the spot to protect and defend Holmes if necessary.
    (B) He believes that what Holmes is doing is wrong and foolish.
    (C) He knows that Holmes's plan has no chance of succeeding.
    (D) He does not trust Holmes to carry out his plan unassisted.
    (E) He does not want to miss out on the excitement of the adventure.

28. The word "precipitate" (line 17) means

    (A) damp and rainy
    (B) hasty and rash
    (C) visible or audible
    (D) honest and open
    (E) brave or daring

29. Holmes believes that breaking into Milverton's house is "morally justifiable" (lines 20–21) because

    (A) he has made a bet with Milverton that he does not want to lose
    (B) he and Milverton do not like one another
    (C) Milverton made him lose face in an earlier encounter
    (D) he wants to prevent Milverton from committing a crime
    (E) Watson once offered to help him take Milverton's pocket-book

30. From the facts in the passage, you can conclude that Milverton is

    (A) a thief
    (B) a murderer
    (C) a blackmailer
    (D) a burglar
    (E) an arsonist

31. Watson is characterized by all of the following EXCEPT

    (A) courage
    (B) loyalty
    (C) honesty
    (D) morality
    (E) impulsiveness

32. Holmes is annoyed at Watson's insistence on joining him because

    I. he does not want to involve Watson in any risks
    II. he prefers to get the better of Milverton on his own
    III. he is not interested in Watson's self-respect or reputation

    (A) I and II only
    (B) II only
    (C) I and III only
    (D) III only
    (E) I, II, and III

33. The fact that Holmes speaks with "concentrated resolution" (line 7) shows that he

    (A) is unlikely to change his mind now that it is made up
    (B) has carefully thought through every detail of his plans
    (C) will insist on carrying out his intentions by himself
    (D) is well aware that he is going into danger
    (E) dislikes the idea of committing a crime

GO ON TO THE NEXT PAGE ⟼

34. Which of the following does NOT describe Holmes's state of mind as he prepares to burgle Milverton's house?

(A) determined
(B) confident
(C) cautious
(D) enthusiastic
(E) reluctant

35. The word "false" (line 32) means

(A) contrary to truth
(B) imprudent
(C) arising from mistaken ideas
(D) not keeping faith
(E) not genuine or real

Questions 36–45. Read the following poem carefully before you choose your answers.

The Second Coming

Turning and turning in the widening gyre
The falcon cannot hear the falconer;
Things fall apart; the center cannot hold;
Mere anarchy is loosed upon the world,
5 The blood-dimmed tide is loosed, and everywhere
The ceremony of innocence is drowned;
The best lack all conviction, and the worst
Are full of passionate intensity.

Surely some revelation is at hand;
10 Surely the Second Coming is at hand.
The Second Coming! Hardly are those words out
When a vast image out of *Spiritus Mundi* [1]
Troubles my sight; somewhere in the sands of the desert
A shape with lion body and the head of a man,
15 A gaze blank and pitiless as the sun,
Is moving its slow thighs, while all about it
Reel shadows of the indignant desert birds.
The darkness drops again; but now I know
That twenty centuries of stony sleep
20 Were vexed to nightmare by a rocking cradle,
And what rough beast, its hour come round at last,
Slouches towards Bethlehem to be born?

(1921)

[1] Literally, "Spirit of the World"; defined by the poet as a collection of universally understood symbols and images

36. The speaker describes anarchy as "mere" (line 4) in order to show that it

(A) is insignificant and unimportant
(B) is total and absolute
(C) is happening in a foreign country
(D) cannot be reversed or halted
(E) is a temporary condition

37. Which is the best explanation of the statement "The best lack all conviction, and the worst / Are full of passionate intensity" (lines 7–8)?

(A) Good people have few followers because they lack enthusiasm; evil people sway crowds by speaking with strong feeling.
(B) Those who seem good are actually evil; those who seem evil are actually good.
(C) The best that can be said of people is that they have strong feelings; the worst that can be said is that they believe in nothing.
(D) It is better to be without strong beliefs and ideals than to have strong and intense emotions.
(E) People pay more attention to a good person who lacks conviction than they pay to an evil person who speaks with passion.

38. Which best describes the tone of the poem?

    (A) disgusted
    (B) angry
    (C) somber
    (D) desperate
    (E) disappointed

39. The passage "A gaze blank and pitiless as the sun, / Is moving its slow thighs, while all about it / Reel shadows of the indignant desert birds / The darkness drops again;" (lines 15–18) contains examples of all of the following EXCEPT

    (A) alliteration
    (B) simile
    (C) personification
    (D) imagery
    (E) rhyme

40. Why does the speaker believe that "some revelation is at hand" (line 9)?

    (A) He has seen a vision of a terrifying future.
    (B) He has heard news of a strange event in the desert.
    (C) He knows that the current state of unrest cannot continue.
    (D) He sees that the world has awakened to a new awareness of danger.
    (E) He feels an inexplicable dread of what is to come.

41. The poem's thematic content is echoed and reflected by which of the following elements?

    I. its lack of rhyme
    II. the rhythmic and metric irregularities in the second stanza
    III. its use of figurative language

    (A) I only
    (B) I, II, and III
    (C) II only
    (D) II and III only
    (E) III only

42. The falcon and falconer in line 1 symbolize

    (A) slave and master
    (B) child and parent
    (C) follower and leader
    (D) lover and beloved
    (E) poet and muse

43. Which best describes the nature of the event the speaker anticipates?

    (A) An evil force will be let loose upon the world.
    (B) All living creatures on earth will die.
    (C) A mysterious lion-man creature will be born in Bethlehem.
    (D) A war between nations will destroy the world.
    (E) People and animals will lose their ability to communicate.

44. When the speaker says "The darkness drops again" (line 18), he means

    (A) chaos and disorder have cast the world into darkness
    (B) the image of the lion-man and birds is frightening and ominous
    (C) the "shadows of the indignant desert birds" create patches of darkness on the sands
    (D) night falls on the lion-man and the birds of the desert
    (E) his momentary vision vanishes from sight

45. The "rocking cradle" (line 20) is a metaphor for which of the following?

    (A) the restless and chaotic state of society
    (B) the manger in which the baby Jesus slept
    (C) the assassination of a major head of state
    (D) the first shot fired in an international war
    (E) the earthquake that awoke the sleeping beast in the desert

GO ON TO THE NEXT PAGE ⟹

Questions 46–52. Read the following passage carefully before you choose your answers.

And so at last we may ask what are the joys of Ignorance. Are they to enjoy what one has, to be molested by no one, to be superior to all cares and annoyance, to live a secure and quiet life in so far as possible? Truly, this is the life of
5 any wild beast or bird that has its little nest in the deepest and most distant forests, as near as possible to the sky, and there rears its nestlings, flies around in search of food with no fear of being hunted, and warbles in its sweet songs at dawn and sunset. Why crave for the heavenly
10 power of the mind in addition to these pleasures? Ergo, let Ignorance throw off her humanity, let her have Circe's cup and betake herself on all fours to the beasts.

To the beasts, indeed? But they refuse to receive such a foul guest, if they have any share in an inferior kind of
15 reason—as many observers have thought that they do— or have an intelligence that is due to some strong instinct, or make use of the arts or of anything resembling the arts among themselves. For, according to Plutarch, dogs in pursuit of game are said to have some sense of logic
20 and to make obvious use of the disjunctive syllogism when they happen to come to a fork in the road. Aristotle notes that the nightingale is in the habit of giving some kind of musical instruction to her young. Almost every beast is its own doctor, and many of them have taught
25 notable medical lessons to mankind. The Egyptian ibis has shown us the value of purges, and the hippopotamus of phlebotomy. Who can deny a knowledge of astronomy to those from whom come so many warnings of winds, rain, floods, and calm weather? With what prudent and
30 stern discipline the geese check their dangerous garrulity with pebbles in their bills when they are flung over Mt. Taurus! Our domestic science owes much to the ants, and our political science to the bees. Military art thanks the cranes for the principle of posting sentinels
35 and forming the triangular phalanx. The beasts are too intelligent to admit Ignorance to their company and fellowship; they put her lower down.

So what then? Must she go to the trees and the stones. The very trees and shrubs, and the entire forest tore away
40 from their roots to run after the elegant music of Orpheus. Often they have had mysterious powers and have given divine oracles, as the oaks at Dodona did. Rocks also respond with some docility to the sacred voice of the poets. And will not even the rocks spurn Ignorance away?

45 And so, since she is lower than every kind of brute, lower than the trees and rocks, lower than every order known to Nature, will it be granted to Ignorance to find rest in the not-being of the Epicureans? No, not there, since it is necessary, that what is worse, what is viler, what is more
50 wretched, what is lower, should be Ignorance.

(1632)

46. The author uses the word "docility" (line 43) to show that the rocks

(A) are made to soften and crumble by the poets' voices
(B) are open and obedient to the poets' teaching
(C) cannot hear or understand what the poets say
(D) refuse to allow Ignorance to come near them
(E) provide the poets with a place to sit and sing their verses

47. According to the author, geese demonstrate "prudent and stern discipline" (lines 29–30) by

(A) always flying along the same safe route
(B) being silent when honking would endanger them
(C) collecting pebbles with which to build shelters
(D) calling to warn each other of nearby predators
(E) avoiding areas where they know they may be hunted

48. The phrase "Let her have Circe's cup" (lines 11–12) is best interpreted as

(A) let her be fatally poisoned
(B) let her fall in love with the first person she sees
(C) let her forget everything she ever knew
(D) let her be transformed into a pig
(E) let her sleep for a hundred years

49. When the author says that dogs can "make obvious use of the disjunctive syllogism" (line 20), he means that

(A) they are easily confused and misled

(B) their minds can grasp complicated instructions

(C) they are highly skilled at tracking their prey

(D) they can find their way home without help

(E) they are capable of choosing the better of two alternatives

50. The third paragraph of the argument might be considered weak because it

(A) relies on evidence from works of imaginative literature

(B) discusses trees and stones

(C) asks several questions of the reader

(D) defines Ignorance as the lowest and most vile element

(E) repeats an earlier statement that Ignorance is lower than the beasts

51. The author proves that animals are not ignorant of any of the following EXCEPT

(A) music

(B) medicine

(C) art

(D) astronomy

(E) logic

52. The speaker implies throughout the passage that "the joys of Ignorance" (line 1) are

(A) contentment

(B) peace

(C) safety

(D) intelligence

(E) nonexistent

Questions 53–60. Read the following poem carefully before you choose your answers.

Another II

As loving hind that (hartless) wants her deer,
Scuds through the woods and fern with hark'ning ear,
Perplext, in every bush and nook doth pry,
Her dearest deer, might answer ear or eye;
5 So doth my anxious soul, which now doth miss
A dearer dear (far dearer heart) than this.
Still wait with doubts, and hopes, and failing eye,
His voice to hear or person to descry.
Or as the pensive dove doth all alone
10 (On withered bough) most uncouthly bemoan
The absence of her love and loving mate,
Whose loss hath made her so unfortunate,

Ev'n thus do I, with many a deep sad groan,
Bewail my turtle true, who now is gone,
15 His presence and his safe return still woos,
With thousand doleful sighs and mournful coos.
Or as the loving mullet, that true fish,
Her fellow lost, nor joy nor life do wish,
But launches on that shore, there for to die,
20 Where she her captive husband doth espy.
Mine being gone, I lead a joyless life,
I have a loving peer, yet seem no wife;
But worst of all, to him can't steer my course,
I here, he there, alas, both kept by force.
25 Return my dear, my joy, my only love,
Unto thy hind, thy mullet, and thy dove,

GO ON TO THE NEXT PAGE ➡

Who neither joys in pasture, house, nor streams,
The substance gone, O me, these are but dreams.
Together at one tree, oh let us browse,
30 And like two turtles roost within one house,
And like the mullets in one river glide,
Let's still remain but one, till death divide.
Thy loving love and dearest dear,
At home, abroad, and everywhere.

(c. 1650)

53. Which line of the poem best sums up the
speaker's message to her husband?

(A) "[I] Bewail my turtle true, who now is gone"
(line 14)
(B) "I have a loving peer, yet seem no wife"
(line 22)
(C) "I here, he there, alas, both kept by force"
(line 24)
(D) "The substance gone, O me, these are but
dreams" (line 28)
(E) "Let's still remain but one, till death divide"
(line 32)

54. The first six lines of the poem are characterized
by which of the following?

(A) extended metaphor
(B) enjambment
(C) wordplay
(D) paradox
(E) literary allusions

55. The author uses the hind, mullet, and turtledove
to symbolize all of the following EXCEPT

(A) longing
(B) loyalty
(C) love
(D) sorrow
(E) fidelity

56. Which best describes the speaker's situation?

(A) She and her husband are temporarily apart.
(B) Her husband has recently died and left her alone.
(C) She has lost her husband's love to
another woman.
(D) She has permanently abandoned her husband.
(E) She no longer loves her husband.

57. The change in meter at line 33 alerts the reader
to which of the following?

(A) a new rhyme scheme
(B) a shift in tone or mood
(C) the conclusion of the poem
(D) a change in speakers
(E) the introduction of a new subject

58. The author uses words like "anxious" (line
5), "doubts" (line 7), "bemoan" (line 10), and
"doleful" (line 16) to contribute to a mood of

(A) despair
(B) mourning
(C) passion
(D) grief
(E) hope

59. The author uses the phrase "failing eye" (line 7)
to show that the speaker

(A) is searching for her mate in a dark forest
(B) is unable to hear any trace of her mate
(C) cannot see what she is looking for
(D) is weeping with unhappiness over her loss
(E) does not know where to look for her mate

60. The speaker's sorrow is best characterized as

(A) shocking and traumatic
(B) momentary and trivial
(C) absolute and total
(D) wistful and loving
(E) bitter and resentful

STOP

If you finish before time is called, you may check your work on this test only.

Do not turn to any other test in this book.

Answer Key

1. D	16. C	31. E	46. B
2. D	17. E	32. A	47. B
3. C	18. A	33. A	48. D
4. A	19. C	34. E	49. E
5. E	20. B	35. B	50. A
6. B	21. A	36. B	51. C
7. C	22. D	37. A	52. E
8. A	23. C	38. D	53. E
9. B	24. E	39. E	54. C
10. C	25. E	40. C	55. D
11. C	26. E	41. B	56. A
12. A	27. A	42. C	57. C
13. E	28. B	43. A	58. D
14. D	29. D	44. E	59. C
15. B	30. C	45. A	60. D

Answers and Explanations

1. **(D)** The author says he frequently wept while listening to slaves singing and that even thinking about the music makes him sad. This context makes it clear that the "expression of feeling" he refers to is another tear trickling down his cheek.

2. **(D)** *Obdurate* is derived from a Latin word meaning "hard." If a person has an *obdurate* heart, he is "hardhearted" or unfeeling.

3. **(C)** In this sense, *rude* means "crude, rough, unrefined." The slaves' songs are not finished compositions by trained musicians; they are made up on the spot.

4. **(A)** The author says that slaves sing in order to relieve the sorrows of the heart.

5. **(E)** All three options are reasonable causes for the slaves to feel happy and excited about going to the Great House Farm.

6. **(B)** The three words in the question all refer to the emotions felt by the singers.

7. **(C)** The author repeatedly expresses his hatred of slavery as an institution. Because this appears to be his major focus, the inference follows that he wants to persuade others to hate slavery as much as he does.

8. **(A)** Most of the author's references to the songs are to their emotional impact on himself as well as on others. He is so strongly affected by the memory of the songs that he believes the effect will be equally strong on other listeners. He believes that this appeal to emotion is stronger than a book's appeal to reason.

9. **(B)** A *glimmering* conception is one that is only faintly comprehended.

10. **(C)** The author calls his fellow poets misers because they are stingy with their words to make them fit into traditional rhyme schemes. Because the argument of the poem is that poets should attempt new rhyme schemes or else poetry will die as an art, choice A must be wrong, because "fail to adhere" indicates that not following traditional rhyme schemes is a negative characteristic. The author argues that poets expand their uses of words, and choice B is the exact opposite of this argument. Choice D is wrong because the author *does* call his fellow poets misers. Choice E is wrong because there is nothing in the poem about how well poetry pays as a profession.

11. **(C)** Most sonnets follow one of two set rhyme schemes—Italian or Shakespearean. This sonnet has an irregular rhyme scheme all its own.

12. **(A)** The speaker says that if we *must* use rhymes in poetry, then we need to find ways to make rhyme contribute more to the artistic effect of the whole poem.

13. **(E)** The speaker is comparing rhyme schemes to sandals. Just as a sandal should perfectly and comfortably fit a person's bare foot, a rhyme scheme should be a perfect and comfortable fit for the language and meaning of a poem. *Poesy* refers to the art and practice of writing poetry.

14. **(D)** The sonnet argues that new and better rhyme schemes are needed to replace the old patterns. It proves its point by employing an irregular rhyme scheme.

15. **(B)** In this context, *jealous* means "distrustful, suspicious." "Dead leaves" is a metaphorical reference to long-established poetic forms and techniques, which the poet believes have outworn their welcome. He says, in effect, that poets should distrust old ways of writing poetry rather than using them unthinkingly or automatically.

16. **(C)** The poet's main argument is not that rhyme should be eliminated but that it should always be adapted to serve the poem's content. He believes that poets should adapt a rhyme scheme to fit the ideas they want to express, rather than making their ideas fit into a set rhyme scheme.

17. **(E)** The context shows that this archaic definition of *meet* is the correct one.

18. **(A)** The poem's overall message is that poets must pay close attention to both the meaning and the sound of their words. The lyre is a musical instrument; the words *lyre, chord,* and *ear* all suggest that in these lines, the poet is primarily concerned with urging his colleagues to think about sound.

19. **(C)** The speaker is first drawn to the lake by its loneliness, but it does not exert a true fascination for him until he sees it at night. In the darkness, it terrifies him, and he exults in the feeling of terror.

20. **(B)** The phrase "tremulous delight" (line 14) implies that the speaker defines fear as an emotion that would drive him away and terror as an emotion that attracts and thrills him.

21. **(A)** The speaker says that terror delights him and that he finds *solace,* or comfort, in the thoughts of his own death by drowning in the lake.

22. **(D)** The speaker is fascinated by thoughts of his own death. *Morbid* comes from a Latin root meaning "death."

23. **(C)** In the Book of Genesis, the Garden of Eden is an earthly paradise where people and animals enjoy untroubled happiness. Only a gloomy and morbid person could compare an isolated lake, with its towering pines and black rocks, to this biblical pleasure garden.

24. **(E)** *Ominousness* is the best choice because an air of foreboding, of approaching disaster, hangs over the poem. The speaker appears to be emotionally unstable, to be attracted to dark and lonely places, and to feel a thrill at the thought of his own death.

25. **(E)** All three are true statements. The speaker's unstable mind has produced a poem with an unstable rhythmic structure. The jerky rhythm of many of the lines affects the reader's impression of everything the speaker describes, including the lake. The irregularities of the rhythm upset the reader's natural expectation that the rhymed couplets will proceed in a smooth and regular rhythm.

26. **(E)** Choices C and D are true statements, but these facts about Watson would not cause a strong emotional reaction, such as the author describes. Watson reacts strongly because he is afraid for Holmes—afraid for the consequences to his career and reputation if he is caught.

27. **(A)** The greatest fear Watson expresses about the burglary is that Holmes may get caught. Therefore, his most probable reason for going along is his friendship for Holmes—he wants to help and protect his friend.

28. **(B)** Holmes explains that his action is not hasty and rash, but rather that he has thought carefully before making his decision.

29. **(D)** Details in the passage show that Milverton intends to commit a crime against Holmes's client, Lady Eva. Holmes intends to prevent a crime by committing one of his own. Because he is stealing nothing except items "which are used for an illegal purpose," he feels that his act is justifiable.

30. **(C)** The references to money, "the letters," and Lady Eva's "ruin" imply that Milverton is blackmailing her—that her letters contain secrets that can destroy her reputation, and that he will publish these letters unless she pays him not to.

31. **(E)** Courage: Watson insists on sharing what he knows to be a serious risk. Loyalty: To help and protect his friend, Watson is willing to set aside his strong sense of right and wrong. Honesty: Watson is open with Holmes about his objections to the plan and clearly disapproves of the crime as a dishonest act, despite the "moral justification." Morality: Watson shows moral disapproval of the planned burglary but also the moral sense to admit that Milverton plans an even worse crime. The caution Watson exhibits in the passage shows that choice E must be the correct answer.

32. **(A)** Holmes's remark, "it's a sporting duel between this fellow Milverton and me," suggests that he wants to defeat Milverton all by himself (the word *duel,* by definition, is a contest between two people). Holmes is well aware that he is about to commit a crime, and naturally he hesitates to involve Watson. Therefore, options I and II are reasonable. Option III cannot be supported, because Holmes's annoyed expression disappears when Watson reminds him that he too has a reputation to consider.

33. **(A)** A *resolute* person is one who is determined—one whose mind is made up and who will not easily be persuaded to change it. Choice C is wrong because this particular phrase involves only the determination to carry out the act; it does not relate to Holmes's original intention of carrying it out alone.

34. **(E)** Determined: Holmes is clearly resolved on his course of action and will change his mind. Confident: He states that Milverton will be asleep and that he expects to "be back here by two," having carried out his plan. Cautious: Holmes has thought the matter through and laid his plans very carefully so as to take no unnecessary risk. Enthusiastic: The phrases "a sporting duel" and "fight it to a finish" show that Holmes is eager to defeat Milverton. This leaves choice E.

35. **(B)** There is nothing untruthful about Holmes's intention to burgle Milverton's house. *Imprudent* means unwise, or ill-advised. In this context, this is the correct answer. Choice C does not make sense because Holmes does not have any mistaken ideas about the risks he is taking. Choice D is wrong because Holmes does not have a trusting relationship with Milverton to betray. Choice E is incorrect because Holmes is not pretending to be something or someone else.

36. **(B)** The context shows that this archaic sense of *mere* must be correct. The line means "Total anarchy is loosed upon the world."

37. **(A)** The first six lines describe a society in chaos. "The best" and "the worst" refers to the political and/or religious leaders who influence and control society for good or evil ends. The speaker observes that the good leaders lose followers because they show no conviction, or belief in their own cause. The evil forces, on the other hand, attract followers by speaking forcefully and with passion.

38. **(D)** The poem is about the author's despair over the decline of Western civilization. Various words and phrases in the poem convey this feeling: "Mere anarchy is loosed upon the world" (line 4) and "The blood-dimmed tide is loosed" (line 5).

39. **(E)** Alliteration: "Darkness drops again" uses a repeating *d* sound to create the effect of a dull thud. Simile: "blank and pitiless *as* the sun." Personification: "indignant desert birds." Imagery: The lines contain vivid visual images. None of the lines rhymes with any of the others, so choice E is correct.

40. **(C)** The speaker believes that the world around him is coming to an end; that the Apocalypse—the end of one world and the beginning of a new one—is near. The speaker compares his own world with that described in the Bible and believes that the biblical prophecy is about to come true and that the world will begin again, in some new fashion.

41. **(B)** The major theme of the poem is the destruction of order in the world. This is mirrored by the poem's lack of structural order—its unrhymed lines and the frequent shift away from the basic meter of iambic pentameter. Option III is wrong because the presence of figurative language in a poem is normal. The figurative language in the poem supports a theme of everything being wrong, chaotic, or out of order.

42. **(C)** The poem describes chaos in two realms: one of faith (the references to the second coming of Jesus) and one of government (the reference to anarchy and "the blood-dimmed tide" of war). Political and religious leaders (falconers) can no longer make their followers (the falcons) hear them, because they "lack all conviction" (line 7) and they have lost control.

43. **(A)** The speaker describes a "rough beast" that "slouches towards Bethlehem to be born." This is a metaphor for some new force that will appear in the world, which the speaker believes will have as much influence as Jesus once had. The language "troubles my sight," "its gaze blank and pitiless," "rough beast," and "slouches" all suggest that the new force will be evil rather than good.

44. **(E)** The vision described in lines 14–17 is an image or picture brightly visible in the speaker's imagination. When it disappears, "the darkness drops again." The mind's eye is once more a blank surface waiting for new impressions.

45. **(A)** The speaker believes that an evil force has been awakened by the "rocking cradle" of a society that is no longer peaceful, ordered, or controlled.

46. **(B)** A *docile* person is teachable, tractable, or obedient.

47. **(B)** *Garrulity* means "talkativeness." The geese carry pebbles in their beaks to stop themselves from honking or calling, when making that noise would endanger them.

48. **(D)** The phrase "betake herself on all fours" is a reference to being turned into an animal. (This allusion refers to Circe, a character in the *Odyssey* who transforms Odysseus' crew into swine, or pigs.)

49. **(E)** The phrase "a fork in the road" is the context clue that tells you the author is referring to a dog's ability to choose the better alternative when confronted with two options. *Disjunctive* refers to two mutually exclusive alternatives, and a *syllogism* is a rule of logic.

50. **(A)** The evidence in the second paragraph is all based on direct observations of animals that can be scientifically proved. The evidence about the intelligence and higher instincts of trees and rocks, however, is drawn from mythology, a form of imaginative literature. The fact that a phenomenon appears in a work of fiction is not solid proof that it exists in reality.

51. **(C)** The author gives specific examples of animal knowledge of the other four choices. He does not suggest that animals are able to create pictures, statues, or other works of visual art.

52. **(E)** In the first paragraph, the author lists several possible "joys of Ignorance," including those described in choices A–C. He then shows that animals are able to live in peace, security, and contentment precisely because they are *not* ignorant. The entire passage implies that Ignorance is a joyless state.

53. **(E)** The speaker addresses her husband directly only in the final ten lines, which eliminates choices A, B, and C. Choice E sums up the main idea toward which the entire poem has been building.

54. **(C)** The poet plays with *hart/heart* and *dear/deer*—words that sound alike but mean different things.

55. **(D)** The author is sorrowful because her husband is away, but the three animals do not symbolize sorrow. They symbolize her feelings of love, loyalty, fidelity, and longing for her absent mate.

56. **(A)** "Let's still remain but one, till death divide" (line 32) implies that the husband is still alive. Nothing in the poem suggests that she and her husband do not love one another. Because the speaker describes herself and her husband as "kept [apart] by force" (line 24), it appears that he has gone away on some necessary business and will return.

57. **(C)** It is a standard poetic technique to signal the end of a poem, or a scene in a verse play, with a rhymed couplet. Because this entire poem is in rhymed couplets, the author has changed the meter instead of the rhyme scheme; the final two lines are one metric foot shorter than the rest of the verse.

58. **(D)** The speaker feels deep grief over the absence of her husband. Despair is too strong a word, because she still feels hope that he will return; mourning is too strong a word because he is still alive.

59. **(C)** "Failing eye" means that her eyes fail to *descry*, or see, his *person*, or physical presence. She cannot see him because he is absent.

60. **(D)** Every line of the poem tells of the speaker's love and her wish that her husband should return soon. The fact that she indulges in wordplay and metaphoric conceits shows that her sorrow cannot be so "absolute and total" that she has lost her wit and sense of fun.

How To Calculate Your Score

Count the number of correct answers and enter the total below.

Count the number of wrong answers. Do NOT include any questions you did not answer.

Multiply the number of wrong answers by 0.25 and enter the total below.

Do the subtraction. The answer is your raw score. Use the scoring scale to find your scaled score.

$$\overline{\hspace{3cm}} - \overline{\hspace{5cm}} = \overline{\hspace{2cm}}$$
(number of correct answers)   (number of wrong answers × 0.25)   (raw score)

RAW SCORE	SCALED SCORE	RAW SCORE	SCALED SCORE	RAW SCORE	SCALED SCORE	RAW SCORE	SCALED SCORE	RAW SCORE	SCALED SCORE
60	800	44	710	28	560	12	420	-4	260
59	800	43	700	27	550	11	410	-5	250
58	800	42	690	26	540	10	400	-6	240
57	800	41	690	25	530	9	390	-7	230
56	800	40	680	24	520	8	380	-8	220
55	800	39	670	23	510	7	370	-9	210
54	790	38	660	22	500	6	360	-10	200
53	790	37	650	21	500	5	350	-11	200
52	780	36	640	20	490	4	340	-12	200
51	770	35	630	19	490	3	330	-13	200
50	760	34	620	18	480	2	320	-14	200
49	750	33	610	17	470	1	310	-15	200
48	740	32	600	16	460	0	300		
47	740	31	590	15	450	-1	290		
46	730	30	580	14	440	-2	280		
45	720	29	570	13	430	-3	270		

Note: This is only a sample scoring scale. Scoring scales differ from exam to exam.

Practice Test 6

The following practice test is designed to be just like the real SAT Literature Test. It matches the actual test in content coverage and degree of difficulty.

Once you finish the practice test, determine your score. Carefully read the answer explanations of the questions you answered incorrectly. Identify any weaknesses in your literature skills by determining the areas in which you made the most errors. Review those sections of this book first. Then, as time permits, go back and review your strengths.

Allow one hour to take the test. Time yourself and work uninterrupted. If you run out of time, take note of where you stopped when time ran out. Remember that you lose a quarter point for each incorrect answer, but you do not lose points for questions you leave blank. Therefore, unless you can eliminate one or more of the five choices, it is best to leave a question unanswered.

Use the following formula to calculate your score:

$$\text{(number of correct answers)} - \tfrac{1}{4} \text{(number of incorrect answers)}$$

If you treat this practice test just like the actual exam, it will accurately reflect how you are likely to perform on test day. Here are some hints on how to create test-taking conditions similar to those of the actual exam:

- Complete the test in one sitting. On test day, you will not be allowed to take a break.
- Tear out the answer sheet and fill in the ovals just as you will on the actual test day.
- Have a good eraser and more than one sharp pencil handy. On test day, you will not be able to go get a new pencil if yours breaks.
- Do not allow yourself any extra time; put down your pencil after exactly one hour, no matter how many questions are left to answer.
- Become familiar with the directions on the test. If you go in knowing what the directions say, you will not have to waste time reading and thinking about them on the actual test day.

Answer Sheet

Tear out this answer sheet and use it to mark your answers.

1. Ⓐ Ⓑ Ⓒ Ⓓ Ⓔ	16. Ⓐ Ⓑ Ⓒ Ⓓ Ⓔ	31. Ⓐ Ⓑ Ⓒ Ⓓ Ⓔ	46. Ⓐ Ⓑ Ⓒ Ⓓ Ⓔ
2. Ⓐ Ⓑ Ⓒ Ⓓ Ⓔ	17. Ⓐ Ⓑ Ⓒ Ⓓ Ⓔ	32. Ⓐ Ⓑ Ⓒ Ⓓ Ⓔ	47. Ⓐ Ⓑ Ⓒ Ⓓ Ⓔ
3. Ⓐ Ⓑ Ⓒ Ⓓ Ⓔ	18. Ⓐ Ⓑ Ⓒ Ⓓ Ⓔ	33. Ⓐ Ⓑ Ⓒ Ⓓ Ⓔ	48. Ⓐ Ⓑ Ⓒ Ⓓ Ⓔ
4. Ⓐ Ⓑ Ⓒ Ⓓ Ⓔ	19. Ⓐ Ⓑ Ⓒ Ⓓ Ⓔ	34. Ⓐ Ⓑ Ⓒ Ⓓ Ⓔ	49. Ⓐ Ⓑ Ⓒ Ⓓ Ⓔ
5. Ⓐ Ⓑ Ⓒ Ⓓ Ⓔ	20. Ⓐ Ⓑ Ⓒ Ⓓ Ⓔ	35. Ⓐ Ⓑ Ⓒ Ⓓ Ⓔ	50. Ⓐ Ⓑ Ⓒ Ⓓ Ⓔ
6. Ⓐ Ⓑ Ⓒ Ⓓ Ⓔ	21. Ⓐ Ⓑ Ⓒ Ⓓ Ⓔ	36. Ⓐ Ⓑ Ⓒ Ⓓ Ⓔ	51. Ⓐ Ⓑ Ⓒ Ⓓ Ⓔ
7. Ⓐ Ⓑ Ⓒ Ⓓ Ⓔ	22. Ⓐ Ⓑ Ⓒ Ⓓ Ⓔ	37. Ⓐ Ⓑ Ⓒ Ⓓ Ⓔ	52. Ⓐ Ⓑ Ⓒ Ⓓ Ⓔ
8. Ⓐ Ⓑ Ⓒ Ⓓ Ⓔ	23. Ⓐ Ⓑ Ⓒ Ⓓ Ⓔ	38. Ⓐ Ⓑ Ⓒ Ⓓ Ⓔ	53. Ⓐ Ⓑ Ⓒ Ⓓ Ⓔ
9. Ⓐ Ⓑ Ⓒ Ⓓ Ⓔ	24. Ⓐ Ⓑ Ⓒ Ⓓ Ⓔ	39. Ⓐ Ⓑ Ⓒ Ⓓ Ⓔ	54. Ⓐ Ⓑ Ⓒ Ⓓ Ⓔ
10. Ⓐ Ⓑ Ⓒ Ⓓ Ⓔ	25. Ⓐ Ⓑ Ⓒ Ⓓ Ⓔ	40. Ⓐ Ⓑ Ⓒ Ⓓ Ⓔ	55. Ⓐ Ⓑ Ⓒ Ⓓ Ⓔ
11. Ⓐ Ⓑ Ⓒ Ⓓ Ⓔ	26. Ⓐ Ⓑ Ⓒ Ⓓ Ⓔ	41. Ⓐ Ⓑ Ⓒ Ⓓ Ⓔ	56. Ⓐ Ⓑ Ⓒ Ⓓ Ⓔ
12. Ⓐ Ⓑ Ⓒ Ⓓ Ⓔ	27. Ⓐ Ⓑ Ⓒ Ⓓ Ⓔ	42. Ⓐ Ⓑ Ⓒ Ⓓ Ⓔ	57. Ⓐ Ⓑ Ⓒ Ⓓ Ⓔ
13. Ⓐ Ⓑ Ⓒ Ⓓ Ⓔ	28. Ⓐ Ⓑ Ⓒ Ⓓ Ⓔ	43. Ⓐ Ⓑ Ⓒ Ⓓ Ⓔ	58. Ⓐ Ⓑ Ⓒ Ⓓ Ⓔ
14. Ⓐ Ⓑ Ⓒ Ⓓ Ⓔ	29. Ⓐ Ⓑ Ⓒ Ⓓ Ⓔ	44. Ⓐ Ⓑ Ⓒ Ⓓ Ⓔ	59. Ⓐ Ⓑ Ⓒ Ⓓ Ⓔ
15. Ⓐ Ⓑ Ⓒ Ⓓ Ⓔ	30. Ⓐ Ⓑ Ⓒ Ⓓ Ⓔ	45. Ⓐ Ⓑ Ⓒ Ⓓ Ⓔ	60. Ⓐ Ⓑ Ⓒ Ⓓ Ⓔ

PRACTICE TEST 6

Time: 60 Minutes

Directions: This test consists of selections from literary works and questions on their content, form, and style. After reading each passage or poem, choose the best answer to each question and then fill in the corresponding oval on the answer sheet.

Note: Pay particular attention to the requirements of questions that contain the words NOT or EXCEPT.

Questions 1–9. Read the following passage carefully before you choose your answers.

"My dear Mr. Bennet," said his lady to him one day, "have you heard that Netherfield Park is let at last?"

Mr. Bennet replied that he had not.

"But it is," returned she; "for Mrs. Long has just been
5 here, and she told me all about it."

Mr. Bennet made no answer.

"Do not you want to know who has taken it?" cried his wife impatiently.

"*You* want to tell me, and I have no objection to
10 hearing it."

This was invitation enough.

"Why, my dear, you must know, Mrs. Long says that Netherfield is taken by a young man of large fortune from the north of England; that he came down on
15 Monday in a chaise-and-four to see the place, and was so much delighted with it that he agreed with Mr. Morris immediately; that he is to take possession before Michaelmas, and some of his servants are to be in the house by the end of next week."

20 "What is his name?"

"Bingley."

"Is he married or single?"

"Oh! single, my dear, to be sure! A single man of large fortune; four or five thousand a year. What a fine thing
25 for our girls!"

"How so? how can it affect them?"

"My dear Mr. Bennet," replied his wife, "how can you be so tiresome! you must know that I am thinking of his marrying one of them."

30 "Is that his design in settling here?"

"Design! nonsense, how can you talk so! But it is very likely that he *may* fall in love with one of them, and therefore you must visit him as soon as he comes."

"I see no occasion for that. You and the girls may go, or
35 you may send them by themselves, which perhaps will be still better, for as you are as handsome as any of them, Mr. Bingley might like you the best of the party."

"My dear, you flatter me. I certainly *have* had my share of beauty, but I do not pretend to be anything extraordinary
40 now. When a woman has five grown-up daughters, she ought to give over thinking of her own beauty."

"In such cases, a woman has not often much beauty to think of."

"But, my dear, you must indeed go and see Mr. Bingley
45 when he comes into the neighborhood."

"It is more than I engage for, I assure you."

"But consider your daughters. Only think what an establishment it would be for one of them. Sir William and Lady Lucas are determined to go, merely on
50 that account, for in general, you know, they visit no

newcomers. Indeed you must go, for it will be impossible for *us* to visit him, if you do not."

"You are over-scrupulous, surely. I dare say Mr. Bingley
55 will be very glad to see you; and I will send a few lines by you to assure him of my hearty consent to his marrying whichever he chooses of the girls; though I must throw in a good word for my little Lizzy."

"I desire you will do no such thing. Lizzy is not a bit better than the others; and I am sure she is not half so
60 handsome as Jane, nor half so good-humored as Lydia. But you are always giving *her* the preference."

"They have none of them much to recommend them," replied he; "they are all silly and ignorant like other girls; but Lizzy has something more of quickness than her
65 sisters."

"Mr. Bennet, how can you abuse your own children in such a way? You take delight in vexing me. You have no compassion on my poor nerves."

"You mistake me, my dear. I have a high respect for your
70 nerves. They are my old friends. I have heard you mention them with consideration these twenty years at least."

"Ah! you do not know what I suffer."

"But I hope you will get over it, and live to see many young men of four thousand a year come into the
75 neighborhood."

"It will be no use to us if twenty such should come, since you will not visit them."

"Depend upon it, my dear, that when there are twenty, I will visit them all."

(1813)

1. From the fact that Lizzy is his favorite daughter, you can conclude that Mr. Bennet

(A) likes talking to people with a sense of humor
(B) values intelligence more than any other quality
(C) enjoys seeing pretty faces around him
(D) avoids argument and conflict within the family
(E) appreciates having good-natured and pretty children

2. The statement "*You* want to tell me, and I have no objection to hearing it" (lines 9–10) implies which of the following?

(A) Mr. Bennet is not much interested in hearing his wife's news.
(B) Mrs. Bennet is disappointed by her husband's objections.
(C) Mr. Bennet already knows what his wife is about to tell him.
(D) Mr. and Mrs. Bennet understand each other without having to say anything.
(E) Mrs. Bennet hesitates to speak without being coaxed and encouraged.

3. Mrs. Bennet uses the word "let" (line 2) to mean that Netherfield Park has been

(A) allowed, permitted
(B) abandoned, left behind
(C) leased, rented
(D) prevented, hindered
(E) assigned, appointed

4. Mrs. Bennet's repeated insistence that Mr. Bennet visit Mr. Bingley reveals all of the following EXCEPT

    (A) she is not a subtle person
    (B) she focuses all her attention on what is most important to her
    (C) she will make every effort to see that her daughters marry well
    (D) she does not understand her husband's character
    (E) she is not practical or realistic by nature

5. Why does Mr. Bennet promise that "when there are twenty, I will visit them all" (lines 78–79)?

    (A) He does not wish to make any effort on his daughters' behalf.
    (B) He enjoys teasing and provoking his wife.
    (C) He will only bestir himself on an extraordinary occasion.
    (D) He sees no point in visiting only one newcomer to the neighborhood.
    (E) He knows one young man cannot marry all five of his daughters.

6. All of the following statements help to reveal Mr. Bennet's sense of humor EXCEPT

    (A) "... you may send them by themselves, which perhaps will be still better, for as you are as handsome as any of them, Mr. Bingley might like you the best of the party." (lines 35–37)
    (B) "I will send a few lines by you to assure him of my hearty consent to his marrying whichever he chooses of the girls." (lines 54–56)
    (C) "... they are all silly and ignorant, like other girls; but Lizzy has something more of quickness than her sisters." (lines 63–65)
    (D) "I have a high respect for your nerves. They are my old friends. I have heard you mention them with consideration these twenty years at least." (lines 69–71)
    (E) "But I hope you will get over it, and live to see many young men of four thousand a year come into the neighborhood." (lines 73–75)

7. Which of the following suggests that Mr. Bennet shares his wife's concern for their daughters' future?

    (A) his wish that his daughters were not silly and ignorant
    (B) his promise to visit twenty young men when they move to the neighborhood
    (C) his suggestion that his wife and daughters should visit Mr. Bingley
    (D) his immediate question as to whether Bingley is married or single
    (E) his promise to consent to Bingley's marrying one of his daughters

8. What accounts for Mrs. Bennet's reaction when Mr. Bennet says "I must throw in a good word for my little Lizzy" (lines 56–57)?

    I. She does not regard Lizzy's quickness as an attractive quality.

    II. She is a little jealous of Mr. Bennet's affection for Lizzy.

    III. She is fonder of Jane and Lydia than she is of Lizzy.

(A) I and II only
(B) I and III only
(C) II and III only
(D) III only
(E) I, II, and III

9. Mr. Bennet's attitude toward Mrs. Bennet is best described as

(A) loving and affectionate
(B) detached and ironic
(C) irritated and contemptuous
(D) suspicious and jealous
(E) cold and indifferent

Questions 10–16. Read the following poem carefully before you choose your answers.

Fear no more the heat o' th' sun,
    Nor the furious winter's rages;
Thou thy worldly task hast done,
    Home art gone, and ta'en thy wages.
5 Golden lads and girls all must,
As chimney-sweepers, come to dust.

Fear no more the frown o' th' great;
    Thou art past the tyrant's stroke.
Care no more to clothe and eat;
10   To thee the reed is as the oak.
The scepter, learning, physic, must
All follow this, and come to dust.

Fear no more the lightning flash,
    Nor th' all-dreaded thunder-stone.
15 Fear not slander, censure rash;
    Thou hast finish'd joy and moan.
All lovers young, all lovers must
Consign to thee, and come to dust.

No exorciser harm thee!
20 Nor no witchcraft charm thee!
Ghost unlaid forbear thee!
Nothing ill come near thee!
Quiet consummation have,
And renownèd be thy grave!

(c. 1609)

10. "Golden lads and girls all must / As chimney-sweepers, come to dust" (lines 5–6) is an example of

(A) a play on words
(B) a metaphor
(C) verbal irony
(D) personification
(E) a tragedy

11. "The scepter" (line 11) symbolizes which of the following?

(A) a doctor
(B) a ghost
(C) a monarch
(D) a poet
(E) a lover

12. The metaphor "Home art gone, and ta'en thy wages" (line 4) implies that the person addressed has

(A) gone home
(B) quit her job
(C) left town
(D) died
(E) abandoned the speaker

13. Which best explains the meaning of "Ghost unlaid forbear thee!" (line 21)?

(A) Let nothing haunt you.
(B) Let ghosts fear you.
(C) Let ghosts help carry your burdens.
(D) Let us always remember you.
(E) Let your spirit rest.

14. The phrase "Quiet consummation have" (line 23) is best paraphrased as

(A) May you find true love and fulfillment.
(B) May you find happiness in marriage.
(C) May you be blessed with peace and happiness.
(D) May you die with courage.
(E) May your dead body lie quietly in the earth.

15. Which best describes the wish the speaker expresses for the person addressed as "thee" in lines 19–24?

(A) that she will sleep peacefully and well
(B) that she will lie quiet and undisturbed in her grave
(C) that she will learn not to fear so many things
(D) that she will forget the haunting memories of the past
(E) that she will return to him one day in the future

16. "To thee the reed is as the oak" (line 10) is the speaker's way of saying that

(A) neither weakness nor strength means anything to you now
(B) you once seemed weak, but you now show great strength
(C) you can no longer tell the difference between a reed and an oak tree
(D) it does not matter to you where we shelter you from the weather
(E) you are just as happy to be poor as to be rich

Questions 17–25. Read the following dramatic excerpt carefully before you choose your answers.

(By learning to speak like a lady, flower-seller Liza Doolittle hopes to make a better life for herself. Speech professor Henry Higgins agrees to house her at his expense during her training. Liza's father, hearing of her good fortune, comes to Higgins and his colleague Pickering to ask them for money.)

DOOLITTLE. What am I, Governors both? I ask you, what am I? I'm one of the undeserving poor: that's what I am. Think of what that means to a man. It means that he's up agen middle-class morality all the time. If there's
5 anything going, and I put in for a bit of it, it's always the same story: "You're undeserving; so you can't have it." But my needs is as great as the most deserving widow's that ever got money out of six different charities in one week for the death of the same husband. I don't need less than
10 a deserving man: I need more. I don't eat less hearty than him; and I drink a lot more. I want a bit of amusement, 'cause I'm a thinking man. I want cheerfulness and a song and a band when I feel low. Well, they charge me just the same for everything as they charge the deserving. What is
15 middle-class morality? Just an excuse for never giving me anything. Therefore, I ask you, as two gentlemen, not to play that game on me. I'm playing straight with you. I ain't pretending to be deserving. I'm undeserving; and I mean to go on being undeserving. I like it; and that's the truth.
20 Will you take advantage of a man's nature to do him out of the price of his own daughter what he's brought up and fed and clothed by the sweat of his brow until she's growed big enough to be interesting to you two gentlemen? Is five pounds unreasonable? I put it to you; and I leave it to you.

25 HIGGINS *[rising, and going over to Pickering]*. Pickering: if we were to take this man in hand for three months, he

could choose between a seat in the Cabinet and a popular pulpit in Wales.

PICKERING. What do you say to that, Doolittle?

30 DOOLITTLE. Not me, Governor, thank you kindly. I've heard all the preachers and all the prime ministers—for I'm a thinking man and game for politics or religion or social reform same as all the other amusements—and I tell you it's a dog's life any way you look at it. Undeserving

35 poverty is my line. Taking one station in society with another, it's—it's—well, it's the only one that has any ginger in it, to my taste.

HIGGINS. I suppose we must give him a fiver.

PICKERING. He'll make a bad use of it, I'm afraid.

40 DOOLITTLE. Not me, Governor, so help me I won't. Don't you be afraid that I'll save it and spare it and live idle on it. There won't be a penny of it left by Monday: I'll have to go to work same as if I'd never had it. It won't pauperize me, you bet. Just one good spree for myself and

45 the missus, giving pleasure to ourselves and employment to others, and satisfaction to you to think it's not been throwed away. You couldn't spend it better.

HIGGINS *[taking out his pocket book and coming between Doolittle and the piano]*. This is irresistible. Let's give him

50 ten. *[He offers two notes to the dustman[1]]*.

DOOLITTLE. No, Governor. She wouldn't have the heart to spend ten; and perhaps I shouldn't neither. Ten pounds is a lot of money: it makes a man feel prudent like; and then goodbye to happiness. You give me what I ask you,

55 Governor: not a penny more, and not a penny less.

(1916)

---

[1] British term for "garbage collector," Doolittle's occupation

17. When Higgins says that Doolittle "could choose between a seat in the Cabinet and a popular pulpit in Wales" (lines 27–28), he acknowledges that Doolittle

    I. is a charming and entertaining speaker
    II. has a natural ability to express himself clearly and well
    III. has strong political convictions and deep religious faith

  (A) I only
  (B) II only
  (C) III only
  (D) I and II only
  (E) II and III only

18. Why does Doolittle believe that feeling "prudent like" means "goodbye to happiness" (lines 53–54)?

  (A) Prudent people save money and thus deprive themselves of the enjoyment it can buy.
  (B) People who are prudent disapprove of many ordinary amusements.
  (C) A prudent person would need more than five pounds for "one good spree."
  (D) Prudent people let their spouses dictate what they will do with their income.
  (E) A prudent person feels that he has no responsibilities to others.

19. In what sense is Doolittle "undeserving" as used in the passage according to the standards of "middle-class morality"?

  (A) He has a job and can thus afford to pay his own way.
  (B) He drinks heavily, relies on his charm, and spends his money freely.
  (C) He does not support his daughter's effort to improve her situation.
  (D) He has never succeeded in borrowing money from a charity.
  (E) He does not want to rise to a higher social rank.

GO ON TO THE NEXT PAGE ⟼

20. Why does Doolittle believe that "undeserving poverty" is the only station in life "that has any ginger in it" (lines 34–37)?

   (A) It qualifies him for assistance from various charities.
   (B) It allows him to talk to those of higher rank as if they were his equals.
   (C) It offers him the chance to rise to a better position in society.
   (D) It lets him depend on others for his support.
   (E) It gives him the freedom to be irresponsible and enjoy himself as he likes.

21. Higgins's use of the word "irresistible" (line 49) shows that he

   (A) is charmed by Doolittle's personality
   (B) is convinced by Doolittle's logic
   (C) feels compassion for Doolittle's poverty
   (D) is angered by Doolittle's request for money
   (E) feels guilty at having to refuse Doolittle's request

22. Doolittle's example of "the most deserving widow that ever got money out of six different charities in one week for the death of the same husband" (lines 7–9) demonstrates his belief that

   (A) widows who apply to charities are not really deserving of help
   (B) charities will not help someone like himself who has a job
   (C) he would have to die before his "missus" could get help from a charity
   (D) middle-class moralists are hypocritical
   (E) the "deserving" poor will always find someone to give them a helping hand

23. Which of the following best supports Doolittle's statement "I'm a thinking man" (line 32)?

   (A) "What am I, Governors both? I ask you, what am I? I'm one of the undeserving poor: that's what I am." (lines 1–3)
   (B) "Well, they charge me just the same for everything as they charge the deserving. What is middle-class morality? Just an excuse for never giving me anything." (lines 13–16)
   (C) "Taking one station in society with another, it's—it's—well, it's the only one that has any ginger in it, to my taste." (lines 35–37)
   (D) "Don't you be afraid that I'll save it and spare it and live idle on it. There won't be a penny of it left by Monday." (lines 41–42)
   (E) "No, Governor. She wouldn't have the heart to spend ten; and perhaps I shouldn't neither." (lines 51–52)

24. What does Doolittle mean by asking, "Will you take advantage of a man's nature to do him out of the price of his own daughter what he's brought up and fed and clothed by the sweat of his brow until she's growed big enough to be interesting to you two gentlemen?" (lines 20–23)

   (A) Higgins and Pickering have deprived him of his daughter through their educational experiment, but have failed to compensate him.
   (B) Higgins and Pickering are training Liza for free, so members of her family would also benefit from their generosity.
   (C) His poverty makes him unable to provide for his daughter.
   (D) Now that Higgins and Pickering are financially supporting Liza, they can also support him.
   (E) He has always struggled to support Liza, and now he needs help to continue to do so.

GO ON TO THE NEXT PAGE ⟶

25. Doolittle's long speech beginning "What am I,
    Governors both" (line 1) represents or includes
    all of the following EXCEPT

    (A) monologue
    (B) dialect
    (C) repetition
    (D) parallel structure
    (E) irony

Questions 26–35. Read the following poem carefully before you choose your answers.

Beat! Beat! Drums!

Beat! beat! drums!—blow! bugles! blow!
Through the windows—through doors—burst like a
                                    ruthless force,
Into the solemn church, and scatter the congregation,
Into the school where the scholar is studying;
5 Leave not the bridegroom quiet—no happiness must he
                                    have now with his bride,
Nor the peaceful farmer any peace, ploughing his field or
                                    gathering his grain,
So fierce you whirr and pound you drums—so shrill you
                                    bugles blow.

Beat! beat! drums!—blow! bugles! blow!
Over the traffic of cities—over the rumble of wheels in
                                    the streets;
10 Are beds prepared for sleepers at night in the houses? no
                                    sleepers must sleep in those beds,
No bargainers' bargains by day—no brokers or
                                    speculators—would they continue?
Would the talkers be talking? would the singer attempt
                                    to sing?
Would the lawyer rise in the court to state his case
                                    before the judge?
Then rattle quicker, heavier drums—you bugles
                                    wilder blow.

15 Beat! beat! drums!—blow! bugles! blow!
Make no parley—stop for no expostulation,
Mind not the timid—mind not the weeper or prayer,
Mind not the old man beseeching the young man,
Let not the child's voice be heard, nor the mother's
                                    entreaties,
20 Make even the trestles to shake the dead where they lie
                                    awaiting the hearses,
So strong you thump O terrible drums—so loud you
                                    bugles blow.
                                    (1861)

26. The poet begins each stanza with the same line
    in order to

    (A) seize and hold the reader's attention
    (B) interrupt the people as they go about their
        everyday business
    (C) emphasize the insistence and urgency of the
        call to arms
    (D) show that everyone must obey the bugles
        and drums
    (E) echo the excitement young men feel as they
        go off to war

27. What is the effect of the regular iambic rhythm
    that characterizes the final line of each stanza?

        I. It reminds the reader of English poetic
           tradition.
       II. It disturbs the reader's expectations of
           irregular rhythms.
      III. It echoes the rhythm of the drumbeats
           that call soldiers to arms.

    (A) I only
    (B) II only
    (C) I and II only
    (D) III only
    (E) I and III only

28. Which best conveys the meaning of the word "expostulation" (line 16)?

    (A) shouting
    (B) protest
    (C) mourning
    (D) pleading
    (E) questions

29. What are the old man, child, and mother (lines 18–19) pleading for?

    (A) a speedy conclusion to the war
    (B) their loved ones not to go into the dangers of battle
    (C) their side of the conflict to be victorious in the end
    (D) peace to be declared before any fighting begins
    (E) the terrible noise of bugles and drums to stop frightening them

30. The personification of the bugles and drums in the opening and closing lines of each stanza

    (A) makes the call to war seem unswerving and pitiless
    (B) shows that the bugles and drums play all by themselves
    (C) demonstrates the seriousness of the call to arms
    (D) underscores the strength and power of the enemy army
    (E) appeals to the reader's sense of sight

31. In the second stanza, why must the drums "rattle quicker, heavier" and the bugles "wilder blow" (line 21)?

    (A) to persuade potential recruits that war is a gallant adventure
    (B) to frighten the soldiers in the enemy army
    (C) to calm the prayers and entreaties of anxious family members
    (D) to make themselves heard over the everyday tasks at which people work
    (E) to drown out arguments made by those who do not want to join up

32. The word "parley" (line 16) is especially appropriate in this poem because of its association with

    (A) musical notation
    (B) literary theory
    (C) poetic form and structure
    (D) American history
    (E) military procedure

33. Which best characterizes the speaker's attitude toward war?

    (A) He feels frightened and uneasy about it.
    (B) He regrets it as a necessary evil.
    (C) He wishes he were young enough to join up.
    (D) He regards it as a destructive force.
    (E) He enthusiastically welcomes and supports it.

34. The imagery throughout the poem appeals most strongly to the sense of

    (A) sight
    (B) hearing
    (C) touch
    (D) taste
    (E) smell

35. In what way does the poem's structure reflect its content?

(A) The content states that the call to arms insists on obedience, and the lines describing the drums and bugles impose their own regularity on an otherwise free-verse poem.

(B) The content describes a variety of people who will be affected by the coming war, and the lines show a variety of rhymes and rhythms.

(C) The structure has three stanzas with the same number of lines, and the content describes three different kinds of people.

(D) The structure is free-verse, and the content describes people's free responses to the call to arms.

(E) The content is about war, and the structure conforms to military regularity.

Questions 36–42. Read the following poem carefully before you choose your answers.

Fair Cynthia, all the homage that I may
Unto a creature, unto thee I pay;
In lonesome woods to meet so kind a guide,
To me's more worth than all the world beside.
5 Some joy I felt just now, when sage got o'er
Yon surly river to this rugged shore,
Deeming rough welcomes from these clownish trees
Better than lodgings with Nereides.
Yet swelling fears surprise; all dark appears—
10 Nothing but light can dissipate those fears.
My fainting vitals can't lend strength to say,
But softly whisper, O I wish 'twere day.
The murmur hardly warmed the ambient air,
Ere thy bright aspect rescues from despair:
15 Makes the old hag her sable mantle loose,
And a bright joy does through my soul diffuse.
The boisterous trees now lend a passage free,
And pleasant prospects thou giv'st light to see.

(1704)

36. Which of the following does the author address as "fair Cynthia" (line 1)?

(A) the sun
(B) the moon
(C) the river
(D) the night
(E) the clouds

37. The words "clownish" (line 7) and "boisterous" (line 17) suggest that the trees

(A) offer safety and shelter from the weather
(B) appear dark and forbidding
(C) are tossing about in the wind
(D) provide welcome shade from the sun
(E) amuse the speaker with their unusual shapes

38. Which of the following best defines "prospects" (line 18)?

(A) plans and intentions
(B) expectations for the future
(C) views of the countryside
(D) people who mine for precious metals
(E) outlines of what is to come

39. Which of the following is responsible for the "swelling fears" (line 9) the speaker feels?

(A) the surly river (line 6)
(B) the rugged shore (line 6)
(C) the clownish trees (line 7)
(D) the ambient air (line 13)
(E) the sable mantle (line 15)

40. Which of the following is NOT an example of personification?

(A) "yon surly river" (line 6)
(B) "these clownish trees" (line 7)
(C) "my fainting vitals" (line 11)
(D) "the ambient air" (line 13)
(E) "the old hag" (line 15)

41. The speaker uses the word "sage" (line 5) to mean

(A) wise from experience
(B) well-behaved
(C) prudent and cautious
(D) spicy and sweet
(E) solemn and grave

42. "Swelling fears surprise" (line 9) is best paraphrased as

(A) I suddenly realize that I feel a growing fear.
(B) I'm surprised to discover that I'm scared.
(C) I'm frightened by the mysterious swelling of the ground.
(D) It surprises me that I'm not at all afraid.
(E) The best way to conquer fear is to surprise it.

Questions 43–51. Read the following passage carefully before you choose your answers.

Amory decided to sit for a while on the front steps, so he bade them good night.

The great tapestries of trees had darkened to ghosts back at the last edge of twilight. The early moon had
5 drenched the arches with pale blue, and, weaving over the night, in and out of the gossamer rifts of moon, swept a song, a song with more than a hint of sadness, infinitely transient, infinitely regretful.

He remembered that an alumnus of the nineties had told
10 him of one of Booth Tarkington's[1] amusements: standing in mid-campus in the small hours and singing tenor songs to the stars, arousing mingled emotions in the couched undergraduates according to the sentiment of their moods.

[1] Princeton alumnus and Pulitzer Prize–winning novelist

15 Now, far down the shadowy line of University Place a white-clad phalanx broke the gloom, and marching figures, white-shirted, white-trousered, swung rhythmically up the street, with linked arms and heads thrown back:

20 *"Going back—going back,*
Going—back—to—Nas-sau—Hall,
Going back—going back—
To the—Best—Old—Place—of—All.
Going back—going back,
25 *From all—this—earth-ly—ball,*
We'll—clear—the—track—as—we—go—back—
Going—back—to—Nas-sau—Hall!"

Amory closed his eyes as the ghostly procession drew near. The song soared so high that all dropped out except
30 the tenors, who bore the melody triumphantly past the

GO ON TO THE NEXT PAGE ⟹

danger-point and relinquished it to the fantastic chorus. Then Amory opened his eyes, half afraid that sight would spoil the rich illusion of harmony.

He sighed eagerly. There at the head of the white platoon
35 marched Allenby, the football captain, slim and defiant, as if aware that this year the hopes of the college rested on him, that his hundred-and-sixty pounds were expected to dodge to victory through the heavy blue and crimson lines.

40 Fascinated, Amory watched each rank of linked arms as it came abreast, the faces indistinct above the polo shirts, the voices blent in a pæan of triumph—and then the procession passed through shadowy Campbell Arch, and the voices grew fainter as it wound eastward over the
45 campus.

The minutes passed and Amory sat there very quietly. He regretted the rule that would forbid freshmen to be outdoors after curfew, for he wanted to ramble through the shadowy scented lanes, where Witherspoon brooded
50 like a dark mother over Whig and Clio, her Attic children, where the black Gothic snake of Little curled down to Cuyler and Patton,[2] these in turn flinging the mystery out over the placid slope rolling to the lake.

(1920)

[2] Witherspoon, Whig, Clio, Little, Cuyler, and Patton Halls—buildings on the Princeton campus

43. Amory thinks of the group of singing students as a "ghostly procession" (line 28) and a "fantastic chorus" (line 31) because

   (A) none of them is a close friend of his
   (B) they are upperclassmen and he is a freshman
   (C) he is eager for the day when he can join their group
   (D) he is captivated by the sound of their singing
   (E) they are indistinct white shapes in the dusk

44. The author uses the words "phalanx" (line 16) and "platoon" (line 34) to compare the students to

   (A) football players
   (B) soldiers
   (C) fraternity brothers
   (D) ghosts
   (E) kings

45. The phrases "gossamer rifts of moon" (line 6), "a hint of sadness" (line 7), "the rich illusion" (line 33), and "he sighed eagerly" (line 34) contribute to the passage's mood of

   (A) nostalgia
   (B) romance
   (C) innocence
   (D) regret
   (E) anxiety

46. Which phrase might be described as a contradiction in terms?

   (A) "infinitely transient" (lines 7–8)
   (B) "mingled emotions" (line 12)
   (C) "ghostly procession" (line 28)
   (D) "rich illusion" (line 33)
   (E) "slim and defiant" (line 35)

47. The author personifies the college buildings in the last paragraph in order to

   (A) clarify why Amory wants to explore the campus after curfew
   (B) provide the reader with visual details of the setting
   (C) emphasize the history and traditions of the university
   (D) contribute to the sense of enchantment Amory feels
   (E) explain why the upperclassmen are so glad to be back on campus

48. "The heavy blue and crimson lines" (lines 38–39) is an allusion to

    (A) bruises the players will acquire during the games
    (B) the colors of rival universities' football teams
    (C) a professor's marks on a highly graded essay or exam
    (D) the valedictory speech that Allenby will make at graduation
    (E) the uniform worn by the Princeton football squad

49. The author's use of the word "mystery" (line 53) contributes to the sense that

    (A) everything on the campus is new and strange to Amory
    (B) Amory has no friends among the upperclassmen
    (C) Amory is afraid he will not do well at Princeton
    (D) the singing students are all unknown to Amory
    (E) Princeton is making Amory homesick and unhappy

50. The author recounts the anecdote about Booth Tarkington in order to

    I. emphasize the sense of tradition and continuity embodied in the university
    II. draw the reader into Amory's emotions as he listens to the upperclassmen singing
    III. poke sly fun at Amory's excitement when he hears the singing

    (A) I only
    (B) II only
    (C) I and II only
    (D) III only
    (E) I, II, and III

51. All of the following details are examples of metaphorical language EXCEPT

    (A) "The great tapestries of trees had darkened to ghosts" (line 3)
    (B) "The early moon had drenched the arches with pale blue" (lines 4–5)
    (C) "weaving over the night . . . swept a song" (lines 5–7)
    (D) "singing tenor songs to the stars" (lines 11–12)
    (E) "the black Gothic snake of Little curled down to Cuyler and Patton" (lines 51–52)

Questions 52–60. Read the following poem carefully before you choose your answers.

Strange Meeting

It seemed that out of battle I escaped
Down some profound dull tunnel, long since scooped
Through granites which titanic wars had groined.
Yet also there encumbered sleepers groaned,
5 Too fast in thought or death to be bestirred.
Then, as I probed them, one sprang up, and stared
With piteous recognition in fixed eyes,
Lifting distressful hands, as if to bless.
And by his smile, I knew that sullen hall—
10 By his dead smile I knew we stood in Hell.
With a thousand pains that vision's face was grained;
Yet no blood reached there from the upper ground,

And no guns thumped, or down the flues made moan.
"Strange friend," I said, "here is no cause to mourn."
15 "None," said that other, "save the undone years,
The hopelessness. Whatever hope is yours,
Was my life also; I went hunting wild
After the wildest beauty in the world,
Which lies not calm in eyes, or braided hair,
20 But mocks the steady running of the hour,
And if it grieves, grieves richlier than here.
For by my glee might many men have laughed,
And of my weeping something had been left,
Which must die now. I mean the truth untold,
25 The pity of war, the pity war distilled.

Now men will go content with what we spoiled,

Or, discontent, boil bloody, and be spilled.

They will be swift with swiftness of the tigress.

None will break ranks, though nations trek from progress.

30 Courage was mine, and I had mystery,

Wisdom was mine, and I had mastery:

To miss the march of this retreating world

Into vain citadels that are not walled.

Then, when much blood had clogged their chariot-wheels,

35 I would go up and wash them from sweet wells

Even with truths that lie too deep for taint.

I would have poured my spirit without stint

But not through wounds; not on the cess of war.

Foreheads of men have bled where no wounds were.

40 I am the enemy you killed, my friend.

I knew you in this dark: for so you frowned

Yesterday through me as you jabbed and killed.

I parried; but my hands were loath and cold.

Let us sleep now . . ."

(1917)

52. The structure of "Strange Meeting" relies on which of the following literary devices?

(A) exact rhyme

(B) free verse

(C) hyperbole

(D) colloquialisms

(E) heroic couplets

53. The speaker believes that "here is no cause to mourn" (line 14) because

  I. he and the stranger are meeting in Hell

  II. they are safe from the weapons and bloodshed of battle

  III. the soldiers around them are peacefully asleep in death

(A) I only

(B) II only

(C) III only

(D) II and III only

(E) I, II, and III

54. What does the stranger mean by saying that beauty "mocks the steady running of the hour" (line 20)?

(A) It prefers to be independent of others.

(B) It laughs at everything that surrounds it.

(C) It refuses to be careful or prudent.

(D) It does not fear the passage of time.

(E) It looks forward eagerly to the future.

55. Which line best expresses the major theme of the poem?

(A) "By his dead smile I knew we stood in Hell." (line 10)

(B) "'Strange friend,' I said, 'here is no cause to mourn.'" (line 14)

(C) "The pity of war, the pity war distilled." (line 25)

(D) "I would go up and wash them from sweet wells" (line 35)

(E) "I am the enemy you killed, my friend." (line 40)

56. When the stranger says "Now men will go content . . . Into vain citadels that are not walled" (lines 26–33), he predicts that

(A) men will continue to make war on one another

(B) his country will be defeated in the war

(C) leaders will come together to make peace

(D) one nation will force the other to retreat

(E) he and the speaker will kill one another

57. When the stranger says that his hands were "loath" (line 43), he means they were

(A) unskilled

(B) unwilling

(C) ugly

(D) wounded

(E) frozen

GO ON TO THE NEXT PAGE ⟼

58. All of the following lines contain opposing or contradictory elements or ideas EXCEPT

    (A) "For by my glee might many men have laughed" (line 22)
    (B) "None will break ranks, though nations trek from progress" (line 29)
    (C) "Into vain citadels that are not walled" (line 33)
    (D) "Foreheads of men have bled where no wounds were" (line 39)
    (E) "I am the enemy you killed, my friend" (line 40)

59. The stranger's desire to share "the truth untold" (line 24) and "truths that lie too deep for taint" (line 36) implies that if he had lived, he would have been

    (A) a politician
    (B) a general
    (C) a clergyman
    (D) a writer
    (E) a doctor

60. Which best expresses the meaning of the word "taint" (line 36)?

    (A) perception, awareness
    (B) expression, utterance
    (C) removing, erasing
    (D) falsehoods, lies
    (E) contamination, corruption

STOP

If you finish before time is called, you may check your work on this test only.

Do not turn to any other test in this book.

Answer Key

1. B	16. A	31. D	46. A
2. A	17. D	32. E	47. D
3. C	18. A	33. D	48. B
4. E	19. B	34. B	49. A
5. B	20. E	35. A	50. A
6. C	21. A	36. B	51. D
7. D	22. D	37. C	52. E
8. E	23. B	38. C	53. B
9. B	24. A	39. E	54. D
10. A	25. E	40. D	55. C
11. C	26. C	41. A	56. A
12. D	27. D	42. A	57. B
13. A	28. B	43. E	58. A
14. E	29. B	44. B	59. D
15. B	30. A	45. B	60. E

Answers and Explanations

1. (B) Mr. Bennet says that "Lizzy has something more of quickness than her sisters." *Quickness* refers to intelligence and wit.

2. (A) "I have no objection to hearing it" indicates that Mr. Bennet feels only the mildest interest in hearing Mrs. Bennet's news.

3. (C) All five are accurate definitions of the word *let*, but the context makes it clear that Mr. Bingley has just leased the house and will soon "take possession," or move in.

4. (E) Mrs. Bennet shows her lack of subtlety by asking straight out for what she wants. The repetition of her demand shows her ability to focus on what she thinks is important—introducing her daughters to a potential husband. If she understood Mr. Bennet better, she would approach the question in a way that would make him respond in a more satisfactory manner. However, she is clearly practical; getting acquainted with Bingley is a necessary first step toward the good marriage she hopes one of her daughters will make.

5. (B) Both of the Bennets know quite well that 20 rich young men will not arrive in the neighborhood. Mrs. Bennet exaggerates out of disappointment, and Mr. Bennet's tone throughout the passage shows that he finds amusement in baiting his wife.

6. (C) Mr. Bennet appears to mean this remark literally, but the other four comments are made to indulge his mildly sarcastic sense of humor and to tease his wife. Her comment "You take delight in vexing me" is truer than she realizes.

7. (D) Because "Is he married or single" is almost the first thing Mr. Bennet asks after hearing his wife say that the newcomer is "a young man of large fortune," it appears he shares her desire to see her daughters well-provided for in marriage.

8. (E) Mrs. Bennet is irritated by her husband's quick wit and intelligence, so she most likely finds the same qualities equally irritating in her daughter. Mr. Bennet teases his wife rather than showing affection for her, so she is probably a little jealous of his affection for Lizzy. She praises Jane and Lydia in comparison to Lizzy, suggesting that she prefers them.

9. (B) Mr. Bennet speaks to his wife with courtesy, irony, and a complete lack of emotional involvement. Most of his statements poke fun at her, gently but sarcastically; as she says, he "takes delight" in teasing her. "Detached" is the best description of this attitude.

10. (A) The author puns on two different definitions of *dust*. Chimney-sweepers find literal dust and ashes in the process of doing their jobs; young people "come to dust" when they die and their bones gradually crumble.

11. (C) A *scepter* is a rod or staff carried by a monarch on ceremonial occasions.

12. (D) The line is a metaphor for death. Several other lines in the poem, such as "And renowned be thy grave," support this. (In the play from which this song is taken, two young men sing it over the body of a beloved friend.)

13. (A) The idiom "to lay one's ghosts" means to come to terms with unresolved issues in one's past. An "unlaid ghost" is one that still haunts or bothers a person. The speaker hopes that all such "ghosts" from the past will *forbear* his friend, or leave her in peace.

14. (E) In this context, *consummation* refers to the completion of a task. The person addressed has completed her life; the speaker hopes that her body will lie quiet and undisturbed in her grave.

15. (B) A careful reading of the poem shows beyond any question that the person addressed is dead. Therefore, only choice B is possible.

16. (A) The person addressed is dead. In almost every line of the poem, the speaker tells her that she has nothing further to worry about. In this line, he says that to the dead, reeds (a symbol of weakness and fragility) and oaks (a symbol of strength and might) are exactly alike; the dead cannot perceive any difference between them.

17. (D) Higgins is impressed on two levels by Doolittle's skill as a speaker. First, Doolittle is amusing and entertaining, as Higgins acknowledges by calling him "irresistible." Second, Doolittle has interesting ideas about life in a rigid class-based society and is able to express those ideas clearly and well.

18. (A) Doolittle finds happiness in enjoying life in the present moment, without thought for the future. A *prudent* person would sacrifice today's pleasure in order to provide for tomorrow's needs.

19. (B) "Middle-class morality" expects people to attend church, behave soberly, support their families, and obey the authorities. Doolittle mentions that he is a heavy drinker and that he is not "prudent" but prefers to spend his money freely; and it is reasonable to conclude that his approach to Higgins is not the first time he has charmed someone out of a small sum of money. This irresponsible, pleasure-loving attitude to life makes him "undeserving."

20. (E) Doolittle thinks that being a prime minister or preacher would be "a dog's life," because these are positions that mean care and responsibility. As a working man, he is free to do what he likes, when he likes.

21. (A) *Charm* is a quality of personality that wins other people over, as Doolittle's frank discussion of his beliefs wins Higgins.

22. (D) Doolittle points out that the middle-class moralists overlook the widow's dishonesty in repeatedly cashing in on her husband's death. He rightly regards this as evidence of hypocrisy.

23. (B) The structure of society and one's own place in that structure are abstract intellectual issues. Choice B shows that Doolittle is "a thinking man" because he has pondered those issues and come to definite conclusions about them.

24. (A) The phrase "do him out of the price of his own daughter" means that Higgins and Pickering are cheating Doolittle of the money his daughter is worth. Choices B and D are wrong because Doolittle does not claim to deserve the same consideration as Liza. Remember that because these answer choices essentially say the same thing, they must be wrong. Choice C is incorrect because Doolittle argues that he has spent his entire life providing for Liza. He claims no desire to continue to support Liza, so choice E is wrong.

25. (E) The speech is a monologue—a long speech made by one actor. Dialect: Doolittle's grammar and vocabulary do not strictly conform to Standard English usage (for example, he says *agen* for *against*). Repetition: "What am I? I ask you, what am I?" Parallel structure: "I put it to you; and I leave it to you." The speech lacks irony; Doolittle is entirely earnest in what he says.

26. (C) The repetition echoes the relentlessness of the authorities' insistence that all young men who hear the call join up and fight. The entire poem insists that no considerations can excuse anyone from answering the call, and the repeated first line underscores this insistence.

27. **(D)** Option I is wrong because nothing in the poem's subject matter relates to literary history or the writing of poetry. Option II is wrong because readers are conditioned to expect regularity in poetry; irregularities are what cause surprise. Option III is correct; it's impossible not to hear the drumbeats when reading the lines aloud.

28. **(B)** To *expostulate* means to protest or argue.

29. **(B)** The phrase "the old man beseeching the young man" and the earlier references to weeping and praying support the idea that fathers, children, wives, and mothers are pleading with young men to stay home where it is safe, not to join up and get killed.

30. **(A)** Even though the bugles and drums are personified, the reader is still aware that they are inanimate objects. It is frightening to think that mechanical objects—objects that cannot feel or think—nonetheless have the power to start a war.

31. **(D)** The second stanza describes ordinary people working at their jobs and ignoring the drums and bugles. The speaker urges them to play more loudly to get the attention of those who are carrying on with their lives.

32. **(E)** When leaders of opposing armies meet to discuss an issue such as a truce or an exchange of prisoners, this is referred to as a *parley*. A military term like this is perfect for a poem about war.

33. **(D)** Words such as *fierce, shrill, terrible,* and *loud* and the portrayal of the call to arms as a force that destroys families and puts an end to peaceful occupations—all show the speaker's negative view of war.

34. **(B)** The drums, bugles, entreaties, prayers, references to conversation, talking, singing, parley, and more are all sound effects, appealing to readers' sense of hearing.

35. **(A)** The content states that the call to arms imposes its inflexible will on everyone. In the same way, in the first and last lines of each stanza, the drums and bugles impose their own regular rhythmic structure on an otherwise free-verse poem.

36. **(B)** A careful reading of the poem shows that "Cynthia" provides light on a dark night. The only choice that matches this is B, the moon.

37. **(C)** *Boisterous* means "noisy and active, unrestrained." Anchored as they are to the ground, trees can only be described this way if they are being blown and tossed about by the wind. *Clownish* also suggests tumbling and movement.

38. **(C)** The context shows that the speaker is talking about the views she can see in the moonlight once she passes through the trees.

39. **(E)** The speaker pays homage to the moon because she is afraid of the dark. The "sable mantle" is a metaphor for the dark sky.

40. **(D)** A river cannot feel surly, trees cannot act clownish, a person's vital organs cannot literally faint, and night is not "an old hag." Only choice D, "the ambient air," is a literal expression; *ambient* means "surrounding."

41. **(A)** Context shows that the speaker feels she is wiser and smarter for having survived the experience of crossing the "surly river."

42. **(A)** The line might be rewritten "I surprise swelling fears." In this sense, *surprise* means "discover." The speaker is saying that she discovers a fear of the darkness rising inside her.

43. **(E)** All five choices are true statements, but only choice E accounts for the connection in Amory's imagination between the upperclassmen and ghosts. Like ghosts, the boys are dimly seen white figures at night.

44. (B) A *phalanx* is a closely massed group of soldiers; a *platoon* is a subdivision of a military company or troop.

45. (B) Amory is captivated by Princeton. He responds strongly to sensory impressions. He feels a sense of mystery, unreality, enchantment, and exultation, very much like falling in love. *Romance* is the choice that best describes this mood.

46. (A) Something *infinite* lasts forever; something *transient* has only a momentary existence or presence.

47. (D) The numerous references to ghosts, shadows, and illusions show that Amory feels almost as if he is caught up in a magic spell. The idea of college buildings as living creatures with human personalities suggests that they too are enchanted by magic.

48. (B) Because Allenby must "dodge through the heavy blue and crimson lines" to achieve victory, the lines must be those of a rival team or teams. (Many readers would know that blue and crimson represent Yale and Harvard, Princeton's two main rivals.)

49. (A) Amory wants to explore the "shadowy scented lanes" so that he will better understand the mysteries of a place that is new and strange to him.

50. (A) The author's main purpose in the passage appears to be to evoke the sounds and sights of a Princeton freshman's first night on campus. Part of this experience is Amory's knowledge of Princeton's traditions—old buildings that have been part of the campus for many years, students singing at night, and football games against other universities.

51. (D) This phrase is intended literally; Tarkington was literally out alone at night, singing to the stars in the sky. The other four choices make imaginative, direct comparisons between two things—for example, songs cannot literally "weave."

52. (E) A heroic couplet is two rhymed lines of iambic pentameter. "Strange Meeting" is composed entirely of such couplets, although they differ from standard heroic couplets because the rhymes are not exact (i.e., *mystery/ mastery, killed/cold*).

53. (B) The lines "no blood reached there from the upper ground, / And no guns thumped or down the flues made moan," show that option II is correct. Finding oneself in Hell is certainly "cause to mourn," and many of the soldiers are groaning, so options I and III are wrong.

54. (D) "The steady running of the hour" refers to the page of time, measured out at a steady rate by a clock. Beauty is so confident that it does not yet fear the future, in which it will grow old and may fade.

55. (C) The pity of war—in which young men who have no personal quarrel kill one another, and the dead are prevented from growing to adulthood and fulfilling their potential for good—is the main theme of the poem.

56. (A) The stranger looks toward the future and predicts that men will either accept the world, which has been spoiled by war, or they will go to war again.

57. (B) To *loathe* is to hate. To be *loath* to do something is to hate having to do it, or to be unwilling to do it.

58. (A) *Progress* implies motion toward something, not away from it. Citadels, by definition, are walled. If foreheads bleed, they must be wounded. A man cannot be both an enemy and a friend.

59. (D) The stranger suggests that he would have made men laugh and weep (lines 22–23) and also that he wants to share the truth. This accurately describes the aim of any creative artist. Therefore, *writer* is the best of the five choices.

60. (E) To *taint* means to infect something with poison or disease. When something is *tainted*, it is contaminated or corrupted.

How To Calculate Your Score

Count the number of correct answers and enter the total below.

Count the number of wrong answers. Do NOT include any questions you did not answer.

Multiply the number of wrong answers by 0.25 and enter the total below.

Do the subtraction. The answer is your raw score. Use the scoring scale to find your scaled score.

$$\overline{\text{(number of correct answers)}} - \overline{\text{(number of wrong answers} \times 0.25)} = \overline{\text{(raw score)}}$$

RAW SCORE	SCALED SCORE	RAW SCORE	SCALED SCORE	RAW SCORE	SCALED SCORE	RAW SCORE	SCALED SCORE	RAW SCORE	SCALED SCORE
60	800	44	710	28	560	12	420	-4	260
59	800	43	700	27	550	11	410	-5	250
58	800	42	690	26	540	10	400	-6	240
57	800	41	690	25	530	9	390	-7	230
56	800	40	680	24	520	8	380	-8	220
55	800	39	670	23	510	7	370	-9	210
54	790	38	660	22	500	6	360	-10	200
53	790	37	650	21	500	5	350	-11	200
52	780	36	640	20	490	4	340	-12	200
51	770	35	630	19	490	3	330	-13	200
50	760	34	620	18	480	2	320	-14	200
49	750	33	610	17	470	1	310	-15	200
48	740	32	600	16	460	0	300		
47	740	31	590	15	450	-1	290		
46	730	30	580	14	440	-2	280		
45	720	29	570	13	430	-3	270		

Note: This is only a sample scoring scale. Scoring scales differ from exam to exam.

Practice Test 7

The following practice test is designed to be just like the real SAT Literature Test. It matches the actual test in content coverage and degree of difficulty.

Once you finish the practice test, determine your score. Carefully read the answer explanations of the questions you answered incorrectly. Identify any weaknesses in your literature skills by determining the areas in which you made the most errors. Review those sections of this book first. Then, as time permits, go back and review your strengths.

Allow one hour to take the test. Time yourself and work uninterrupted. If you run out of time, take note of where you stopped when time ran out. Remember that you lose a quarter point for each incorrect answer, but you do not lose points for questions you leave blank. Therefore, unless you can eliminate one or more of the five choices, it's best to leave a question unanswered.

Use the following formula to calculate your score:

(number of correct answers) – ¼ (number of incorrect answers)

If you treat this practice test just like the actual exam, it will accurately reflect how you are likely to perform on test day. Here are some hints on how to create test-taking conditions similar to those of the actual exam:

- Complete the test in one sitting. On test day, you will not be allowed to take a break.
- Tear out the answer sheet and fill in the ovals just as you will on the actual test day.
- Have a good eraser and more than one sharp pencil handy. On test day, you will not be able to go get a new pencil if yours breaks.
- Do not allow yourself any extra time; put down your pencil after exactly one hour, no matter how many questions are left to answer.
- Become familiar with the directions on the test. If you go in knowing what the directions say, you will not have to waste time reading and thinking about them on the actual test day.

Answer Sheet

Tear out this answer sheet and use it to mark your answers.

1. Ⓐ Ⓑ Ⓒ Ⓓ Ⓔ	16. Ⓐ Ⓑ Ⓒ Ⓓ Ⓔ	31. Ⓐ Ⓑ Ⓒ Ⓓ Ⓔ	46. Ⓐ Ⓑ Ⓒ Ⓓ Ⓔ
2. Ⓐ Ⓑ Ⓒ Ⓓ Ⓔ	17. Ⓐ Ⓑ Ⓒ Ⓓ Ⓔ	32. Ⓐ Ⓑ Ⓒ Ⓓ Ⓔ	47. Ⓐ Ⓑ Ⓒ Ⓓ Ⓔ
3. Ⓐ Ⓑ Ⓒ Ⓓ Ⓔ	18. Ⓐ Ⓑ Ⓒ Ⓓ Ⓔ	33. Ⓐ Ⓑ Ⓒ Ⓓ Ⓔ	48. Ⓐ Ⓑ Ⓒ Ⓓ Ⓔ
4. Ⓐ Ⓑ Ⓒ Ⓓ Ⓔ	19. Ⓐ Ⓑ Ⓒ Ⓓ Ⓔ	34. Ⓐ Ⓑ Ⓒ Ⓓ Ⓔ	49. Ⓐ Ⓑ Ⓒ Ⓓ Ⓔ
5. Ⓐ Ⓑ Ⓒ Ⓓ Ⓔ	20. Ⓐ Ⓑ Ⓒ Ⓓ Ⓔ	35. Ⓐ Ⓑ Ⓒ Ⓓ Ⓔ	50. Ⓐ Ⓑ Ⓒ Ⓓ Ⓔ
6. Ⓐ Ⓑ Ⓒ Ⓓ Ⓔ	21. Ⓐ Ⓑ Ⓒ Ⓓ Ⓔ	36. Ⓐ Ⓑ Ⓒ Ⓓ Ⓔ	51. Ⓐ Ⓑ Ⓒ Ⓓ Ⓔ
7. Ⓐ Ⓑ Ⓒ Ⓓ Ⓔ	22. Ⓐ Ⓑ Ⓒ Ⓓ Ⓔ	37. Ⓐ Ⓑ Ⓒ Ⓓ Ⓔ	52. Ⓐ Ⓑ Ⓒ Ⓓ Ⓔ
8. Ⓐ Ⓑ Ⓒ Ⓓ Ⓔ	23. Ⓐ Ⓑ Ⓒ Ⓓ Ⓔ	38. Ⓐ Ⓑ Ⓒ Ⓓ Ⓔ	53. Ⓐ Ⓑ Ⓒ Ⓓ Ⓔ
9. Ⓐ Ⓑ Ⓒ Ⓓ Ⓔ	24. Ⓐ Ⓑ Ⓒ Ⓓ Ⓔ	39. Ⓐ Ⓑ Ⓒ Ⓓ Ⓔ	54. Ⓐ Ⓑ Ⓒ Ⓓ Ⓔ
10. Ⓐ Ⓑ Ⓒ Ⓓ Ⓔ	25. Ⓐ Ⓑ Ⓒ Ⓓ Ⓔ	40. Ⓐ Ⓑ Ⓒ Ⓓ Ⓔ	55. Ⓐ Ⓑ Ⓒ Ⓓ Ⓔ
11. Ⓐ Ⓑ Ⓒ Ⓓ Ⓔ	26. Ⓐ Ⓑ Ⓒ Ⓓ Ⓔ	41. Ⓐ Ⓑ Ⓒ Ⓓ Ⓔ	56. Ⓐ Ⓑ Ⓒ Ⓓ Ⓔ
12. Ⓐ Ⓑ Ⓒ Ⓓ Ⓔ	27. Ⓐ Ⓑ Ⓒ Ⓓ Ⓔ	42. Ⓐ Ⓑ Ⓒ Ⓓ Ⓔ	57. Ⓐ Ⓑ Ⓒ Ⓓ Ⓔ
13. Ⓐ Ⓑ Ⓒ Ⓓ Ⓔ	28. Ⓐ Ⓑ Ⓒ Ⓓ Ⓔ	43. Ⓐ Ⓑ Ⓒ Ⓓ Ⓔ	58. Ⓐ Ⓑ Ⓒ Ⓓ Ⓔ
14. Ⓐ Ⓑ Ⓒ Ⓓ Ⓔ	29. Ⓐ Ⓑ Ⓒ Ⓓ Ⓔ	44. Ⓐ Ⓑ Ⓒ Ⓓ Ⓔ	59. Ⓐ Ⓑ Ⓒ Ⓓ Ⓔ
15. Ⓐ Ⓑ Ⓒ Ⓓ Ⓔ	30. Ⓐ Ⓑ Ⓒ Ⓓ Ⓔ	45. Ⓐ Ⓑ Ⓒ Ⓓ Ⓔ	60. Ⓐ Ⓑ Ⓒ Ⓓ Ⓔ

PRACTICE TEST 7

Time: 60 Minutes

Directions: This test consists of selections from literary works and questions on their content, form, and style. After reading each passage or poem, choose the best answer to each question and then fill in the corresponding oval on the answer sheet.

Note: Pay particular attention to the requirements of questions that contain the words NOT or EXCEPT.

Questions 1–8. Read the following passage carefully before you choose your answers.

An author ought to consider himself, not as a gentleman who gives a private or eleemosynary treat, but rather as one who keeps a public ordinary, at which all persons are welcome for their money. In the former case, it is well
5 known that the entertainer provides what fare he pleases; and though this should be very indifferent, and utterly disagreeable to the taste of his company, they must not find any fault; nay, on the contrary, good breeding forces them outwardly to approve and to commend whatever
10 is set before them. Now the contrary of this happens to the master of an ordinary. Men who pay for what they eat will insist on gratifying their palates, however nice and whimsical these may prove; and if everything is not agreeable to their taste, will challenge a right to censure, to
15 abuse, and to d—n their dinner without control.

To prevent, therefore, giving offence to their customers by any such disappointment, it hath been usual with the honest and well-meaning host to provide a bill of fare which all persons may peruse at their first entrance into
20 the house; and having thence acquainted themselves with the entertainment which they may expect, may either stay and regale with what is provided for them, or may depart to some other ordinary better accommodated to their taste.

25 As we do not disdain to borrow wit or wisdom from any man who is capable of lending us either, we have condescended to take a hint from these honest victuallers, and shall prefix not only a general bill of fare to our whole entertainment, but shall likewise give the reader

30 particular bills to every course which is to be served up in this and the ensuing volumes.

The provision, then, which we have here made is no other than *Human Nature.* Nor do I fear that my sensible reader, though most luxurious in his taste, will start,
35 cavil, or be offended, because I have named but one article. The tortoise—as the alderman of Bristol, well learned in eating, knows by much experience—besides the delicious calipash and calipee, contains many different kinds of food; nor can the learned reader be
40 ignorant, that in Human Nature, though here collected under one general name, is such prodigious variety, that a cook will have sooner gone through all the several species of animal and vegetable food in the world, than an author will be able to exhaust so extensive a subject.

45 An objection may perhaps be apprehended from the more delicate, that this dish is too common and vulgar; for what else is the subject of all the romances, novels, plays, and poems, with which the stalls abound? Many exquisite viands might be rejected by the epicure, if it was
50 a sufficient cause for his contemning of them as common and vulgar, that something was to be found in the most paltry alleys under the same name. In reality, true nature is as difficult to be met with in authors as the Bayonne ham, or Bologna sausage, is to be found in the shops.

55 But the whole, to continue the same metaphor, consists in the cookery of the author; for, as Mr Pope[1] tells us—

---

[1] Mr Pope: 18th-century English poet Alexander Pope.

GO ON TO THE NEXT PAGE ⟼

Practice Test

"True wit is nature to advantage drest;
What oft was thought, but ne'er so well exprest."

The same animal which hath the honour to have some part of
60 his flesh eaten at the table of a duke, may perhaps be degraded
in another part, and some of his limbs gibbeted, as it were,
in the vilest stall in town. Where, then, lies the difference
between the food of the nobleman and the porter, if both are
at dinner on the same ox or calf, but in the seasoning, the
65 dressing, the garnishing, and the setting forth? Hence the one
provokes and incites the most languid appetite, and the other
turns and palls that which is the sharpest and keenest.

In like manner, the excellence of the mental
entertainment consists less in the subject than in
70 the author's skill in well dressing it up. How pleased,
therefore, will the reader be to find that we have, in the
following work, adhered closely to one of the highest
principles of the best cook which the present age, or
perhaps that of Heliogabalus[2], hath produced. This great
75 man, as is well known to all lovers of polite eating, begins
at first by setting plain things before his hungry guests,
rising afterwards by degrees as their stomachs may be
supposed to decrease, to the very quintessence of sauce
and spices. In like manner, we shall represent Human
80 Nature at first to the keen appetite of our reader, in that
more plain and simple manner in which it is found in
the country, and shall hereafter hash and ragout it with
all the high French and Italian seasoning of affectation
and vice which courts and cities afford. By these means, we
85 doubt not but our reader may be rendered desirous to read
on forever, as the great person just above-mentioned is
supposed to have made some persons eat.

Having premised thus much, we will now detain those
who like our bill of fare no longer from their diet, and
90 shall proceed directly to serve up the first course of our
history for their entertainment.

(1749)

[2] Heliogabalus: ruler of the Roman Empire 218–222 C.E.

1. Which best defines the word "nice" as it is used in the last sentence of the first paragraph (line 12)?

   (A) pleasant, likeable
   (B) finicky, particular
   (C) delicate, subtle
   (D) scrupulous, exact
   (E) foolish, silly

2. Why did the author include this introductory passage in his book?

   (A) to persuade the reading public to buy the book
   (B) to describe the book's contents in detail
   (C) to explain to potential readers why he wrote the book
   (D) to give readers a general idea of what the book is about
   (E) to defend his decision to write the book

3. Details in the text imply that this passage is the introduction to

   (A) a cookbook
   (B) a travel guide
   (C) a work of fiction
   (D) a work of literary criticism
   (E) a history book

4. The author suggests that country life is

   (A) less varied and entertaining than court and city life
   (B) less wholesome than court and city life
   (C) less satisfying than court and city life
   (D) less complicated than court and city life
   (E) less violent than court and city life

5. According to the author, who or what deserves the credit if the book is good?

   (A) the reader
   (B) the author
   (C) the introduction
   (D) the theme
   (E) the plot

GO ON TO THE NEXT PAGE ⟼

6. The author suggests that a writer and a victualler have all these things in common EXCEPT

   (A) both depend on public goodwill for their prosperity
   (B) both must offer literature/food of the best quality
   (C) both must be honest with their paying customers
   (D) both should produce what will please the greatest possible number
   (E) both face a great variety of demands from the public

7. From the author's statement that his book is about "Human Nature" (line 40), a reader might expect it to contain which of the following?

   (A) an exciting plot
   (B) reliable information
   (C) exotic settings
   (D) poetic use of language
   (E) realistic, believable characters

8. In the paragraph that begins "In like manner" (line 68), the author suggests that he will satisfy his readers and hold their interest by making his history increasingly

   (A) more varied and exciting
   (B) more comic and amusing
   (C) more tragic and pathetic
   (D) more mysterious and intriguing
   (E) more preachy and moralistic

Questions 9–17. Read the following poem carefully before you choose your answers.

Since brass, nor stone, nor earth, nor boundless sea,
But sad mortality o'ersways their power,
How with this rage shall beauty hold a plea,
Whose action is no stronger than a flower?
5 O, how shall summer's honey breath hold out
Against the wrackful siege of batt'ring days,
When rocks impregnable are not so stout,
Nor gates of steel so strong, but Time decays?
O fearful meditation! Where, alack,
10 Shall Time's best jewel from Time's chest lie hid?
Or what strong hand can hold his swift foot back?
Or who his spoil of beauty can forbid?
  O, none! unless this miracle have might,
  That in black ink my love may still shine bright.

(1609)

9. Which of the following refers to the speaker's beloved?

   (A) summer's honey breath (line 5)
   (B) the wrackful siege (line 6)
   (C) fearful meditation (line 9)
   (D) Time's best jewel (line 10)
   (E) this miracle (line 13)

10. Which of the following does the speaker claim is the most powerful?

   (A) stone (line 1)
   (B) rocks impregnable (line 7)
   (C) gates of steel (line 8)
   (D) Time (line 8)
   (E) black ink (line 14)

11. Which best sums up the speaker's main idea?

    (A) True beauty always outlasts the ravages of time.
    (B) Death destroys all memory of beauty.
    (C) A poet has the power to make beauty last forever.
    (D) Time is more powerful than anything in nature.
    (E) Love lasts only for a short time.

12. The speaker uses the phrase "O fearful meditation!" (line 9) to mean

    (A) the thought of time's destructive power frightens him.
    (B) the process of serious thinking intimidates him.
    (C) he tries his best not to think about his lost love.
    (D) he is afraid in the merciless face of nature.
    (E) he is afraid of what will happen to him in the course of time.

13. The speaker characterizes Time as all of the following EXCEPT

    (A) miserly
    (B) patient
    (C) furious
    (D) brutal
    (E) destructive

14. The poet capitalizes "Time" throughout the poem for which of the following reasons?

    I. to make Time seem more powerful
    II. to show that poetry outlasts Time
    III. to help personify Time

    (A) II only
    (B) I and II only
    (C) III only
    (D) I and III only
    (E) II and III only

15. The poem addresses all the following themes EXCEPT

    (A) the endurance of art
    (B) the inevitability of death
    (C) the fleeting nature of beauty
    (D) the omnipotence of time
    (E) the fear of loneliness

16. Over which issue does the speaker express some doubt?

    (A) whether his poem will outlast the ravages of time
    (B) whether true beauty is really spoiled by the passage of time
    (C) whether time can destroy steel gates or towering rocks
    (D) whether death must come to all things in nature
    (E) whether summer can last beyond its natural time span

17. "The wrackful siege of batt'ring days" (line 6) suggests that Time is most like which of the following?

    (A) a storm at sea
    (B) an invading army
    (C) a stonemason or bricklayer
    (D) a king in a castle
    (E) an evil giant

Questions 18–25. Read the following passage carefully before you choose your answers.

On a late spring afternoon Ella McCarthy sat on a green-painted chair in Kensington Gardens, staring listlessly at an uninteresting stretch of park landscape that blossomed suddenly into tropical radiance as an expected figure
5 appeared in the middle distance.

"Hullo, Bertie!" she exclaimed sedately, when the figure arrived at the painted chair that was the nearest neighbor to her own, and dropped into it eagerly, yet with a certain due regard for the set of its trousers; "hasn't it been a
10 perfect spring afternoon?"

The statement was a distinct untruth as far as Ella's own feelings were concerned; until the arrival of Bertie the afternoon had been anything but perfect.

Bertie made a suitable reply, in which a questioning note
15 seemed to hover.

"Thank you ever so much for those lovely handkerchiefs," said Ella, answering the unspoken question; "they were just what I've been wanting. There's only one thing spoilt my pleasure in your gift," she added, with a pout.

20 "What was that?" asked Bertie anxiously, fearful that perhaps he had chosen a size of handkerchief that was not within the correct feminine limit.

"I should have liked to have written and thanked you for them as soon as I got them," said Ella, and Bertie's sky
25 clouded at once.

"You know what mother is," he protested; "she opens all my letters, and if she found I'd been giving presents to anyone there'd have been something to talk about for the next fortnight."

30 "Surely, at the age of twenty—" began Ella.

"I'm not twenty till September," interrupted Bertie.

"At the age of nineteen years and eight months," persisted Ella, "you might be allowed to keep your correspondence private to yourself."

35 "I ought to be, but things aren't always what they ought to be. Mother opens every letter that comes into the house, whoever it's for. My sisters and I have made rows about it time and again, but she goes on doing it."

"I'd find some way to stop her if I were in your place,"
40 said Ella valiantly, and Bertie felt that the glamour of his anxiously deliberated present had faded away in the disagreeable restriction that hedged round its acknowledgment.

"Is anything the matter?" asked Bertie's friend Clovis when
45 they met that evening at the swimming-bath.

"Why do you ask?" said Bertie.

"When you wear a look of tragic gloom in a swimming-bath," said Clovis, "it's especially noticeable from the fact that you're wearing very little else. Didn't she like the
50 handkerchiefs?"

Bertie explained the situation.

"It is rather galling, you know," he added, "when a girl has a lot of things she wants to write to you and can't send a letter except by some roundabout, underhand way."

55 "One never realizes one's blessings while one enjoys them," said Clovis; "now I have to spend a considerable amount of ingenuity inventing excuses for not having written to people."

"It's not a joking matter," said Bertie resentfully: "you
60 wouldn't find it funny if your mother opened all your letters."

"The funny thing to me is that you should let her do it."

"I can't stop it. I've argued about it—"

"You haven't used the right kind of argument, I expect.
65 Now, if every time one of your letters was opened you lay on your back on the dining-table during dinner and had a fit, or roused the entire family in the middle of the night to hear you recite one of Blake's 'Poems of Innocence,' you would get a far more respectful hearing for future
70 protests. People yield more consideration to a mutilated mealtime or a broken night's rest, than ever they would to a broken heart."

"Oh, dry up," said Bertie crossly, inconsistently splashing Clovis from head to foot as he plunged into the water.

(1919)

GO ON TO THE NEXT PAGE ⟹

18. By saying that the park landscape "blossomed suddenly into tropical radiance" (lines 3–4), the author means that

    (A) the sun just came out from behind the clouds
    (B) the flowers in the park are growing rapidly
    (C) the weather was cloudy and overcast earlier in the day
    (D) Ella is annoyed about the handkerchiefs
    (E) Ella is delighted to see Bertie

19. Which phrase surprises the reader by associating two contradictory ideas or images?

    (A) staring listlessly (line 2)
    (B) blossomed suddenly (lines 3–4)
    (C) exclaimed sedately (line 6)
    (D) disagreeable restriction (line 42)
    (E) tragic gloom (line 47)

20. Which best sums up Clovis's advice to Bertie?

    (A) Bertie should invent excuses to avoid writing to Ella.
    (B) Bertie should behave unpleasantly whenever his mother opens his mail.
    (C) Bertie should ask his mother never to open his letters without his express permission.
    (D) Bertie should ask his sisters' advice about an appropriate gift for Ella.
    (E) Bertie should tell his mother she is breaking his heart by reading his mail.

21. All these details establish or maintain a humorous tone EXCEPT

    (A) Bertie's care for the set of his trousers when sitting down beside Ella
    (B) Ella's assertion that she would find a way to stop the opening of her mail
    (C) Clovis's statement that not being able to write letters can be a blessing
    (D) Clovis' specific suggestions of how Bertie might solve his problem
    (E) Bertie's saying "Oh, dry up" just as he splashes Clovis with water

22. From their conversation, you can infer that Bertie and Clovis

    (A) met each other for the first time only a few weeks ago
    (B) are members of the same large extended family
    (C) have been close friends for a long time
    (D) know each other casually but not intimately
    (E) are members of the same swim team

23. Which best describes Clovis' personality?

    (A) He is imaginative and resourceful.
    (B) He is compassionate and sympathetic.
    (C) He is cheerful and optimistic.
    (D) He is courteous and thoughtful.
    (E) He is dreamy and impractical.

24. The reader may reasonably infer all of these things about Bertie's mother EXCEPT

    (A) she is curious to the point of being nosy
    (B) she is determined to control her children
    (C) she does not get much mail of her own
    (D) she does not have a job outside of her home
    (E) she is a loving and concerned parent

25. You can guess that Ella is genuinely interested in Bertie because

    I. she is deliberately lying in wait for him in Kensington Gardens

    II. she is pleased with the present he sent her

    III. she urges him to defy his mother

(A) I only
(B) II only
(C) I and II only
(D) I and III only
(E) I, II, and III

Questions 26–35. Read the following passage carefully before you choose your answers.

However much we may admire the orator's occasional bursts of eloquence, the noblest written words are commonly as far behind or above the fleeting spoken language as the firmament with its stars is behind the
5 clouds. *There* are the stars, and they who can may read them. The astronomers forever comment on and observe them. They are not exhalations like our daily colloquies and vaporous breath. What is called eloquence in the forum is commonly found to be rhetoric in the study. The
10 orator yields to the inspiration of a transient occasion, and speaks to the mob before him, to those who can *hear* him; but the writer, whose more equable life is his occasion, and who would be distracted by the event and the crowd which inspire the orator, speaks to the intellect and health of
15 mankind, to all in any age who can *understand* him.

No wonder that Alexander[1] carried the *Iliad* with him on his expeditions in a precious casket. A written word is the choicest of relics. It is something at once more intimate with us and more universal than any other
20 work of art. It is the work of art nearest to life itself. It may be translated into every language, and not only be read but actually breathed from all human lips; not be represented on canvas or in marble only, but be carved out of the breath of life itself. The symbol of an ancient
25 man's thought becomes a modern man's speech. Two thousand summers have imparted to the monuments of Grecian literature, as to her marbles, only a maturer golden and autumnal tint, for they have carried their own serene and celestial atmosphere into all lands to
30 protect them against the corrosion of time. Books are the treasured wealth of the world and the fit inheritance of generations and nations. Books, the oldest and the best, stand naturally and rightfully on the shelves of every cottage. They have no cause of their own to plead,
35 but while they enlighten and sustain the reader his common sense will not refuse them. Their authors are a natural and irresistible aristocracy in every society, and, more than kings or emperors, exert an influence on mankind. When the illiterate and perhaps scornful
40 trader has earned by enterprise and industry his coveted leisure and independence, and is admitted to the circles of wealth and fashion, he turns inevitably at last to those still higher but yet inaccessible circles of intellect and genius, and is sensible only of the
45 imperfection of his culture and the vanity and insufficiency of all his riches, and further proves his good sense by the pains which be takes to secure for his children that intellectual culture whose want he so keenly feels; and thus it is that he becomes the founder
50 of a family.

Those who have not learned to read the ancient classics in the language in which they were written must have a very imperfect knowledge of the history of the human race; for it is remarkable that no transcript of them has ever been

---

[1] Alexander: Alexander III "the Great," ruler of the Macedonian Empire from 336–323 B.C.E.

GO ON TO THE NEXT PAGE ⟼

55 made into any modern tongue, unless our civilization itself may be regarded as such a transcript. Homer has never yet been printed in English, nor Aeschylus, nor Virgil even—works as refined, as solidly done, and as beautiful almost as the morning itself; for later writers, 60 say what we will of their genius, have rarely, if ever, equaled the elaborate beauty and finish and the lifelong and heroic literary labors of the ancients. They only talk of forgetting them who never knew them. It will be soon enough to forget them when we have the learning and the 65 genius which will enable us to attend to and appreciate them. That age will be rich indeed when those relics which we call Classics, and the still older and more than classic but even less known Scriptures of the nations, shall have still further accumulated, when the Vaticans 70 shall be filled with Vedas and Zendavestas and Bibles, with Homers and Dantes and Shakespeares, and all the centuries to come shall have successively deposited their trophies in the forum of the world. By such a pile we may hope to scale heaven at last.

(1854)

26. The word "scale" in the final sentence means

(A) climb to, ascend to
(B) play a series of musical notes
(C) remove the protective plates from a fish
(D) reduce according to a fixed ratio
(E) represent in proportion to actual size

27. According to the author, what makes a literary work "the work of art nearest to life itself" (line 20)?

(A) It can be found on the shelves of every cottage.
(B) Its physical form is more durable than canvas, paint, marble, or any other form of visual art.
(C) It can be translated into many languages and thus potentially understood by everyone, not only the people of one nation.
(D) It is easier to always have by your side, and to carry with you, than a painting or statue.
(E) It represents and reflects the actual thoughts and emotions of a real person.

28. When the author says in lines 55–56 that "our civilization itself may be regarded as a transcript" of the ancient classics, he means

(A) that the time has come to translate the classics into modern languages
(B) that the classics still exist because people faithfully copied and printed them
(C) that human civilization exists because the classics were written
(D) that the classics have shaped and influenced humankind through the ages
(E) that people of the present day understand and appreciate the classics

29. The author believes that great literary works are like stars because they share the quality of

(A) enduring beauty
(B) profound thought
(C) visual brilliance
(D) vast distance
(E) fleeting existence

30. Which of the following best states the meaning of the sentence "They only talk of forgetting them who never knew them" (lines 62–63)?

(A) People cannot remember texts that they never read in the first place.
(B) It is impossible to forget what one has not carefully read.
(C) The only people who think the classics are not worthwhile have never actually read them.
(D) People may talk about having forgotten the classics, but in fact they remember them well.
(E) Those who have never read the classics have nothing to forget.

31. Which of the following comes closest to expressing the main argument of the essay?

    (A) "*There* are the stars, and they who can may read them." (lines 5–6)
    (B) "What is called eloquence in the forum is commonly found to be rhetoric in the study." (lines 8–9)
    (C) "The symbol of an ancient man's thought becomes a modern man's speech." (lines 24–25)
    (D) "Books are the treasured wealth of the world and the fit inheritance of generations and nations." (lines 30–32)
    (E) "Homer has never yet been printed in English, nor Aeschylus, nor Virgil even." (lines 56–58)

32. Why does the author believe that the influence of the best books is greater than that of "kings or emperors" (line 38)?

    (A) because monarchs are evil tyrants, while books are benevolent
    (B) because monarchs live only a short time, while books endure through many generations
    (C) because monarchs must compromise with advisers, while authors can write what they please
    (D) because a monarch can only affect his or her own people, while a book can be read all over the world
    (E) because monarchs are not necessarily well read, but authors of great books are

33. The author's habit of pairing of ideas or concepts, such as "comment on and observe," "golden and autumnal," and "illiterate and perhaps scornful," has which of the following effects?

    I. It adds emphasis to a particular point.
    II. It provides additional descriptive details.
    III. It unifies the essay by its frequent use.

    (A) I only
    (B) I and II only
    (C) II only
    (D) II and III only
    (E) I, II, and III

34. According to the author, what makes the trader feel that his riches are vain and insufficient?

    (A) They have not won him a place in good society.
    (B) They have not allowed him to marry and raise a family.
    (C) They have not taught him anything true and everlasting about life.
    (D) They have not given him the means of getting an education.
    (E) They have not provided him with material comforts.

35. Why does the author believe that great books are "the treasured wealth of the world" (line 31)?

    (A) because books contain all human wisdom and imagination
    (B) because early books are beautifully lettered and illustrated
    (C) because many books have expensive and handsome bindings
    (D) because old books can be found in libraries
    (E) because old or antique books are worth a lot of money

Questions 36–43. Read the following poem carefully before you choose your answers.

Out From Behind This Mask (To Confront a Portrait)

1

Out from behind this bending rough-cut mask,
These lights and shades, this drama of the whole,
This common curtain of the face contain'd in me for me,
   in you for you, in each for each,
5 (Tragedies, sorrows, laughter, tears—O heaven!
The passionate teeming plays this curtain hid!)
This glaze of God's serenest purest sky,
This film of Satan's seething pit,
This heart's geography's map, this limitless small
   continent, this soundless sea;
10 Out from the convolutions of this globe,
This subtler astronomic orb than sun or moon, than
   Jupiter, Venus, Mars,
This condensation of the universe, (nay here the only
   universe,
Here the idea, all in this mystic handful wrapt;)
These burin'd¹ eyes, flashing to you to pass to
   future time,
15 To launch and spin through space revolving sideling, from
   these to emanate,
To you whoe'er you are—a look.

2

A traveler of thoughts and years, of peace and war,
Of youth long sped and middle age declining,
(As the first volume of a tale perused and laid away, and
   this the second,
20 Songs, ventures, speculations, presently to close,)
Lingering a moment here and now, to you I opposite turn,
As on the road or at some crevice door by chance, or
   open'd window,
Pausing, inclining, baring my head, you specially I greet,
To draw and clinch your soul for once inseparably
   with mine,
25 Then travel travel on.

                            (1891)

¹burin'd: engraved or incised

36. The implied extended metaphor in lines 1–6 of the poem relates to

   (A) music
   (B) theater
   (C) poetry
   (D) painting
   (E) mystery

37. The speaker compares his face to all of the following EXCEPT

   (A) a rough-cut mask (line 1)
   (B) a curtain (line 3)
   (C) a passionate play (line 6)
   (D) a glaze (line 7)
   (E) a film (line 8)

38. The speaker uses the word "common" (line 3) in the sense of

   (A) ordinary, usual
   (B) coarse, ill-bred
   (C) universal, shared by all
   (D) habitual, frequent
   (E) second-rate, substandard

39. Which best describes the speaker's idea about the purpose of the human face?

   (A) It reveals a person's true and essential nature.
   (B) It conceals the thoughts, emotions, and passions of the inner person.
   (C) It acts as a mirror in which other people see themselves reflected.
   (D) It is the reason we are either attracted or repelled by one another when we meet.
   (E) It is the best means of assessing another person's qualities.

GO ON TO THE NEXT PAGE ⟹

40. The speaker uses the images of "God's serenest purest sky" and "Satan's seething pit" (lines 7–8) to convey which of the following ideas?

    I. The soul has both noble and evil impulses.

    II. A person's past history can contain both heroic and villainous acts.

    III. Memory is both a curse and a blessing.

(A) I only
(B) II only
(C) I and II only
(D) II and III only
(E) I, II, and III

41. How does the speaker of this poem seem to feel about himself?

(A) He sees himself clearly and is comfortable with himself.
(B) He thinks he is better and more perceptive than other people.
(C) He thinks poorly of his own negative thoughts and emotions.
(D) He is anxious to present an attractive appearance to others.
(E) He does not want to acknowledge his true nature to himself.

42. The word "portrait" in the title refers to

(A) the speaker's face
(B) a painting of someone's face
(C) the face of a chance-met person
(D) a mirror
(E) the poem

43. What happens in the poem?

(A) The speaker looks into a mirror and muses about his features.
(B) The speaker exchanges a friendly glance with another person.
(C) The speaker comes face to face with a portrait in a museum.
(D) The speaker describes his long acting career in a series of plays.
(E) The speaker recounts the experiences of many journeys.

Questions 44–50. Read the following passage carefully before you choose your answers.

As love is the most noble and divine passion of the soul, so is it that to which we may justly attribute all the real satisfactions of life; and without it, man is unfinished, and unhappy.

5 There are a thousand things to be said of the advantages this generous passion brings to those whose hearts are capable of receiving its soft impressions, for 'tis not everyone that can be sensible of its tender touches. How many examples, from history and observation, could

10 I give of its wondrous power; nay, even to a degree of transmigration? How many idiots has it made wise? How many fools eloquent? How many homebred squires accomplished? How many cowards brave? And there is no sort or species of mankind on whom it cannot

15 work some change and miracle, if it be a noble, well-grounded passion, except on the fop in fashion; the hardened, incorrigible fop, so often wounded but never reclaimed. For still, by a dire mistake, conducted by vast opinionatreism[1], and a greater portion of self-love, than

20 the rest of the race of man, he believes that affectation in his mien and dress, that mathematical movement, that formality in every action, that face managed with care, and softened into ridicule, the languishing turn, the toss, and the back-shake of the periwig, is the direct way

25 to the heart of the fine person he adores, and instead of curing love in his soul, serves only to advance his folly, and the more he is enamored, the more industriously he assumes (every hour) the coxcomb. These are Love's playthings, a sort of animals with whom he sports, and

30 whom he never wounds but when he is in good humor and always shoots laughing. 'Tis the diversion of the little god to see what a fluttering and bustle one of these sparks, new-wounded, makes; to what fantastic fooleries he has recourse. The glass is every moment called to counsel, the

35 valet consulted and plagued for new invention of dress, the footman and *scrutore*[2] perpetually employed; billet-doux and madrigals take up all his mornings, till playtime in dressing, till night in gazing; still, like a sunflower turned towards the beams of the fair eyes of his Celia,

40 adjusting himself in the most amorous posture he can assume, his hat under his arm, while the other hand is put

carelessly into his bosom, as if laid upon his panting heart; his head a little bent to one side, supported with a world of cravat-string, which he takes mighty care not to put into

45 disorder, as one may guess by a never-failing and horrid stiffness in his neck, and if he have an occasion to look aside, his whole body turns at the same time, for fear the motion of the head alone should incommode the cravat or periwig. And sometimes the glove is well-managed, and

50 the white hand displayed. Thus, with a thousand other little motions and formalities, all in the common place or road of foppery, he takes infinite pains to show himself to the pit and boxes, a most accomplished ass. This is he, of all humankind, on whom love can do no miracles, and

55 who can nowhere, and upon no occasion, quit one grain of his refined foppery, unless in a duel or a battle, if ever his stars should be so severe and ill-mannered to reduce him to the necessity of either. Fear then would ruffle that fine form he had so long preserved in nicest order, with grief

60 considering that an unlucky, chance wound in his face, if such a dire misfortune should befall him, would spoil the sale of it forever.

Perhaps it will be urged that, since no metamorphosis can be made in a fop by love, you must consider him one of those

65 that only talks of love, and thinks himself that happy thing, a lover, and wanting fine sense enough for the real passion, believes what he feels to be it. There are in the quiver of the god a great many different darts; some that wound for a day, and others for a year. They are all fine, painted, glittering

70 darts, and show as well as those made of the noblest metal, but the wounds they make reach the desire only, and are cured by possessing, while the short-lived passion betrays the cheats. But 'tis that refined and illustrious passion of the soul, whose aim is virtue, and whose end is honor, that has

75 the power of changing nature, and is capable of performing all those heroic things of which history is full.

(1688)

[1] opinionatreism: high opinion of oneself, conceit, vanity
[2] scrutore: writing-desk

44. Which is NOT one reason for the common comparison, used in the passage, of falling in love to being struck by a dart or arrow?

    (A) because both only happen by chance
    (B) because both affect everything about the way a person feels
    (C) because both can distract a person from all other thoughts or activities
    (D) because both can cause genuine pain
    (E) because both usually strike a person without warning

45. The author's suggestion that a facial wound would "spoil the sale" of the fop's face (lines 61–62) is an implied metaphor likening the fop to

    (A) a student
    (B) a soldier
    (C) a prostitute
    (D) a coward
    (E) a lover

46. What reason(s) does the author suggest for her belief that a fop is incapable of true love?

        I. He thinks only about himself and his appearance.
        II. He always acts from calculation, never from impulse.
        III. He is irritable and easily annoyed.

    (A) I and II only
    (B) II and III only
    (C) I and III only
    (D) I only
    (E) III only

47. Details in the passage suggest that the author believes fops are

    (A) vicious and evil
    (B) good-natured and friendly
    (C) heartless and cold
    (D) silly and pathetic
    (E) cynical and jaded

48. Which best describes the "dire mistake" (line 18) the author believes the fop makes in his approach to romance?

    (A) He thinks about himself instead of about his beloved.
    (B) He takes care with his personal appearance.
    (C) He shrinks from taking part in a fight.
    (D) He attends a variety of brilliant social gatherings.
    (E) He does not know when he looks foolish.

49. In the phrase "if ever his stars should be so severe" (lines 56–57), the word *stars* refers to the fop's

    (A) military rank
    (B) fortune or fate
    (C) bright eyes
    (D) celebrity status
    (E) sparkling jewelry

50. Why does the author say that the fop is "like a sunflower" (line 38)?

    (A) because he is showy and dresses in bright colors
    (B) because he is tall and handsome
    (C) because he is attracted to the light
    (D) because he is most active at night
    (E) because he requires care and cultivation

GO ON TO THE NEXT PAGE ⟹

Questions 51–60. Read the following passage carefully before you choose your answers.

On a January evening of the early seventies, Christine Nilsson was singing in *Faust* at the Academy of Music in New York.

Though there was already talk of the erection, in remote
5 metropolitan distances "above the Forties," of a new Opera House which should compete in costliness and splendor with those of the great European capitals, the world of fashion was still content to reassemble every winter in the shabby red and gold boxes of the sociable
10 old Academy. Conservatives cherished it for being small and inconvenient, and thus keeping out the "new people" whom New York was beginning to dread and yet be drawn to; and the sentimental clung to it for its historic associations, and the musical for its excellent acoustics,
15 always so problematic a quality in halls built for the hearing of music.

It was Madame Nilsson's first appearance that winter, and what the daily press had already learned to describe as "an exceptionally brilliant audience" had gathered to hear her,
20 transported through the slippery, snowy streets in private broughams, in the spacious family landau, or in the humbler but more convenient "Brown coupe." To come to the Opera in a Brown coupe was almost as honorable a way of arriving as in one's own carriage; and departure by
25 the same means had the immense advantage of enabling one (with a playful allusion to democratic principles) to scramble into the first Brown conveyance in the line, instead of waiting till the cold-and-gin congested nose of one's own coachman gleamed under the portico of the
30 Academy. It was one of the great livery-stableman's most masterly intuitions to have discovered that Americans want to get away from amusement even more quickly than they want to get to it.

When Newland Archer opened the door at the back of the
35 club box the curtain had just gone up on the garden scene. There was no reason why the young man should not have come earlier, for he had dined at seven, alone with his mother and sister, and had lingered afterward over a cigar in the Gothic library with glazed black-walnut bookcases
40 and finial-topped chairs which was the only room in the house where Mrs. Archer allowed smoking. But, in the

first place, New York was a metropolis, and perfectly aware that in metropolises it was "not the thing" to arrive early at the opera; and what was or was not "the
45 thing" played a part as important in Newland Archer's New York as the inscrutable totem terrors that had ruled the destinies of his forefathers thousands of years ago.

The second reason for his delay was a personal one. He had dawdled over his cigar because he was at heart a
50 dilettante, and thinking over a pleasure to come often gave him a subtler satisfaction than its realization. This was especially the case when the pleasure was a delicate one, as his pleasures mostly were; and on this occasion the moment he looked forward to was so rare and exquisite
55 in quality that—well, if he had timed his arrival in accord with the prima donna's stage-manager he could not have entered the Academy at a more significant moment than just as she was singing: "He loves me—he loves me not— HE LOVES ME!—" and sprinkling the falling daisy petals
60 with notes as clear as dew.

She sang, of course, "*M'ama!*" and not "he loves me," since an unalterable and unquestioned law of the musical world required that the German text of French operas sung by Swedish artists should be translated into Italian for the
65 clearer understanding of English-speaking audiences. This seemed as natural to Newland Archer as all the other conventions on which his life was molded: such as the duty of using two silver-backed brushes with his monogram in blue enamel to part his hair, and of never appearing
70 in society without a flower (preferably a gardenia) in his buttonhole.

(1920)

51. Which best describes the author's attitude toward New York society of the 1870s?

(A) ironic
(B) nostalgic
(C) bitter
(D) amused
(E) admiring

52. Newland Archer's character is best described as

(A) passionate and restless
(B) exacting and hard to please
(C) mild and pleasant
(D) conservative and conventional
(E) intellectual and artistic

53. Which sentence uses a paradox in order to make a point?

(A) "The world of fashion was still content to reassemble every winter in the shabby red and gold boxes of the sociable old Academy" (lines 7–10)
(B) "What the daily press had already learned to describe as 'an exceptionally brilliant audience' had gathered to hear her" (lines 18–19)
(C) "To come to the Opera in a Brown coupe was almost as honorable a way of arriving as in one's own carriage" (lines 22–24)
(D) "New York was a metropolis, and . . . in metropolises it was 'not the thing' to arrive early at the opera" (lines 42–44)
(E) "If he had timed his arrival in accord with the prima donna's stage-manager he could not have entered the Academy at a more significant moment" (lines 55–57)

54. The detail that Newland considers it a "duty" to use a certain kind of hairbrush is significant because it shows that

(A) he is a fop who thinks only about his own personal appearance
(B) he allows social conventions to govern his private behavior
(C) he appreciates and enjoys possessing nice things
(D) he enjoys anticipation more than reality
(E) he does whatever his mother tells him

55. "An unalterable and unquestioned law of the musical world required that the German text of French operas sung by Swedish artists should be translated into Italian for the clearer understanding of English-speaking audiences" (lines 62–65) is an example of

(A) metaphor
(B) hyperbole
(C) irony
(D) allusion
(E) foreshadowing

56. Which of the following does NOT support the author's implication that New Yorkers of the 1870s have little genuine interest in opera?

(A) "there was already talk . . . of a new Opera House which should compete in costliness and splendor with those of the great European capitals" (lines 4–7)
(B) "Conservatives cherished it for being small and inconvenient, and thus keeping out the 'new people'" (lines 10–11)
(C) "Americans want to get away from amusement even more quickly than they want to get to it" (lines 31–33)
(D) "he could not have entered the Academy at a more significant moment than just as she was singing: 'He loves me'" (lines 56–58)
(E) "New York was a metropolis, and . . . in metropolises it was 'not the thing' to arrive early at the opera" (lines 42–44)

57. The word "dilettante" (line 50) shows that Newland Archer's interest in music is

(A) passionate
(B) well informed
(C) professional
(D) polite
(E) superficial

GO ON TO THE NEXT PAGE ⟹

58. "Sprinkling the falling daisy petals" (line 59) is an allusion to

    (A) a newspaper review
    (B) a children's game
    (C) a social gaffe
    (D) a French opera
    (E) a joke about gardening

59. The comparison between the social conventions of 1870s New York and the "inscrutable totem terrors" (line 46) of primitive man suggests that the modern conventions are

    (A) not reasonable or logical
    (B) the result of superstition
    (C) permanent and binding
    (D) punitive and harsh
    (E) based on natural human impulses

60. What does their concern over the costliness and splendor of the potential new Opera House imply about the New York opera-goers?

    I. They disagree over the best location for the new Opera House.
    II. Their primary goal is to impress outsiders.
    III. They are not interested in how the music will sound.

    (A) II only
    (B) I and II only
    (C) II only
    (D) II and III only
    (E) III only

STOP

If you finish before time is called, you may check your work on this test only.

Do not turn to any other test in this book.

Answer Key

1. B	16. A	31. D	46. A
2. D	17. B	32. B	47. D
3. C	18. E	33. E	48. A
4. A	19. C	34. C	49. B
5. B	20. B	35. A	50. C
6. D	21. B	36. B	51. A
7. E	22. C	37. C	52. D
8. A	23. A	38. C	53. B
9. D	24. E	39. B	54. B
10. E	25. E	40. C	55. C
11. C	26. A	41. A	56. D
12. A	27. E	42. C	57. E
13. B	28. D	43. B	58. B
14. D	29. A	44. A	59. A
15. E	30. C	45. C	60. D

Answers and Explanations

1. **(B)** A person with a *nice* palate is one who is fussy or choosy about what he eats.

2. **(D)** Although the author compares his introduction to a menu that sets forth the bill of fare in a restaurant, his introduction is much less specific than a menu; it tells the reader only that the work is a story of "Human Nature" with both urban and rural settings.

3. **(C)** The word *history* in the last sentence is used in the sense of "narrative" or "story." The many mentions of cooks, restaurants, and so on are only used for purposes of comparison.

4. **(A)** Since the author describes city life in terms of "high French and Italian seasoning," he considers that it has more variety and, metaphorically speaking, more flavor than country life.

5. **(B)** The author says that "the excellence of the book consists less in the subject than in the author's skill." Thus, the book will only be good if it is well written, no matter what the plot and theme are like.

6. **(D)** The author never suggests that either writer or victualler should create books or meals that cater to specific demands from the public. He states instead that the writer should choose his own subject and the victualler his own menu, as long as they explain clearly to the customer what they are offering, so he will know whether to buy it or instead "depart to some other ordinary better accommodated to his taste."

7. **(E)** "Human nature" refers to the way people think, feel, and behave. Therefore, it relates to character, not to plot, accuracy, setting, or writing style.

8. **(A)** The author explains that a smart cook will begin with plain dishes and build a meal to spicier and more flavorful ones. In the same way, he will make his story progressively more varied and exciting in its characters and settings.

9. **(D)** "Summer's honey breath" refers literally to summer. "The wrackful siege" refers to the damage wrought by the passage of time. "Fearful meditation" refers literally to a thought that awes or frightens the speaker. "This miracle" refers to the possibility that the speaker's poem will outlast the passage of time. "Time's best jewel" refers to the beloved, as the most precious of all living things.

10. **(E)** In the last line, the speaker expresses the belief that "black ink"—in other words, his poem—may give his love eternal life, despite Time's best efforts to destroy her as Time must destroy all life. Therefore ink is more powerful than Time.

11. **(C)** The first twelve lines observe that Time destroys everything that lives, no matter how strong it appears. The last two lines, however, point out that there is one thing that can outlast Time—the written word. By writing about beauty, the poet can make it last forever.

12. **(A)** The speaker expresses fear at the notion that Time can destroy everything, no matter how strong and enduring it seems—heavy rocks, steel gates, and so on.

13. **(B)** Time is miserly because he keeps a chest of jewels. The words *wrackful seige, batt'ring,* and *swift foot* suggest brutality. The word *rage* also suggests fury. Many images, including *spoil of beauty and decays*, suggest destruction. The only choice left is B; the speaker does not characterize Time as patient.

14. **(D)** Option I is correct because the capital *T* does convey a sense of power and authority; it makes the word *Time* stand out and call attention to itself. Option II is wrong because capitalizing Time shows Time's strength, not his one weakness. Option III is correct because only proper nouns—names of specific people or things—are usually capitalized; the effect is as though Time is a great giant, not a disembodied concept.

15. **(E)** The speaker claims that his poem may outlast the ravages of Time, which rules out choice A. The poem describes several examples of death, decay, or destruction wrought by time, which rules out choices B and D. The poem mentions Time's "spoil of beauty," which rules out choice C.

16. **(A)** The word *may* in the final line tells you that choice A is correct. The speaker does not say that his poem *will* last forever; he hopes it *may* last.

17. **(B)** The words *siege* and *batt'ring* (battering) create an image of war, with a hostile army surrounding a town or fortress, battering against its walls, and keeping its people or soldiers trapped inside with no means of escape.

18. **(E)** The phrase is used metaphorically. The weather has been sunny and pleasant all along; were it otherwise, Ella would not sit outdoors in the park. The day becomes beautiful to Ella when Bertie appears because she is happy to see him.

19. **(C)** Exclamations are usually loud, hearty, and strong—the opposite of *sedate*.

20. **(B)** Clovis outlines two ways in which Bertie might make his mother drop her bad habits—both ways involve creating an uproar that will disturb and annoy everyone in the house.

21. **(B)** Choice A is funny because Bertie should be thinking only about Ella, not about his appearance. Choices C and E are funny because both involve paradoxes. Choice D is funny because the suggestions are creative, specific, vivid, and unexpected.

22. **(C)** Bertie confides in Clovis and also tells him to "dry up." If the young men were recent acquaintances or only casual friends, they would likely be more polite and aloof with one another; they would not talk about intimate concerns. A further clue to their close friendship is the fact that Clovis knew that Bertie was giving the handkerchiefs to Ella.

23. **(A)** The two suggestions Clovis offers as solutions to Bertie's difficulty prove that he is good at solving problems, and that his solutions are the unique and original products of a wild imagination.

24. **(E)** Only a nosy person would open mail that was not addressed to her. Only a controlling person would read her children's private correspondence once the children are grown (Bertie is almost 20). Only someone who did not get much mail of her own would have the time or interest to read other people's mail. Only someone who did not have a day job would be at home every day when the mail is delivered. A loving and concerned parent would be more likely to ask direct questions of her children if she wanted to know anything, rather than spying on them by reading their mail.

25. **(E)** Ella clearly went to the Gardens specifically to meet Bertie. She says the handkerchiefs are "just what I've been wanting." The fact that she encourages Bertie to take charge shows that she cares about him and wants him to be strong.

26. **(A)** The reference to heaven makes it clear that the author means *scale* in the sense of ascending to a high place.

27. **(E)** The author goes on to explain that the written word reflects life in a way that other arts do not, because in life words are the basic means of human communication, "actually breathed from all human lips." Only a few people paint pictures or sculpt statues or compose music, but *all* people express their thoughts and emotions in words.

28. **(D)** In the second paragraph, the author states that writers have had more influence on humankind than kings or emperors. In other words, the classics have shaped and affected people's ways of thinking about and experiencing life, in every generation down to the author's own time.

29. **(A)** Stars do not contain profound thoughts (or any thoughts), which rules out choice B. Written works are not visually interesting or brilliant, which rules out choice C. Written works are close at hand, which rules out choice D. Both stars and literary classics have a permanent, not fleeting, existence, which rules out choice E. The author makes the comparison because like a star, a literary work endures; and just as stars fascinate with visual beauty, books fascinate with the beauty of language, images and ideas.

30. **(C)** The sentence is a little confusing because *they* refers to people and *them* refers to the literary classics. The author says "The only people who suggest we should forget about studying or reading the classics are the people who never read them in the first place." This is closest in phrasing and meaning to choice C.

31. **(D)** The main idea of the essay is the author's praise of great works of literature. He supports his argument by showing that speeches are inferior to written texts, and by praising the ancient classics and explaining why they are of lasting importance. Choice D best sums up the essay's argument, or thesis. Choices A, B, and C support the main argument.

32. **(B)** Choice A is wrong because not all monarchs are evil tyrants and not all books are good. Choice C is wrong because a monarch's influence is changed, not lessened, by the need to compromise. Choice D is wrong because monarchs' decisions, such as declaring war, can affect many nations outside their own. Choice E is wrong because poorly-educated monarchs are rare, but many great writers (Homer, Aesop, and Shakespeare are examples) did not get good educations. The author believes that a monarch's influence is less because the monarch is mortal; later monarchs can undo or overturn his decisions, and he may be forgotten in time. A book, on the other hand, lasts forever.

33. **(E)** Option I is correct because the second item in each pair does indeed add emphasis to the idea being expressed—for instance, "the elaborate beauty" is not as strong as "the elaborate beauty and finish" (line 61). Option II is correct because each word after "and" does add detail that the first word did not provide by itself: for instance, the trader's riches are not merely vain, they are vain and insufficient. Option III is correct because the author uses this device throughout the essay, thus giving his prose a particular rhythm and balance. The stylistic device pulls all parts of the essay together into a unified, consistent whole.

34. **(C)** Once the trader makes his fortune, he begins to mix with good society; then he tries to talk to people of "intellect and genius" and quickly realizes they know and understand things he does not know and that his money cannot buy for him. Therefore, he makes sure that his children acquire the "intellectual culture" he never had time for in his working life. This best fits choice C.

35. **(A)** The author values books, and believes that other people value them, because of the thoughts and ideas inside them, not because of the beauty of illustrations or fine leather bindings or because they are worth large sums of money.

36. **(B)** The words *mask, drama, curtain, tragedies,* and *plays* all show that the poet is implying a comparison to theater.

37. **(C)** The face is the mask behind which the essence of the person is concealed. The speaker also uses the words *curtain, glaze,* and *film* to evoke the idea of an outer covering used to hide what is behind it. The "passionate teeming plays" are the essence of the person that is concealed BEHIND the face, or "curtain."

38. **(C)** These are all correct definitions of *common,* but the speaker clearly refers to the human face as "a common curtain," meaning that his statement applies to all people. "In each for each" is a further clue that he means *common* in the sense of "common to us all."

39. **(B)** The images of the mask and curtain (lines 1 and 3) show that the speaker believes the face exists in order to hide the thoughts and feelings in the mind of the person.

40. **(C)** The speaker compares a person's deepest inner self to both God's sky (heaven) and Satan's pit (hell). In other words, he suggests that inside each person can be found both good and evil impulses, memories of one's own noble and base deeds. This fits options I and II. Option III does not fit because the poem is not saying "I both love and hate my memories"—it is saying "my face conceals both good and bad memories."

41. **(A)** The speaker does not boast about himself, nor does he criticize. This eliminates choices B, C, and D. He describes himself as an older person (see the start of stanza 2) who seems to take great joy in honest communication with chance-met individuals as described at the end of both stanzas. This fits choice A. Since the poem is all about describing and perceiving one's own true nature, choice E cannot be correct.

42. **(C)** The word *confront* suggests that the speaker comes face to face with the portrait. This best fits his encounter with the person he addresses as "you"—the chance-met stranger on the road. This person's face (and perhaps his or her soul as well, as hinted in line 24) is the portrait. Portraits often reveal the subject's inner essence, not just his or her features.

43. **(B)** The poem contains only one action, which is described in the second stanza: during his travels, the speaker turns to the chance-met person and greets him or her as one human being to another, then moves on. In the first stanza, the speaker explains everything he reveals in his greeting; his whole self, looking through his eyes out of the concealing mask of his face.

44. **(A)** Love happens only by chance, but being struck by an arrow is usually the result of the archer's deliberate aim. The other four choices accurately describe something that applies equally well to being physically wounded and to being emotionally overcome: it affects all your feelings, it distracts you, it hurts, and it often comes without warning.

45. **(C)** The passage shows that the fop's main occupation is to "sell" his appearance to the ladies he tries to fascinate. The only person among the options who lives by selling himself or herself is the prostitute, choice C.

46. (A) Option I is correct because every detail of the long second paragraph shows how self-absorbed the fop is, especially over his outward appearance. Option II is correct because the author points out that the fop is affected, that he strikes poses, that he manages his facial expressions, and so on. Option III is wrong because the fop is not defined by irritability; an irritable person might be listed with the fool, the coward, and the others at the start of the second paragraph who are redeemed and transformed by love.

47. (D) The author pokes fun at the fops of society. She finds them harmless, foolish, and laughable.

48. (A) At the start of the long second paragraph, the author lists several categories of people—the coward, the idiot, the fool—who are deeply flawed, but who can be redeemed by the power of love. She excludes the fop from this list because he is too self-absorbed to feel love; he loves himself too much ever to love anyone else. This best fits choice A.

49. (B) The author uses the word *stars* to mean destiny, fortune or fate. Many people in the author's time believed—as many people believe today—that a person's life was predetermined by the position of the stars in the heavens at his or her birth.

50. (C) The author specifically makes the comparison to illustrate the fop responding to the light and warmth in his beloved's eyes, just as a sunflower responds to the light and warmth of the sun. Choice A is true of both the fop and the bright yellow flower, but a glance at the passage shows that this is not the shared quality that made the author write the simile.

51. (A) The idea that singing *Faust* in Italian makes it easier for an English-speaking audience to understand it is only one of several examples of irony in the passage. The author shows no desire to return to the time of the early 1870s; instead, she subtly pokes fun at its cherished customs.

52. (D) Archer follows the conventions: he goes late to the opera, wears a gardenia in his buttonhole, parts his hair properly, and so on. The author says that these conventions seem "natural" to him. People who follow social conventions without question are inherently conservative. Nothing in the passage supports choices A or B. Choice C may be true, but only one detail—Newland's obedience to his mother's wishes about smoking—supports it, while several details support choice D. The word dilettante undercuts choice E.

53. (B) *Exceptionally* means "unusually," yet the daily papers apparently use the phrase "exceptionally brilliant" to describe *all* New York audiences. This is a paradox—a statement with a self-contradictory quality. The author suggests that in fact the audience is not exceptional at all, but that it nonetheless insists on being *described* as exceptional.

54. (B) The focus of the passage is on the conventions that govern a person's behavior. A person's choice of hairbrush is an intimate personal detail that would only be known to himself and perhaps to others living in his house—yet Newland still allows society to dictate this very private choice. The word *duty* shows that he considers this a social obligation. Therefore his society feels free to dictate people's private lives, not only their public actions.

55. (C) The statement implies the opposite of what it says; that in fact the English-speaking audience will understand the opera less clearly, not more clearly, when it is sung in a foreign language.

Practice Test 7   **287**

56. **(D)** Choice A shows that the audience cares what the new Opera House will look like, but not about musical concerns such as the acoustics. Choice B shows that they like the old Academy not because it is a good place to hear music, but because it doesn't have too many seats. Choice C shows that although crowds go to the opera, they are eager to leave it. Choice E shows that people prefer arriving too late to hear the beginning of the performance—obviously something no music lover would ever do.

57. **(E)** A *dilettante* is a person who feels a superficial interest in the arts, one who likes to dabble in poetry, music, and so on, but who does not pursue any of the arts passionately or thoroughly. The word indicates that Newland genuinely enjoys opera—he does not attend performances out of mere politeness—but that he is not a passionate, deeply knowledgeable fan.

58. **(B)** Picking the petals from a flower while reciting "He (or she) loves me; he loves me not" is a common children's game in many cultures. The author does not explain the allusion because she expects her readers to recognize it. In the opera *Faust*, the character sung by Christine Nilsson plays this game as part of the scene on stage.

59. **(A)** To *scrutinize* something means to examine or study it closely. The prefix *in-* means "not." Therefore, *inscrutable* conventions are those that cannot be understood by study or examination—those that are incomprehensible. In other words, the conventions have no basis in reason or logic; that is what makes them similar to ancient superstitions. This fits choice A.

60. **(D)** Option I is wrong because the location of the new Opera House is not relevant to its costliness or splendor. Option II is correct because costliness and splendor are surface, visible characteristics and they are the only concerns the author mentions; the patrons evidently are NOT concerned with acoustics, size, or comfort, for instance. Option III is correct because costliness and splendor have nothing to do with the actual purpose of the Opera House, which is to perform and enjoy musical works.

How To Calculate Your Score

Count the number of correct answers and enter the total below.

Count the number of wrong answers. Do NOT include any questions you did not answer.

Multiply the number of wrong answers by 0.25 and enter the total below.

Do the subtraction. The answer is your raw score. Use the scoring scale to find your scaled score.

$$\overline{\text{(number of correct answers)}} - \overline{\text{(number of wrong answers} \times 0.25)} = \overline{\text{(raw score)}}$$

RAW SCORE	SCALED SCORE	RAW SCORE	SCALED SCORE	RAW SCORE	SCALED SCORE	RAW SCORE	SCALED SCORE	RAW SCORE	SCALED SCORE
60	800	44	710	28	560	12	420	–4	260
59	800	43	700	27	550	11	410	–5	250
58	800	42	690	26	540	10	400	–6	240
57	800	41	690	25	530	9	390	–7	230
56	800	40	680	24	520	8	380	–8	220
55	800	39	670	23	510	7	370	–9	210
54	790	38	660	22	500	6	360	–10	200
53	790	37	650	21	500	5	350	–11	200
52	780	36	640	20	490	4	340	–12	200
51	770	35	630	19	490	3	330	–13	200
50	760	34	620	18	480	2	320	–14	200
49	750	33	610	17	470	1	310	–15	200
48	740	32	600	16	460	0	300		
47	740	31	590	15	450	–1	290		
46	730	30	580	14	440	–2	280		
45	720	29	570	13	430	–3	270		

Note: This is only a sample scoring scale. Scoring scales differ from exam to exam.

Practice Test 8

The following practice test is designed to be just like the real SAT Literature Test. It matches the actual test in content coverage and degree of difficulty.

Once you finish the practice test, determine your score. Carefully read the answer explanations of the questions you answered incorrectly. Identify any weaknesses in your literature skills by determining the areas in which you made the most errors. Review those sections of this book first. Then, as time permits, go back and review your strengths.

Allow one hour to take the test. Time yourself and work uninterrupted. If you run out of time, take note of where you stopped when time ran out. Remember that you lose a quarter point for each incorrect answer, but you do not lose points for questions you leave blank. Therefore, unless you can eliminate one or more of the five choices, it's best to leave a question unanswered.

Use the following formula to calculate your score:

(number of correct answers) – ¼ (number of incorrect answers)

If you treat this practice test just like the actual exam, it will accurately reflect how you are likely to perform on test day. Here are some hints on how to create test-taking conditions similar to those of the actual exam:

- Complete the test in one sitting. On test day, you will not be allowed to take a break.
- Tear out the answer sheet and fill in the ovals just as you will on the actual test day.
- Have a good eraser and more than one sharp pencil handy. On test day, you will not be able to go get a new pencil if yours breaks.
- Do not allow yourself any extra time; put down your pencil after exactly one hour, no matter how many questions are left to answer.
- Become familiar with the directions on the test. If you go in knowing what the directions say, you will not have to waste time reading and thinking about them on the actual test day.

Practice Test 8

Answer Sheet

Tear out this answer sheet and use it to mark your answers.

1. Ⓐ Ⓑ Ⓒ Ⓓ Ⓔ	16. Ⓐ Ⓑ Ⓒ Ⓓ Ⓔ	31. Ⓐ Ⓑ Ⓒ Ⓓ Ⓔ	46. Ⓐ Ⓑ Ⓒ Ⓓ Ⓔ
2. Ⓐ Ⓑ Ⓒ Ⓓ Ⓔ	17. Ⓐ Ⓑ Ⓒ Ⓓ Ⓔ	32. Ⓐ Ⓑ Ⓒ Ⓓ Ⓔ	47. Ⓐ Ⓑ Ⓒ Ⓓ Ⓔ
3. Ⓐ Ⓑ Ⓒ Ⓓ Ⓔ	18. Ⓐ Ⓑ Ⓒ Ⓓ Ⓔ	33. Ⓐ Ⓑ Ⓒ Ⓓ Ⓔ	48. Ⓐ Ⓑ Ⓒ Ⓓ Ⓔ
4. Ⓐ Ⓑ Ⓒ Ⓓ Ⓔ	19. Ⓐ Ⓑ Ⓒ Ⓓ Ⓔ	34. Ⓐ Ⓑ Ⓒ Ⓓ Ⓔ	49. Ⓐ Ⓑ Ⓒ Ⓓ Ⓔ
5. Ⓐ Ⓑ Ⓒ Ⓓ Ⓔ	20. Ⓐ Ⓑ Ⓒ Ⓓ Ⓔ	35. Ⓐ Ⓑ Ⓒ Ⓓ Ⓔ	50. Ⓐ Ⓑ Ⓒ Ⓓ Ⓔ
6. Ⓐ Ⓑ Ⓒ Ⓓ Ⓔ	21. Ⓐ Ⓑ Ⓒ Ⓓ Ⓔ	36. Ⓐ Ⓑ Ⓒ Ⓓ Ⓔ	51. Ⓐ Ⓑ Ⓒ Ⓓ Ⓔ
7. Ⓐ Ⓑ Ⓒ Ⓓ Ⓔ	22. Ⓐ Ⓑ Ⓒ Ⓓ Ⓔ	37. Ⓐ Ⓑ Ⓒ Ⓓ Ⓔ	52. Ⓐ Ⓑ Ⓒ Ⓓ Ⓔ
8. Ⓐ Ⓑ Ⓒ Ⓓ Ⓔ	23. Ⓐ Ⓑ Ⓒ Ⓓ Ⓔ	38. Ⓐ Ⓑ Ⓒ Ⓓ Ⓔ	53. Ⓐ Ⓑ Ⓒ Ⓓ Ⓔ
9. Ⓐ Ⓑ Ⓒ Ⓓ Ⓔ	24. Ⓐ Ⓑ Ⓒ Ⓓ Ⓔ	39. Ⓐ Ⓑ Ⓒ Ⓓ Ⓔ	54. Ⓐ Ⓑ Ⓒ Ⓓ Ⓔ
10. Ⓐ Ⓑ Ⓒ Ⓓ Ⓔ	25. Ⓐ Ⓑ Ⓒ Ⓓ Ⓔ	40. Ⓐ Ⓑ Ⓒ Ⓓ Ⓔ	55. Ⓐ Ⓑ Ⓒ Ⓓ Ⓔ
11. Ⓐ Ⓑ Ⓒ Ⓓ Ⓔ	26. Ⓐ Ⓑ Ⓒ Ⓓ Ⓔ	41. Ⓐ Ⓑ Ⓒ Ⓓ Ⓔ	56. Ⓐ Ⓑ Ⓒ Ⓓ Ⓔ
12. Ⓐ Ⓑ Ⓒ Ⓓ Ⓔ	27. Ⓐ Ⓑ Ⓒ Ⓓ Ⓔ	42. Ⓐ Ⓑ Ⓒ Ⓓ Ⓔ	57. Ⓐ Ⓑ Ⓒ Ⓓ Ⓔ
13. Ⓐ Ⓑ Ⓒ Ⓓ Ⓔ	28. Ⓐ Ⓑ Ⓒ Ⓓ Ⓔ	43. Ⓐ Ⓑ Ⓒ Ⓓ Ⓔ	58. Ⓐ Ⓑ Ⓒ Ⓓ Ⓔ
14. Ⓐ Ⓑ Ⓒ Ⓓ Ⓔ	29. Ⓐ Ⓑ Ⓒ Ⓓ Ⓔ	44. Ⓐ Ⓑ Ⓒ Ⓓ Ⓔ	59. Ⓐ Ⓑ Ⓒ Ⓓ Ⓔ
15. Ⓐ Ⓑ Ⓒ Ⓓ Ⓔ	30. Ⓐ Ⓑ Ⓒ Ⓓ Ⓔ	45. Ⓐ Ⓑ Ⓒ Ⓓ Ⓔ	60. Ⓐ Ⓑ Ⓒ Ⓓ Ⓔ

PRACTICE TEST 8
Time: 60 Minutes

Directions: This test consists of selections from literary works and questions on their content, form, and style. After reading each passage or poem, choose the best answer to each question and then fill in the corresponding oval on the answer sheet.

Note: Pay particular attention to the requirements of questions that contain the words NOT or EXCEPT.

Questions 1–9. Read the following poem carefully before you choose your answers.

And what is love? It is a doll dressed up
For idleness to cosset, nurse, and dandle;
A thing of soft misnomers, so divine
That silly youth doth think to make itself
5 Divine by loving, and so goes on
Yawning and doting a whole summer long,
Till Miss's comb is made a perfect tiara,
And common Wellingtons turn Romeo boots;
Till Cleopatra lives at Number Seven,
10 And Antony resides in Brunswick Square.
Fools! if some passions high have warmed the world,
If queens and soldiers have played deep for hearts,
It is no reason why such agonies
Should be more common than the growth of weeds.
15 Fools! make me whole again that weighty pearl
The queen of Egypt melted, and I'll say
That ye may love in spite of beaver hats.

(1818)

1. By calling love "a thing of soft misnomers" (line 3), the speaker implies that

(A) no one has ever said "I love you" sincerely
(B) all lovers in the history of the world have been young and foolish
(C) love is an emotion that only fools ever feel
(D) lovers call each other by exaggerated and unmerited nicknames
(E) love is not a genuine emotion, but a false one

2. The tone of the poem is best described as

(A) mocking and scornful
(B) bitter and ironic
(C) cheerful and optimistic
(D) anguished and desperate
(E) neutral and objective

3. Which best sums up the speaker's attitude toward love?

(A) It does not really exist.
(B) It has the power to make ordinary people divine.
(C) It is only truly felt by a very few extraordinary individuals.
(D) It makes people happy and contented.
(E) It makes heroes into fools.

4. The speaker uses "common Wellingtons" (line 8) to symbolize

(A) everyday garments
(B) ordinary young people
(C) ancient heroes
(D) love letters
(E) magic tricks

GO ON TO THE NEXT PAGE ⟹

5. In line 2, the speaker personifies idleness as

(A) a lyric poet
(B) a lover
(C) a silly youth
(D) a powerful queen
(E) a little girl

6. Why does the speaker consider that the youth of his own day are silly fools?

(A) They think falling in love will transform them into heroes or heroines.
(B) They think Antony and Cleopatra are still alive.
(C) They want to be in love because it is painful, not because it is pleasurable.
(D) They are eager to experience love as a natural part of growing up.
(E) They do not understand that love is a common, universal emotion.

7. Which best paraphrases the point the speaker makes by challenging the young lovers to "make me whole again that weighty pearl / The queen of Egypt melted" (lines 15–16)?

(A) Explain why the love of Antony and Cleopatra made them famous.
(B) Prove to me that you really are divine, as you claim to be.
(C) Compare your love for your beloved to Cleopatra's love for Antony.
(D) See if you understand my historical allusion to Cleopatra's pearl.
(E) Persuade me verbally that your love really has made you heroic.

8. Which of the following major themes does the poem address?

  I. the foolishness of callow youth
 II. the grandeur and pageant of the long past
III. the conflict between generations

(A) I and III
(B) II only
(C) II and III only
(D) III only
(E) I, II, and III

9. What is the most likely reason the poet did not choose to write this poem in the sonnet form?

(A) because it is a narrative rather than a lyric poem
(B) because the sonnet is commonly associated with love poetry
(C) because a sonnet must conform to a specific rhyming pattern
(D) because a sonnet is written in iambic pentameter
(E) because it expresses a specific emotion

GO ON TO THE NEXT PAGE ⟹

Questions 10–17. Read the following passage carefully before you choose your answers.

Mr. James Duffy lived in Chapelizod because he wished to live as far as possible from the city of which he was a citizen and because he found all the other suburbs of Dublin mean, modern and pretentious. He lived in an
5 old sombre house and from his windows he could look into the disused distillery or upwards along the shallow river on which Dublin is built. The lofty walls of his uncarpeted room were free from pictures. He had himself bought every article of furniture in the room: a black iron
10 bedstead, an iron washstand, four cane chairs, a clothes-rack, a coal-scuttle, a fender and irons and a square table on which lay a double desk. A bookcase had been made in an alcove by means of shelves of white wood. The bed was clothed with white bedclothes and a black and scarlet
15 rug covered the foot. A little hand-mirror hung above the washstand and during the day a white-shaded lamp stood as the sole ornament of the mantelpiece. The books on the white wooden shelves were arranged from below upwards according to bulk. A complete Wordsworth stood at
20 one end of the lowest shelf and a copy of the *Maynooth Catechism*, sewn into the cloth cover of a notebook, stood at one end of the top shelf. Writing materials were always on the desk. In the desk lay a manuscript translation of Hauptmann's *Michael Kramer*, the stage directions
25 of which were written in purple ink, and a little sheaf of papers held together by a brass pin. In these sheets a sentence was inscribed from time to time and, in an ironical moment, the headline of an advertisement for Bile Beans had been pasted on to the first sheet. On
30 lifting the lid of the desk a faint fragrance escaped—the fragrance of new cedarwood pencils or of a bottle of gum or of an overripe apple which might have been left there and forgotten.

Mr. Duffy abhorred anything which betokened physical
35 or mental disorder. A medieval doctor would have called him saturnine. His face, which carried the entire tale of his years, was of the brown tint of Dublin streets. On his long and rather large head grew dry black hair and a tawny moustache did not quite cover
40 an unamiable mouth. His cheekbones also gave his face a harsh character; but there was no harshness in the eyes which, looking at the world from under their tawny eyebrows, gave the impression of a man ever alert to greet a redeeming instinct in others but often disappointed.
45 He lived at a little distance from his body, regarding his own acts with doubtful side-glances. He had an odd autobiographical habit which led him to compose in his mind from time to time a short sentence about himself containing a subject in the third person and a predicate
50 in the past tense. He never gave alms to beggars and walked firmly, carrying a stout hazel.

He had been for many years cashier of a private bank in Baggot Street. Every morning he came in from Chapelizod by tram. At midday he went to Dan Burke's
55 and took his lunch—a bottle of lager beer and a small trayful of arrowroot biscuits. At four o'clock he was set free. He dined in an eating-house in George's Street where he felt himself safe from the society of Dublin's gilded youth and where there was a certain plain honesty
60 in the bill of fare. His evenings were spent either before his landlady's piano or roaming about the outskirts of the city. His liking for Mozart's music brought him sometimes to an opera or a concert: these were the only dissipations of his life.

65 He had neither companions nor friends, church nor creed. He lived his spiritual life without any communion with others, visiting his relatives at Christmas and escorting them to the cemetery when they died. He performed these two social duties for old dignity's sake
70 but conceded nothing further to the conventions which regulate the civic life. He allowed himself to think that in certain circumstances he would rob his bank but, as these circumstances never arose, his life rolled out evenly—an adventureless tale.

(1916)

10. All of the following details support the idea that Mr. Duffy is not a sociable man EXCEPT

    (A) "he wished to live as far as possible from the city of which he was a citizen" (lines 1–3)
    (B) he was "ever alert to greet a redeeming instinct in others but often disappointed" (lines 43–44)
    (C) "he dined . . . where he felt himself safe from the society of Dublin's gilded youth" (lines 57–59)
    (D) "his liking for Mozart's music brought him sometimes to an opera or a concert" (lines 62–63)
    (E) "he lived his spiritual life without any communion with others" (lines 66–67)

11. What can you conclude from the detail that "a sentence was inscribed from time to time" (line 27) in Mr. Duffy's translation of *Michael Kramer*?

    (A) He has no serious goal of completing the translation.
    (B) He only recently began working on the translation.
    (C) He has been commissioned to translate the script for a fee.
    (D) He does not understand the language in which the play is written.
    (E) He enjoys spending his spare time writing at his desk.

12. Which of the following can you conclude about Mr. Duffy from the way he has furnished his room?

    I. He is austere by nature and inclination.
    II. Material possessions hold no particular value for him.
    III. He spends very little time in his room.

    (A) I only
    (B) I and II only
    (C) II only
    (D) II and III only
    (E) I, II, and III

13. By saying "A medieval doctor would have called him saturnine" (lines 35–36), the author means that Mr. Duffy is

    (A) truculent and brutal
    (B) irritable and belligerent
    (C) impulsive and rash
    (D) cheerful and optimistic
    (E) gloomy and grave

14. Which detail suggests that Mr. Duffy is not comfortable with himself?

    (A) "Mr. Duffy abhorred anything which betokened physical or mental disorder" (lines 34–35)
    (B) "a tawny moustache did not quite cover an unamiable mouth" (lines 39–40)
    (C) his eyes "gave the impression of a man ever alert to greet a redeeming instinct in others" (lines 43–44)
    (D) "he lived at a little distance from his body, regarding his own acts with doubtful side-glances" (lines 45–46)
    (E) "he lived his spiritual life without any communion with others" (lines 66–67)

15. When the author says that Mr. Duffy's face "carried the entire tale of his years" (lines 36–37), he means that Mr. Duffy

    (A) has a very ordinary appearance
    (B) is as harsh as he appears on the surface
    (C) can accurately be summed up in a glance
    (D) likes to tell stories to chance-met acquaintances
    (E) shows his constant habit of worrying

16. This short-story excerpt provides you with which of the following stages of the story's entire plot?

(A) the exposition
(B) the rising action
(C) the climax
(D) the falling action
(E) the resolution or conclusion

17. Which best describes the attitude of the narrating voice toward Mr. Duffy?

(A) contemptuous
(B) pitying
(C) admiring
(D) distasteful
(E) neutral

Questions 18–24. Read the following poem carefully before you choose your answers.

Wild, wild the storm, and the sea high running;
Steady the roar of the gale, with incessant undertone
                              muttering;
Shouts of demoniac laughter fitfully piercing and pealing;
Waves, air, midnight, their savagest trinity lashing;
5 Out in the shadows there, milk-white combs careering;
On beachy slush and sand, spurts of snow fierce slanting—
Where through the murk the easterly death-wind breasting,
Through cutting swirl and spray, watchful and firm
                              advancing
(That in the distance! is that a wreck? is the red signal
                              flaring?),
10 Slush and sand of the beach, tireless till daylight wending,
Steadily, slowly, through hoarse roar never remitting,
Along the midnight edge, by those milk-white combs
                              careering,
A group of dim, weird forms, struggling, the night
                              confronting,
That savage trinity warily watching.

                              (1891)

18. In which of the following excerpts does the poet use the sound of the words to convey their meaning?

(A) Wild, wild the storm (line 1)
(B) Waves, air, midnight (line 4)
(C) milk-white combs careering (line 5)
(D) beachy slush and sand (line 6)
(E) dim, weird forms, struggling (line 13)

19. Which of these might a literary scholar cite to defend the idea that this poem might be considered a sonnet?

　I. its rhyme scheme and meter
　II. its number of lines
　III. its subject matter and tone

(A) I only
(B) II only
(C) I and II only
(D) I and III only
(E) II and III only

20. The word "remitting" (line 11) is used here to mean

(A) transmitting, sending
(B) forgiving, pardoning
(C) submitting, presenting
(D) lessening, slackening
(E) refraining, holding back

21. Which of the following effects does the poet achieve by ending each line with an -*ing* word and a pause?

    I. He makes every line rhyme.
    II. He echoes the sound of the waves washing up on the shore.
    III. He gives the poem an irregular rhythm.

  (A) I only
  (B) I and II only
  (C) II only
  (D) II and III only
  (E) III only

22. Which best describes the speaker's reaction to the storm he describes?

  (A) He is frightened by its noise.
  (B) He is impressed by its drama and power.
  (C) He is sobered by its destructiveness.
  (D) He is thankful not to be out in it.
  (E) He is emotionally unaffected by it.

23. You can reasonably infer that the "dim, weird forms" (line 13) are

  (A) shore patrolmen or watchmen
  (B) wrecked sailors
  (C) idle tourists
  (D) the speaker and his friends
  (E) fishermen waiting to go out

24. How is the repetition of several phrases in the poem (such as "milk-white combs careering" in lines 5 and 12) linked to its subject matter?

  (A) It echoes the repeated wash of waves breaking on the shore.
  (B) It emphasizes the similarity of the sounds made by the waves and the wind.
  (C) It shows that the speaker has seen a great many storms at sea.
  (D) It demonstrates that each moment of a storm is unlike all the others.
  (E) It creates an image of a disturbance of nature that will never end.

Questions 25–33. Read the following passage carefully before you choose your answers.

After the arrival of coffee the Major was rallying Eugene upon some rival automobile shops lately built in a suburb, and already promising to flourish.

"I suppose they'll either drive you out of the business,"
5 said the old gentleman, "or else the two of you'll drive all the rest of us off the streets."

"If we do, we'll even things up by making the streets five or ten times as long as they are now," Eugene returned.

"How do you propose to do that?"

10 "It isn't the distance from the center of a town that counts," said Eugene; "it's the time it takes to get there. This town's already spreading; bicycles and trolleys have been doing their share, but the automobile is going to carry city streets clear out to the county line...."

15 "Well, well!" the Major laughed. "You have enough faith in miracles, Eugene—granting that trolleys and bicycles and automobiles are miracles. So you think they're to change the face of the land, do you?"

"They're already doing it, Major; and it can't be stopped.
20 Automobiles—"

At this point he was interrupted. George was the interrupter. He had said nothing since entering the dining room, but now he spoke in a loud and peremptory voice, using the tone of one in authority who checks idle prattle
25 and settles a matter forever.

"Automobiles are a useless nuisance," he said.

There fell a moment's silence.

Isabel gazed incredulously at George, color slowly heightening upon her cheeks and temples, while Fanny
30 watched him with a quick eagerness, her eyes alert

and bright. But Eugene seemed merely quizzical, as if
not taking this brusquerie to himself. The Major was
seriously disturbed.

"What did you say, George?" he asked, though George had
35 spoken but too distinctly.

"I said all automobiles were a nuisance," George
answered, repeating not only the words but the tone in
which he had uttered them. And he added, "They'll never
amount to anything but a nuisance. They had no business
40 to be invented."

The Major frowned. "Of course you forget that Mr.
Morgan[1] makes them, and also did his share in
inventing them. If you weren't so thoughtless he might
think you rather offensive."

45 "That would be too bad," said George coolly. "I don't
think I could survive it."

Again there was a silence, while the Major stared at his
grandson, aghast. But Eugene began to laugh cheerfully.

"I'm not sure he's wrong about automobiles," he said.
50 "With all their speed forward they may be a step
backward in civilization—that is, in spiritual civilization.
It may be that they will not add to the beauty of the
world, nor to the life of men's souls. I am not sure. But
automobiles have come, and they bring a greater change
55 in our life than most of us suspect. They are here, and
almost all outward things are going to be different
because of what they bring. They are going to alter
war, and they are going to alter peace. I think men's
minds are going to be changed in subtle ways because
60 of automobiles; just how, though, I could hardly guess.
But you can't have the immense outward changes that
they will cause without some inward ones, and it may
be that George is right, and that the spiritual alteration
will be bad for us. Perhaps, ten or twenty years from now,
65 if we can see the inward change in men by that time, I
shouldn't be able to defend the gasoline engine, but would
have to agree with him that automobiles 'had no business
to be invented.'" He laughed good-naturedly, and looking
at his watch, apologized for having an engagement which
70 made his departure necessary when he would so much

[1]Mr. Morgan: Eugene

prefer to linger. Then he shook hands with the Major, and
bade Isabel, George, and Fanny a cheerful good-night—a
collective farewell cordially addressed to all three of them
together—and left them at the table.

(1918)

25. You can reasonably conclude that Eugene leaves
the dinner at the end of the excerpt because

(A) he truly does have another engagement, as
he claims
(B) he is angry and embarrassed over George's
insults
(C) he doesn't understand that George wants
him to go
(D) he is too proud to stay where he knows he is
not entirely welcome
(E) he had always intended to leave right
after dinner

26. The author of the passage uses the automobile as
a symbol of

(A) progress
(B) change
(C) stability
(D) youth
(E) passion

27. Which is the most likely reason George remains
silent throughout the meal until he interrupts
Eugene?

(A) He is not feeling well.
(B) He did not want to come to dinner in the
first place.
(C) He is unwilling to speak politely or civilly to
his guest.
(D) He is lost in thought.
(E) He does not understand the topic of
conversation.

GO ON TO THE NEXT PAGE ⟹

28. From her reaction to George's statements, you can conclude that Fanny is

    (A) shocked
    (B) pleased
    (C) distressed
    (D) uncomprehending
    (E) furious

29. The word "rallying" (line 1) is closest in meaning to

    (A) encouraging
    (B) informing
    (C) lecturing
    (D) teasing
    (E) scolding

30. Why does the author set off the sentence "There fell a moment's silence" (line 27) as a separate paragraph all to itself?

    (A) to distract the reader from George's rude remark
    (B) to emphasize the shocked reaction of the listeners
    (C) to show that Eugene is deeply offended
    (D) to contrast George's mood with that of the other diners
    (E) to help the reader understand why George speaks as he does

31. Which of the following motivates Eugene to say a collective good-night to Isabel, George, and Fanny instead of speaking to each one separately?

        I. He does not want to upset anyone any further than George already has.
        II. He is too proud to speak in a friendly way to George as an individual.
        III. He does not know any of the three of them very well as individuals.

    (A) I only
    (B) II only
    (C) I and II only
    (D) II and III only
    (E) III only

32. The parallel structure that characterizes Eugene's final speech in the passage has all these effects EXCEPT

    (A) it shows that this moment is the climax of the entire passage
    (B) it adds a solemnity and weight to the ideas he expresses
    (C) it suggests that he uses a formal tone of voice
    (D) it makes his words linger in the reader's memory
    (E) it makes the reader feel that what he is saying is important

33. What do the words *peremptory, brusquerie, coolly,* and *offensive* imply about George's motivation for speaking as and when he does?

    (A) that he loathes automobiles
    (B) that he disagrees with Eugene's point of view
    (C) that he intensely dislikes Eugene
    (D) that he feels contempt for the Major
    (E) that he is bored with the conversation

Questions 34–39. Read the following passage carefully before you choose your answers.

Shakespeare is, above all writers, at least above all
modern writers, the poet of nature; the poet that holds
up to his readers a faithful mirrour of manners and of
life. His characters are not modified by the customs of
5 particular places, unpractised by the rest of the world;
by the peculiarities of studies or professions, which can
operate but upon small numbers; or by the accidents of
transient fashions or temporary opinions: they are the
genuine progeny of common humanity, such as the world
10 will always supply, and observation will always find. His
persons act and speak by the influence of those general
passions and principles by which all minds are agitated,
and the whole system of life is continued in motion. In
the writings of other poets a character is too often an
15 individual; in those of Shakespeare it is commonly a
species. . . .

It will not easily be imagined how much Shakespeare
excells in accommodating his sentiments to real life,
but by comparing him with other authours. It was
20 observed of the ancient schools of declamation, that the
more diligently they were frequented, the more was the
student disqualified for the world, because he found
nothing there which he should ever meet in any other
place. The same remark may be applied to every stage
25 but that of Shakespeare. The theatre, when it is under
any other direction, is peopled by such characters as
were never seen, conversing in a language which was
never heard, upon topicks which will never arise in the
commerce of mankind. But the dialogue of this authour
30 is often so evidently determined by the incident which
produces it, and is pursued with so much ease and
simplicity, that it seems scarcely to claim the merit of
fiction, but to have been gleaned by diligent selection out
of common conversation, and common occurrences. . . .

35 Other dramatists can only gain attention by hyperbolical
or aggravated characters, by fabulous and unexampled
excellence or depravity, as the writers of barbarous
romances invigorated the reader by a giant and a dwarf;
and he that should form his expectations of human affairs
40 from the play, or from the tale, would be equally deceived.
Shakespeare has no heroes; his scenes are occupied only by

men, who act and speak as the reader thinks that he should
himself have spoken or acted on the same occasion: Even
where the agency is supernatural the dialogue is level with
45 life. Other writers disguise the most natural passions and
most frequent incidents: so that he who contemplates them
in the book will not know them in the world: Shakespeare
approximates the remote, and familiarizes the wonderful;
the event which he represents will not happen, but if it
50 were possible, its effects would be probably such as he has
assigned; and it may be said, that he has not only shewn
human nature as it acts in real exigencies, but as it would
be found in trials, to which it cannot be exposed. This
therefore is the praise of Shakespeare, that his drama is the
55 mirrour of life; that he who has mazed his imagination, in
following the phantoms which other writers raise up before
him, may here be cured of his delirious extasies, by reading
human sentiments in human language; by scenes from
which a hermit may estimate the transactions of the world,
60 and a confessor predict the progress of the passions.

His adherence to general nature has exposed him to
the censure of criticks, who form their judgments upon
narrower principles. Dennis and Rymer[1] think his Romans
not sufficiently Roman; and Voltaire censures his kings as
65 not completely royal. Dennis is offended, that Menenius,
a senator of Rome[2], should play the buffoon; and Voltaire
perhaps thinks decency violated when the Danish
Usurper[3] is represented as a drunkard. But Shakespeare
always makes nature predominate over accident; and if
70 he preserves the essential character, is not very careful
of distinctions superinduced and adventitious. His story
requires Romans or kings, but he thinks only on men.
He knew that Rome, like every other city, had men of
all dispositions; and wanting a buffoon, he went into
75 the senate-house for that which the senate-house would
certainly have afforded him. He was inclined to shew an
usurper and a murderer not only odious but despicable,

[1] John Dennis and Thomas Rymer: 18th-century critics of
Shakespeare's plays
[2] Menenius: a character in Shakespeare's play *Coriolanus*
[3] the Danish Usurper: King Claudius in Shakespeare's
play *Hamlet*

GO ON TO THE NEXT PAGE

he therefore added drunkenness to his other qualities,
knowing that kings love wine like other men, and that
80 wine exerts its natural power upon kings. These are the
petty cavils of petty minds; a poet overlooks the casual
distinction of country and condition, as a painter, satisfied
with the figure, neglects the drapery.

(1765)

34. What does the author mean by saying that
Shakespeare "holds up a faithful mirror" to his
readers (lines 2–3)?

(A) that Shakespeare wrote many
autobiographical plays

(B) that Shakespeare's plays are often about
real people

(C) that Shakespeare's characters seem real and
familiar

(D) that Shakespeare accurately reflected the
customs of his own times

(E) that Shakespeare often employed audience
members in his performances

35. What similarity does the author see between
the poet and painter he compares in the final
sentence of the passage?

(A) Both look only at the outer surface of a
character or a model.

(B) Both depend for success on the goodwill of
the public.

(C) Both create works of art or literature for
their personal pleasure.

(D) Both consider art or literature to be difficult,
demanding work.

(E) Both are primarily interested in the essence
of a character or model.

36. Which best explains the meaning of the
sentence "Even where the agency is supernatural
the dialogue is level with life" (lines 43–45)?

(A) Even a nonmortal character in a
Shakespearean play will speak dialogue in a
language the audience can understand.

(B) Even in the fantasy plays of Shakespeare, the
dialogue holds the audience's interest.

(C) Shakespeare has a gift for writing
lively, believable dialogue that is almost
supernatural.

(D) Even Shakespeare's nonhuman characters
(such as phantom, god, or sprite) reveal
natural, human thoughts and emotions in
their speech.

(E) Audiences always find Shakespeare's
characters human and true, even when the
plays are given alien or futuristic settings.

37. According to the author of the passage, what is
the basis of the objections that Dennis, Rymer,
and Voltaire make to Shakespeare's plays?

(A) The characters are not realistic human
beings.

(B) The authority figures are not dignified
enough.

(C) The critics are made into buffoons.

(D) The characters' behavior is based on
their rank.

(E) The plots rely too much on accidental
happenings.

38. "He who has mazed his imagination"
(line 55) has

(A) corrupted it

(B) made it dull

(C) exercised it

(D) stimulated it

(E) baffled it

39. The word "cavils" (line 81) means approximately the same thing as

(A) speeches, comments
(B) judgments, conclusions
(C) objections, criticisms
(D) fears, apprehensions
(E) puzzles, riddles

Questions 40–45. Read the following poem carefully before you choose your answers.

I lived with visions for my company
Instead of men and women, years ago,
And found them gentle mates, nor thought to know
A sweeter music than they played to me—
5 But soon their trailing purple was not free
Of this world's dust; —their lutes did silent grow,
And I myself grew faint and blind below
Their vanishing eyes. Then *thou* didst come . . . to *be*,
Beloved, what they *seemed*. Their shining fronts,
10 Their songs, their splendors . . . (better, yet the same . . .
As river-water hallowed into fonts . . .)
Met in thee, and, from out thee, overcame
My soul with satisfaction of all wants—
Because God's gifts put man's best dreams to shame.

(1850)

40. Who are the speaker's "gentle mates" (line 3)?

(A) her childhood friends
(B) her brothers and sisters
(C) creatures of her imagination
(D) ghosts of people who died
(E) her dolls, toys, and pets

41. What does the speaker mean by saying "I myself grew faint and blind" (line 7)?

(A) She became seriously ill.
(B) She lost her eyesight.
(C) Her visions changed from happy dreams to nightmares.
(D) She felt less real and alive as her visions faded.
(E) Her imagination began to lose its power.

42. What does the poem state or imply about the speaker's past life?

    I. She was lonely and isolated.
    II. She loved music.
    III. She reveled in her imagination.

(A) I only
(B) I and II only
(C) II and III only
(D) III only
(E) I and III only

43. The word "faint" (line 7) is used to mean

(A) unconscious
(B) hard to hear
(C) difficult to see
(D) cowardly
(E) physically weak

44. What does the phrase "God's gifts put man's best dreams to shame" (line 14) mean?

(A) Actual, living human beings are much more wonderful than characters in dreams.

(B) People should be ashamed of hanging on to their dreams.

(C) No person can imagine any gift worthy of being offered up as a sacrifice to God.

(D) People should not waste their time dreaming; they should be active in the real world.

(E) Real people are only pale imitations of the wonders created by the human imagination.

45. Why did the speaker's visions grow silent and begin to vanish?

(A) She acquired many friends.

(B) She found happiness and fulfillment in love.

(C) She acquired adult responsibilities.

(D) She began to feel that visions were not enough for her.

(E) She lost the power to imagine.

Questions 46–53. Read the following passage carefully before you choose your answers.

[Enter Quince the carpenter, and Snug the joiner, and Bottom the weaver, and Flute the bellows mender, and Snout the tinker, and Starveling the tailor.]

QUINCE. Is all our company here?

BOTTOM. You were best to call them generally, man by man, according to the scrip.

QUINCE. Here is the scroll of every man's name which
5 is thought fit, through all Athens, to play in our interlude before the Duke and the Duchess on his wedding-day at night.

BOTTOM. First, good Peter Quince, say what the play treats on, then read the names of the actors, and so grow
10 to a point.

QUINCE. Marry, our play is "The most lamentable comedy and most cruel death of Pyramus and Thisby."

BOTTOM. A very good piece of work, I assure you, and a merry. Now, good Peter Quince, call forth your actors by
15 the scroll. Masters, spread yourselves.

QUINCE. Answer as I call you. Nick Bottom, the weaver.

BOTTOM. Ready. Name what part I am for, and proceed.

QUINCE. You, Nick Bottom, are set down for Pyramus.

BOTTOM. What is Pyramus? A lover, or a tyrant?

20 QUINCE. A lover, that kills himself most gallant for love.

BOTTOM That will ask some tears in the true performing of it: if I do it, let the audience look to their eyes. I will move storms; I will condole in some measure. To the

rest—yet my chief humor is for a tyrant. I could play Ercles
25 rarely, or a part to tear a cat in, to make all split.

"The raging rocks
And shivering shocks
Shall break the locks
Of prison gates;
30 And Phibbus' car
Shall shine from far
And make and mar
The foolish Fates."

This was lofty! Now name the rest of the players. This is
35 Ercles' vein, a tyrant's vein. A lover is more condoling.

QUINCE. Francis Flute, the bellows-mender.

FLUTE. Here, Peter Quince.

QUINCE. Flute, you must take Thisby on you.

FLUTE. What is Thisby? A wandering knight?

40 QUINCE. It is the lady that Pyramus must love.

FLUTE. Nay, faith, let me not play a woman. I have a beard coming.

QUINCE. That's all one. You shall play it in a mask, and you may speak as small as you will.

45 BOTTOM. An I may hide my face, let me play Thisby too. I'll speak in a monstrous little voice. "Thisne, Thisne!" "Ah, Pyramus, my lover dear! Thy Thisby dear, and lady dear!"

QUINCE. No, no; you must play Pyramus: and, Flute,
50 you Thisby.

BOTTOM. Well, proceed.

QUINCE. Robin Starveling, the tailor.

STARVELING. Here, Peter Quince.

QUINCE. Robin Starveling, you must play Thisby's
55 mother. Tom Snout, the tinker.

SNOUT. Here, Peter Quince.

QUINCE. You, Pyramus' father; myself, Thisby's father;
Snug, the joiner, you the lion's part; and, I hope, here is a
play fitted.

60 SNUG. Have you the lion's part written? Pray you, if it be,
give it me, for I am slow of study.

QUINCE. You may do it extempore, for it is nothing but
roaring.

BOTTOM. Let me play the lion too. I will roar that I will
65 do any man's heart good to hear me; I will roar, that I
will make the Duke say "Let him roar again, let him roar
again!"

QUINCE. An you should do it too terribly, you would
fright the Duchess and the ladies, that they would shriek;
70 and that were enough to hang us all.

ALL. That would hang us, every mother's son.

BOTTOM. I grant you, friends, if that you should fright
the ladies out of their wits, they would have no more
discretion but to hang us; but I will aggravate my voice so
75 that I will roar you as gently as any sucking dove; I will
roar you an 'twere any nightingale.

QUINCE. You can play no part but Pyramus; for
Pyramus is a sweet-fac'd man, a proper man as one shall
see in a summer's day, a most lovely gentleman-like man.
80 Therefore you must needs play Pyramus.

BOTTOM. Well, I will undertake it. What beard were I
best to play it in?

QUINCE. Why, what you will.

BOTTOM. I will discharge it in either your straw-color
85 beard, your orange-tawny beard, your purple-in-grain
beard, or your French-crown-color beard, your perfect
yellow.

QUINCE. Some of your French crowns have no hair at
all, and then you will play bare-faced. But, masters, here
90 are your parts. And I am to entreat you, request you,
and desire you, to con them by to-morrow night; and
meet me in the palace wood, a mile without the town, by

moonlight. There will we rehearse; for if we meet in the
city, we shall be dogg'd with company, and our devices
95 known. In the meantime I will draw a bill of properties,
such as our play wants. I pray you, fail me not.

BOTTOM. We will meet, and there we may rehearse
most obscenely and courageously. Take pains, be
perfect: adieu.

100 QUINCE. At the Duke's oak we meet.

BOTTOM. Enough. Hold, or cut bow-strings.

[Exeunt]

(1595)

46. Which character appears to be the most shy?

(A) Bottom
(B) Flute
(C) Quince
(D) Snug
(E) Starveling

47. The characters misuse all these words in the dialogue EXCEPT

(A) generally (line 2)
(B) interlude (line 5)
(C) comedy (line 12)
(D) aggravate (line 74)
(E) obscenely (line 98)

48. You can assume that Flute is the youngest of the characters because

(A) he is a bellows-mender
(B) he is growing a beard
(C) he is cast as a young woman
(D) he wants to play a knight
(E) he is an experienced actor

49. Which detail does NOT support the suggestion that Bottom has a masterful personality?

(A) He wants to perform every role in the play.
(B) He insists on having the last word in the scene.
(C) He throws himself energetically into each part.
(D) He tries to take over Quince's role of director.
(E) He asks for advice about a beard for his character.

50. When Quince tells Snug "You may do it extempore," he means

(A) you may roar as loudly as you like
(B) you don't have to learn any lines
(C) you can learn the part quickly
(D) your role in the play is silent
(E) you don't have to be in the play

51. What quality does Quince seem to possess that makes him a good choice to direct "Pyramus and Thisby"?

(A) good judgment
(B) forcefulness
(C) anxiety
(D) acting ability
(E) creativity

52. Why is Bottom's line "A very good piece of work, I assure you, and a merry" (lines 13–14) ironic?

(A) because he does not know the play
(B) because the play was just written
(C) because Bottom is cast in the leading role
(D) because the play is a comedy
(E) because the play will be rehearsed in secret

53. Which of the following aspects of the scene contribute to its humor?

    I. the misuse or incorrect use of words
    II. the demonstrations of Bottom's acting ability
    III. Flute's objection to playing Thisby because he is growing a beard

(A) I only
(B) I and II only
(C) II only
(D) II and III only
(E) I, II, and III

Questions 54–60. Read the following passage carefully before you choose your answers.

"Jane," said Mrs. Tyke, as the three ladies sat over a late breakfast, the Doctor having already retreated to the laboratory and his newspaper: "Jane, I think you have made a conquest."

5   Jane looked down in silence, with a conscious simper. Catherine spoke rather anxiously: "Indeed, Cousin Lucy, I have noticed what you allude to, and I have spoken to Jane about not encouraging Mr. Durham. He is not at all a man she can really like, and she ought to be most careful not to
10   let herself be misunderstood. Jane, you ought indeed."

But Jane struck merrily in: "Mr. Durham is old enough and—ahem!—handsome enough to take care of himself, sister. And, besides"—with a touch of mimicry, which recalled his pompous manner—"Orpingham Place, my
15   dear madam, Orpingham Place is a very fine place, a very fine place indeed. Our pineapples can really hardly be got rid of, and our prize pigs can't see out of their eyes; they can't indeed, my dear young lady, though it's not pretty talk for a pretty young lady to listen to .
20   . . Very well, if the pines and the pigs are smitten, why shouldn't I marry the pigs and the pines?"

GO ON TO THE NEXT PAGE ⟶

"Why not?" cried Mrs. Tyke with a laugh; but Miss
Charlmont, looking disturbed, rejoined: "Why not,
certainly, if you like Mr. Durham; but do you like Mr.
25 Durham? And, whether or not, you ought not to laugh
at him."

Jane pouted: "Really one would think I was a child still!
As to Mr. Durham, when he knows his own mind and
speaks, you may be quite sure I shall know my own mind
30 and give him his answer . . . Orpingham Place, my dear
Miss Catherine, the finest place in the county; the finest
place in three counties, whatever my friend the Duke
may say. A charming neighborhood, Miss Catherine:
her Grace the Duchess, the most affable woman you can
35 imagine, and my lady the Marchioness, a fine woman—a
very fine woman. But they can't raise such pines as
my pines; they can't do it, you know; they haven't the
means, you know. . . Come now, sister, don't look cross;
when I'm Mrs. Durham, you shall have your slice of the
40 pigs and the pines."

(1870)

54. Catherine (Miss Charlmont) is best
characterized as

(A) timid
(B) scrupulous
(C) sarcastic
(D) practical
(E) outspoken

55. Why does Catherine say that Jane "ought not to
laugh at" Mr. Durham (lines 25–26)?

(A) because Catherine likes and respects
Mr. Durham
(B) because Jane is engaged to marry
Mr. Durham
(C) because Mr. Durham is a wealthy man
(D) because Mr. Durham is not an
amusing person
(E) because Jane's laughter is mocking
and unkind

56. You can reasonably conclude that Jane is
encouraging Mr. Durham's attentions because

I. he is wealthy and owns a fine large
house
II. his wit and cleverness make her laugh
III. he is on friendly terms with members of
the aristocracy

(A) I and II only
(B) II and III only
(C) I and III only
(D) I only
(E) III only

57. Details in the passage imply all of the following
about Mr. Durham EXCEPT

(A) he is a member of the nobility
(B) he is substantially older than Jane
(C) he is very proud of his country home
(D) he wants people to know that dukes and
duchesses are his friends
(E) he is not good at concealing his emotions

58. Which of the following does NOT describe Jane?

(A) mercenary
(B) pragmatic
(C) clever
(D) heartless
(E) impulsive

59. What does it mean to say that Jane reacted "with a conscious simper" (line 5)?

(A) Jane smiled with genuine pleasure.

(B) Jane gave an affected smirk.

(C) Jane produced a wry, uncomfortable smile.

(D) Jane broke into a wide grin of amusement.

(E) Jane gave a big, beaming smile.

60. Mr. Durham's continued boasting about his house and the produce of his estate imply that he is

(A) honest

(B) persuasive

(C) insecure

(D) haughty

(E) industrious

STOP

If you finish before time is called, you may check your work on this test only.

Do not turn to any other test in this book.

Answer Key

1. D	16. A	31. C	46. E
2. A	17. E	32. A	47. B
3. C	18. D	33. C	48. C
4. B	19. E	34. C	49. E
5. E	20. D	35. E	50. B
6. A	21. C	36. D	51. A
7. B	22. B	37. B	52. A
8. E	23. A	38. E	53. E
9. B	24. A	39. C	54. B
10. D	25. D	40. C	55. E
11. A	26. B	41. D	56. C
12. B	27. C	42. E	57. A
13. E	28. B	43. C	58. E
14. D	29. D	44. A	59. B
15. C	30. B	45. D	60. C

Answers and Explanations

1. **(D)** A *misnomer* is literally "a wrong name." The speaker says that common endearments such as *angel* are misnomers because people are ordinary mortals, not angels.

2. **(A)** The speaker scoffs at lovers who think their passion is as great as that of Antony and Cleopatra, but his tone is mocking (choice A) rather than bitter (choice B). The comparison of Wellingtons to "Romeo boots" and the statement "ye may love in spite of beaver hats" show that the speaker has not lost his sense of humor.

3. **(C)** Lines 11–12 show that the poet believes that some people have felt true love, so you can rule out choice A. Since the lovers he cites are Antony (commander of the Roman army) and Cleopatra (pharaoh of Egypt), you know he believes that only extraordinary people feel what he recognizes as love.

4. **(B)** Choice A is wrong because *symbolize* means "stand for something beyond their literal identity." Wellingtons are heavy, waterproof boots; they literally ARE everyday garments of the poet's own day. "Common Wellingtons turn Romeo boots" means "the prosaic becomes picturesque." Love turns a dull, everyday young man into a romantic hero. Therefore choice B is correct.

5. **(E)** The person most likely to "cosset, nurse, and dandle" a doll is a little girl, choice E.

6. **(A)** The speaker says that "silly youth doth think to make itself / Divine by loving" (lines 4–5). In other words, the mere act of falling in love will make them great heroes like Antony or queens like Cleopatra.

7. **(B)** The speaker points out that Cleopatra was such a great heroine and queen that she was literally able to melt a pearl. He challenges the lover of his own day to prove himself or herself equal to Cleopatra by making the pearl whole again. If the "silly youth" has indeed been made "divine by loving," this should be possible. Choice E comes close to the meaning, but the speaker wants to see actions, not words.

8. **(E)** Option I is correct because the speaker repeatedly states that youth is foolish in both its behavior and its emotions. Option II is correct because the young lovers want to feel like Antony and Cleopatra—they want to identify with the glamorous and exciting past, not the prosaic present in which people wear Wellington boots and beaver hats. Option III is correct because the speaker's point of view is clearly that of someone older than the "silly youth" he scorns so much.

9. **(B)** Choices A and C are false statements. This is not a narrative poem, and although sonnets commonly follow one of three rhyme schemes, they can have their own individual rhyming patterns or even be unrhymed. Choices D and E make no sense because this poem is written in iambic pentameter and most sonnets, like this poem, express a specific emotion. This leaves choice B, which makes perfect sense. When a poet mocks the behavior of young lovers, he should not undercut his own point by stating it in the form of a love poem.

10. **(D)** A person who goes to operas and concerts will be surrounded by fellow audience-members who probably share his tastes and whose company he might enjoy. The other four choices all show that Mr. Duffy prefers to spend his time alone—away from downtown Dublin and its "gilded youth," often disappointed in people, and preferring to pray and worship in private.

11. **(A)** If choice C were true, Duffy could not afford to work only "from time to time." If choice D were true, he would not be translating the play at all. If choice E were true, he would get more work done on the project. Choice B might or might not be true; he might easily have been writing "from time to time" over a long period of months or years. Choice A is the only answer that fits; a person not serious about completing a project will work on it sporadically, as Duffy does.

12. **(B)** Option I is correct because *austere* means "plain and unadorned," which exactly describes Duffy's room. Option II is correct because Duffy has very few personal possessions; a few books, a writing desk, a lamp, clothes, and a few necessary pieces of furniture. Option III is wrong because nothing suggests that the room is uncomfortable or neglected; since Duffy chose all the furniture himself, it presumably reflects his personal taste and is thus a place where he can relax and feel comfortable.

13. **(E)** You can certainly rule out choices C and D because details within the passage show that these choices do not accurately describe Duffy. A *saturnine* person has a heavy, gloomy, serious manner or personality.

14. **(D)** A person who is comfortable in his own skin, who is at ease with himself and likes himself, does not give his own body or actions any thought one way or the other.

15. **(C)** The "tale of Duffy's years" is his life. The author says that Duffy's face reflects the kind of life he has led, using a version of the common idiom "you can read his face like a book."

16. **(A)** Even without having read the story, you should be able to identify this excerpt as expository material. The excerpt introduces and describes someone who is clearly the story's main character (because he is described in great detail) and it describes the story's setting. These are two of the main purposes of a story's exposition. Rising action would build toward a climax; this passage does not do that. The climax would be a moment of high interest and excitement; this passage is descriptive rather than action-packed. Falling action would lead toward a conclusion; and a conclusion would resolve a major conflict.

17. **(E)** The narrating voice describes Duffy; it allows the reader to draw his or her own conclusions. It provides information but does not express any opinion, either favorable or unfavorable.

18. **(D)** The *ch, sh,* and *s* sounds of "beachy slush and sand" precisely convey the experience of trudging through it. Your feet make the sound "slush" when you trudge through wet snow or wet sand. *Slush* is an example of onomatopoeia—a word whose sound and meaning are identical.

19. **(E)** Option I is wrong because this is a free-verse poem; it is unrhymed and the lines are of different lengths. (The -*ing* words at the ends of the lines are not rhyming words, because their stressed syllables do not rhyme.) Option II is correct because, like all sonnets, this poem has 14 lines. Option III is correct because a sonnet is a lyric poem, whose purpose is not necessarily to tell a story, but to capture a particular emotion, often by descriptive means.

20. **(D)** These are all accurate definitions of the word *remitting*, but it is clear from the context that the poet means "the hoarse roar is continuing, it is not slackening or ceasing or growing quieter." This echoes the word *incessant* in line 2.

21. **(C)** Option I is wrong because in order for words to rhyme, they must have the same vowel sound on the stressed syllable: RUN-ning, PEAL-ing, ad-VANc-ing, and so on do not have the same vowel sound. The only rhyme occurs when "careering" is repeated. Option II is correct because waves wash up on the shore with the same LOUD-soft rhythmic pattern as the -ing words: LOUD as they break on the shore, and soft as they recede. Option III is wrong because the poem has a generally regular rhythm of six stressed syllables per line (except for the short final line); the -ing words contribute to this rhythmic regularity.

22. **(B)** The tone of the poem is one of awe and exultation at the impressive spectacle of nature showing its powers. There is nothing to indicate fear; the speaker seems to take a certain pleasure in the storm. The speaker describes the storm so vividly that he cannot be unaffected by it.

23. **(A)** The speaker tells you that the dim, weird forms are struggling, confronting the night, and warily watching the "savage trinity" of waves, air, and midnight. They are keeping track of the course of the storm. This makes it most likely that they are shore patrol. Tourists would not be out in such weather. The speaker is clearly not one of the group; he sees them only dimly, so they must be some distance away from him. Neither wrecked sailors nor fishermen would have any reason to watch the storm through the night.

24. **(A)** The sound of waves breaking on the shore is repetitious; each wave sounds like the previous one. The poem uses the device of repetition to recreate that sound for the reader and thus to make the scene come alive.

25. **(D)** The other engagement is almost certainly a polite fiction; if it really existed, Eugene would almost certainly have come to dinner on another night, or told his hosts in advance that he would have to leave right after the meal. This eliminates choices A and E. George's rudeness is impossible to miss, which eliminates choice C. Eugene's speech and behavior don't reflect anger or embarrassment—he seems very forgiving—but naturally he does not want to linger where it is clear that one of his hosts hates and resents him.

26. **(B)** The Major and Eugene both comment on changes that the automobile has brought to their city. Eugene clearly states in his long final speech that automobiles represent change, but that not all change is positive—that is, not all change can be called progress. Therefore, choice A cannot be correct.

27. **(C)** George's statements are relevant to the table conversation, so you can rule out choices D and E. Nothing in the passage supports choice A. Choice C is better than choice B because it is more specific. It pinpoints the most likely reason for George's long silence—his dislike of Eugene prevents him from speaking until he finds an opportunity to be openly rude. Choice B is true up to a point—George probably did not look forward to sharing a meal with Eugene—but the passage shows that he preferred to come to dinner and be rude rather than stay away.

28. **(B)** Fanny's eagerness and bright eyes are most consistent with pleasurable excitement. On some level, she is pleased by the incident.

29. **(D)** The conversation between Eugene and the Major is pleasant; this eliminates choices C and E. As an auto manufacturer, Eugene would almost certainly already know of the suburban shop, so choice B is unlikely. Context shows that choice D makes the best sense. The Major is in a teasing, friendly mood; he puns on the double meaning of the verb *drive*, and a later paragraph shows him laughing.

30. (B) Readers naturally pause for a moment as one paragraph ends and their eyes shift back to the left margin of the page to start the next paragraph. In reading aloud, there is also a natural slight pause at the end of each paragraph. By adding this brief pause before and after the sentence, the author literally lengthens the moment of silence he describes—a silence caused by the shock of hearing a rude remark suddenly dropped into the middle of a pleasant conversation.

31. (C) Option I is correct because Eugene's primary motivation in the last half of the passage is clearly to smooth over George's rudeness and not make a scene or start a fight. His cordial farewell to all three people indicates that he wishes to show no special resentment toward George. Option II is correct because George's insulting words are much too clear for Eugene to misunderstand, and he understandably does not wish to show special friendliness to one who has just been inexcusably rude to him. Option III is wrong because, as a dinner guest in their home, Eugene is clearly on close terms with the whole family.

32. (A) Parallel structure is a literary device in which an author repeats grammatical patterns for emphasis: "speed forward/step backward," "going to alter war/going to alter peace." This way of speaking, which is based on classical rhetoric, does indeed add to the weight of the speaker's ideas and make them seem more important than if they were more casually expressed. Repetition always makes words easier to remember. Choice A is the correct answer because this is the one thing parallel structure does not achieve in this speech; it does not highlight a climax in the action of a plot.

33. (C) Although choices A and B are true, and choice E is probable, they do not go far enough to account for George's deliberate rudeness to a dinner guest. Choice D is wrong because the Major is not the target of George's comments. Intense personal dislike is the only choice that satisfactorily accounts for George's behavior.

34. (C) To hold up a mirror to the reader means "to show the reader his or her own reflection." The author means that all readers recognize themselves in Shakespeare; in other words, that the characters in Shakespeare's plays speak and behave like ordinary human beings.

35. (E) Choices B–D are wrong because they make points that the author of the passage does not address. Choices A and E have opposite meanings, and choice E is what the author says. The poet pays no attention to a character's label or category, such as "senator" or "Roman"; instead, the poet looks at the man behind the label. In the same way, the painter looks at the bones and muscles of the model's body, not at the clothing covering the body.

36. (D) The *agency* of dialogue is the means by which it is spoken; in this case, the agent is the actor. "Level with life" means that the dialogue is lifelike; that the gods, goddesses, fairies, and other non-mortal characters in Shakespeare's plays speak with the same feelings and the same expressions human beings would use. Choice D most closely matches this.

37. (B) Dennis feels that a Roman senator should not behave like a buffoon; Voltaire feels that a king should not be a drunkard. In other words, both critics believe that characters who hold a high position of authority should not behave like realistic human beings; they should be more dignified and more admirable.

38. (E) The archaic word *mazed* means "bewildered, confused." The author means that the unrealistic and fantastical characters of other playwrights will baffle and bewilder the reader, but when he meets Shakespeare's characters on the page or the stage, he will recognize himself and his neighbors in them, and feel right at home.

39. (C) To *cavil* at something means to find fault with it; therefore, a "petty cavil" is a nitpicking criticism. The context of the entire paragraph makes the meaning clear.

40. (C) The words *visions* (line 1) and *dreams* (line 14) makes it clear that the speaker refers to imaginary friends—people she invented to keep her company "years ago."

41. (D) As the speaker grows older, her visions begin to fade and she begins to feel that she too is fading; she is growing less real, less substantial, and less visible to others. The visions have always kept her company; when they are gone she feels alone, as though she has been forgotten.

42. (E) Option I is correct because the speaker clearly states in the first two lines that she had only imaginary companions in the past, not real ones. Option II is wrong because the music the speaker refers to in lines 4, 6, and 10 is metaphorical, not literal. Option III is correct because any person who can be content with imaginary friends must have an active and creative imagination that she takes pleasure in using.

43. (C) Since the speaker grows faint "below their vanishing eyes," she "becomes difficult for them to see." In other words, her image or outline is blurry, indistinct, or vague.

44. (A) To "put a dream to shame" means "to compare favorably to a dream." "God's gifts" are real people; "man's best dreams" are the imaginary characters people create for themselves. The author says that the real people are greatly superior to the imaginary ones.

45. (D) You can rule out choices A and B because the speaker finds love only after the visions have already faded. You can rule out choice C because nothing in the poem supports it. You can rule out choice E because the act of expressing herself in verse shows clearly that the speaker has not lost her imagination. Choice D makes sense; many people who live only on visions and daydreams eventually find them stale and frustrating, and long for real human companionship.

46. (E) Starveling must logically be the most shy character because he has the least to say of the five choices. Shy people like to remain inconspicuous.

47. (B) *Generally* means "all together" but Bottom uses it to mean the opposite, "one by one." A *comedy* is a humorous play; a "lamentable" story of a cruel death is a tragedy. To *aggravate* the voice means to raise it; Bottom uses it incorrectly to mean "lower my voice." Whatever Bottom might mean by *obscenely*, the word's actual meaning makes no sense in this line, particularly given the players' care not to shock the ladies in the audience. The only word used correctly is *interlude*, which in this case refers to a short play being performed in a series of entertainments.

48. (C) In Shakespeare's theater, men and boys played all the female roles; young boys whose voices had not yet broken were most likely to be cast as young girls. Choices A, B, and D are all true statements about Flute, but are not relevant to his appropriateness to play Thisby.

49. (E) A masterful person is one who takes charge. Bottom's forceful, masterful personality shows in his command of the scene, his attempts to tell Quince how to do his job, and his eagerness to play every character in the piece. The one moment when he gives up control is when he asks "What beard were I best to play it in?"

50. (B) *Extempore* means "without previous study." Quince is telling Snug that there are no verbal lines for him to memorize; he will only have to roar like a lion at the right moments. You can rule out choice A because the actors have expressed concern over frightening the ladies, C because Snug has said he is "slow of study," D because it is made clear that the lion in the play must roar, and E because nothing in the scene supports the idea that Snug is quitting the play.

51. **(A)** Good judgment enables Quince to assign each role according to his actors' interests and abilities. Bottom plays the hero because he likes to show off and has plenty of energy; Snug, who is slow to learn lines, is given a role with no lines to learn. There is nothing in the scene to support any of the other four choices.

52. **(A)** Bottom praises the play without knowing the story. If he knew the story, he would not ask "What is Pyramus? A lover, or a tyrant?"

53. **(E)** Option I is correct because malapropisms—instances of incorrect word usage by the characters—are a traditional way to make the audience laugh. Option II is correct because Bottom's impersonations of Ercles, Pyramus, Thisby, and the lion are done with great zest, partly to amuse his friends. Option III is correct because the juxtaposition of the tragedy's heroine Thisby and Flute's beard is funny.

54. **(B)** A scrupulous person is one who behaves with integrity and a sense of fairness. Catherine clearly believes that Jane should not lead Mr. Durham on, and that she should also not be so unkind and rude as to make fun of him.

55. **(E)** Catherine clearly does not care much for Mr. Durham since she thinks her sister cannot possibly like him. Her objection is on the grounds of good manners; in Catherine's view, it is not proper to mock and make fun of other people.

56. **(C)** Option I is correct because Jane describes the fine house, with its hothouse pineapples and its prize pigs. Option II is wrong because it is not Mr. Durham's clever wit, but his pompous and silly boasting, that make Jane laugh. Option III is correct because the last paragraph quotes Mr. Durham's comments on his titled neighbors. Friends in high places and a stately country home seem likely to appeal to Jane, as they would appeal to many young women of her time.

57. **(A)** Choice B is wrong because Mr. Durham calls Jane a "pretty young lady" and "my dear young lady"; this implies that he is an older man. Choices C and D are wrong because Jane quotes his manner of boasting about his house and his titled friends. Choice E is wrong because Lucy, Catherine, and Jane all noticed his interest in Jane. This leaves choice A, which is correct because if Mr. Durham were a nobleman he would have a title rather than being called *Mr.*

58. **(E)** Choice A is wrong because Jane clearly is attracted by the idea of becoming a rich man's wife. Choice B is wrong because a wealthy husband is indeed a practical choice. Choice C is wrong because her talent for mimicry shows cleverness and wit. Choice D is wrong because her impatient dismissal of Catherine's genuine concern for her, and her scheme for marrying a man she clearly despises, indicate a lack of heart. This leaves choice E, which does NOT characterize Jane because her actions are the result of careful planning.

59. **(B)** A *simper* is an affected, silly smile; it does not show any genuine emotion, but is an expression a person assumes for effect. Jane simpers to show what she does not feel—modest pleasure in acknowledging her conquest.

60. **(C)** Boasting is a very common characteristic of people who fear that others are looking down on them, or that other people are better than they are. In addition, clues in the passage tell you the story is set in England, a class-conscious society at the date the passage was written (1870). In this setting, there was general agreement that aristocrats were superior to commoners, even—perhaps especially—wealthy commoners. Mr. Durham boasts about his material possessions to prove to himself, as much as to others, that he deserves respect.

How To Calculate Your Score

Count the number of correct answers and enter the total below.

Count the number of wrong answers. Do NOT include any questions you did not answer.

Multiply the number of wrong answers by 0.25 and enter the total below.

Do the subtraction. The answer is your raw score. Use the scoring scale to find your scaled score.

$$\overline{\text{(number of correct answers)}} - \overline{\text{(number of wrong answers} \times 0.25)} = \overline{\text{(raw score)}}$$

RAW SCORE	SCALED SCORE	RAW SCORE	SCALED SCORE	RAW SCORE	SCALED SCORE	RAW SCORE	SCALED SCORE	RAW SCORE	SCALED SCORE
60	800	44	710	28	560	12	420	−4	260
59	800	43	700	27	550	11	410	−5	250
58	800	42	690	26	540	10	400	−6	240
57	800	41	690	25	530	9	390	−7	230
56	800	40	680	24	520	8	380	−8	220
55	800	39	670	23	510	7	370	−9	210
54	790	38	660	22	500	6	360	−10	200
53	790	37	650	21	500	5	350	−11	200
52	780	36	640	20	490	4	340	−12	200
51	770	35	630	19	490	3	330	−13	200
50	760	34	620	18	480	2	320	−14	200
49	750	33	610	17	470	1	310	−15	200
48	740	32	600	16	460	0	300		
47	740	31	590	15	450	−1	290		
46	730	30	580	14	440	−2	280		
45	720	29	570	13	430	−3	270		

Note: This is only a sample scoring scale. Scoring scales differ from exam to exam.

Literary Resources

Authors and Texts Used in *McGraw-Hill Education SAT Subject Test: Literature*

Diagnostic

Practice Test 1

Practice Test 2

Practice Test 3

Practice Test 4

Practice Test 5

Practice Test 6

- Jane Austen: from *Pride and Prejudice*—p. 239–240
- William Shakespeare: "Fear no more the heat o' the sun" from *Cymbeline*—p. 242
- George Bernard Shaw: from *Pygmalion*—p. 243–244
- Walt Whitman: "Beat! Beat! Drums!" from *Leaves of Grass*—p. 246
- Sarah Kemble Knight: poem from *The Private Journal of Sarah Kemble Knight*—p. 248
- F. Scott Fitzgerald: from *This Side of Paradise*—p. 249–250
- Wilfred Owen: "Strange Meeting"—p. 251–252

Practice Test 7

- Henry Fielding: from Introduction to *Tom Jones*—p. 265–266
- William Shakespeare: Sonnet LXV—p. 267
- Saki (H. H. Munroe): from "Shock Tactics"—p. 269
- Henry David Thoreau: from "On Reading" from *Walden*—p. 271–272
- Walt Whitman: "Out from Behind This Mask (To Confront a Portrait)" from *Leaves of Grass*—p. 274
- Aphra Behn: from *The Fair Jilt*—p. 276
- Edith Wharton: from *The Age of Innocence*—p. 278

Practice test 8

- John Keats: lyric poem—p. 293
- James Joyce: from "A Painful Case" from *Dubliners*—p. 295
- Walt Whitman: poem from *Leaves of Grass*—p. 297
- Booth Tarkington: from *The Magnificent Ambersons*—p. 298–299
- Samuel Johnson: from Preface to *The Plays of William Shakespeare*—p. 301–302
- Elizabeth Barret Browning: sonnet from *Sonnets from the Portuguese*—p. 303
- Shakespeare: from *A Midsummer Night's Dream*—p. 304–305
- Christina Rossetti: from *Commonplace*—p. 306–307

NOTES

NOTES

NOTES

NOTES

NOTES